W9-DAN-441

Praise for *War Is a Lie*

"If you stop and think, and genuinely wonder, and long for a new, better world, I urge you to read a book I've just finished. It's...brilliantly and passionately written, and while being truthful is full of hope of destroying the military-in-dustrial-media-congressional-imperialpresidential-complex. It's *War Is a Lie* by David Swanson, a Virginia author."

—MUMIA ABU-JAMAL, author, radio commentator

"David Swanson is the most consistently great writer of this generation."

—JEAN ATHEY, peace activist

"David Swanson's *War Is a Lie* should be required reading. It lays bare the hypocrisy of American 'do-as-I-say, not-as-I-do' foreign policy, exposing the lies and the deliberate glorification of military disasters. Swanson advocates for endless diplomacy rather than endless war, a much cheaper and less bloody alternative to present U.S. militarism. *War Is a Lie* gives you the arguments, outrage and inspiration you need to take action. Read it."

—MEDEA BENJAMIN, author, peace activist

"Five years ago, David Swanson let us all in on a little secret: Everything we believe to be true about war is a big fat lie...actually, a series of lies that are intertwined and reinforce each other until the lies are the only thing we can see. In this second edition of *War Is a Lie*, Swanson provides an epilogue describing how the war lies have continued perpetuating war over the past five years, describing one instance after another of unnecessary, immoral and illegal military conflict. Still, Swanson is hopeful. He believes that war can be eradicated by exposing the lies that nurture it, and through the coordinated resistance of the world's citizens."

—LEAH BOLGER, activist, veteran

"I've been reading a bit of this book every night since I got it. The effect it's having on me is hard to explain. Like I've been born into a cult whether or not I want it, but now the lies are being washed away by the rain."

—JOHN BOSTROM, peace activist

"Debunks every argument you've heard used to justify, glorify, instigate, promote, prolong, and expand war."

—KIM CARLYLE, peace activist, veteran

"If decisions to go to war were really made on the basis of reason and facts, rather than greed and power, David Swanson's brilliant new book would put a stop to them. Those of us who know David understand that he writes quickly and eloquently, speaks honestly and powerfully, and follows a logical point all the way to its conclusion. He has a philosopher's mind with a computer's precision. And he always maintains a justifiable moral outrage at the lies of the war criminals—calling out their crimes, detailing their carnage, poking holes in their excuses. Reading *War Is a Lie* is like reading Mark Twain's 'War Prayer,' only in book form."

—STEVE COBBLE, political strategist

"This updated version of David Swanson's classic, *War Is a Lie*, dispels any notion that the Obama administration has been more truthful or law-abiding than Bush and Co. On the most critical issue of our time, 'hope and change' have meant only more sophisticated lies, secrets, and war propaganda, not a new commitment to peace."

—NICOLAS J. S. DAVIES, author of *Blood on Our Hands: The American Invasion and Destruction of Iraq*

"*War Is a Lie* is a must read for anyone who wants to break the centuries-long cycle of a perennially war-waging United States. In this carefully researched book, Mr. Swanson exposes the falsehoods that a willing government sells to a gullible public to gain support for one unnecessary war after another. The profit motives, power plays, and perennial chest-thumping, that have all been given more importance than human lives, are exposed in all their ugliness. This book should be required reading in every high school history class in the country."

—ROBERT FANTINA, author, peace activist

"Our times cry out for a smart, witty and courageous Populist who hasn't forgotten how to play offense. Luckily we have David Swanson."

—MIKE FERNER, author, peace activist, veteran

"This book is a nonviolent assault on the acceptance and justification of war, of all wars. For those of us who already are familiar with the uncountable arguments supporting Swanson's position, he was successful in compiling them in a very readable work which also serves as a reference book. For those of us who more or less blindly accept our culture of militarism, I am hopeful that the exposure to the clear, compelling, evidence-based debunking of general war myths and lies laid out by Swanson will open new windows of understanding."

—PATRICK HILLER, conflict transformation scholar, director of the War Prevention Initiative by the Jubitz Family Foundation

"No one has worked harder than David Swanson to free the U.S. from the grip of militarism. His recently updated book, *War Is a Lie*, brilliantly exposes just our profound addiction to war. I hope it jumpstarts a conversation about how we can achieve enduring peace."

—JOHN HORGAN, science journalist, author, *The End of War*

"In his usual meticulous, forthright style, Swanson does us a tremendous service by outlining, in detail and with a large body of examples, the lies behind all the U.S. wars, the money behind them, and the politicians who sell them to the public. If you want to know why and how U.S. wars are truly waged, read this critically important book."

—DAHR JAMAIL, journalist, author of *Beyond the Green Zone: Dispatches from an Unembedded Journalist in Occupied Iraq*

"David Swanson is one of the greatest peace strategists alive today. You will find *War Is a Lie* to be engaging, insightful, inspirational, and useful."

—MICHAEL D. KNOX, PhD, chair, U.S. Peace Memorial Foundation

"Not since General Smedley Butler's *War Is a Racket* has a simpler, more brilliant, or truer book been published."

—GEOFFREY MILLARD, peace activist, veteran

"A vital guide to understanding deadly propaganda, *War Is a Lie* maps out the deceptive terrain where people fall into accepting perpetual war as necessary. David Swanson has done the difficult work of making it easy for readers to grasp the extent of the lies—and the horrific consequences. With meticulous research and moral clarity, this book could transform your view of war and the real possibilities for peace."

—NORMAN SOLOMON, author, film maker, activist

"While Americans elect leaders whom they trust are honest, truthful, and really care about the kids they send to kill for our country, *War Is a Lie* reveals decade after decade the sordid side of our history: that our elected officials lie us into war with stunning and embarrassing regularity and are little concerned about the harm to innocent civilians, much less to members of our own military."

—ANN WRIGHT, peace activist, author, veteran

Just World Books

Timely Books for Changing Times

Just World Books exists to expand the discourse in the United States and worldwide on issues of vital international concern. We are committed to building a more just, equitable, and peaceable world. We uphold the equality of all human persons. We aim for our books to contribute to increasing understanding across national, religious, ethnic, and racial lines; to share more broadly the reflections, analyses, and policy prescriptions of pathbreaking activists for peace; and to help to prevent war.

To learn about our existing and upcoming titles, to find our terms for bookstores or other bulk purchasers, or to buy our books, visit our website:

www.JustWorldBooks.com

Also, follow us on Facebook, Twitter, and Instagram!

Our recent titles include:

- *Survival and Conscience: From the Shadows of Nazi Germany to the Jewish Boat to Gaza*, by Lillian Rosengarten
- *The People Make the Peace: Lessons from the Vietnam Antiwar Movement*, edited by Karín Aguilar-San Juan and Frank Joyce
- *Gaza Unsilenced*, edited by Refaat Alareer and Laila El-Haddad
- *Baddawi*, by Leila Abdelrazaq
- *Chaos and Counterrevolution: After the Arab Spring*, by Richard Falk
- *Palestine: The Legitimacy of Hope*, by Richard Falk
- *Chief Complaint: A Country Doctor's Tales of Life in Galilee*, by Hatim Kanaaneh
- *In Our Power: U.S. Students Organize for Justice in Palestine*, by Nora Barrows-Friedman
- *Gaza Writes Back: Short Stories from Young Writers in Gaza, Palestine*, edited by Refaat Alareer
- *The Gaza Kitchen: A Palestinian Culinary Journey*, by Laila El-Haddad and Maggie Schmitt
- *On the Brink: Israel and Palestine on the Eve of the 2014 Gaza Invasion*, by Alice Rothchild

WAR IS A LIE

Second Edition

David Swanson

Just World Books
Charlottesville, Virginia

Timely Books for Changing Times

Just World Books is an imprint of Just World Publishing, LLC.

Copyright © 2016 David Swanson

All rights reserved. No part of this book, except brief passages for review purposes, may be reproduced or transmitted in any form or by any means, electronic or mechanical, including photocopying, recording, or exporting from any information storage system, without permission in writing from the publisher. Such permission may be requested via the email or physical address listed at www.justworldbooks.com/contact.

Cover design by CStudio Design
Typesetting by Diana Ghazzawi for Just World Publishing, LLC.

Publisher's Cataloging in Publication
(Provided by Quality Books, Inc.)

Swanson, David, 1969 December 1- author.
　　War is a lie / by David Swanson. -- Second edition.
　　pages cm
　　Includes bibliographical references and index.
　　LCCN 2015953890
　　ISBN 9781682570005
　　ISBN 978-1-935982-86-9 (EPUB)
　　ISBN 978-1-935982-87-6 (Mobi)

　　1. War (Philosophy) 2. War--Moral and ethical
aspects.　 I. Title.

U21.2.S93 2016　　　　303.6'6
　　　　　　　　　　QBI15-600238

CONTENTS

PREFACE

The first edition of this book was published in 2010. Reading through it five years later, I've found that I wanted to make very few changes. Principally, I've added an epilogue that addresses the state of wars and of war lies five years on. I've also updated Chapter 14 and made a few other very minor changes throughout.

I had thought that I might produce a new edition of this book with each new war, but I quickly realized that I could not possibly keep up with all the new wars. So this is an edition that, in the epilogue, applies the lessons of the book to several new and ongoing wars at once.

This approach also allows me to examine, in the epilogue, the current and evolving ability of the public to recognize and reject war lies. Improving that ability is, of course, the entire purpose of this book.

—David Swanson
July 2015, Charlottesville, VA

INTRODUCTION

Not a single thing that we commonly believe about wars that helps keep them around is true. Wars cannot be good or glorious. Nor can they be justified as a means of achieving peace or anything else of value. The reasons given for wars, before, during, and after them (often three very different sets of reasons for the same war) are all false. It is common to imagine that, because we'd never go to war without a good reason, having gone to war, we simply must have a good reason. This needs to be reversed. Because there can be no good reason for war, having gone to war, we are participating in a lie.

A very intelligent friend recently told me that prior to 2003 no American president had ever lied about reasons for war. Another, only slightly better informed, told me that the United States had not had any problems with war lies or undesirable wars between 1975 and 2003. I hope that this book will help set the record straight. "A war based on lies" is just a long-winded way of saying "a war." The lies are part of the standard package.

Lies have preceded and accompanied wars for millennia, but in the past century war has become far more deadly. Its victims are now primarily non-participants, often almost exclusively on one side of the war. Even the participants from the dominant side can be drawn from a population coerced into fighting and isolated from those making the decisions about or benefitting from the war. Participants who survive war are far more likely now to have been trained and conditioned to do things they cannot live with having done. In short, war ever more closely resembles mass murder, a resemblance put into our legal system by the banning of war in the Kellogg-Briand Peace Pact in 1928, the United Nations Charter in 1945, and the International Criminal Court's (limited and tentative) decision in 2010 to prosecute crimes of aggression at a future date. Arguments that might have sufficed to justify

11

wars in the past might not do so now. War lies are now far more dangerous things. But, as we will see, wars were never justifiable.

While all war making is illegal under the Kellogg-Briand Pact, a defensive war is widely understood to be legal under the UN Charter, even if not necessarily moral. But any defensive war is also a war of illegal aggression from the other side. All sides in all wars, even wars with two clear aggressors, always claim to be acting defensively. Some actually are. When a powerful military attacks a weak and impoverished nation halfway around the globe, those who fight back may tell lies—about the aggressors, about their own prospects for victory, about atrocities they commit, about rewards for martyrs in paradise, etc.—but they do not have to lie the war into existence; it has come to them. The lies that create wars, and the lies that allow war to remain one of our tools of public policy, must be addressed before any others.

This book focuses, not exclusively but heavily, on the United States' wars, because the United States is where I live and because it is the leading war maker in the world right now. Many people in this country are inclined to a healthy skepticism or even fanatical certainty of disbelief when it comes to statements our government makes about anything other than wars. On taxes, Social Security, healthcare, or schools it simply goes without saying: elected officials are a pack of liars.

When it comes to wars, however, some of the same people are inclined to believe every fantastical claim that comes out of Washington, D.C., and to imagine they thought it up for themselves. Others argue for an obedient and non-questioning attitude toward "our commander-in-chief," following a pattern of behavior common among soldiers. They forget that in a democracy "we the people" are supposed to be in charge. They also forget what the United States and its allies did to German and Japanese soldiers following World War II, despite their honest defense of having followed their commanders' orders. Still other people are just not sure what to think about arguments made in support of wars. This book is, of course, addressed to those who are thinking it through for themselves.

The word "war" conjures up in many people's minds the U.S. Civil War or World War I. We hear constant references to "the battlefield" as if wars still primarily involve pairs of armies lined up against each other in an open space. Some of today's wars are more usefully referred to as "occupations" and can be visualized more as a Jackson Pollock painting with three colors splattered everywhere, one representing the occupying army, a second representing the enemy, and a third representing innocent civilians—with the second and third colors only distinguishable from each other using a microscope.

But hot occupations involving constant violence must be distinguished from the many cold occupations consisting of foreign troops stationed permanently in allied nations. And what to make of operations involving the steady bombing of a nation from unmanned drones piloted by men and women on the other side of the world? Is that war? Are secret assassination squads sent into yet other nations to work their will also taking part in war? What about arming a proxy state and encouraging it to launch attacks on a neighbor or its own people? What about selling weaponry to hostile nations around the world or facilitating the spread of nuclear weapons? Perhaps not all unjustifiable warlike actions are actually acts of war. But many are actions to which domestic and international laws of war should be applied and which we should have public knowledge of and control over. In the U.S. system of government, the legislature shouldn't cede the constitutional power of war to presidents simply because the appearance of wars has changed. The people shouldn't lose their right to know what their government is doing, simply because its actions are warlike without actually being war.

While this book focuses on the justifications that have been offered for wars, it is also an argument against silence. People should not permit congress members to campaign for office without explaining their positions on the funding of wars, including undeclared wars consisting of repeated drone strikes or bombings into foreign nations, including quick wars that come and go in the course of a term of Congress, and including very long wars that our televisions forget to remind us are still going on.

The U.S. public may be more opposed to wars now than ever before, the culmination of a process that has taken over a century and a half. Antiwar sentiment was extremely high between the two world wars, but it is now more firmly established. However, it fails when confronted with wars in which few Americans die. The steady drip of a handful of U.S. deaths each week in a war without end has become part of our national scenery. Preparation for war is everywhere and rarely questioned.

We are more saturated with militarism than ever before. The military and its support industries eat up an increasingly larger share of the economy, providing jobs intentionally spread across all congressional districts. Military recruiters and recruitment advertising are ubiquitous. Sporting events on television welcome "members of the United States armed forces viewing in 177 nations around the world" and nobody blinks. When wars begin, the government does whatever it has to do to persuade enough of the public to support the wars. Once the public turns against wars, the government just as effectively resists pressure to bring them to a swift end. Some years into the wars in Afghanistan and Iraq, a majority of Americans told pollsters it had been a mistake to begin either of those wars. But easily manipulated majorities had supported those mistakes when they were made.

Up through the two world wars, nations demanded ever greater sacrifices from the majority of their populations to support war. Today, the case for war must overcome people's resistance to arguments that they know have fooled them in the past. But, in order to support war, people need not be convinced to make great sacrifices, enlist, register for a draft, grow their own food, or curtail their consumption. They just have to be convinced to do nothing at all, or at most to tell pollsters on the phone that they support a war. The presidents who took us into the two world wars and deeper into the Vietnam War were elected claiming they'd keep us out, even as they also saw political advantages to getting in.

By the time of the Gulf War (and following British prime minister Margaret Thatcher's patriotic boost of support during her speedy 1982 war with Argentina over the Falkland Islands) the prospect of electoral gains, at least from quick wars, had come to dominate political thinking. President Bill Clinton was widely suspected, accurately or not, of launching military actions to distract from his personal scandals. George W. Bush made no secret of his hunger for war when running for president, blurting out at a December 1999 six-way New Hampshire Primary debate, which the media concluded he'd won, "I'd take him out, take out the weapons of mass destruction.... I'm surprised he's still there." Bush later told the *New York Times* he'd meant "take 'em out" referring to the weapons, not the ruler of Iraq. Presidential candidate Barack Obama promised to end one war but escalate another and enlarge the war-making machine.

That machine has changed over the years, but some things haven't. This book looks at examples of what I take to be the main categories of war lies, examples taken from around the world and through the centuries. I could have arranged this story in chronological order and named each chapter for a particular war. Such a project would have been both endless and repetitive. It would have produced an encyclopedia when what I thought was needed was a guidebook, a how-to manual to be employed in preventing and ending wars. If you want to find everything I've included about a particular war, the index at the back of the book will be useful. I recommend, however, reading the book straight through in order to follow the debunking of common themes in the war-lying business, lies that keep coming back like zombies that just won't die.

This book is aimed at exposing the falsehood of all the more and less coherent rationales that have been offered for wars. If this book succeeds in its intent, the next time a war is proposed there will be no need to wait to see whether the justifications turn out to be false. We will know that they are false, and we will know that even if true they can not serve as justifications.

Some of us knew there were no weapons in Iraq and that even if there had been that could not have legally or morally sanctioned war.

Going forward, our goal should be war preparedness in a particular sense: we should be prepared to reject lies that might launch or prolong a war. This is just what the overwhelming mass of Americans did by rejecting lies about Iran for years following the invasion of Iraq. Our preparedness should include a ready response to that most difficult argument to refute: silence. When there's no debate at all over whether to bomb Pakistan, the pro-war side automatically wins. We should mobilize not only to halt but also to prevent wars, both actions which require applying pressure to those in power, a very different thing from persuading honest observers.

Yet, persuading honest observers is the place to start. War lies come in all shapes and sizes, and I have grouped them into what I see as the dominant themes in the chapters that follow. The idea of "the big lie" is that people who would themselves more readily tell small fibs than giant whoppers will be more reluctant to doubt a big lie from someone else than to doubt a small one. But it's not strictly the size of the lie that matters, I think, so much as the type. It can be painful to realize that people you look up to as leaders recklessly waste human lives for no good reason. It can be more pleasant to suppose they would never do such a thing, even if supposing this requires erasing some well-known facts from your consciousness. The difficulty is not in believing that they would tell enormous lies, but in believing that they would commit enormous crimes.

The reasons often given for wars are not all legal reasons and not all moral reasons. They don't always agree with each other, but they are usually offered in combination nonetheless, since they appeal to different groups of potential war supporters. Wars, we are told, are fought against evil demonic peoples or dictators who have already attacked us or might soon do so. Thus, we are acting in defense. Some of us prefer to see the enemy's entire population as evil, and others to place the blame only on their government. For some people to offer their support, wars must be seen as humanitarian, fought on behalf of the very people other supporters of the same war would like to see wiped off the face of the earth. Despite wars becoming such acts of generosity, we are nonetheless careful to pretend that they are unavoidable. We are told and believe that there is no other choice. War may be a horrible thing, but we have been forced into it. Our warriors are heroes, while those who set the policy have the noblest of motives and are better qualified than the rest of us to make the critical decisions.

Once a war is underway, however, we don't continue it in order to defeat the evil enemies or to bestow benefits on them; we continue wars primarily for the good of our own soldiers currently deployed on the "battlefield," a process we call "supporting the troops." And if we want to end an unpopular war, we do that by escalating it. Thus we achieve "victory," which we can trust our televisions to accurately inform us of. Thus do we make a better world and uphold the rule of law. We prevent future wars by continuing the existing ones and preparing for ever more.

Or so we like to believe.

1

WARS ARE NOT FOUGHT AGAINST EVIL

One of the oldest excuses for war is that the enemy is irredeemably evil. He worships the wrong god, has the wrong skin and language, commits atrocities, and cannot be reasoned with. The long-standing tradition of making war on foreigners and converting those not killed to the proper religion "for their own good" is similar to the current practice of killing hated foreigners for the stated reason that their governments ignore women's rights. From among the rights of women encompassed by such an approach, one is missing: the right to life, as women's groups in Afghanistan have tried to explain to those who use their plight to justify the war. The believed evil of our opponents allows us to avoid counting the non-American women or men or children killed. Western media reinforce our skewed perspective with endless images of women in burqas, but they never risk offending us with pictures of women and children killed by our troops and air strikes.

Imagine if war were really fought for strategic, principled, humanitarian goals, the "march of freedom," and the "spread of democracy." Wouldn't we count the foreign dead in order to make some sort of rough calculation of whether the good we were trying to do outweighed the damage? We don't do so, for the obvious reason that we consider the enemy evil and worthy of death and believe that any other thought would constitute a betrayal of our own side. We used to count the enemy dead, in Vietnam and earlier wars, as a measure of progress. In 2010, Gen. David Petraeus revived a bit of that in Afghanistan, without including civilian dead. For the most part now, however, the higher the number of dead is, the more criticism there is of the war. But by avoiding counting and estimating, we give the game away: we still place a negative or empty value on those lives.

But just as the supposedly irredeemable heathen were converted to the correct religion when the screaming and dying stopped, so too do our wars eventually come to an end, or at least to a permanent occupation of a pacified puppet state. At that point, the irredeemably evil opponents become admirable or at least tolerable allies. Were they evil to begin with or did saying so just make it easier to take a nation to war and persuade its soldiers to aim and fire? Did the people of Germany become subhuman monsters each time we (the U.S. government and those persuaded to identify with it) had to make war on them, and then revert to being full humans when peace came? How did our Russian allies become an evil empire the moment they stopped doing the good humanitarian work of killing Germans? Or were we only pretending they were good, when actually they were evil all along? Or were we pretending they were evil when they were only somewhat confused human beings, just like us? How did Afghans and Iraqis all become demonic when a group of Saudis flew airplanes into buildings in the United States, and how did the Saudi people stay human? Don't look for logic.

Belief in a crusade against evil remains a strong motivator of war supporters and participants. Some supporters and participants in U.S. wars are motivated, in fact, by a desire to kill and convert non-Christians. But none of this is central to the real, or at least the primary and surface-level, motivations of war planners, which will be discussed in Chapter 6. Their bigotry and hatred, if they have any, may ease their minds, but do not typically drive their agenda. War planners do, however, find fear, hatred, and revenge to be powerful motivators of the public and of military recruits. Our violence-saturated popular culture makes us overestimate the danger of violent attack, and our government plays on that fear with threats, warnings, color-coded danger levels, airport searches, and decks of playing cards with faces of the most evil enemies on them.

Evil vs. Harm

The worst causes of preventable death and suffering in the world include wars. But here in the United States, the leading causes of preventable death are not foreign cultures, foreign governments, or terrorist groups. They are illnesses, accidents, car crashes, and suicides. The "war on poverty," "war on obesity," and other such campaigns have been failed attempts to bring to bear on other great causes of harm and loss of life the same passion and urgency usually associated with wars against evil. Why is heart disease not evil? Why is cigarette smoking or the lack of workplace safety enforcement not evil? Among the rapidly growing unhealthy factors impacting our life chances is global warming. Why do we not launch urgent all-out efforts to combat these causes of death?

The reason is one that makes no moral sense, but makes emotional sense to us all. If someone tried to hide the danger of cigarettes, knowing this would result in much suffering and death, he would have done so to make a buck, not to hurt me personally. Even if he did act for the sadistic joy of hurting lots of people, though his acts might be counted evil, he still would not have specifically set out to hurt me in particular through a violent act.

Athletes and adventurers put themselves through fear and danger just for the thrill. Civilians enduring bombing raids experience fear and danger, but not the trauma suffered by soldiers. When soldiers return from wars psychologically damaged, it is not primarily because they have been through fear and danger. The top causes of stress in war are having to kill other human beings and having to directly face other human beings who want to kill you. The latter is described by Lt. Col. Dave Grossman in his book *On Killing* as "the wind of hate." Grossman explains:

> We want desperately to be liked, loved, and in control of our lives; and intentional, overt, human hostility and aggression—more than anything else in life—assaults our self-image, our sense of control, our sense of the world as a meaningful and comprehensible place, and, ultimately, our mental and physical health.... It is not fear of death and injury from disease or accident but rather acts of personal depredation and domination by our fellow human beings that strike terror and loathing in our hearts.[1]

This is why drill sergeants are pseudo-evil toward trainees. They are inoculating them, conditioning them to face, handle, and believe they can survive the wind of hate. Most of us, fortunately, have not been so trained. The airplanes of September 11, 2001, did not hit most of our homes, but the terrorized belief that the next ones might hit us made fear an important force in politics, one that many politicians only encouraged. We were then shown images of foreign, dark-skinned, Muslim, non-English speaking prisoners being treated like wild beasts and tortured because they could not be reasoned with. And for years we bankrupted our economy to fund the killing of "rag heads" and "hadji" long after Saddam Hussein had been driven out of power, captured, and killed. This illustrates the power of belief in opposing evil. You will not find the eradication of evil anywhere in the papers of the Project for the New American Century, the think tank that pushed hardest for a war on Iraq. Opposing evil is a way to get those who will not profit in any way from a war on board with promoting it.

Atrocities

In any war, both sides claim to be fighting for good against evil. (During the Gulf War, President George H. W. Bush mispronounced Saddam Hussein's first name to sound like Sodom, while Hussein spoke of "Devil Bush.") While one side could be telling the truth, clearly both parties in a war cannot be on the side of pure goodness against absolute evil. In most cases, something evil can be pointed to as evidence. The other side has committed atrocities that only evil beings would commit. And if it hasn't really done so, then some atrocities can easily be invented. Harold Lasswell's 1927 book *Propaganda Technique in the World War* includes a chapter on "Satanism," which states:

> A handy rule for arousing hate is, if at first they do not enrage, use an atrocity. It has been employed with unvarying success in every conflict known to man. Originality, while often advantageous, is far from indispensable. In the early days of the War of 1914 [later known as World War I] a very pathetic story was told of a seven-year old youngster, who had pointed his wooden gun at a patrol of invading Uhlans, who had dispatched him on the spot. This story had done excellent duty in the Franco-Prussian war over forty years before.[2]

Other atrocity stories have more bases in fact. But usually similar atrocities can also be found in many other nations against which ours has not chosen to make war. Sometimes the U.S. government makes war on behalf of dictatorships that are themselves guilty of atrocities. Other times the United States is guilty of the same atrocities or even played a role in the atrocities of its new enemy and former ally. Even the primary offense against which the United States is going to war can be one it is guilty of. It is as important, in selling a war, to deny or excuse one's own atrocities as to highlight or invent the enemy's. President Theodore Roosevelt alleged atrocities by the Filipinos, while dismissing those committed by U.S. troops in the Philippines as of no consequence and no worse than what had been done at the massacre of the Sioux at Wounded Knee, as if mere mass murder were the standard of acceptability. One U.S. atrocity in the Philippines involved slaughtering over 600, mostly unarmed, men, women, and children trapped in the crater of a dormant volcano. The general in command of that operation openly favored the extermination of all Filipinos.

In selling the war on Iraq, it became important to stress that Saddam Hussein had used chemical weapons, and equally important to avoid the fact that he had done so with U.S. assistance. George Orwell wrote in 1948:

> Actions are held to be good or bad, not on their own merits but according to who does them, and there is almost no kind of outrage—torture, the use of hostages, forced labor, mass deportations, imprisonment without

trial, forgery, assassination, the bombing of civilians—which does not change its moral color when it is committed by "our" side.... The nationalist not only does not disapprove of atrocities committed by his own side, but he has a remarkable capacity for not even hearing about them.[3]

At some point we have to raise the question of whether the atrocities are the real motivation of the war planners, which should lead us to also look into the question of whether war is the best tool for preventing atrocities.

A Plank in Our Own Eye

The record of the United States, sadly, is one of big lies. We are told that Mexico has attacked us, when in reality the United States attacked them. Spain was denying Cubans and Filipinos their liberty, when we should have been the ones denying them their liberty. Germany was practicing imperialism, which was interfering with British, French, and U.S. empire building. Howard Zinn quotes from a 1939 skit in his *A People's History of the United States*:

> We, the governments of Great Britain and the United States, in the name of India, Burma, Malaya, Australia, British East Africa, British Guiana, Hongkong, Siam, Singapore, Egypt, Palestine, Canada, New Zealand, Northern Ireland, Scotland, Wales, as well as Puerto Rico, Guam, the Philippines, Hawaii, Alaska, and the Virgin Islands, hereby declare most emphatically, that this is not an imperialist war.[4]

Britain's Royal Air Force kept busy between the two world wars dropping bombs on India and took the prime responsibility for policing Iraq by firebombing tribes who did not or could not pay their taxes. When Britain declared war on Germany, the British imprisoned thousands of people in India for opposing World War II. Were the British fighting imperialism in World War II, or just German imperialism?

The original enemies of bands of human warriors may have been large cats, bears, and other beasts that preyed on our ancestors. Cave drawings of these animals may be some of the oldest military recruitment posters, but the new ones haven't changed much. During World War II the Nazis used a poster depicting their enemies as gorillas, copying a poster that the American government had produced for the first world war to demonize or sub-humanize the Germans. The American version carried the words "Destroy This Mad Brute," and had been copied from an earlier poster by the British. U.S. posters during World War II also depicted the Japanese as gorillas and bloodthirsty monsters.

The British and U.S. propaganda that persuaded Americans to fight in World War I focused on demonization of the Germans for fictional atrocities committed in Belgium.[5] The Committee on Public Information, run by George Creel on behalf of President Woodrow Wilson, organized "Four Minute Men" who gave pro-war speeches in movie theaters during the four minutes it took to change reels. A sample speech printed in the committee's *Four Minute Men Bulletin* on January 2, 1918, read:

> While we are sitting here tonight enjoying a picture show, do you realize that thousands of Belgians, people just like ourselves, are languishing in slavery under Prussian masters? ...Prussian "Schrecklichkeit" (the deliberate policy of terrorism) leads to almost unbelievable besotten brutality. The German soldiers...were often forced against their wills, they themselves weeping, to carry out unspeakable orders against defenseless old men, women, and children.... For instance, at Dinant the wives and children of 40 men were forced to witness the execution of their husbands and fathers.[6]

Those who commit or are believed to have committed such atrocities can be treated as less than human (while Germans committed atrocities in Belgium and throughout the war, those that received the most attention are now known to have been fabricated or remain unsubstantiated and very much in doubt).[7]

In 1938 Japanese entertainers falsely described Chinese soldiers as failing to clear away their dead bodies after battles, leaving them to the beasts and the elements.[8] This apparently helped justify the Japanese in making war on China. German troops invading the Ukraine during World War II could have converted surrendering Soviet troops to their side, but they were unable to accept their surrender because they were unable to see them as human.[9] U.S. demonization of the Japanese during World War II was so effective that the U.S. military found it hard to stop its troops from killing Japanese soldiers who were trying to surrender.[10] There were also incidents of Japanese pretending to surrender and then attacking, but those do not explain away this phenomenon.

Japanese atrocities were numerous and hideous, and did not require fabrication. U.S. posters and cartoons depicted Japanese as insects and monkeys. Australian Gen. Sir Thomas Blamey told the *New York Times*, "Fighting Japs is not like fighting normal human beings. The Jap is a little barbarian.... We are not dealing with humans as we know them. We are dealing with something primitive. Our troops have the right view of the Japs. They regard them as vermin."[11]

A U.S. Army poll in 1943 found that roughly half of all GIs believed it would be necessary to kill every Japanese on earth. War correspondent Edgar L. Jones wrote in the February 1946 *Atlantic Monthly*, "What kind of war do civilians suppose we fought anyway? We shot prisoners in cold blood, wiped out hospitals, strafed lifeboats, killed or mistreated enemy civilians, finished off the enemy wounded, tossed the dying into a hole with the dead, and in the Pacific boiled flesh off enemy skulls to make table ornaments for sweethearts, or carved their bones into letter openers."[12]

Soldiers don't do that sort of thing to human beings. They do it to evil beasts.

In fact, enemies in war are not just less than human. They are demonic. During the U.S. Civil War, Herman Melville maintained that the North was fighting for heaven and the South for hell, referring to the South as "the helmed dilated Lucifer."[13] During the Vietnam War, as Susan Brewer recounts in her book *Why America Fights*:

> War correspondents frequently did "citizen soldier" interviews with articulate young officers who would be identified by name, rank, and hometown. The soldier would talk about being "here to do a job" and express confidence in eventually getting it done.... In contrast, the enemy was routinely dehumanized in news coverage. American troops referred to the enemy as "gooks," "slopes," or "dinks."[14]

A Gulf War editorial cartoon in the *Miami Herald* depicted Saddam Hussein as a giant fanged spider attacking the United States. Hussein was frequently compared to Adolf Hitler. On October 9, 1990, a 15-year-old Kuwaiti girl told a U.S. congressional committee that she'd seen Iraqi soldiers take 15 babies out of an incubator in a Kuwaiti hospital and leave them on the cold floor to die. Some Congress members, including the late Tom Lantos (D-CA), knew but did not tell the U.S. public that the girl was the daughter of the Kuwaiti ambassador to the United States, that she'd been coached by a major U.S. public relations company paid by the Kuwaiti government, and that there was no other evidence for the story.[15] President George H. W. Bush used the dead babies story 10 times in the next 40 days, and seven senators used it in the Senate debate on whether to approve military action. The Kuwaiti disinformation campaign for the Gulf War would be successfully reprised by Iraqi groups favoring Iraqi regime change 12 years later.

Are such fibs just a necessary part of the process of stirring up weak souls' emotions for the truly necessary and noble work of war? Are we all, each and every one of us, wise and knowing insiders who must tolerate being lied to because others just don't understand? This line of thinking would be more persuasive if wars did any good that could not be done without them and if they did it without all the harm. Two intense wars and many years of bombing and deprivation later, the evil ruler of Iraq was gone, but we'd spent trillions of dollars; a million Iraqis were dead; four million were displaced and desperate and abandoned; violence was everywhere; sex trafficking was on the rise; the basic infrastructure of electricity, water, sewage, and healthcare was in ruins (in part because of the U.S. intention to privatize Iraq's resources for profit); life expectancy had dropped; cancer rates in Fallujah surpassed those in Hiroshima; anti-U.S. terrorist groups were using the occupation of Iraq as a recruiting tool; there was no functioning government in Iraq; and most Iraqis said they'd been better off with Saddam Hussein in power. We have to be lied to for this? Really?

Of course, Saddam Hussein did evil things. He murdered and tortured. But he caused the most suffering through a war against Iran in which the United States assisted him. He could have been the pure essence of evil, without our own nation's needing to qualify as the epitome of unstained goodness. But why did Americans, twice, somehow choose the precise moments in which our government wanted to make war to become outraged at Saddam Hussein's evil? Why are the rulers of Saudi Arabia, just next door, never any cause for distress in our humanitarian hearts? Are we emotional opportunists, developing hatred only for those we have a chance to unseat or kill? Or are those who are instructing us as to whom we should hate this month the real opportunists?

Bigoted Racist Jingoism Helps the Medicine Go Down

What makes the most fantastic and undocumented lies credible are differences and prejudices, against others and in favor of our own. Without religious bigotry, racism, and patriotic jingoism, wars would be harder to sell.

Religion has long been a justification for wars, which were fought for gods before they were fought for pharaohs, kings, and emperors. If Barbara Ehrenreich has it right in her book *Blood Rites: Origins and History of the Passions of War*, the earliest precursors to wars were battles against lions, leopards, and other ferocious predators of people.[16] In fact, those predatory beasts may be the base material from which gods were invented—and unmanned drones named (e.g., "the Predator"). The "ultimate sacrifice" in war may be intimately connected with the practice of human sacrifice as it existed before wars, as we know them, came to be. The emotions (not the creeds or accomplishments, but some of the sensations) of religion and war may be so similar, if not identical, because the two practices have a common history and have never been far apart.

The crusades and colonial wars and many other wars have had religious justifications. Americans fought religious wars for many generations prior to the war for independence from England. Captain John Underhill in 1637 described his own heroic war making against the Pequot:

> Captaine Mason entering into a Wigwam, brought out a fire-brand, after hee had wounded many in the house; then hee set fire to the West-side...my selfe set fire on the South end with a traine of Powder, the fires

of both meeting in the center of the Fort blazed most terribly, and burnt all in the space of halfe an houre; many couragious fellowes were unwilling to come out, and fought most desperately...so as they were scorched and burnt...and so perished valiantly.... Many were burnt in the Fort, both men, women, and children.[17]

This Underhill explains as a holy war: "The Lord is pleased to exercise his people with trouble and afflictions, that hee might appeare to them in mercy, and reveale more cleerely his free grace unto their soules."[18]

Underhill means his own soul, and the Lord's people are of course the white folks. The Native Americans may have been courageous and valiant, but they were not recognized as people in the full sense. Two and a half centuries later, many Americans had developed a far more enlightened outlook, and many had not. President William McKinley viewed Filipinos as in need of military occupation for their own good.

By his own account, McKinley in 1899 told a gathering of Methodists he hadn't wanted the Philippines, and "when they came to us, as a gift from the gods, I did not know what to do with them." McKinley said he had prayed and received the following enlightenment. It would be "cowardly and dishonorable" to give the Philippines back to Spain, "bad business" to give them to Germany or France, and would supposedly create "anarchy and misrule" to leave the Philippines to the Filipinos. So, by divine guidance, McKinley saw that he had no choice: "There was nothing left for us to do but to take them all, and to educate the Filipinos, and uplift and civilize and Christianize them." McKinley was proposing to civilize a nation with a university older than Harvard and to Christianize a population that was largely Roman Catholic.[19]

It is doubtful many members of the delegation of Methodists questioned McKinley's wisdom. As Harold Lasswell noted in 1927, "The churches of practically every description can be relied upon to bless a popular war, and to see in it an opportunity for the triumph of whatever godly design they choose to further." All that was needed, Lasswell said, was to get "conspicuous clerics" to support the war, and "lesser lights will twinkle after." Propaganda posters in the United States during World War I showed Jesus wearing khaki and sighting down a gun barrel. Lasswell had lived through a war fought against Germans, people who predominantly belonged to the same religion as Americans.[20] How much easier it is to use religion in wars against Muslims in the 21st century. Karim Karim, an associate professor at Carleton University's School of Journalism and Communication, writes:

The historically entrenched image of the 'bad Muslim' has been quite useful to Western governments planning to attack Muslim-majority lands. If public opinion in their countries can be convinced that Muslims

are barbaric and violent, then killing them and destroying their property appears more acceptable.[21]

In reality, of course, nobody's religion justifies making war on them,
and U.S. presidents no longer claim it does (though in 2015-2016, some presidential candidates did). But Christian proselytization is common in the U.S.
military, and so is hatred of Muslims. Soldiers have reported to the Military
Religious Freedom Foundation that when seeking mental health counseling,
they have been sent to chaplains instead who have counseled them to stay on
the "battlefield" to "kill Muslims for Christ."[22]

Religion can be used to encourage the belief that what you are doing is
good even if it makes no sense to you. A higher being understands it, even if
you don't. Religion can offer life after death and a belief that you are killing
and risking death for the highest possible cause. But religion is not the only
group difference that can be used to promote wars. Any difference of culture
or language will do, and the power of racism to facilitate the worst sorts of
human behavior is well established. Senator Albert J. Beveridge (R-IN) offered the Senate his own divinely guided rationale for war on the Philippines:

> God has not been preparing the English-speaking and Teutonic peoples
> for a thousand years for nothing but vain and idle self-contemplation
> and self-admiration. No! He has made us the master organizers of the
> world to establish system where chaos reigns.[23]

The two world wars in Europe, while fought between nations now typically thought of as "white," involved racism on all sides as well. The French
newspaper *La Croix* on August 15, 1914, celebrated "the ancient élan of the
Gauls, the Romans, and the French resurging within us," and declared that
"The Germans must be purged from the left bank of the Rhine. These infa-
mous hordes must be thrust back within their own frontiers. The Gauls of
France and Belgium must repulse the invader with a decisive blow, once and
for all. The race war appears."[24]

Three years later it was the United States' turn to lose its mind. On
December 7, 1917, Congressman Walter Chandler (D-TN) declared on the
floor of the House:

> It has been said that if you will analyze the blood of a Jew under the
> microscope, you will find the Talmud and the Old Bible floating around
> in some particles. If you analyze the blood of a representative German
> or Teuton you will find machine guns and particles of shells and bombs
> floating around in the blood.... Fight them until you destroy the whole
> bunch.[25]

This kind of thinking helps not only in easing the war-funding check-books out of the pockets of Congress members, but also in allowing the young people they send to war to do the killing. As we'll see in Chapter 5, killing does not come easily. About 98 percent of people tend to be very resistant to killing other people. More recently, a psychiatrist developed a methodology to allow the U.S. Navy to better prepare assassins to kill. It includes techniques, "to get the men to think of the potential enemies they will have to face as inferior forms of life [with films] biased to present the enemy as less than human: the stupidity of local customs is ridiculed, local personalities are presented as evil demigods."[26]

It is much easier for a U.S. soldier to kill a hadji than a human being, just as it was easier for Nazi troops to kill *Untermenschen* than real people. William Halsey, who commanded the United States' naval forces in the South Pacific during World War II, thought of his mission as "Kill Japs, kill Japs, kill more Japs," and had vowed that when the war was over, the Japanese language would be spoken only in hell.[27]

If war evolved as a way for the men who killed giant beasts to keep busy killing other men as those animals died out, as Ehrenreich theorizes, its partnership with racism and all other distinctions between groups of people is a long one. But nationalism is the most recent, powerful, and mysterious source of mystical devotion aligned with war, and the one that itself grew out of war making. While knights of old would die for their own glory, modern men and women will die for a fluttering piece of colored cloth that itself cares nothing for them. The day after the United States declared war on Spain in 1898, the first state (New York) passed a law requiring that school children salute the U.S. flag. Others would follow. Nationalism was the new religion.[28]

Samuel Johnson reportedly remarked that patriotism is the last refuge of a scoundrel, while others have suggested that, on the contrary, it is the first. When it comes to motivating warlike emotions, if other differences fail, there is always this: the enemy does not belong to our country and salute our flag. When the United States was lied more deeply into the Vietnam War, all but two senators voted for the Gulf of Tonkin resolution. One of the two, Wayne Morse (D-OR) told other senators that he had been told by the Pentagon that the alleged attack by the North Vietnamese had been provoked. As will be discussed in Chapter 2, Morse's information was correct. Any attack would have been provoked. But, as we will see, the attack itself was fictional. Morse's colleagues did not oppose him on the grounds that he was mistaken, however. Instead, a senator told him, "Hell, Wayne, you can't get into a fight with the president when *all the flags are waving* and we're about to go to a national convention. All [President] Lyndon [Johnson] wants is a piece of paper telling him we did right out there, and we support him."[29]

As the war ground on for years, pointlessly destroying millions of lives, senators on the Foreign Relations Committee discussed in secret their concern that they had been lied to. Yet they chose to keep quiet, and records of some of those meetings were not made public until 2010.[30] The flags had apparently been waving through all the intervening years.

War is as good for patriotism as patriotism is for war. When World War I began, many socialists in Europe rallied to their various national flags and abandoned their struggle for the international working class.[31] Still today, nothing drives American opposition to international structures of government like U.S. interest in war and insistence that U.S. soldiers never be subject to any authority other than Washington, D.C.

That's Not Ten Million People, That's Adolf Hitler

But wars are not fought against flags or ideas, nations or demonized dictators. They are fought against people, 98 percent of whom are resistant to killing, and most of whom had little or nothing to do with bringing on the war. One way to dehumanize those people is to replace all of them with an image of a single monstrous individual.

Marlin Fitzwater, White House press secretary for Presidents Ronald Reagan and George H. W. Bush, said that war is "easier for people to understand if there's a face to the enemy." He gave examples: "Hitler, Ho Chi Minh, Saddam Hussein, Milosevic." Fitzwater might well have included the name Manuel Antonio Noriega. When the first President Bush sought, among other things, to prove he was no "wimp" by attacking Panama in 1989, the most prominent justification was that Panama's leader was a mean, drug-crazed, weirdo with a pockmarked face who liked to commit adultery. An important article in the very serious *New York Times* on December 26, 1989, began "The United States military headquarters here, which has portrayed General Manuel Antonio Noriega as an erratic, cocaine-snorting dictator who prays to voodoo gods, announced today that the deposed leader wore red underwear and availed himself of prostitutes."

Never mind that Noriega had worked for the U.S. Central Intelligence Agency (CIA), including at the time he'd stolen the 1984 election in Panama. Never mind that his real offense was refusing to back U.S. war making against Nicaragua. Never mind that the United States had known about Noriega's drug trafficking for years and continued working with him. This man snorted cocaine in red underwear with women not his wife. "That is aggression as surely as Adolf Hitler's invasion of Poland 50 years ago was aggression," declared Deputy Secretary of State Lawrence Eagleburger of Noriega's drug trafficking.[32] The invading U.S. liberators even claimed to find a big stash of cocaine in one of Noriega's homes, although it turned out to be tamales wrapped in banana leaves. And what if the tamales really had been cocaine? Would that, like the discovery of actual "weapons of mass destruction" in Baghdad in 2003 have justified *war*?

Fitzwater's reference to "Milosevic" was, of course, to Slobodan Milosevic, then president of Serbia, whom David Nyhan of the *Boston Globe* in January 1999 called "the closest thing to Hitler Europe has confronted in the last half century." Except, you know, for all the other ones. By 2010, the practice in U.S. domestic politics of comparing anyone you disagreed with to Hitler had become almost comical, but it is a practice that has helped launch many wars and may still launch more. However, it takes two to tango: in 1999, Serbs were calling the president of the United States "Bill Hitler."[33]

In the spring of 1914, in a movie theater in Tours, France, an image of Wilhelm II, the Emperor of Germany, came on the screen for a moment. All hell broke loose.

"Everybody yelled and whistled, men, women, and children, as if they had been personally insulted. The good natured people of Tours, who knew no more about the world and politics than what they had read in their newspapers, had gone mad for an instant," according to Stefan Zweig.[34] But the French would not be fighting Kaiser Wilhelm II. They would be fighting ordinary people who happened to be born a little ways away from themselves in Germany.

Increasingly, over the years, we've been told that wars are not against people, but purely against bad governments and their evil leaders. Time after time we fall for tired rhetoric about new generations of "precision" weapons that our leaders pretend can target oppressive regimes without harming the people we think we're liberating. And we fight wars for "regime change." If the wars don't end when the regime has been changed, that's because we have a responsibility to take care of the "unfit" creatures, the little children, whose regimes we've changed. Yet, there's no established record of this doing any good. The United States and its allies did relatively well by Germany and Japan following World War II, but could have done so for Germany following World War I and skipped the sequel. Germany and Japan were reduced to rubble, and U.S. troops have yet to leave. That's hardly a useful model for new wars.

With wars or warlike actions the United States has overthrown governments in Hawaii, Cuba, Puerto Rico, the Philippines, Nicaragua, Honduras, Iran, Guatemala, Vietnam, Chile, Grenada, Panama, Afghanistan, and Iraq, not to mention the Congo (1960); Ecuador (1961 and 1963); Brazil (1961 and 1964); the Dominican Republic (1961 and 1963); Greece (1965 and 1967); Bolivia (1964 and 1971); El Salvador (1961); Guyana (1964); Indonesia (1965);

Ghana (1966); and of course Haiti (1991 and 2004). We've replaced democracy with dictatorship, dictatorship with chaos, and local rule with U.S. domination and occupation. In no case has a U.S. war clearly reduced evil. In most cases, including Iran and Iraq, U.S. invasions and U.S.-backed coups have led to severe repression, disappearances, extra-judicial executions, torture, corruption, and prolonged setbacks for the democratic aspirations of ordinary people.

The focus on rulers in wars is not motivated by humanitarianism so much as propaganda. People enjoy fantasizing that a war is a duel between great leaders. This requires demonizing one and glorifying another.

If You're Not for War, You're for Tyrants, Slavery, and Nazism

The United States was born out of a war against the figure of King George, whose crimes are listed in the *Declaration of Independence*. George Washington was correspondingly glorified. King George of England and his government were guilty of the crimes alleged, but other colonies gained their rights and independence without a war. As with all wars, no matter how old and glorious, the American Revolution was driven by lies. The story of the Boston Massacre, for example, was distorted beyond recognition, including in an engraving by Paul Revere that depicted the British as butchers. Benjamin Franklin produced a fake issue of the *Boston Independent* in which the British boasted of scalp hunting.[35] Thomas Paine and other pamphleteers sold the colonists on war, but not without misdirection and false promises. Howard Zinn describes what happened:

> Around 1776, certain important people in the English colonies made a discovery that would prove enormously useful for the next two hundred years. They found that by creating a nation, a symbol, a legal unity called the United States, they could take over land, profits, and political power from favorites of the British Empire. In the process, they could hold back a number of potential rebellions and create a consensus of popular support for the rule of a new, privileged leadership.[36]

As Zinn notes, prior to the revolution, there had been 18 uprisings against colonial governments, six black rebellions, and 40 riots, and the political elites saw a possibility for redirecting anger toward England. Still, the poor who would not profit from the war or reap its political rewards had to be compelled by force to fight in it. Many, including slaves promised greater liberty by the British, deserted or switched sides. Punishment for infractions in the Continental Army was 100 lashes. When George Washington, the richest man in America, was unable to convince Congress to raise the legal limit to 500 lashes, he considered using hard labor as a punishment instead, but dropped that idea because the hard labor would have been indistinguishable from regular service in the Continental Army. Soldiers also deserted because they needed food, clothing, shelter, medicine, and money. They signed up for pay, were not paid, and endangered their families' wellbeing by remaining in the Army unpaid. About two-thirds of them were ambivalent to or against the cause for which they were fighting and suffering.[37] Popular rebellions, like Shays' Rebellion in Massachusetts, would follow the revolutionary victory.

The American revolutionaries were also able to open up the West to expansion and wars against the Native Americans, something the British had been forbidding. The American Revolution, the very act of birth and liberation for the United States, was also a war of expansion and conquest. King George, according to the *Declaration of Independence*, had "endeavoured [*sic*] to bring on the inhabitants of our frontiers, the merciless Indian Savages." Of course, those were people fighting in defense of their lands and lives. Victory at Yorktown was bad news for their future, as England signed their lands over to the new nation.

Another sacred war in U.S. history, the Civil War, was fought—so many believe—in order to put an end to the evil of slavery. In reality, that goal was a belated excuse for a war already well underway, much like spreading democracy to Iraq became a belated justification for a war begun in 2003 overwhelmingly in the name of eliminating fictional weaponry. In fact, the mission of ending slavery was required to justify a war that had become too horrifying to be justified solely by the empty political goal of "union." Patriotism had not yet been puffed up into quite the enormity it is today. Casualties were mounting sharply: 25,000 at Shiloh, 20,000 at Bull Run, 24,000 in a day at Antietam. A week after Antietam, Lincoln issued the Emancipation Proclamation, which freed the slaves only where Lincoln could not free the slaves except by winning the war. (His orders freed slaves only in southern states that had seceded, not in border states that remained in the union.) Yale historian Harry Stout explains why Lincoln took this step: "By Lincoln's calculation, the killing must continue on ever grander scales. But for that to succeed, the people must be persuaded to shed blood without reservation. This, in turn, required a moral certitude that the killing was just. Only emancipation—Lincoln's last card—would provide such certitude."[38] The Proclamation also worked against England's entering the war on the side of the South.

We can't know for certain what would have happened to the colonies without the Revolution or to slavery without the Civil War. But we know that much of the rest of the hemisphere ended colonial rule and slavery without wars. Had Congress found the decency to end slavery through legislation, perhaps the nation would have ended it without division. Had the American

South been permitted to secede in peace, and the Fugitive Slave Law been easily repealed by the North, it seems unlikely slavery would have lasted much
longer.[39] In fact, widespread slavery in the South continued in a slightly different form right up until World War II, and was openly defended as being
justified by the cruelty of the North during and following the Civil War.[40]

The Mexican-American War, which was fought in part in order to expand slavery—an expansion that may have helped lead to the Civil War—is
less talked about. When the United States, in the course of that war, forced
Mexico to give up its northern territories, American diplomat Nicholas Trist
negotiated most firmly on one point. He wrote to the U.S. secretary of state:

> I assured [the Mexicans] that if it were in their power to offer me the
> whole territory described in our project, increased ten-fold in value,
> and, in addition to that, covered a foot thick all over with pure gold,
> upon the single condition that slavery should be excluded therefrom, I
> could not entertain the offer for a moment.[41]

Was that war fought against evil, too?

The most sacred and unquestionable war in U.S. history, however, is
World War II. I'll save a full discussion of this war for Chapter 4, but note
here only that in the minds of many Americans today, World War II was justified because of the degree of evilness of Adolf Hitler, and that evilness is to
be found above all in the holocaust.

But you won't find any recruitment posters of Uncle Sam saying, "I Want
You...to Save the Jews." When a resolution was introduced in the U.S. Senate
in 1934 expressing "surprise and pain" at Germany's actions, and asking that
Germany restore rights to Jews, the State Department "caused it to be buried
in committee."[42]

By 1937 Poland had developed a plan to send Jews to Madagascar, and
the Dominican Republic had a plan to accept them as well. Prime Minister
Neville Chamberlain of Great Britain came up with a plan to send Germany's
Jews to Tanganyika in East Africa. Representatives of the United States,
Britain, and South American nations met at Lake Geneva in July 1938 and all
agreed that none of them would accept the Jews.

On November 15, 1938, reporters asked President Franklin Roosevelt
what could be done. He replied that he would refuse to consider allowing
more immigrants than the standard quota system allowed. Bills were introduced in Congress to allow 20,000 Jews under the age of 14 to enter the
United States. Senator Robert Wagner (D-NY) said, "Thousands of American
families have already expressed their willingness to take refugee children into
their homes." First Lady Eleanor Roosevelt set aside her anti-Semitism to support the legislation, but her husband successfully blocked it for years.

In July, 1940, Adolf Eichman, "architect of the holocaust," intended to send all Jews to Madagascar, which now belonged to Germany, France having been occupied. The ships would need to wait only until the British, which now meant Winston Churchill, ended their blockade. That day never came. On November 25, 1940, the French ambassador asked the U.S. secretary of state to consider accepting German Jewish refugees then in France. On the 21st of December, the secretary of state declined. By July 1941, the Nazis had determined that a final solution for the Jews could consist of genocide rather than expulsion.

In 1942, with the assistance of the Census Bureau, the United States locked up 110,000 Japanese Americans and Japanese in various internment camps, primarily on the West Coast, where they were identified by numbers rather than names. This action, taken by President Roosevelt, was supported two years later by the U.S. Supreme Court.

In 1943 off-duty white U.S. troops attacked Latinos and African Americans in Los Angeles's "zoot suit riots," stripping and beating them in the streets in a manner that would have made Hitler proud. The Los Angeles City Council, in a remarkable effort to blame the victims, responded by banning the style of clothing worn by Mexican immigrants called the zoot suit.

When U.S. troops were crammed onto the *Queen Mary* in 1945 headed for the European war, blacks were kept apart from whites and stowed in the depths of the ship near the engine room, as far as possible from fresh air, in the same location in which blacks had been brought to America from Africa centuries before.[43] African-American soldiers who survived World War II could not legally return home to many parts of the United States if they had married white women overseas. White soldiers who had married Asians were up against the same anti-miscegenation laws in 15 states.

It is simply preposterous to suggest that the United States fought World War II against racial injustice or to save the Jews. What we are told wars are for is extremely different from what they are really for.

Modern Variations

In this age of supposedly fighting against rulers and on behalf of oppressed peoples, the Vietnam War offers an interesting case in which the U.S. policy was to avoid overthrowing the enemy government but to work hard to kill its people. To overthrow the government in Hanoi, it was feared, would draw China or Russia into the war, something the United States hoped to avoid. But destroying the nation ruled by Hanoi was expected to cause it to submit to U.S. rule.[44]

The Afghanistan War, already the longest war in U.S. history and entering its 10th year at the time this book was written, is another interesting case, in that the demonic figure used to justify it, terrorist leader Osama bin Laden, was not the ruler of the country. He was someone who had spent time in the country, and in fact had been supported there by the United States in a war against the Soviet Union. He had allegedly planned the crimes of September 11, 2001, in part in Afghanistan. Other planning, we knew, had gone on in Europe and the United States. But it was Afghanistan that apparently needed to be punished for its role as host to this criminal.

For the previous three years, the United States had been asking the Taliban, the political group in Afghanistan allegedly sheltering bin Laden, to turn him over. The Taliban wanted to see evidence against bin Laden and to be assured that he would receive a fair trial in a third country and not face the death penalty. According to the British Broadcasting Corporation (BBC), the Taliban warned the United States that bin Laden was planning an attack on American soil. Former Pakistani foreign secretary Niaz Naik told the BBC that senior U.S. officials had told him at a UN-sponsored summit in Berlin in July, 2001 that the United States would take military action against the Taliban by mid-October. Naik "said it was doubtful that Washington would drop its plan even if bin Laden were to be surrendered immediately by the Taliban."[45]

This was all before the crimes of September 11, for which the war would supposedly be revenge. When the United States attacked Afghanistan on October 7, 2001, the Taliban again offered to negotiate for the handing over of bin Laden. When President Bush again refused, the Taliban dropped its demand for evidence of guilt and offered simply to turn bin Laden over to a third country. President George W. Bush rejected this offer and continued bombing.[46] At a March 13, 2002, press conference, Bush said of bin Laden, "I truly am not that concerned about him." For at least several more years, with bin Laden and his group, al Qaeda, no longer believed to be in Afghanistan, the war of revenge against him continued to afflict the people of that land. In contrast to Iraq, the War in Afghanistan was often referred to between 2003 and 2009 as "the good war."

The case made for the Iraq War in 2002 and 2003 appeared to be about "weapons of mass destruction," as well as more revenge against bin Laden, who in reality had no connections to Iraq at all. If Iraq didn't give the weapons up, there would be war. And since Iraq did not have them, there was war. But this was fundamentally an argument that Iraqis, or at least Saddam Hussein, embodied evil. After all, few nations possessed anywhere near as many nuclear, biological, or chemical weapons as the United States, and we didn't believe anyone had the right to make war on us. The United States helped other nations acquire such weapons and did not make war on them. In fact, the United States had helped Iraq acquire biological and chemical weapons years before, which had laid the basis for the pretenses that it still had them.

Ordinarily, a nation's possessing weapons can be immoral, undesirable, or illegal, but it cannot be grounds for a war. Aggressive war is itself the most immoral, undesirable, and illegal act possible. So, why was the debate over whether to attack Iraq a debate over whether Iraq had weapons? Apparently, we had established that Iraqis were so evil that if they had weapons then they would use them, possibly through Saddam Hussein's fictional ties to al Qaeda. If someone else had weapons, we could talk to them. If Iraqis had weapons we needed to wage war against them. They were part of what President George W. Bush called "an axis of evil." That Iraq was most blatantly not using its alleged weapons and that the surest way to provoke their use would be to attack Iraq were inconvenient thoughts, and therefore they were set aside and forgotten, because our leaders knew full well that Iraq really had no such capability.

Fighting Fire with Gasoline

A central problem with the idea that wars are needed to combat evil is that there is nothing more evil than war. War causes more suffering and death than anything war can be used to combat. Wars don't cure diseases or prevent car accidents or reduce suicides. (In fact, as we'll see in Chapter 5, they drive suicides through the roof.) No matter how evil a dictator or a people may be, they cannot be more evil than war. Had he lived to be a thousand, Saddam Hussein could not have done the damage to the people of Iraq or the world that the war to eliminate his fictional weapons has done. War is not a clean and acceptable operation marred here and there by atrocities. War is all atrocity, even when it purely involves soldiers obediently killing soldiers. Rarely, however, is that all it involves. Gen. Zachary Taylor reported on the Mexican-American War (1846–1848) to the U.S. War Department:

> I deeply regret to report that many of the twelve months' volunteers, in their route hence of the lower Rio Grande, have committed extensive outrages and depredations upon the peaceable inhabitants. THERE IS SCARCELY ANY FORM OF CRIME THAT HAS NOT BEEN REPORTED TO ME AS COMMITTED BY THEM.[47]

If Gen. Taylor did not want to witness outrages, he should have stayed out of war. And if the American people felt the same way, they should not have made him a hero and a president for going to war. Rape and torture are not the worst part of war. The worst part is the acceptable part: the killing. The torture engaged in by the United States during its recent wars on Afghanistan and Iraq is part, and not the worst part, of a larger crime. The Jewish holocaust took nearly 6 million lives in the most horrible way imaginable, but World War II took, in total, about 70 million—of which about 24 million were military. We don't hear much about the 9 million Soviet soldiers whom the Germans killed. But they died facing people who wanted to kill them, and they themselves were under orders to kill. There are few things worse in the world. Missing from U.S. war mythology is the fact that by the time of the D-Day invasion, 80 percent of the German army was busy fighting the Russians. But that does not make the Russians heroes; it just shifts the focus of a tragic drama of stupidity and pain eastward.

Most supporters of war admit that war is hell. But most human beings like to believe that all is fundamentally right with the world, that everything is for the best, that all actions have a divine purpose. Even those who lack religion tend, when discussing something horribly sad or tragic, not to exclaim, "How sad and awful!" but to express—and not just under shock but even years later—their inability to "understand" or "believe" or "comprehend" it, as though pain and suffering were not as clearly comprehensible facts as joy and happiness are. We want to pretend with Dr. Pangloss that all is for the best, and the way we do this with war is to imagine that our side is battling against evil for the sake of good, and that war is the only way such a battle can be waged. If we have the means with which to wage such battles, then as Senator Beveridge remarked above, we must be expected to use them. Senator William Fulbright (D-AK) explained this phenomenon:

> Power tends to confuse itself with virtue and a great nation is peculiarly susceptible to the idea that its power is a sign of God's favor, conferring upon it a special responsibility for other nations—to make them richer and happier and wiser, to remake them, that is, in its own shining image.[48]

Madeline Albright, secretary of state when Bill Clinton was president, was more concise: "What's the point of having this superb military that you're always talking about if we can't use it?"[49]

The belief in a divine right to wage war seems to only grow stronger when great military power runs up against resistance too strong for military power to overcome. In 2008 a U.S. journalist wrote about Gen. David Petraeus, then commander in Iraq, "God has apparently seen fit to give the U.S. Army a great general in this time of need."[50]

On August 6, 1945, President Harry S. Truman announced:

Sixteen hours ago an American airplane dropped one bomb on Hiroshima, an important Japanese Army base. That bomb had more power than 20,000 tons of T.N.T. It had more than two thousand times the blast power of the British "Grand Slam" which is the largest bomb ever yet used in the history of warfare.[51]

When Truman lied to America that Hiroshima was a military base rather than a city full of civilians, people no doubt wanted to believe him. Who would want the shame of belonging to the nation that commits a whole new kind of atrocity? (Will naming lower Manhattan "ground zero" erase the guilt?) And when we learned the truth, we wanted and still want desperately to believe that war is peace, that violence is salvation, that our government dropped nuclear bombs in order to save lives, or at least to save American lives.

We tell each other that the bombs shortened the war and saved more lives than the some 200,000 they took away. And yet, weeks before the first bomb was dropped, on July 13, 1945, Japan sent a telegram to the Soviet Union expressing its desire to surrender and end the war. The United States had broken Japan's codes and read the telegram. Truman referred in his diary to "the telegram from Jap Emperor asking for peace." Truman had been informed through Swiss and Portuguese channels of Japanese peace overtures as early as three months before Hiroshima. Japan objected only to surrendering unconditionally and giving up its emperor, but the United States insisted on those terms until after the bombs fell, at which point it allowed Japan to keep its emperor.

Presidential advisor James Byrnes had told Truman that dropping the bombs would allow the United States to "dictate the terms of ending the war." Secretary of the Navy James Forrestal wrote in his diary that Byrnes was "most anxious to get the Japanese affair over with before the Russians got in." Truman wrote in his diary that the Soviets were preparing to march against Japan and "Fini Japs when that comes about." Truman ordered the bomb dropped on Hiroshima on August 6 and another type of bomb, a plutonium bomb, which the military also wanted to test and demonstrate, on Nagasaki on August 9. Also on August 9, the Soviets attacked the Japanese. During the next two weeks, the Soviets killed 84,000 Japanese while losing 12,000 of their own soldiers, and the United States continued bombing Japan with non-nuclear weapons. Then the Japanese surrendered. The United States Strategic Bombing Survey concluded that, "certainly prior to 31 December, 1945, and in all probability prior to 1 November, 1945, Japan would have surrendered even if the atomic bombs had not been dropped, even if Russia had not entered the war, and even if no invasion had been planned or contemplated."[52]

One dissenter who had expressed this same view to the Secretary of War prior to the bombings was Gen. Dwight Eisenhower. The Chairman of the Joint Chiefs of Staff Admiral William D. Leahy agreed: "The use of this barbarous weapon at Hiroshima and Nagasaki was of no material assistance in our war against Japan. The Japanese were already defeated and ready to surrender."[53]

Whatever dropping the bombs might possibly have contributed to ending the war, it is curious that the approach of *threatening* to drop them, the approach used during a half-century of Cold War to follow, was never tried. An explanation may perhaps be found in Truman's comments suggesting the motive of revenge:

> Having found the bomb we have used it. We have used it against those who attacked us without warning at Pearl Harbor, against those who have starved and beaten and executed American prisoners of war, and against those who have abandoned all pretense of obeying international law of warfare.[54]

Truman could not, incidentally, have chosen Tokyo as a target—not because it was a city, but because the United States had already reduced it to rubble.

The nuclear catastrophes may have been, not the ending of a World War, but the theatrical opening of the Cold War, aimed at sending a message to the Soviets. Many low- and high-ranking officials in the U.S. military, including commanders-in-chief, have been tempted to nuke more cities ever since, beginning with Truman threatening to nuke China in 1950. A myth developed, in fact, that Eisenhower's enthusiasm for nuking China led to the rapid conclusion of the Korean War. Belief in that myth led President Richard Nixon, decades later, to imagine he could end the Vietnam War by pretending to be crazy enough to use nuclear bombs. Even more disturbingly, he actually was crazy enough. "The nuclear bomb, does that bother you?...I just want you to think big, Henry, for Christsakes," Nixon said to Henry Kissinger in discussing options for Vietnam.[55]

President George W. Bush oversaw the development of smaller nuclear weapons that might be used more readily, as well as much larger non-nuclear bombs, blurring the line between the two. President Barack Obama established in 2010 that the United States might strike first with nuclear weapons, but only against Iran or North Korea. The United States alleged, without evidence, that Iran was not complying with the Nuclear Nonproliferation Treaty (NPT), even though the clearest violation of that treaty is the United States' own failure to work on disarmament and the United States' Mutual Defense Agreement with the United Kingdom, by which the two countries share nuclear weapons in violation of Article 1 of the NPT, and even though the United States' first strike nuclear weapons policy violates yet another treaty: the UN Charter.

Americans may never admit what was done in Hiroshima and Nagasaki, but our country had been in some measure prepared for it. After Germany had invaded Poland, Britain and France had declared war on Germany. Britain in 1940 had broken an agreement with Germany not to bomb civilians, before Germany retaliated in the same manner against England—although Germany had itself bombed Guernica, Spain, in 1937, and Warsaw, Poland, in 1939, and Japan meanwhile was bombing civilians in China. Then, for years, Britain and Germany had bombed each other's cities before the United States joined in, bombing German and Japanese cities in a spree of destruction unlike anything ever previously witnessed. When the United States was firebombing Japanese cities, *Life* magazine printed a photo of a Japanese person burning to death and commented, "This is the only way." By the time of the Vietnam War, such images were highly controversial. By the time of the 2003 war on Iraq, such images were not shown, just as enemy bodies were no longer counted. That development, arguably a form of progress, still leaves us far from the day when atrocities will be displayed with the caption "There has to be another way."

Combating evil is what peace activists do. It is not what wars do. And it is not, at least not obviously, what motivates the masters of war, those who plan the wars and bring them into being. But it is tempting to think so. It is very noble to make brave sacrifices, even the ultimate sacrifice of one's life, in order to end evil. It is perhaps even noble to use other people's children to vicariously put an end to evil, which is all that most war supporters do. It is righteous to become part of something bigger than oneself. It can be thrilling to revel in patriotism. It can be momentarily pleasurable I'm sure, if less righteous and noble, to indulge in hatred, racism, and other group prejudices. It's nice to imagine that your group is superior to someone else's. And the patriotism, racism, and other -isms that divide you from the enemy, can thrillingly unite you, for once, with all of your neighbors and compatriots across the now meaningless boundaries that usually hold sway.

If you are frustrated and angry, if you long to feel important, powerful, and dominating, if you crave the license to lash out in revenge either verbally or physically, you may cheer for a government that announces a vacation from morality and open permission to hate and to kill. You'll notice that the most enthusiastic war supporters sometimes want nonviolent war opponents killed and tortured along with the vicious and dreaded enemy; the hatred is far more important than its object. If your religious beliefs tell you that war is good, then you've really gone big time. Now you're part of God's plan. You'll live after death, and perhaps we'll all be better off if you bring on the death of us all.

But simplistic beliefs in good and evil don't match up well with the real world, no matter how many people share them unquestioningly. They do not make you a master of the universe. On the contrary, they place control of your fate in the hands of people cynically manipulating you with war lies. And the hatred and bigotry don't provide lasting satisfaction, but instead breed bitter resentment.

Are you above all that? Have you outgrown racism and other such ignorant beliefs? Do you support wars because they, in fact, have honorable motivations as well? Do you suppose that wars, whatever base emotions also get attached to them, are fought in defense of victims against aggressors and to preserve the most civilized and democratic ways of life? Let's take a look at that in Chapter 2.

2

WARS ARE NOT
LAUNCHED IN DEFENSE

Creating war propaganda is the world's second oldest profession, and its old-est line is "they started it." Wars have been fought for millennia in defense against aggressors and in defense of the way of life of various states. Athenian historian Thucydides's record of Athenian general Pericles's oration at the mass funeral of a year's worth of war dead is still widely praised by proponents of war. Pericles tells the assembled mourners that Athens has the greatest fighters because they are motivated to defend their superior and more dem-ocratic way of life, and that to die in its defense is the best fate anyone could hope for. Pericles is describing Athenians fighting in other states for imperial gain, and yet he depicts that fighting as the defense of something more valu-able than the peoples of those other states could even comprehend—the very same something that President George W. Bush would much later say drove terrorists to attack the United States: freedom.

"They hate our freedoms, our freedom of religion, our freedom of speech, our freedom to vote and assemble and disagree with each other," Bush said on September 20, 2001, hitting a theme he would return to again and again.[1]

Captain Paul K. Chappell in his book *The End of War* writes that people who have freedom and prosperity can be easier to persuade to support wars, because they have more to lose.[2] I don't know whether that's true or how to test it, but it is predominantly those with the least to lose within our society who are sent to fight our wars. In any case, talk of fighting wars "in defense" often refers to defense of our standard of living and way of life, a point that rhetorically helps to blur the question of whether we are fighting against or as an aggressor.

In response to the pro-war argument that we must defend our standard of living by protecting oil supplies, a common statement on posters at antiwar marches in 2002 and 2003 was "How did our oil get under their sand?" To some Americans "securing" oil reserves was a "defensive" action. Others had been convinced the war had nothing to do with oil whatsoever.

Defensive wars can be seen as defending peace. Wars are launched and waged in the name of peace, while no one has yet promoted peace for the sake of war. A war in the name of peace can please proponents of both war and peace, and can justify war in the eyes of those who think it requires justification. "For the preponderating majority in any community," wrote Harold Lasswell nearly a century ago, "the business of beating the enemy in the name of security and peace suffices. This is the great war aim, and in single-hearted devotion to its achievement they find that 'peacefulness of being at war.'"[3]

While all wars are described as defensive in some way by all parties involved, it is only by fighting a war in actual self-defense that a war can be made legal under the UN Charter, though nothing can make it legal under the Kellogg-Briand Pact. Under the UN Charter, unless the Security Council has agreed to a special authorization, only those fighting back against an attack are fighting war legally. In the United States the Department of War was renamed the Department of Defense in 1948, appropriately enough the same year in which George Orwell wrote *Nineteen Eighty-Four*. Since then, Americans have dutifully referred to anything their military or most other militaries do as "defense." Peace advocates who want to slash three quarters of the military's budget, which they believe is either immoral aggression or pure waste, publish papers calling for reduced spending on "defense." They've lost that struggle before opening their mouths. The very last thing people will part with is "defense."

But if what the Pentagon does is primarily defensive, Americans require a sort of defending unlike any previously seen or currently sought by any other people. Nobody else has divided the globe, plus outer space and cyberspace, into zones and created a military command to control each one. Nobody else has several hundred, perhaps over a thousand, military bases spread around the earth in other people's countries. Almost nobody else has *any* bases in other people's countries. Most countries do not have nuclear, biological, or chemical weapons. The U.S. military does. Americans spend more money on our military than any other nation, amounting to about 45 percent of the whole world's military expenditures. The top 15 nations account for 83 percent of the world's military spending, and the United States spends more than numbers 2 through 15 combined.[4] The United States spends 72 times what Iran and North Korea spend combined.[5]

Our "Defense Department," under its old and new names, has taken large and small military actions abroad, some 250 times, not counting covert actions or the installation of permanent bases. For only 31 years, or 14 percent, of U.S. history have there been no U.S. troops engaged in any significant actions abroad. Acting in defense, to be sure, the United States has attacked, invaded, policed, overthrown, or occupied 62 other nations.[6] John Quigley's excellent 1992 book *The Ruses for War* analyzes 25 of the United States' most significant military actions following World War II, concluding that each was promoted with lies.[7]

U.S. troops have been attacked while stationed abroad, but there has never been an attack on the United States, at least not since 1815. When the Japanese attacked U.S. ships at Pearl Harbor, Hawaii was not a U.S. state, but rather an imperial territory, made such by the U.S. overthrow of the queen on behalf of sugar plantation owners. When terrorists attacked the World Trade Center in 2001, they were committing a most serious crime, but they were not launching a war. In the lead-up to the War of 1812, the British and Americans exchanged attacks along the Canadian border and in the open seas. Native Americans also exchanged attacks with U.S. settlers, although who was invading whom is a question we've never wanted to face.

What we have seen from the United States and every other war-making state are wars *in the name of defense* that use massive aggression to respond to minor injuries or insults, that use massive aggression for the sake of revenge, that follow successful provocations of aggression by the enemy, that follow merely the pretense that there has been aggression from the other side, and that ostensibly defend allies or imperial possessions or other nations treated as puzzle pieces in a global game in which allegiances are imagined to fall like dominoes. There have even been wars of humanitarian aggression. In the end, most of these wars are wars of aggression—plain and simple.

But They Looked at Us Funny

An instance of transforming skirmishes, maritime offenses, and trade disagreements into a full-blown, utterly useless and destructive war is the now-forgotten War of 1812, the main accomplishment of which, other than death and misery, seems to have been getting Washington burned. Honest charges could be laid against the British. And, unlike many U.S. wars, this one was authorized by—and in fact promoted primarily by—Congress, as opposed to the president. But it was the United States, not Britain, that declared war, and one goal of many war supporters was not especially defensive: the conquest of Canada! Congressman Samuel Taggart (F-MA), in protest of a closed-door debate, published a speech in the *Alexandria Gazette* on June 24, 1812, in which he remarked:

> The conquest of Canada has been represented to be so easy as to be little more than a party of pleasure. We have, it has been said, nothing to do

but to march an army into the country and display the standard of the United States, and the Canadians will immediately flock to it and place themselves under our protection. They have been represented as ripe for revolt, panting for emancipation from a tyrannical Government, and longing to enjoy the sweets of liberty under the fostering hand of the United States.[8]

Taggart went on to present reasons why such a result was by no means to be expected, and of course he was right. But being right is of little value when war fever takes hold. Vice President Dick Cheney, on March 16, 2003, made a similar claim about Iraqis, despite himself having pointed out its error on television nine years earlier when he had explained why the United States had not invaded Baghdad during the Gulf War. (Cheney, at that time, may have left some factors unstated, such as the real fear back then of chemical or biological weapons, as compared with the *pretense* of that fear in 2003.) Cheney said of his coming second attack on Iraq: "Now, I think things have gotten so bad inside Iraq, from the standpoint of the Iraqi people, my belief is we will, in fact, be greeted as liberators."[9]

A year earlier, Ken Adelman, former arms control director for President Ronald Reagan said, "Liberating Iraq would be a cakewalk." This expectation, whether a pretense or sincere and truly stupid, didn't work out in Iraq or two centuries ago in Canada. The Soviets went into Afghanistan in 1979 with the same stupid expectation of being welcomed as friends,[10] and the United States repeated the same mistake there beginning in 2001. Of course, such expectations would never work out for a foreign army in the United States either, no matter how admirable the people invading us might be or how miserable they might find us.

What if Canada and Iraq had indeed welcomed U.S. occupations? Would that have produced anything to outweigh the horror of the wars? Norman Thomas, author of *War: No Glory, No Profit, No Need*, speculated as follows:

> [S]uppose the United States in the War of 1812 had succeeded in its very blundering attempt to conquer all or part of Canada. Unquestionably we should have school histories to teach us how fortunate was the result of that war for the people of Ontario and how valuable a lesson it finally taught the British about the need for enlightened rule! Yet, to-day the Canadians who remain within the British Empire would say they have more real liberty than their neighbors to the south of the border![11]

A great many wars, including numerous U.S. wars against the native peoples of North America, were wars of escalation. Just as the Iraqis—or, anyway, some people from the Middle East with funny sounding names—had killed 3,000 people in the United States, making the slaughter of a million Iraqis a defensive measure, the American Indians had always killed some number of settlers, against which actions a war could be understood as retaliation. But such wars are glaringly wars of choice, because numerous minor incidents identical to those that provoke wars are allowed to pass without wars.

Through decades of Cold War, the United States and the Soviet Union allowed minor incidents, such as the shooting down of spy planes, to be handled with tools other than serious war. When the Soviet Union shot down a U-2 spy plane in 1960, relations with the United States were seriously damaged, but no war was launched. The Soviet Union traded the pilot they'd shot down for one of their own spies in an exchange that was far from unusual. And a U.S. radar operator for the top-secret U-2, a man who had defected to the Soviet Union six months earlier and reportedly told the Russians everything he knew, was welcomed back by the United States government and never prosecuted. On the contrary, the government loaned him money and later issued him a new passport overnight. His name was Lee Harvey Oswald.[12]

Identical incidents would have served as excuses for war in other circumstances, namely any circumstances in which government leaders wanted a war. In fact, on January 31, 2003, President George W. Bush proposed to British Prime Minister Tony Blair that painting U-2 aircraft with United Nations colors, flying them low over Iraq, and getting them shot at, could provide an excuse for war.[13] Meanwhile, while publicly threatening war on Iraq over its fictional "weapons of mass destruction," the United States ignored an interesting development: the actual acquisition of nuclear weapons by North Korea. Wars don't go where the offenses are; the offenses are found or concocted to fit the desired wars. If the United States and the Soviet Union can avoid war because they don't want to destroy the world, then all nations can avoid all wars by choosing not to destroy pieces of the world.

Damsels in Distress

Often one of the initial excuses for military action is to defend Americans in a foreign country who have supposedly been put at risk by recent events. This excuse was used, along with the usual variety of other excuses, by the United States when invading the Dominican Republic in 1965, Grenada in 1983, and Panama in 1989, in examples that have been written about by John Quigley as well as Norman Solomon in his book *War Made Easy*. In the case of the Dominican Republic, U.S. citizens who wanted to leave (1,856 of them) had been evacuated prior to the military action. Neighborhoods in Santo Domingo where Americans lived were free of violence and the military was not needed in order to evacuate anyone. All the major Dominican factions had agreed to help evacuate any foreigners who wanted to leave.

In the case of Grenada (an invasion that the United States banned the U.S. media from covering) there were supposedly U.S. medical students to rescue. But U.S. State Department official James Budeit, two days before the invasion, learned that the students were not in danger. When about 100 to 150 students decided they wanted to leave, their reason was fear of the U.S. attack. The parents of 500 of the students sent President Reagan a telegram asking him not to attack, letting him know their children were safe and free to leave Grenada if they chose to do so.

In the case of Panama, a real incident could be pointed to, one of a sort that has been found everywhere foreign armies have ever occupied someone else's country. Some drunk Panamanian soldiers had beaten up a U.S. navy officer and threatened his wife. While George H. W. Bush claimed that this and other new developments prompted the war, the war plans had actually begun months prior to the incident.[14]

The Empire Strikes Back

A curious variation on the justification of defense is the justification of revenge. There can be an implication in cries of "they attacked us first" that they will do so again if we don't attack them. But often the emotional punch is in the cry for revenge, while the possibility of future attacks is far from certain. In fact, launching a war guarantees counter-attacks, against troops if not territory, and launching a war against a nation in response to the actions of terrorists can serve as recruitment advertising for more terrorists. Launching such a war also constitutes the supreme crime of aggression, motives of revenge notwithstanding. Revenge is a primitive emotion, not a legal defense for war.

The murderers who flew airplanes into buildings on September 11, 2001, died in the process. There was no way to launch a war against them, and they represented no nation whose territory (as it has been commonly if falsely believed since World War II) could be freely and legally bombed in the course of a war. Possible co-conspirators in the crimes of September 11 who were among the living should have been sought out through all national, foreign, and international channels, and prosecuted in open and legitimate courts— as bin Laden and others were indicted *in absentia* in Spain. They still should be. Claims that the terrorists were themselves "retaliating" defensively against U.S. actions should also have been investigated. If the stationing of U.S. troops in Saudi Arabia and U.S. military aid to Israel were destabilizing the Middle East and endangering innocent people, those and similar policies should have been reviewed to determine whether any advantages outweighed the damage being done. Most U.S. troops were pulled out of Saudi Arabia two years later, but by then many more had been sent into Afghanistan and Iraq.

The president withdrawing those troops in 2005, George W. Bush, was the son of the president who had, in 1990, sent them in on the basis of the lie that Iraq was about to attack Saudi Arabia. The vice president in 2003, Dick Cheney, had been the secretary of "defense" in 1990, when he had been assigned the task of persuading the Saudis to allow the U.S. troop presence despite their not believing the lie.[15]

There was little reason to believe that launching a war on Afghanistan would lead to the capture of suspected terrorist leader Osama bin Laden, and, as we have seen, that was clearly not the top priority for the U.S. government, which rejected an offer to put him on trial. Instead, the war itself was the priority. And the war was certain to be counter-productive in terms of preventing terrorism. David Wildman and Phyllis Bennis provide the background:

> Previous U.S. decisions to respond militarily to terrorist attacks have all failed for the same reasons. One, they have killed, injured, or rendered even more desperate already-impoverished innocents. Two, they haven't worked to stop terrorism. In 1986 Ronald Reagan ordered the bombing of Tripoli and Benghazi to punish Libyan leader Muammar Ghadafi for an explosion in a discotheque in Germany that had killed two GIs. Ghadafi survived, but several dozen Libyan civilians, including Ghadafi's three-year-old daughter, were killed.
>
> Just a couple of years later came the Lockerbie disaster, for which Libya would take responsibility. In 1999, in response to the attacks on U.S. embassies in Kenya and Tanzania, U.S. bombers attacked Osama bin Laden's training camps in Afghanistan and an allegedly bin Laden-linked pharmaceutical factory in the Sudan. It turned out the Sudanese factory had no connection to bin Laden, but the U.S. attack had destroyed the only producer of vital vaccines for children growing up in the profound scarcity of central Africa. And the attack on the camps in the Afghan mountains clearly did not prevent the attacks of September 11, 2001.[16]

The "global war on terrorism" that was launched in late 2001 with the war on Afghanistan and continued with the war on Iraq followed the same pattern. By 2007, we could document a shocking sevenfold increase in fatal jihadist attacks around the world, meaning hundreds of additional terrorist attacks and thousands of additional dead civilians in predictable if criminal response to the latest "defensive" wars by the United States, wars that had produced nothing of value to weigh against that harm.[17] The U.S. State Department responded to the dangerous escalation in worldwide terrorism by discontinuing its annual report on terrorism.

Two years later, President Barack Obama escalated the war in Afghanistan, with the understanding that al Qaeda was not present in Afghanistan; that the most hated group likely to claim any share of power in Afghanistan, the Taliban, was not closely allied with al Qaeda; and that al Qaeda was otherwise occupied launching terrorist attacks in other countries. The war needed to press forward, nonetheless, because...well, because...um, actually nobody was really sure why. On July 14, 2010, the president's representative to Afghanistan, Richard Holbrooke, testified before the Senate Foreign Relations Committee. Holbrooke seemed fresh out of justifications. Senator Bob Corker (R-TN) told the *Los Angeles Times* during the hearing, "A lot of folks on both sides of the aisle think this effort is adrift. A lot of folks you'd consider the strongest hawks in the country are scratching their heads in concern."[18]

Corker complained that after listening for 90 minutes to Holbrooke he had, "no earthly idea what our objectives are on the civilian front. So far, this has been an incredible waste of time."[19] The possibility that the United States was under attack and fighting this distant pointless war in self-defense was not even imaginable as a plausible explanation, so the topic was never discussed by anyone other than the occasional radio host throwing out the mindless claims that amount to "we've gotta fight 'em there so we don't hafta fight 'em here." The closest Holbrooke or the White House came to a justification for keeping the war going or escalating it was always that if the Taliban forces won they would bring in al Qaeda, and if al Qaeda were in Afghanistan that would endanger the United States. But numerous experts, including Holbrooke, at other times admitted there was no evidence for either claim. The Taliban was no longer on good terms with al Qaeda, and al Qaeda could plot anything it wanted to plot in any number of other countries.

Two months earlier, on May 13, 2010, the following exchange had taken place at a Pentagon press conference with Gen. Stanley McChrystal who was then running the war in Afghanistan:

> REPORTER: [I]n Marja there are reports—credible reports—of intimidation and even beheading of local people who work with your forces. Is that your intelligence? And if so, does it worry you?
>
> GEN. MCCHRYSTAL: Yeah. It absolutely is things that we see. But it's absolutely predictable.[20]

Read that again.

If you're in somebody else's country, and the locals who help you happen, as a matter of course, to get their heads sliced off, it might be time to reconsider what you're doing, or at least to come up with some justification for it, no matter how fantastic.

A Provocative Strategy

Another type of "defensive" war is one that follows a successful provocation of aggression from the desired enemy. This method was used to begin, and repeatedly to escalate, the Vietnam War, as recorded in the Pentagon Papers.

Setting aside until Chapter 4 the question of whether the United States should have entered World War II, in either Europe or the Pacific or both, the fact is that the United States was unlikely to enter unless attacked. In 1928 the U.S. Senate had voted 85 to 1 to ratify the Kellogg-Briand Pact, a treaty that bound—and still binds—our nation and many others never again to engage in war.

British Prime Minister Winston Churchill's fervent hope for years was that Japan would attack the United States. This would permit the United States (not legally, but politically) to fully enter the war in Europe, as its president wanted to do, as opposed to merely providing weaponry, as it had been doing. On April 28, 1941, Churchill wrote a secret directive to his war cabinet: "It may be taken as almost certain that the entry of Japan into the war would be followed by the immediate entry of the United States on our side."[21]

On May 11, 1941, Robert Menzies, the prime minister of Australia, met with Roosevelt and found him "a little jealous" of Churchill's place in the center of the war. While Roosevelt's cabinet all wanted the United States to enter the war, Menzies found that Roosevelt, "trained under Woodrow Wilson in the last war, waits for an incident, which would in one blow get the USA into war and get R. out of his foolish election pledges that 'I will keep you out of war.'"[22]

On August 18, 1941, Churchill met with his cabinet at 10 Downing Street. The meeting had some similarity to the July 23, 2002, meeting at the same address, the minutes of which became known as the Downing Street Minutes. Both meetings revealed secret U.S. intentions to go to war. In the 1941 meeting, Churchill told his cabinet, according to the minutes: "The President had said he would wage war but not declare it." In addition, "Everything was to be done to force an incident."

Japan was certainly not averse to attacking others and had been busy creating an Asian empire. And the United States and Japan were certainly not living in harmonious friendship. But what could bring the Japanese to attack?

When President Franklin Roosevelt visited Pearl Harbor on July 28, 1934, seven years before the Japanese attack, the Japanese military expressed apprehension. General Kunishiga Tanaka wrote in the *Japan Advertiser*, objecting to the build-up of the American fleet and the creation of additional bases in Alaska and the Aleutian Islands: "Such insolent behavior makes us most suspicious. It makes us think a major disturbance is purposely being encouraged in the Pacific. This is greatly regretted."[23]

Whether it was actually regretted or not is a separate question from whether this was a typical and predictable response to military expansionism, even when done in the name of "defense." The great unembedded (as we would today call him) journalist George Seldes was suspicious as well. In October, 1934, he wrote in *Harper's Magazine*: "It is an axiom that nations do not arm for war but for *a* war." Seldes asked an official at the Navy League:

> "Do you accept the naval axiom that you prepare to fight a specific navy?"
>
> The man replied "Yes."
>
> "Do you contemplate a fight with the British navy?"
>
> "Absolutely, no."
>
> "Do you contemplate war with Japan?"
>
> "Yes."[24]

In 1935, the most decorated U.S. marine in history at the time, Brigadier Gen. Smedley D. Butler, published with enormous success a short book called *War Is a Racket*. He saw perfectly well what was coming and warned the nation:

> At each session of Congress the question of further naval appropriations comes up. The swivel-chair admirals...don't shout that "We need lots of battleships to war on this nation or that nation." Oh, no. First of all, they let it be known that America is menaced by a great naval power. Almost any day, these admirals will tell you, the great fleet of this supposed enemy will strike suddenly and annihilate our 125,000,000 people. Just like that. Then they begin to cry for a larger navy. For what? To fight the enemy? Oh my, no. Oh, no. For defense purposes only. Then, incidentally, they announce maneuvers in the Pacific. For defense. Uh, huh.
>
> The Pacific is a great big ocean. We have a tremendous coastline in the Pacific. Will the maneuvers be off the coast, two or three hundred miles? Oh, no. The maneuvers will be two thousand, yes, perhaps even thirty-five hundred miles, off the coast.
>
> The Japanese, a proud people, of course will be pleased beyond expression to see the United States fleet so close to Nippon's shores. Even as pleased as would be the residents of California were they to dimly discern, through the morning mist, the Japanese fleet playing at war games off Los Angeles.[25]

In March 1935, Roosevelt bestowed Wake Island on the U.S. Navy and gave Pan Am Airways a permit to build runways on Wake Island, Midway Island, and Guam. Japanese military commanders announced that they were disturbed and viewed these runways as a threat. So did peace activists in the United States. By the next month, Roosevelt had planned war games and maneuvers near the Aleutian Islands and Midway Island. By the following month, peace activists were marching in New York advocating friendship with Japan. Norman Thomas wrote in 1935: "The Man from Mars who saw how men suffered in the last war and how frantically they are preparing for the next war, which they know will be worse, would come to the conclusion that he was looking at the denizens of a lunatic asylum."[26]

The U.S. Navy spent the next few years working up plans for war with Japan, the March 8, 1939, version of which described "an offensive war of long duration" that would destroy the military and disrupt the economic life of Japan. In January, 1941, eleven months before the attack, the *Japan Advertiser* expressed its outrage over Pearl Harbor in an editorial, and the U.S. ambassador to Japan wrote in his diary: "There is a lot of talk around town to the effect that the Japanese, in case of a break with the United States, are planning to go all out in a surprise mass attack on Pearl Harbor. Of course I informed my government."[27]

On February 5, 1941, Rear Admiral Richmond Kelly Turner wrote to Secretary of War Henry Stimson to warn of the possibility of a surprise attack at Pearl Harbor.

As early as 1932, the United States had been talking with China about providing airplanes, pilots, and training for its war with Japan. In November 1940, Roosevelt loaned China 100 million dollars for war with Japan, and after consulting with the British, U.S. Secretary of the Treasury Henry Morgenthau made plans to send the Chinese bombers with U.S. crews to use in bombing Tokyo and other Japanese cities. On December 21, 1940, two weeks shy of a year before the Japanese attack on Pearl Harbor, China's Minister of Finance T.V. Soong and Colonel Claire Chennault, a retired U.S. Army flier who was working for the Chinese and had been urging them to use American pilots to bomb Tokyo since at least 1937, met in Henry Morgenthau's dining room to plan the firebombing of Japan. Morgenthau said he could get men released from duty in the U.S. Army Air Corps if the Chinese could pay them $1,000 per month. Soong agreed.

On May 24, 1941, the *New York Times* reported on U.S. training of the Chinese air force, and the provision of "numerous fighting and bombing planes" to China by the United States. "Bombing of Japanese Cities is Expected" read the subhead. By July, the Joint Army-Navy Board had approved a plan called JB 355 to firebomb Japan. A front corporation would buy American planes to be flown by American volunteers trained by Chennault and paid by another front group. Roosevelt approved, and his China expert Lauchlin Currie, in the words of Nicholson Baker, "wired Madame Chiang

Kai-Shek and Claire Chennault a letter that fairly begged for interception by Japanese spies." Whether or not that was the entire point, this was the letter:

> I am very happy to be able to report today the President directed that sixty-six bombers be made available to China this year with twenty-four to be delivered immediately. He also approved a Chinese pilot training program here. Details through normal channels. Warm regards.[28]

The U.S. ambassador had said "in case of a break with the United States" the Japanese would bomb Pearl Harbor. I wonder if this qualified!

The 1st American Volunteer Group (AVG) of the Chinese Air Force, also known as the Flying Tigers, moved ahead with recruitment and training immediately and first saw combat on December 20, 1941, twelve days (local time) after the Japanese attacked Pearl Harbor.[29]

On May 31, 1941, at the Keep America Out of War Congress, William Henry Chamberlin gave a dire warning: "A total economic boycott of Japan, the stoppage of oil shipments for instance, would push Japan into the arms of the Axis. Economic war would be a prelude to naval and military war." The worst thing about peace advocates is how many times they turn out to be right.

On July 24, 1941, President Roosevelt remarked, "If we cut the oil off, [the Japanese] probably would have gone down to the Dutch East Indies a year ago, and you would have had a war. It was very essential from our own selfish point of view of defense to prevent a war from starting in the South Pacific. So our foreign policy was trying to stop a war from breaking out there."

Reporters noticed that Roosevelt said "was" rather than "is." The next day, Roosevelt issued an executive order freezing Japanese assets. The United States and Britain cut off oil and scrap metal to Japan. Radhabinod Pal, an Indian jurist who served on the war crimes tribunal after the war, called the embargoes a "clear and potent threat to Japan's very existence," and concluded the United States had provoked Japan.

On August 7th, four months before the attack, the *Japan Times Advertiser* wrote:

> First there was the creation of a superbase at Singapore, heavily reinforced by British and Empire troops. From this hub a great wheel was built up and linked with American bases to form a great ring sweeping in a great area southwards and westwards from the Philippines through Malaya and Burma, with the link broken only in the Thailand peninsula. Now it is proposed to include the narrows in the encirclement, which proceeds to Rangoon.

WARS ARE NOT LAUNCHED IN DEFENSE   53

By September the Japanese press was outraged that the United States had begun shipping oil right past Japan to reach Russia. Japan, its newspapers said, was dying a slow death from "economic war."

What might the United States have been hoping to gain by shipping oil past a nation in desperate need of it?

In late October, U.S. spy Edgar Mower was doing work for Colonel William Donovan who spied for Roosevelt. Mower spoke with a man in Manila named Ernest Johnson, a member of the Maritime Commission, who said he expected "The Japs will take Manila before I can get out." When Mower expressed surprise, Johnson replied "Didn't you know the Jap fleet has moved eastward, presumably to attack our fleet at Pearl Harbor?"[30]

On November 3, 1941, the U.S. ambassador tried again to get something through his government's thick skull, sending a lengthy telegram to the State Department warning that the economic sanctions might force Japan to commit "national hara-kiri." He wrote, "An armed conflict with the United States may come with dangerous and dramatic suddenness."

Why do I keep recalling the headline of the memo given to President George W. Bush prior to the September 11, 2001, attacks? "Bin Laden Determined to Strike in U.S."

Apparently nobody in Washington wanted to hear it in 1941 either. On November 15, Army Chief of Staff George Marshall briefed the media on something we do not remember as "the Marshall Plan." In fact we don't remember it at all. "We are preparing an offensive war against Japan," Marshall said, asking the journalists to keep it a secret, which as far as I know they dutifully did.

Ten days later Secretary of War Henry Stimson wrote in his diary that he'd met in the Oval Office with Marshall, President Roosevelt, Secretary of the Navy Frank Knox, Admiral Harold Stark, and Secretary of State Cordell Hull. Roosevelt had told them the Japanese were likely to attack soon, possibly next Monday. That would have been December 1, six days before the attack actually came. "The question," Stimson wrote, "was how we should maneuver them into the position of firing the first shot without allowing too much danger to ourselves. It was a difficult proposition."[31]

Was it? One obvious answer was to keep the whole fleet in Pearl Harbor and keep the sailors stationed there in the dark while fretting about them from comfortable offices in Washington. In fact, that was the solution our suit-and-tied heroes went with.

The day after the attack, Congress voted for war. Congresswoman Jeannette Rankin (R-MT), the first woman ever elected to Congress, and who had voted against World War I, stood alone in opposing World War II (just as Congresswoman Barbara Lee [D-CA] would stand alone against attacking

Afghanistan 60 years later). One year after the vote, on December 8, 1942, Rankin put extended remarks into the Congressional Record explaining her opposition. She cited the work of a British propagandist who had argued in 1938 for using Japan to bring the United States into the war. She cited Henry Luce's reference in *Life* magazine on July 20, 1942, to "the Chinese for whom the U.S. had delivered the ultimatum that brought on Pearl Harbor." She introduced evidence that at the Atlantic Conference on August 12, 1941, Roosevelt had assured Churchill that the United States would bring economic pressure to bear on Japan. "I cited," Rankin later wrote, "the State Department Bulletin of December 20, 1941, which revealed that on September 3 a communication had been sent to Japan demanding that it accept the principle of 'nondisturbance of the status quo in the Pacific,' which amounted to demanding guarantees of the inviolateness of the white empires in the Orient."[32]

Rankin found that the Economic Defense Board had gotten economic sanctions under way less than a week after the Atlantic Conference. On December 2, 1941, the *New York Times* had reported, in fact, that Japan had been "cut off from about 75 percent of her normal trade by the Allied blockade." Rankin also cited the statement of Lieutenant Clarence E. Dickinson, U.S.N., in the *Saturday Evening Post* of October 10, 1942, that on November 28, 1941, nine days *before* the attack, Vice Admiral William F. Halsey, Jr., (he of the slogan "kill Japs, kill Japs!") had given instructions to him and others to "shoot down anything we saw in the sky and to bomb anything we saw on the sea."[33]

Whether World War II was the "good war" we are so often told it was, I will defer to Chapter 4. That it was a defensive war because our innocent imperial outpost in the middle of the Pacific was attacked out of the clear blue sky is a myth that deserves to be buried.

Why Provoke When You Can Just Pretend?

One of the least defensible forms of supposedly defensive wars is the war based only on the pretense of aggression by the other side. This was how the United States got into the war through which it stole its southwestern states from Mexico. Before Abraham Lincoln became, as president, the celebrated abuser of war powers who has served to excuse similar abuses by so many of his successors, he was a congressman aware that the Constitution had given the power to declare war to the Congress. In 1847, Congressman Lincoln accused President James Polk of lying the nation into a war by blaming Mexico for aggression when that charge rightly should have been made against the U.S. Army and Polk himself. Lincoln joined with former president and then-current Congressman John Quincy Adams in seeking a formal investigation of Polk's actions and the formal sanctioning of Polk for lying the nation into war.

Polk responded, as Harry Truman and Lyndon Johnson would later do, by announcing that he would not seek a second term. Both houses of Congress then passed a resolution honoring Major Gen. Zachary Taylor for his performance "in a war unnecessarily and unconstitutionally begun by the president of the United States."[34] It was a common understanding that the Constitution did not sanction aggressive wars, but only wars of defense. Ulysses S. Grant considered the Mexican War, in which he nonetheless fought, "one of the most unjust ever waged by a stronger against a weaker nation. It was an instance of a republic following the bad example of European monarchies, in not considering justice in their desire to acquire additional territory."[35]

Lincoln's speech on the floor of the House on January 12, 1848, is a high point of war debate in American history and included these phrases:

> Let him [President James Polk] remember he sits where Washington sat, and so remembering, let him answer as Washington would answer. As a nation should not, and the Almighty will not, be evaded, so let him attempt no evasion—no equivocation. And if, so answering, he can show that the soil was ours where the first blood of the war was shed—that it was not within an inhabited country, or, if within such, that the inhabitants had submitted themselves to the civil authority of Texas or of the United States, and that the same is true of the site of Fort Brown—then I am with him for his justification.... But if he can not or will not do this—if on any pretense or no pretense he shall refuse or omit it—then I shall be fully convinced of what I more than suspect already—that he is deeply conscious of being in the wrong, that he feels the blood of this war, like the blood of Abel, is crying to Heaven against him.... How like the half-insane mumbling of a fever dream, is the whole war part of his late message![36]

I can't imagine most members of Congress speaking of a war-making president with such honesty today. I also can't imagine wars ever coming to an end until that sort of thing happens with some regularity and is backed up by cutting off the funds.

Even while denouncing a war based on lies whose blood was crying to heaven, Lincoln and his fellow Whigs voted repeatedly to fund it.[37] On June 21, 2007, Senator Carl Levin (D-MI) cited Lincoln's example in the *Washington Post* as justification for his own stance as an "opponent" of the war on Iraq who would continue to fund it through eternity as a means of "supporting the troops." Interestingly, regiments from Virginia, Mississippi, and North Carolina sent to risk their lives killing innocent Mexicans in the war that

Lincoln funded on their behalf mutinied against their officers. And at least 9,000 U.S. soldiers, enlisted and volunteer, deserted from the Mexican War.[38]

Some hundreds, in fact, including Irish immigrants, switched their allegiance and enlisted on the Mexican side, forming the Saint Patrick's Battalion. According to Robert Fantina, in his book *Desertion and the American Soldier*, "Perhaps more than in any previous war, in the Mexican-American War lack of belief in the cause was a major reason for deserting."[39] Wars seldom end— except through complete destruction of one side—without that kind of resistance among those sent to do the fighting. When the United States paid Mexico for the vast territory it was taking, the *Whig Intelligencer* wrote, apparently without irony, "We take nothing by conquest.... Thank God."[40]

Many years later, David Rovics would pen these song lyrics:

It was there in the pueblos and hillsides
That I saw the mistake I had made
Part of a conquering army
With the morals of a bayonet blade
So in the midst of these poor, dying Catholics
Screaming children, the burning stench of it all
Myself and two hundred Irishmen
Decided to rise to the call
From Dublin City to San Diego
We witnessed freedom denied
So we formed the Saint Patrick Battalion
And we fought on the Mexican side[41]

In 1898, the *USS Maine* blew up in Havana Harbor, and U.S. newspapers quickly blamed the Spanish, crying out "Remember the Maine! To hell with Spain!" Newspaper owner William Randolph Hearst did his best to fan the flames of a war he knew would boost circulation.[42] Who actually blew the ship up? Nobody knew. Certainly Spain denied it, Cuba denied it, and the United States denied it. Spain didn't just casually deny it either. Spain conducted an investigation and found that the explosion had been inside the ship. Realizing that the United States would reject this finding, Spain proposed a joint investigation by both countries and offered to submit to binding arbitration by an impartial international panel. The United States wasn't interested. Whatever caused the explosion, Washington wanted war.

More recent investigations raise the distinct possibility that the Maine was indeed sunk by an explosion, whether accidental or intentional, that occurred within it, rather than by a mine outside it. But no experts have proven one theory over another to the satisfaction of all, and I'm not sure what good it would do. The Spanish could have found a way to plant a bomb inside the ship. Americans could have found a way to place a mine outside it. Knowing where the explosion took place won't tell us who, if anyone, caused it. But even if we knew for certain who caused it, how, and why, none of that information would change the basic account of what happened in 1898.

The nation went mad for war in response to an attack by Spain for which there was no evidence, merely conjecture. An American ship had blown up, Americans had been killed, and there was a possibility that Spain might be responsible. In combination with other grievances against Spain, this was reason (or excuse) enough to bang the war drums. The pretense of certainty that Spain was to blame was nothing other than a pretense. That fact would remain unaltered even if proof were somehow to emerge that Spain in fact blew up the Maine, just as President George W. Bush's crew would have been lying about its certainty that Iraq had weapons in 2003 even if some weapons had later been found. This alleged atrocity—the sinking of the *Maine*—was used to launch a war "in defense of" Cuba and the Philippines that involved attacking and occupying Cuba and the Philippines, and Puerto Rico for good measure.

Remember those lines from Smedley Butler that I quoted above about how pleased the Japanese would be to see the U.S. fleet playing war games near Japan? These were the next lines in that same passage: "The ships of our navy, it can be seen, should be specifically limited, by law, to within 200 miles of our coastline. Had that been the law in 1898 the Maine would never have gone to Havana Harbor. She never would have been blown up. There would have been no war with Spain with its attendant loss of life."[43]

Butler has a point, even if it's not a mathematical one. It works if we think of Miami as the closest U.S. land to Cuba, but Key West is much closer—only 106 miles from Havana—and the U.S. military had claimed it in 1822, built a base, and held it for the North even during the Civil War. Key West was the largest and wealthiest city in Florida when the *Maine* blew up. Ernest Hemingway wrote *A Farewell to Arms* there, but the military has yet to leave Key West.

Perhaps the height of dishonest pretense in manufacturing a so-called defensive war is to be found in the example of Nazi Germany's actions when it was ready to invade Poland. Heinrich Himmler's SS men staged a series of incidents. In one, a group of them dressed in Polish uniforms, barged into a German radio station in a border town, forced the employees into the base-ment, and announced their anti-German intentions in Polish on the air while firing guns. They brought along a German who actually sympathized with the Poles, killed him, and left him behind to look as if he'd been shot while taking part in their effort. Adolf Hitler told the German Army that force would have to be met with force, and proceeded to attack Poland.[44]

By 2008, the Bush-Cheney administration had been pushing a case for war on Iran unsuccessfully for years. Tales of Iranian support for the Iraqi resistance, Iranian development of nuclear weapons, Iranian ties to terrorists, and so forth were trotted out with great regularity, and completely ignored or rejected by the American people, over 90 percent of whom remained opposed to attacking Iran. Vice President Dick Cheney and his staff, apparently growing desperate, dreamed up, but never acted on, a scheme that would have made Hitler proud. The idea was to build four or five boats that would look like Iranian PT boats and put Navy Seals on them with "a lot of arms." They could start a firefight with a U.S. ship in the Straight of Hormuz, and *voila*, you'd have a war with Iran. The proposal was reportedly dropped because it would have required Americans to fire on Americans.[45]

That concern had not stopped the Joint Chiefs of Staff in 1962 from sending the secretary of "defense" a plan called Operation Northwoods that called for attacking U.S. cities and blaming the attacks on Cuba. That these plans were not acted upon does not diminish their value as clues to the thinking of the people from whose brains they emerged. These were people hunting for excuses for war.

When Britain began bombing civilian targets in Germany in 1940, this was supposed to be seen as retaliation even though Germany had not yet bombed British civilian targets. To accomplish this feat, Winston Churchill told his new minister of information to "arrange that discreet reference should be made in the press to the killing of civilians in France and the Low Countries, in the course of the German air attacks." Britain had actually declared war on Germany in response to Germany's invasion of Poland. This is a common way in which nations that have not been attacked claim to be engaging in "defensive" wars. Wars are launched in defense of allies (something that agreements like the one that created the North Atlantic Treaty Organization [NATO] bind nations to do).

Some wars are launched in "preemptive" defense against the possibility that a nation might attack ours if ours doesn't attack theirs first. "Do unto others, before they can do unto you" is, I believe, how Jesus put it. In modern militaristic parlance this comes out as "fight 'em over there so we don't halfta fight 'em here."

The first problem with this approach is that we have only the vaguest notion of who "them" is. Terrified of a small group of Saudi terrorists, we launch wars on Afghanistan and Iraq. Fantasizing that the enemy, whoever it is, hates us for our freedoms, we fail to realize that they hate us for our government's bombs and bases. So our solution just makes the situation worse.

Since our Civil War, the United States has not fought wars at home. We're used to the U.S. government fighting wars far away and out of sight.

The television cameras in Vietnam were a brief interruption to this pattern, and realistic images even of that war were the exception to the rule.[46] In the two world wars and many wars since, we've been told we might be attacked at home if we didn't go and attack others abroad. In the case of World War I, we were told that Germany had attacked our good and innocent allies, might eventually attack us, and had in fact attacked innocent American civilians aboard a ship called the *Lusitania*.

German submarines had been giving warnings to civilian ships, allowing passengers to abandon them before they were sunk. When this exposed the U-boats to counterattacks, however, the Germans began attacking without warning. That was how they sank the *Lusitania* on May 7, 1915, killing 1,198 people, including 128 Americans. But, through other channels, the Germans had already warned those passengers. The *Lusitania* had been built to specifications of the British Navy, which listed it as an auxiliary cruiser. On its final voyage, the *Lusitania* was packed with American-made war materiel. Before the *Lusitania* left New York, the German Embassy published in New York newspapers a warning that the ship would be subject to attack.[47]

Upon the sinking of the *Lusitania*, those same newspapers, and all other American newspapers, declared the attack murder and omitted any mention of, or rejected German claims as to, what the ship had carried. When President Wilson protested to the German government, pretending the *Lusitania* had not contained any weapons and faulting only Germany, with no criticism of the British blockade, his secretary of state resigned in protest of Wilson, professing a desire to prevent war. The British and U.S. governments lied so effectively that many people today imagine there is doubt over whether the *Lusitania* had weapons on board. Or they imagine that dive crews discovering arms in the wreckage of the ship in 2008 were resolving a long-standing mystery. Here's an excerpt from a report aired on National Public Radio on November 22, 2008:

> When the *Lusitania* went down, it left a mystery behind....In his hands lie pieces of history: seven gleaming rounds of .303 ammunition.... Ammunition that for decades British and American officials said didn't exist. Yet all around Andrews are mountains of jumbled rifle cartridges that glint like pirate's treasure....[48]

Never mind that the contents of the ship had been reported by Germany and were immediately widely suspected of having contributed to the speed at which the ship sank, official lies are given their expected place in the "balanced" media coverage that surrounds us so completely we can't detect it... even 90 years later.

Also left out of our usual understanding of this story is the fact that Winston Churchill's interest in bringing the United States into World War I was similar to what his interest would be in bringing the United States into World War II. He had written, prior to Britain taking numerous steps to fail to provide standard protection to the *Lusitania*, "It is most important to attract neutral shipping to our shores in the hope especially of embroiling the United States with Germany."[49]

If It Were Defense, Would We Have to Be Drafted?

German propaganda efforts in the United States failed miserably in the face of a superior approach by the British and American governments during World War I. The British actually cut the telegraph cable between Germany and the United States so that Americans would get their war news only from Britain. That news was of horrible atrocities—a battle between civilization and the barbarian hordes (those being the Germans, of course). Not only could readers learn about Germans slicing the hands off children and boiling their own troops' corpses for glycerin, and other horrifying fantasies, but the British were apparently winning every battle in a quite enjoyable fashion. While British war correspondents were strictly censored, they needn't have been, as they viewed their own role as hiding the war from the public in order to boost military recruitment in Britain. The *Times* of London explained: "A principle aim of the war policy of [the *Times*] was to increase the flow of recruits. It was an aim that would get little help from accounts of what happened to recruits once they became soldiers."[50]

President Wilson's sales team for the war, the Committee on Public Information (CPI), exercised the power of censorship and would end up banning images of dead Americans while the postmaster general did his part by banning all radical magazines. The CPI also convinced people that fighting the Germans would amount to a defense of democracy in the world and that German defeat in war, as opposed to difficult and serious diplomacy, would create world democracy.

Wilson needed a million soldiers, but in the first six weeks after declaring war, only 73,000 volunteered. Congress was forced, and not for the first time, to create a draft. Daniel Webster had eloquently denounced a draft as unconstitutional in 1814 when it had been attempted unsuccessfully by President James Madison, but drafts had been used on both sides during the Civil War, albeit with the allowance that rich men could pay poor men to go and die in their place. Not only did Americans have to be forced to fight in World War I (and subsequent wars), but in addition 1,532 of the most vocal opponents had to be thrown into prison. The fear of being shot for treason had to be spread throughout the land (as former Secretary of War Elihu Root proposed in the *New York Times*) before the flag waving and military music could proceed uninterrupted. War opponents were, in some cases, lynched, and the mobs acquitted.

The story of this clampdown on free speech—its echoes reverberating through the October 2010 FBI raids on peace activists' homes in Minneapolis, Chicago, and other cities—is well told in Norman Thomas's 1935 book, *War: No Glory, No Profit, No Need*, and in Chris Hedges's 2010 book, *The Death of the Liberal Class*. Four-time presidential candidate Eugene Debs was locked up and sentenced to 10 years for suggesting that working people had no interest in the war. The *Washington Post* called him a "public menace," and applauded his incarceration.[51] He would run for president a fifth time from prison and receive 913,664 votes. At his sentencing Debs remarked:

> Your honor, years ago I recognized my kinship with all living beings, and I made up my mind that I was not one bit better than the meanest on earth. I said then, and I say now, that while there is a lower class, I am in it; while there is a criminal element, I am of it; while there is a soul in prison, I am not free.[52]

The United States was manipulated into World War I to come to the aid of Britain and France, but the people of those countries were not all going along with the war. At least 132,000 Frenchmen opposed the war, refused to take part, and were exiled.[53]

After two world wars with a depression in between, none of which Americans had submitted to voluntarily, President Harry S. Truman had some bad news. If we didn't set off immediately to fight communists in Korea, they would shortly invade the United States. That this was recognized as patent nonsense is perhaps suggested by the fact that, once again, Americans had to be drafted if they were going to go off and fight. The Korean War was waged in supposed defense of the way of life in the United States and in supposed defense of South Korea against aggression by North Korea as part of a global communist conspiracy. Of course it had been the arrogant genius of the Allies to slice the Korean nation in half at the end of World War II.

On June 25, 1950, the north and the south each claimed the other side had invaded. The first reports from U.S. military intelligence were that the south had invaded the north. Both sides agreed that the fighting began near the west coast at the Ongjin peninsula, meaning that Pyongyang was a logical target for an invasion by the south, but an invasion by the north there made little sense as it led to a small peninsula and not to Seoul. Also on June 25, both sides announced the capture by the south of the northern city of Haeju, and the U.S. military confirmed that. On June 26 the U.S. ambassador sent a cable confirming a southern advance: "Northern armor and artillery are withdrawing all along the line."[54]

South Korean President Syngman Rhee had been conducting raids of the north for a year and had announced in the spring his intention to invade the north, moving most of his troops to the 38th parallel, the line along which the north and south had been divided. In the north, only a third of available troops were positioned near the border.

Nonetheless, Americans were told that North Korea had attacked South Korea and had done so at the behest of the Soviet Union as part of a plot to take over the world for communism. Arguably, whichever side attacked (and the consensus is that it was the North to first launch a successful major invasion, regardless of which side initially attacked),[55] this was a civil war. The Soviet Union was not involved, and the United States ought not to have been. South Korea was not the United States, and was not in fact anywhere near the United States. Nonetheless, the United States entered another "defensive" war that had been built up to and provoked by both sides of a small, distant, and divided country.

The U.S. government persuaded the United Nations that military action had to be taken against North Korea, something the Soviet Union might have been expected to veto had it been behind the war, but the Soviet Union was boycotting the United Nations and took no interest. The United States won some countries' votes at the United Nations by lying to them that the south had captured tanks manned by Russians. U.S. officials publicly declared Soviet involvement but privately doubted it.

The Soviet Union, in fact, did not want a war, and on July 6, its deputy foreign minister told the British ambassador in Moscow that it wanted a peaceful settlement. The U.S. ambassador in Moscow thought this was genuine. Washington didn't care. The North, the U.S. government said, had violated the 38th parallel, that sacred line of national sovereignty. But as soon as U.S. Gen. Douglas MacArthur got the chance, he proceeded, with President Truman's approval, right across that line, into the north, and up to the border of China. MacArthur had been drooling for a war with China and threatening it, and asked for permission to attack, which the Joint Chiefs of Staff refused. Eventually, Truman fired MacArthur. Attacking a power plant in North Korea that supplied China, and bombing a border city, was the closest MacArthur got to what he wanted.[56]

But the U.S. threat to China, or at least the U.S. threat to defeat North Korea, brought the Chinese and Russians into the war, a war that cost Korea two million civilian lives and the United States 37,000 soldiers, while turning Seoul and Pyongyang both into piles of rubble. Many of the dead had been killed at close range, slaughtered unarmed and in cold-blood by both sides. And the border was right back where it had been, but the hatred directed across that border greatly increased. When the war ended, having accomplished no good for anyone but weapons makers, "people emerged from a mole-like existence in caves and tunnels to find a nightmare in the bright of day."[57]

Brainwashing

I cannot resist mentioning here one of the most ludicrous ever means of rejecting unwanted information about a war, which arose in the United States during the Korean War. Here in our little U.S. bubble we've heard of a couple of versions of a film called *The Manchurian Candidate*. We've heard of the general concept of "brainwashing" and may even associate it with something evil that the Chinese supposedly did to U.S. prisoners during the Korean War.

I'd be willing to bet that the majority of people who've heard of these things have at least a vague sense that they're not actually real. In fact, people cannot actually be programed like the Manchurian candidate, which was a work of fiction. There was never the slightest evidence that China or North Korea had done any such thing. And the CIA spent decades trying to do such a thing, and finally gave up.

I'd also be willing to bet that very few people know what it was that the U.S. government promoted the myth of "brainwashing" to cover up. During the Korean War, the United States bombed virtually all of North Korea and a good bit of the South, killing hundreds of thousands of people. It dropped massive quantities of napalm. It bombed dams, bridges, villages, and houses. This was all-out mass-slaughter. But there was something the U.S. government didn't want known, something deemed unethical in this genocidal madness.

It is well documented that the United States dropped on China and North Korea insects and feathers carrying anthrax, cholera, encephalitis, and bubonic plague.[58] This was supposed to be a secret at the time, and the Chinese response of mass vaccinations and insect eradication probably contributed to the project's general failure (hundreds were killed, but not millions). But members of the U.S. military taken prisoner by the Chinese confessed to what they had been a part of. Some of them had felt guilty to begin with. Some had been shocked at China's decent treatment of prisoners after U.S. depictions of the Chinese as savages. For whatever reasons, they confessed, and their confessions were highly credible, were borne out by independent scientific reviews, and have stood the test of time.

There isn't any debate that the United States had been working on bio-weapons for years, at Fort Detrick—then Camp Detrick—and numerous other locations. Nor is there any question that the United States employed the top bio-weapons killers from among both the Japanese and the Nazis from the end of World War II onward. Nor is there any question that the United States tested such weapons on the city of San Francisco and numerous other locations around the United States, and on U.S. soldiers. There's a museum in Havana featuring evidence of years of U.S. bio-warfare against Cuba. We know that Plum Island, off the tip of Long Island, was used to test the weaponization of insects, including the ticks that created the ongoing outbreak of Lyme disease.[59] Dave Chaddock's book *This Must Be the Place* collects the evidence that the United States indeed tried to wipe out millions of Chinese and North Koreans with deadly diseases.

The propaganda struggle was intense. The support of the Guatemalan government for the reports of U.S. germ warfare in China were part of the U.S. motivation for overthrowing the Guatemalan government; and the same cover-up was likely part of the motivation for the CIA's murder of a man named Frank Olson.[60]

How to counter reports of the confessions? The answer for the CIA and the U.S. military and their allies in the corporate media was "brainwashing," which conveniently explained away whatever prisoners said as false narratives implanted in their brains by brainwashers. Millions of Americans more or less believe this craziest-ever dog-ate-my-homework concoction to this day. It's safe to say that Americans wouldn't believe in Chinese "brainwashing" if the stories had been about the U.S. government rather than the Chinese.

Cold Blooded War

The U.S. government was just warming up. When President Truman spoke to a joint session of Congress and over the radio on March 12, 1947, he divided the world into two opposing forces, the free world, and the world of the communists and totalitarians. Men like Winston Churchill and Allen Dulles had viewed the Soviet Union as the real enemy before, during, and after World War II. Churchill even proposed recruiting former Nazi troops within days of Germany's surrender to launch a new war against the Soviet Union. Dulles betrayed his own government and Soviet allies to arrange a separate peace with German forces in Italy, and then spent a great deal of effort rescuing former top Nazis from criminal prosecution. The U.S. military and growing spy service quickly recruited large numbers of former Nazis to work against the Soviet Union. President Roosevelt's somewhat cooperative relationship with the Soviet Union died with him. Truman's address concocted a crisis so urgent there was no time to debate or negotiate. He demonized the Soviets. And he laid the groundwork for justifying the creation of the Marshall Plan, the CIA, the National Security Council, the Federal Employee Loyalty Program, and NATO.[61]

These changes, especially the creation of the CIA which Truman would come to regret, increased presidential control over war powers and facilitated secret and unaccountable warlike operations, such as the overthrow of Iran's democracy in 1953, at which time U.S. officials invented the fiction that Iran's democratically elected president was a communist, as Teddy Roosevelt's grandson and Norman Schwarzkopf's father orchestrated a coup and replaced *Time* magazine's 1951 Man of the Year with a dictator.

Next on the block was Guatemala. Edward Bernays had been hired in 1944 by United Fruit. A veteran of the Committee on Public Information which had marketed World War I, nephew of Sigmund Freud, and father of the noble profession of exploiting and encouraging human irrationality through "public relations," Bernays, had published a book in 1928 called simply *Propaganda*, which actually propagandized for the merits of propaganda. Bernays helped United Fruit's Sam Zemurray (who had overthrown the president of Honduras in 1911) by creating a PR campaign beginning in 1951 in the United States against the overly democratic government of Guatemala. The *New York Times* and other media outlets followed Bernays's lead, depicting the noble United Fruit as suffering under the rule of a Marxist dictatorship—which was actually an elected government implementing New Deal-type reforms.

Senator Henry Cabot Lodge Jr. (R-MA) led the effort in Congress. He was the great-great-great-grandson of Senator George Cabot (F-MA) and grandson of Senator Henry Cabot Lodge (R-MA) who had pushed the country into the Spanish-American War and World War I, defeated the League of Nations, and built up the Navy. Henry Cabot Lodge Jr. would go on to serve as ambassador to South Vietnam, in which position he would help maneuver the nation into the Vietnam War. While the Soviet Union had no relations with Guatemala, the father of the CIA Allen Dulles was certain or claimed to be certain that Moscow was directing Guatemala's fictional march toward communism. With President Dwight Eisenhower's approval, the CIA overthrew Guatemala's government on behalf of United Fruit. Key to the operation was the work of Howard Hunt, who would later break into the Watergate for President Richard Nixon, and later still—on his death bed—confess to a role in the assassination of President John F. Kennedy. None of this would have surprised Smedley Butler.

And then—following a missile crisis in Cuba during which the war planners nearly destroyed the planet to make a point, and various other exciting adventures—came Vietnam, a war of aggression in which we were falsely told, as we may also have been in Korea, that the North had started it. We could save South Vietnam or watch all of Asia and then our own nation fall victim to the communist threat, we were told. Presidents Eisenhower and John F.

Kennedy said the nations of Asia (and even Africa and Latin America too, according to Gen. Maxwell Taylor) could fall like dominoes. This was another piece of nonsense that would be recycled in modified form in the "global war on terrorism" waged by Presidents G.W. Bush and Obama. According to blogger Juan Cole, Obama, when arguing in March 2009 for the escalation of the war on Afghanistan which a growing majority of Americans opposed, "described the same sort of domino effect that Washington elites used to ascribe to international communism." Cole added, "In the updated, al-Qaida version, the Taliban might take...Afghanistan, and might...then threaten the shores of the United States. He even managed to add an analog to Cambodia... [namely] Pakistan."[62]

The dramatic incident, however, that was used to escalate the Vietnam War was a fictional attack on U.S. ships in the Gulf of Tonkin on August 4, 1964. These were U.S. war ships off the coast of North Vietnam that were engaged in military actions against North Vietnam. President Lyndon Johnson knew he was lying when he claimed the August 4 attack was unprovoked. Had it happened, it could not have been unprovoked. The same ship that was supposedly attacked on August 4 had damaged three North Vietnamese boats and killed four North Vietnamese sailors two days earlier, in an action where the evidence suggests the United States fired first, although the opposite was claimed. In fact, in a separate operation days earlier, the United States had begun shelling the mainland of North Vietnam.

But the supposed attack on August 4 was actually, at most, a misreading of U.S. sonar. The ship's commander cabled the Pentagon claiming to be under attack, and then immediately cabled to say his earlier belief was in doubt and no North Vietnamese ships could be confirmed in the area. President Johnson was not sure there had been any attack when he told the American public there had been. Months later he admitted privately: "For all I know, our navy was just shooting at whales out there."[63] But by then Johnson had the authorization from Congress for the war he'd wanted.

In fact, by then he'd also lied the United States into an additional little military action in the Dominican Republic to defend Americans and prevent the imagined spread of communism. As we have seen, no Americans were actually in danger. But that justification had been cooked up as a substitute for the claim of combating communism, which Johnson knew to be baseless and couldn't be sure would fly. In a closed session of the Senate Foreign Relations Committee, Assistant Secretary of State Thomas Mann later explained that the U.S. ambassador had asked the head of the Dominican military if he'd be willing to play along with the alternative lie: "All we requested was whether he would be willing to change the basis for this from one of fighting communism to one of protecting American lives."[64]

That same year, President Johnson made his humanitarian and democratic motivations clear in a comment to the Greek ambassador, whose country had unforgivably elected a liberal prime minister not favored by the United States, and dared to squabble with Turkey and oppose U.S. plans to partition Cyprus. Johnson's comment, sure to be remembered as fondly as Lincoln's Gettysburg Address, was:

> Fuck your parliament and your constitution. America is an elephant, Cyprus is a flea. If these two fleas continue itching the elephant, they may just get whacked by the elephant's trunk, whacked good. We pay a lot of good American dollars to the Greeks, Mr. Ambassador. If your Prime Minister gives me a talk about democracy, parliament, and constitutions, he, his parliament, and his constitution may not last very long.[65]

The project of choosing the excuses for a war sometimes seems to be shaped by bureaucratic infighting. Shortly after the invasion of Iraq in 2003, when people who had believed the lies were asking where all the weapons were, Deputy "Defense" Secretary Paul Wolfowitz told *Vanity Fair*, "The truth is that for reasons that have a lot to do with the U.S. government bureaucracy, we settled on the one issue that everyone could agree on which was weapons of mass destruction as the core reason."[66]

In a 2003 documentary called *The Fog of War*, Robert McNamara, who had been secretary of "defense" at the time of the Tonkin lies, admitted that the August 4 attack did not happen and that there had been serious doubts at the time. He did not mention that on August 6 he had testified in a joint closed session of the Senate Foreign Relations and Armed Services Committees along with Gen. Earl Wheeler. Before the two committees, both men claimed with absolute certainty that the North Vietnamese had attacked on August 4. McNamara also did not mention that just days after the Tonkin Gulf non-incident, he had asked the Joint Chiefs of Staff to provide him with a list of further U.S. actions that might provoke North Vietnam. He obtained the list and advocated for those provocations in meetings prior to Johnson's ordering such actions on September 10. These actions included resuming the same ship patrols and increasing covert operations, and by October ordering ship-to-shore bombardment of radar sites.[67]

A 2000–2001 National Security Agency (NSA) report concluded there had been no attack at Tonkin on August 4 and that the NSA had deliberately lied. The Bush Administration did not allow the report to be published until 2005, due to concern that it might interfere with lies being told to get the Afghanistan and Iraq wars started. On March 8, 1999, *Newsweek* had published the mother of all lies: "America has not started a war in this century."[68] No doubt Team Bush thought it best to leave that pretense undisturbed.

I discussed the lies that launched the war on Iraq in my previous book, *Daybreak*, and they don't need review here, except to note that the extensive propaganda effort used to market that war drew from the entire repertoire of past war lies including the work of President George W. Bush's predecessor and promoter of humanitarian aggression, President Bill Clinton. Since occupying Cuba to liberate it, the United States has overthrown numerous governments for the supposed good of their people. In recent decades, it has become almost routine for presidents to launch air strikes against suspected terrorists or with the stated goal of preventing crimes against humanity. Clinton developed this presidential prerogative by using NATO, in violation of the UN Charter and unconstitutionally in defiance of congressional opposition, to bomb the former Yugoslavia in 1999.

The legal danger of such humanitarian bombing missions is that, if the United Nations is circumvented, any nation can claim the same right to start dropping bombs as long as it proclaims humanitarian purposes. The constitutional danger is that any president can take such actions without the approval of the people's representatives in Congress. In fact, the House of Representatives voted not to authorize the bombing in 1999, and the executive went ahead with it anyway. The human danger of these bombing "campaigns" is that the harm done can be as heavy as any that might be prevented. The International Criminal Tribunal for the Former Yugoslavia found that NATO's bombing may have increased, rather than diminished, the war crimes it was justified by—most of which occurred during and not prior to the bombing.

Meanwhile, numerous humanitarian crises, such as the Rwandan genocide of 1994, are ignored because they are not considered to be of strategic value or because no easy military solution is seen. (In the case of Rwanda, allowing the horrors to continue brought to power the military leader whose warmaking the United States had been backing for years.) We think of crises of all sorts (from hurricanes to oil spills to genocides) as only solvable with the often inappropriate tool of the military. If a war is already going on, the excuse of disaster relief isn't needed. In 2003 in Iraq, for example, U.S. troops guarded the oil ministry while institutions of cultural and humanitarian value were looted and destroyed. In 2010 U.S. troops in Pakistan prioritized protecting an air base rather than aiding flood victims. Of course the environmental and human disasters created by one's own wars are quietly ignored, for example the Iraqi refugee crisis or the creation of ISIS.

Then there's the danger of not knowing what we're doing because we're being lied to. With war, this is not so much a danger as a near-certainty. Using a tool that kills great numbers of people and is always justified with lies seems a dubious proposition even on humanitarian grounds. When, in 1995, Croatia had slaughtered or "ethnically cleansed" Serbs with Washington's blessing, driving 150,000 people from their homes, we weren't supposed to notice, much less drop bombs to prevent it. The bombing was saved for Milosevic, who—we were told in 1999—refused to negotiate peace and therefore had to be bombed. We were not told that the United States was insisting on an agreement that no nation in the world would voluntarily agree to, one giving NATO complete freedom to occupy all of Yugoslavia with absolute immunity from laws for all of its personnel. In the June 14, 1999, issue of *The Nation*, George Kenney, a former State Department Yugoslavia desk officer, reported:

> An unimpeachable press source who regularly travels with Secretary of State Madeleine Albright told this [writer] that, swearing reporters to deep-background confidentiality at the Rambouillet talks, a senior State Department official had bragged that the United States "deliberately set the bar higher than the Serbs could accept." The Serbs needed, according to the official, a little bombing to see reason.[69]

Jim Jatras, a foreign policy aide to Senate Republicans, reported in a May 18, 1999, speech at the Cato Institute in Washington that he had it "on good authority" that a "senior Administration official told media at Rambouillet, under embargo" the following: "We intentionally set the bar too high for the Serbs to comply. They need some bombing, and that's what they are going to get."[70]

In interviews with FAIR (Fairness and Accuracy in Reporting), both Kenney and Jatras asserted that these were actual quotes transcribed by reporters who spoke with a U.S. official.

Negotiating for the impossible, and falsely accusing the other side of non-cooperation, is a handy way to launch a "defensive" war.[71] Behind that scheme in 1999 was special U.S. envoy Richard Holbrooke, whom we encountered above in 2010 defending an aggressive war on Afghanistan.

Atrocities against the same group of people can be grounds for humanitarian war or matters of no concern at all, depending on whether the perpetrator is an ally of the U.S. government. Saddam Hussein could murder Kurds until he fell out of favor, at which point murdering Kurds became horrific and galvanizing—unless Turkey did it, in which case it was nothing to worry about. In 2010, the year I wrote the first edition of this book, Turkey was risking its status, however. Turkey and Brazil had taken steps to facilitate peace between the United States and Iran, which of course angered many in Washington. And then Turkey had assisted aid ships seeking to bring food and supplies to the people of Gaza who were being blockaded and starved by the government of Israel. This caused the Israel-right-or-wrong lobby in Washington to reverse a longstanding position and support the idea of Congress "recognizing" the 1915 Armenian Genocide. Had the Armenians suddenly become full humans? Of course not. It had simply become desirable to accuse Turkey, a century too late, of genocide, precisely because Turkey was attempting to alleviate the present-day strangulation of a people.[72]

Former president Jimmy Carter, whom Noam Chomsky calls our least violent president since World War II, has bravely denounced his fair share of atrocities, including those committed by Israel, but not the slaughter of the East Timorese by Indonesia for which his administration provided much of the weaponry, or the slaughter of Salvadorans by their government for which his administration did the same. Atrocious behavior is sanctioned and kept quiet when strategic. It is highlighted and used to justify wars only when the makers of wars want a war for some other set of reasons. Those who obediently cheer for the pretended reasons for a war are being used.

There is one war in U.S. history that we openly refer to as aggression and do not try to defend as defensive. Or, rather, some of us do. Many Southerners refers to it as the War of Northern Aggression, and the North calls it the Civil War. It was a war the South fought for the right to leave and the North fought to prevent states from leaving, not to defend itself against a foreign assault. We've come a long way in terms of the justifications we require of war makers. Although I doubt the U.S. government would allow a state to leave peacefully even today, any war today must be justified in humanitarian terms unknown in previous centuries.

As we will see in Chapter 4, wars have become more deadly and horrific. But the justifications put forward to explain or excuse them have become more benevolent and altruistic. The U.S. government now fights wars for the benefit of the world out of kindness, love, and generosity.

At least that's what I've heard and what we'll examine in Chapter 3.

3

WARS ARE NOT
WAGED OUT OF GENEROSITY

The idea that wars are waged out of humanitarian concern may not at first appear even worthy of response. Wars kill humans. What can be humanitarian about that? But look at the sort of rhetoric that successfully sells new wars: "This conflict started August 2, when the dictator of Iraq invaded a small and helpless neighbor. Kuwait, a member of the Arab League and a member of the United Nations, was crushed, its people brutalized. Five months ago, Saddam Hussein started this cruel war against Kuwait; tonight, the battle has been joined."[1]

Thus spoke President Bush the elder upon launching the Gulf War in 1991. He didn't say he wanted to kill people. He said he wanted to liberate helpless victims from their oppressors, an idea that would be considered leftist in domestic politics, but an idea that seems to create genuine support for wars. And here's President Clinton speaking about Yugoslavia eight years later:

> When I ordered our armed forces into combat, we had three clear goals: to enable the Kosovar people, the victims of some of the most vicious atrocities in Europe since the Second World War, to return to their homes with safety and self-government; to require Serbian forces responsible for those atrocities to leave Kosovo; and to deploy an international security force, with NATO at its core, to protect all the people of that troubled land, Serbs and Albanians alike.[2]

Look also at the rhetoric that is used to successfully keep wars going for years:

> We will not abandon the Iraqi people.

> —Secretary of State Colin Powell, August 13, 2003.

The United States will not abandon Iraq.

—President George W. Bush, March, 21, 2006.

If I break into your house, smash the windows, bust up the furniture, and kill half your family, do I have a moral obligation to stay and spend the night? Would it be cruel and irresponsible for me to "abandon" you, even when you encourage me to leave? Or is it my duty, on the contrary, to depart immediately and turn myself in at the nearest police station? Once the wars in Afghanistan and Iraq had begun, a debate began that resembled this one. As you can see, these two approaches are many miles apart, despite both being framed as humanitarian. One says that we have to *stay* out of generosity, the other that we have to *leave* out of shame and respect. Which is right?

Prior to the invasion of Iraq, Secretary of State Colin Powell reportedly told President Bush "You are going to be the proud owner of 25 million people. You will own all their hopes, aspirations, and problems. You'll own it all." According to Bob Woodward, "Powell and Deputy Secretary of State Richard Armitage called this the Pottery Barn rule: You break it, you own it." Senator John Kerry cited the rule when running for president, and it was and is widely accepted as legitimate by Republican and Democratic politicians in Washington.[3]

The Pottery Barn is a store that has no such rule, at least not for accidents. It's illegal in many U.S. states to have such a rule, except for cases of gross negligence and willful destruction. That description, of course, fits the invasion of Iraq to a T. The doctrine of "shock and awe," of imposing such massive destruction that the enemy is paralyzed with fear and helplessness had long since been proven as hopeless and nonsensical as it sounds. It hadn't worked in World War II or since. Americans parachuting into Japan following the nuclear bombs were not bowed down to; they were lynched. People have always fought back and always will, just as you probably would. But shock and awe is designed to include the complete destruction of infrastructure, communication, transportation, food production and supply, water supply, and so forth. In other words: the illegal imposition of great suffering on an entire population. If that's not willful destruction, I don't know what is.

The invasion of Iraq was also intended as a "decapitation," a "regime change." The dictator was removed from the scene, eventually captured, and later executed following a deeply flawed trial that avoided evidence of U.S. complicity in his crimes. Many Iraqis were delighted with the removal of Saddam Hussein, but quickly began to demand the withdrawal of the U.S. military from their country. Was this ingratitude? "Thank you for deposing our tyrant. Don't let the doorknob hit you in the ass on your way out!" Hmm. That makes it sound as if the United States wanted to stay, and as if the Iraqis owed us the favor of letting us stay. That's quite different from staying reluctantly to fulfill our moral duty of ownership. Which is it?

Owning People

How does one manage to own people? It's striking that Powell, an African American, some of whose ancestors were owned as slaves in Jamaica, told the president he would own people, dark-skinned people against whom many Americans held some degree of prejudice. Powell was arguing against the invasion, or at least warning of what would be involved. But did owning people necessarily have to be involved? If the United States and its fig-leaf "coalition" of minor contingents from other nations had pulled out of Iraq when George W. Bush declared "mission accomplished" in a flight suit on an aircraft carrier in San Diego Harbor on May 1, 2003, and not disbanded the Iraqi military, and not laid siege to towns and neighborhoods, not inflamed ethnic tensions, not prevented Iraqis from working to repair the damage, and not driven millions of Iraqis out of their homes, then the result might not have been ideal, but it almost certainly would have involved less misery than what was actually done, following the Pottery Barn rule.

Or what if the United States had congratulated Iraq on its disarmament, of which the U.S. government was fully apprised? What if the United States had removed its military from the area, eliminated the no-fly zones, and ended the economic sanctions, the sanctions Secretary of State Madeleine Albright had been discussing in 1996 in this exchange on the television program *60 Minutes*:

> LESLEY STAHL: We have heard that a half million children have died. I mean, that's more children than died in Hiroshima. And, you know, is the price worth it?

> ALBRIGHT: I think this is a very hard choice, but the price—we think the price is worth it.[4]

Was it? So much was accomplished that a war was still needed in 2003? Those children couldn't have been spared for seven more years and identical political results? What if the United States had worked with the demilitarized Iraq to encourage a demilitarized Middle East, including all its nations in a nuclear-free zone, encouraging Israel to dismantle its nuclear stockpile instead of encouraging Iran to try to acquire one? George W. Bush had lumped Iran, Iraq, and North Korea into "an axis of evil," attacked unarmed Iraq, ignored nuclear-armed North Korea, and begun threatening Iran. If you were Iran, what would you have wanted?

What if the United States had provided economic aid to Iraq, Iran, and other nations in the region, and led an effort to provide them with (or at least lifted sanctions that are preventing the construction of) windmills, solar panels, and a sustainable energy infrastructure, thus bringing electricity to more, rather than fewer people? Such a project could not possibly have cost anything like the trillions of dollars wasted on war between 2003 and 2010. For an additional relatively tiny expense, we could have created a major program of student exchange between Iraqi, Iranian, and U.S. schools. Nothing discourages war like bonds of friendship and family. Why wouldn't such an approach have been at least as responsible and serious and moral as announcing our ownership of somebody else's country just because we'd bombed it?

Part of the disagreement, I think, arises over a failure to imagine what the bombing looked like. If we think of it as a clean and harmless series of blips on a video game, during which "smart bombs" improve Baghdad by "surgically" removing its evildoers, then moving on to the next step of fulfilling our duties as the new landlords is easier. If, instead, we imagine the actual and horrific mass-murder and maiming of children and adults that went on when Baghdad was bombed, then our thoughts turn to apologies and reparations as our first priority, and we begin to question whether we have the right or the standing to behave as owners of what remains. In fact, smashing a pot at the Pottery Barn would result in our paying for the damage and apologizing, not overseeing the smashing of more pots.

Racist Generosity

Another major source of the disagreement between pro- and anti-Pottery Barners, I think, comes down to a powerful and insidious force discussed in Chapter 1: racism. Remember President McKinley's proposing to govern the Philippines because the poor Filipinos couldn't possibly do it themselves? William Howard Taft, the first American governor-general of the Philippines, called the Filipinos "our little brown brothers." In Vietnam, when the Vietcong appeared willing to sacrifice a great many of their lives without surrendering, that became evidence that they placed little value on life, which became evidence of their evil nature, which became grounds for killing even more of them.

If we set aside the Pottery Barn rule for a moment and think, instead, of the golden rule, we get a very different sort of guidance. "Do unto others as you would have them do unto you." If another nation invaded our country, and the result was immediately chaos; if it was unclear what form of government, if any, would emerge; if the nation was in danger of breaking into pieces; if there might be civil war or anarchy; and if nothing was certain, what is the very first thing we would want the invading military to do? That's right: get the hell out of our country! And in fact that's what the majority of Iraqis in numerous polls told the United States to do for years. For example, a 2006 poll by the Program on International Policy Attitudes found that most Iraqis believed U.S. troops had no plans to ever leave. A large majority favored setting a date for U.S. military departure. Almost half of all Iraqis favored violent attacks on U.S. troops, and 9 out of 10 Sunnis favored such attacks.[5]

Of course, those puppets and politicians benefitting from an occupation prefer to see it continue. But even within the puppet government, the Iraqi Parliament refused to approve the treaty that Presidents Bush and Maliki drew up in 2008 to extend the occupation for three years, unless the people were given a chance to vote it up or down in a referendum. That vote was later repeatedly denied precisely because everyone knew what the outcome would have been. Owning people out of the kindness of our hearts is one thing, I believe, but doing it against their will is quite another. And who has ever willfully chosen to be owned?

Are We Generous?

Is generosity really a motivator behind U.S. wars, whether the launching of them or the prolonging of them? If a nation is generous toward other nations, it seems likely it would be so in more than one way. Yet, if you examine a list of nations ranked by the charity they give to others and a list of nations ranked by their military expenditures, there's no correlation. In a list of the wealthiest two-dozen countries, ranked in terms of foreign giving, the United States is near the bottom, and a significant chunk of the "aid" the U.S. government gives to other countries is actually weaponry. If private giving is factored in with public giving, the United States moves only slightly higher in the list. If the money that recent immigrants send to their own families were included, the United States might move up a bit more, although that seems like a very different kind of giving.

When you look at the top nations in terms of military spending per-capita, none of the wealthy nations from Europe, Asia, or North America make it anywhere near the top of the list, with the single exception of the United States. The United States comes in 11th, with the 10 nations above it in military spending per capita all from the Middle East, North Africa, or central Asia. Greece comes in 23rd, South Korea 36th, and the United Kingdom 42nd, with all other European and Asian nations further down the list. In addition, the United States is the top exporter of private arms sales, with Russia the only other country in the world that comes even remotely close to it.

More importantly, of the 22 major wealthy countries, most of which give more to foreign charity than do we in the United States, 20 haven't started any wars in generations, if ever, and at most have taken small roles in U.S.-dominated war coalitions; one of the other two countries, South Korea, only engages in hostilities with North Korea with U.S. approval; and the last country, the United Kingdom, primarily follows the U.S. lead.

Civilizing the heathen was always viewed as a generous mission (except by the heathen). Manifest destiny was believed to be an expression of God's love. According to anthropologist Clark Wissler, "when a group comes into a new solution to one of its important cultural problems, it becomes zealous to spread that idea abroad, and is moved to embark upon an era of conquest to force the recognition of its merits."[6] Spread? Spread? Where have we heard something about spreading an important solution? Oh, yes, I remember:

> And the second way to defeat the terrorists is to spread freedom. You see, the best way to defeat a society that is—doesn't have hope, a society where people become so angry they're willing to become suiciders, is to spread freedom, is to spread democracy.
>
> —President George W. Bush, June 8, 2005.[7]

This isn't a stupid idea because Bush speaks hesitantly and invents the word "suiciders." It's a stupid idea because freedom and democracy cannot be imposed at gunpoint by a foreign force that thinks so little of the newly free people that it is willing to recklessly murder them. A democracy that is required beforehand to remain loyal to the United States is not a representative government, but rather some sort of strange hybrid with dictatorship. A democracy imposed in order to demonstrate to the world that our way is the best way is unlikely to create a government of, by, and for the people.

U.S. Commander Stanley McChrystal described a planned but failed attempt to create a government in Marjah, Afghanistan, in 2010; he said he would bring in a hand-picked puppet and a set of foreign handlers as "a government in a box." Wouldn't you want a foreign army to bring one of those to your town?

With 86 percent of Americans in a February 2010 CNN poll saying our own government is broken, do we have the know-how, never mind the authority, to impose a model of government on someone else? And if we did, would the military be the tool with which to do it?

What Do You Mean You Already Had a Nation?

Judging from past experience, creating a new nation by force usually fails. We generally call this activity "nation building" even though it usually does not build a nation. In May 2003, two scholars at the Carnegie Endowment for International Peace released a study of past U.S. attempts at nation building, examining—in chronological order—Cuba, Panama, Cuba again, Nicaragua, Haiti, Cuba yet again, the Dominican Republic, West Germany, Japan, the Dominican Republic again, South Vietnam, Cambodia, Grenada, Panama again, Haiti again, and Afghanistan. Of these 16 attempts at nation building, in only four, the authors concluded, was a democracy sustained as long as 10 years after the departure of U.S. forces.

By "departure" of U.S. forces, the authors of the above study clearly meant reduction, since U.S. forces have never actually departed. Two of the four countries were the completely destroyed and defeated Japan and Germany. The other two were U.S. neighbors—tiny Grenada and Panama. The so-called nation building in Panama is considered to have taken 23 years. That same length of time would carry the occupations of Afghanistan and Iraq to 2024 and 2026, respectively.

Never, the authors found, has a surrogate regime supported by the United States, such as those in Afghanistan and Iraq, made the transition to democracy. The authors of this study, Minxin Pei and Sara Kasper, also found that creating lasting democracies had never been the primary goal:

> The primary goal of early U.S. nation-building efforts was in most cases strategic.... Only later did America's political ideals and its need to sustain domestic support for nation building impel it to try to establish democratic rule in target nations.[8]

Do you think an endowment for peace might be biased against war? Surely the Pentagon-created RAND Corporation must be biased *in favor* of war. And yet a RAND study of occupations and insurgencies in 2010, a study produced for the U.S. Marine Corps, found that 90 percent of insurgencies against weak governments, like Afghanistan's, succeed. In other words, the nation building, whether or not imposed from abroad, fails.[9]

In fact, even as war supporters were telling us to escalate and "stay the course" in Afghanistan in 2009 and 2010, experts from across the political spectrum were in agreement that doing so couldn't accomplish anything, much less bestow generous benefits on Afghans. U.S. Ambassador Karl Eikenberry opposed an escalation in leaked cables. Numerous former officials in the military and the CIA favored withdrawal. Matthew Hoh, a senior U.S. civilian diplomat in Zabul Province and former marine captain, resigned and backed withdrawal. So did former diplomat Ann Wright who had helped reopen the embassy in Afghanistan in 2001. The National Security Advisor thought more troops would "just be swallowed up." A majority of the U.S. public opposed the war, and the opposition was even stronger among the

Afghan people, especially in Kandahar, where a U.S. Army-funded survey found that 94 percent of Kandaharis wanted negotiations, not assault, and 85 percent said they viewed the Taliban as "our Afghan brothers."[10]

Chairman of the Senate Foreign Relations Committee, and funder of the escalation, John Kerry noted that an assault on Marja that had been a test run for a larger assault on Kandahar had failed miserably. Kerry also noted that Taliban assassinations in Kandahar had begun when the United States announced a coming assault there. How then, he asked, could the assault stop the killings? Kerry and his colleagues, just before dumping another $33.5 billion into the Afghanistan escalation in 2010, pointed out that terrorism had been increasing globally during the "global war on terrorism." The 2009 escalation in Afghanistan had been followed by an 87 percent increase in violence, according to the Pentagon.

The military had developed, or rather revived from Vietnam days, a strategy for Iraq four years into that war that was also applied to Afghanistan, a kind-hearted strategy known as counter-insurgency. On paper, this required an 80 percent investment in civilian efforts at "winning hearts and minds" and 20 percent in military operations. But in both countries, this strategy was only applied to rhetoric, not reality. Actual investment in non-military operations in Afghanistan never topped five percent, and the man in charge of it, Richard Holbrooke, described the civilian mission as "supporting the military."

Rather than "spreading freedom" with bombs and guns, what would have been wrong with spreading knowledge? If learning leads to the development of democracy, why not spread education? Why not provide funding for children's health and schools, instead of melting the skin off children with white phosphorous? Nobel Peace Laureate Shirin Ebadi proposed, following the September 11, 2001, terrorism, that instead of bombing Afghanistan, the United States could build schools in Afghanistan, each named for and honoring someone killed in the World Trade Center, thus building appreciation for generous aid and understanding of the damage done by violence. Whatever you think of such an approach, it's hard to argue it wouldn't have been generous and perhaps even in line with the principle of loving one's enemies.

Let Me Help You Out of That

The hypocrisy of generously imposed occupations is perhaps most apparent when done in the name of uprooting previous occupations. When Japan kicked European colonialists out of Asian nations only to occupy them itself, or when the United States liberated Cuba or the Philippines in order to dominate those countries itself, the contrast between word and deed jumped out at you. In both of these examples, Japan and the United States offered civilization, culture, modernization, leadership, and mentoring, but they offered them at the barrel of a gun whether anyone wanted them or not. And if anyone did, well, their story got top play back home. When Americans were hearing tales of German barbarity in Belgium and France during World War I, Germans were reading accounts of how dearly the occupied French loved their benevolent German occupiers. And when can you not count on the *New York Times* to locate an Iraqi or an Afghan who's worried that the Americans might leave too soon?

Any occupation must work with some elite group of natives, who in turn will of course support the occupation. But the occupier should not mistake such support for majority opinion, as the United States has been in the habit of doing since at least 1899. Nor should a "native face" on a foreign occupation be expected to fool people: "The British, like the Americans...believed that native troops would be less unpopular than foreigners. That proposition is... dubious: if native troops are perceived to be puppets of foreigners, they may be even more violently opposed than the foreigners themselves."[11]

Native troops may also be less loyal to the occupier's mission and less trained in the ways of the occupying army. This soon leads to blaming the same deserving people on whose behalf the U.S. government has attacked their country for the inability of the U.S. military to leave it. They are now "violent, incompetent, and untrustworthy," as the McKinley White House portrayed the Filipinos,[12] and as the Bush and Obama White Houses portrayed Iraqis and Afghans.

In an occupied nation with its own internal divisions, minority groups may truly fear mistreatment at the hands of the majority should the foreign occupation end. That problem is a reason for future Bushes to heed the advice of future Powells and not invade in the first place. It's a reason not to inflame internal divisions, as occupiers tend to do, much preferring that the people kill each other than that they unite against foreign forces. And it's a reason to encourage international diplomacy and positive influence on the nation while withdrawing and paying reparations.

The feared post-occupation violence is not, however, usually a persuasive argument for extending the occupation. For one thing, it's an argument for permanent occupation. For another, the bulk of the violence that is depicted back in the imperial nation as a civil war is still usually violence directed against the occupiers and their collaborators. When the occupation ends, so does much of the violence. This has been demonstrated in Iraq as troops have reduced their presence; the violence has decreased accordingly. Most of the violence in Basra ended when the British troops there ceased patrolling to control the violence. The plan for withdrawal from Iraq that

George McGovern and William Polk (the former senator and a descendant of former President Polk, respectively) published in 2006 proposed a temporary bridge to complete independence, advice that went unheeded:

> The Iraqi government would be wise to request the short-term services of an international force to police the country during and immediately after the period of American withdrawal. Such a force should be on only temporary duty, with a firm date fixed in advance for withdrawal. Our estimate is that Iraq would need it for about two years after the American withdrawal is complete. During this period, the force probably could be slowly but steadily cut back, both in personnel and in deployment. Its activities would be limited to enhancing public security.... It would have no need for tanks or artillery or offensive aircraft.... It would not attempt...to battle the insurgents. Indeed, after the withdrawal of American and British regular troops and the roughly 25,000 foreign mercenaries, the insurgency, which was aimed at achieving that objective, would lose public support.... Then gunmen would either put down their weapons or become publicly identified as outlaws. This outcome has been the experience of insurgencies in Algeria, Kenya, Ireland (Eire), and elsewhere.[13]

Cops of the World Benevolence Society

It's not just the continuation of wars that is justified as generosity. Initiating fights with evil forces in defense of justice, even while it inspires less than angelic sentiments in some war supporters, is generally also presented as pure selflessness and benevolence. "He is keeping the World safe for Democracy. Enlist and Help Him," read a U.S. World War I poster, fulfilling President Wilson's directive that the Committee on Public Information present the "absolute justice of America's cause," and the "absolute selflessness of America's aims." When President Franklin Roosevelt persuaded Congress to create a military draft and to allow the "lending" of weaponry to Britain before the United States entered World War II, he compared his Lend-Lease program to loaning a hose to a neighbor whose house was on fire.

Then, in the summer of 1941, Roosevelt pretended to go fishing and actually met with Prime Minister Churchill off the coast of Newfoundland. FDR came back to Washington, describing a moving ceremony during which he and Churchill had sung "Onward Christian Soldiers." FDR and Churchill released a joint statement created without the peoples or legislatures of either country that laid out the principles by which the two leaders' nations would fight the war and shape the world afterwards, despite the fact that the United States was still not in the war. This statement, which came to be called the

Atlantic Charter, made clear that Britain and the United States favored peace, freedom, justice, and harmony and had no interest whatsoever in building empires. These were noble sentiments on behalf of which millions could engage in horrible violence.

Until it entered World War II, the United States generously provided the machinery of death to Britain. Following this model, both weapons and soldiers sent to Korea and subsequent actions have for decades been described as "military aid." Thus the idea that war is doing someone a favor was built into the very language used to name it. The Korean War, as a UN-sanctioned "police action," was described not only as charity, but also as the world community's hiring a sheriff to enforce the peace, just as good Americans would have done in a Western town. But being the world's policeman never won over those who believed it was well intentioned yet didn't think the world deserved the favor. Nor did it win over those who saw it as just the latest excuse for war. A generation after the Korean War, Phil Ochs was singing about the United States being the "cops of the world."

By 1961, the cops of the world were in Vietnam, but President Kennedy's representatives there thought a lot more cops were needed and knew the public and the president would be resistant to sending them. For one thing, you couldn't keep up your image as the cops of the world if you sent in a big force to prop up an unpopular regime. What to do? What to do? Ralph Stavins, co-author of an extensive account of Vietnam War planning, recounts that Gens. Maxwell Taylor and Walt W. Rostow, "wondered how the United States could go to war while appearing to preserve the peace. While they were pondering this question, Vietnam was suddenly struck by a deluge. It was as if God had wrought a miracle. American soldiers, acting on humanitarian impulses, could be dispatched to save Vietnam not from the Viet Cong, but from the floods."[14]

For the same reason that Smedley Butler suggested restricting U.S. military ships to within 200 miles of the United States, one might suggest restricting the U.S. military to fighting wars. Troops sent for disaster relief have a way of creating new disasters. U.S. aid is often suspect, even if well-intended by U.S. citizens, because it comes in the form of a fighting force ill equipped and ill prepared to provide aid. Whenever there's a hurricane in Haiti, nobody can tell whether the United States has provided aid workers or imposed martial law. In many disasters around the world the cops of the world don't come at all, suggesting that where they do arrive the purpose may not be entirely pure.

In 1995 the cops of the world stumbled into Yugoslavia out of the goodness of their hearts. President Clinton explained: "America's role will not be about fighting a war. It will be about helping the people of Bosnia to secure their own peace agreement.... In fulfilling this mission, we will have the chance to help stop the killing of innocent civilians, especially children...."[15]

Twenty years later, it's hard to see how Bosnians have secured their own peace. U.S. and other foreign troops have never left, and the place is governed by a European-backed Office of High Representative.

Dying for Women's Rights

Women gained rights in Afghanistan in the 1970s, before the United States intentionally provoked the Soviet Union to invade and arm the likes of Osama bin Laden to fight back. There has been little good news for women since. The Revolutionary Association of the Women of Afghanistan (RAWA) was established in 1977 as an independent political/social organization of Afghan women in support of human rights and social justice. In 2010, RAWA released a statement commenting on the American pretense of occupying Afghanistan for the sake of its women, pointing out that the United States and its allies "empowered the most brutal terrorists of the Northern Alliance and the former Russian puppets...and imposed a puppet government. [I]nstead of uprooting its Taliban and Al-Qaeda creations, the United States and NATO continue to kill our innocent and poor civilians, mostly women and children, in their vicious air raids."[16]

In the view of many women leaders in Afghanistan, the invasion and occupation have done no good for women's rights, and have achieved that result at the cost of bombing, shooting, and traumatizing thousands of women. That's not an unfortunate and unexpected side effect. That is the essence of war, and it was perfectly predictable. The Taliban's tiny force succeeds in Afghanistan because people support it. This results in the United States indirectly supporting it as well.

At the time of this writing, for many months and likely for years, at least the second largest and probably the largest source of revenue for the Taliban has been U.S. taxpayers. We lock people away for giving a pair of socks to the enemy,[17] while our own government serves as chief financial sponsor. *WARLORD, INC.: Extortion and Corruption Along the U.S. Supply Chain in Afghanistan*, is a 2010 report from the Majority Staff of the Subcommittee on National Security and Foreign Affairs in the U.S. House of Representatives. The report documents payoffs to the Taliban for safe passage of U.S. goods, payoffs very likely greater than the Taliban's profits from opium, its other big money maker. This has long been known by top U.S. officials, who also know that Afghans, including those fighting for the Taliban, often sign up to receive training and pay from the U.S. military and then depart, and in some cases sign up again and again.[18]

This must be unknown to Americans supporting the war. You can't support a war in which you're funding both sides, including the side against which you are supposedly defending Afghanistan's women.

Is Ceasing a Crime Reckless?

Senator Barack Obama campaigned for the presidency in 2007 and 2008 on a platform that called for escalating the war in Afghanistan. He did just that shortly after taking office, even before devising any plan for what to do in Afghanistan. Just sending more troops was an end in itself. But candidate Obama focused on opposing the other war—the war on Iraq—and promising to end it. He won the Democratic primary largely because he was lucky enough not to have been in Congress in time to vote for the initial authorization of the Iraq war. That he voted over and over again to fund it was never mentioned in the media, as senators are simply expected to fund wars whether they approve of them or not.

Obama did not promise a speedy withdrawal of all troops from Iraq. In fact, there was a period in which he never let a campaign stop go by without declaring, "We have to be as careful getting out as we were careless getting in."[19] He must have mumbled this phrase even in his sleep. During the same election a group of Democratic candidates for Congress published what they titled "A Responsible Plan to End the War in Iraq." The need to be responsible and careful was premised on the idea that ending a war quickly would be irresponsible and careless. This notion had served to keep the Afghanistan and Iraq wars going for years already and would help keep them going for years to come.

But ending wars and occupations is necessary and just, not reckless and cruel. And it need not amount to "abandonment" of the world. Our elected officials find it hard to believe, but there are ways other than war of relating to people and governments. When a petty crime is underway, our top priority is to stop it, after which we look into ways of setting things right, including deterring future crimes of the same sort and repairing the damage. When the largest crime we know of is underway, we do not need to be as slow about ending it as possible. We need to end it immediately. That is the kindest thing we can do for the people of the country we are at war with. We owe them that favor above all others. We know their nation may have problems when U.S. soldiers leave, and that the U.S. government is to blame for some of those problems. But we also know that they will have no hope of good lives as long as the occupation continues. RAWA's position on the occupation of Afghanistan is that the post-occupation period will be worse the longer the occupation continues. So, the first priority is to immediately end the war.

War kills people, and there is nothing worse. As we will see in Chapter 8, war primarily kills civilians, although the value of the military-civilian distinction seems limited. If another nation occupied the United States, surely we would not approve of killing those Americans who fought back and thereby lost their status as civilians. War kills children, above all, and horrifically traumatizes many of the children it does not kill or maim. This is not exactly news, yet it must be constantly relearned as a corrective to frequent claims that wars have been sanitized and bombs made "smart" enough to kill only the people who really need killing.

In 1890, a U.S. veteran told his children about a war he'd been part of in 1838, a war against Cherokee Indians:

> In another home was a frail Mother, apparently a widow and three small children, one just a baby. When told that she must go, the Mother gathered the children at her feet, prayed a humble prayer in her native tongue, patted the old family dog on the head, told the faithful creature goodbye, with a baby strapped on her back and leading a child with each hand started on her exile. But the task was too great for that frail Mother. A stroke of heart failure relieved her suffering. She sunk and died with her baby on her back, and her other two children clinging to her hands.
>
> Chief Junaluska who had saved President [Andrew] Jackson's life at the battle of Horse Shoe witnessed this scene, the tears gushing down his cheeks and lifting his cap he turned his face toward the heavens and said, 'Oh my God, if I had known at the battle of the Horse Shoe what I know now, American history would have been differently written.[20]

In a video produced in 2010 by Rethink Afghanistan, Zaitullah Ghiasi Wardak describes a night raid in Afghanistan. Here's the English translation:

> I am the son of Abdul Ghani Khan. I am from the Wardak Province, Chak District, Khan Khail Village. At approximately 3:00 a.m. the Americans besieged our home, climbed on top of the roof by ladders.... They took the three youngsters outside, tied their hands, put black bags over their heads. They treated them cruelly and kicked them, told them to sit there and not move.
>
> At this time, one group knocked on the guest room. My nephew said: "When I heard the knock I begged the Americans: 'My grandfather is old and hard of hearing. I will go with you and get him out for you.'" He was kicked and told not to move. Then they broke the door of the guest room. My father was asleep but he was shot 25 times in his bed.... Now I don't know, what was my father's crime? And what was the danger from him? He was 92 years old.[21]

War would be the greatest evil on earth even if it cost no money, used up no resources, left no environmental damage, expanded rather than curtailed the rights of citizens back home, and even if it accomplished something worthwhile. Of course, none of those conditions are possible.

The problem with wars is not that soldiers aren't brave or well intentioned, or that their parents didn't raise them well. Ambrose Bierce, who survived the U.S. Civil War to write about it decades later with a brutal honesty and lack of romanticism that was new to war stories, defined "Generous" in his *Devil's Dictionary* as follows: "Originally this word meant noble by birth and was rightly applied to a great multitude of persons. It now means noble by nature and is taking a bit of a rest."[22]

Cynicism is funny, but not accurate. Generosity is very real, which is of course why war propagandists falsely appeal to it on behalf of their wars. Many young Americans actually signed up to risk their lives in the "global war on terrorism" believing they would be defending their nation from a hideous fate. That takes determination, bravery, and generosity. Those badly deceived young people, as well as those less befuddled who nonetheless enlisted for the latest wars, were not sent off as traditional cannon fodder to fight an army in a field. They were sent to occupy countries in which their supposed enemies looked just like everyone else. They were sent into the land of SNAFU, from which many never return in one piece.

SNAFU is, of course, the army acronym for the state of war: Situation Normal: All Fucked Up.

WARS ARE
NOT UNAVOIDABLE

Wars are given so many glorious and righteous justifications, including the spreading of civilization and democracy around the world, that you wouldn't think it would be necessary to also claim that each war was unavoidable. Who would demand that such good deeds be avoided? And yet there has probably never been a war that hasn't been explained as an absolutely necessary, inevitable, and unavoidable last resort. That this argument always has to be used is a measure of how horrible wars actually are. Like so much else related to war, its unavoidability is a lie, each and every time. War is never the only choice and is always the worst one.

But It's in Our Genes

If war is avoidable, then we can and must eliminate war. And if we can eliminate war, why have no societies done so? The short answer is that they have. But let's be clear. Even if every human and pre-human society had always had war that would be no reason why we have to have it too. Your ancestors may have always eaten meat, but if vegetarianism becomes necessary for survival on this little planet won't you choose to survive rather than insist that you must do what your ancestors did? Of course you *can* do what your ancestors did, and in many cases it may be the best thing to do, but you do not *have* to. Did they all have religion? Some people no longer do. Was animal sacrifice once central to religion? It isn't anymore.

War, too, has changed dramatically just in the past decades and centuries. Would a medieval knight fighting on horseback recognize any kinship with a drone pilot using a joystick at a desk in Nevada to kill a suspected bad guy and nine innocent people in Pakistan? Would the knight think that the drone piloting, even once it was explained to him, was an act of war? Would the drone pilot think the knight's activities were acts of war? If war can change into something unrecognizable, why can't it change into nothingness? As far as we know, wars involved only men for millennia. Now women take part. If women can start participating in war, why can't men stop doing so? Of course, they can. But for the weak-willed and those who have replaced religion with bad science, it is essential before people can do something to prove that they have *already* done it.

OK, if you insist. Anthropologists have, in fact, found dozens of human societies in all corners of the world that have not known, or have abandoned, warfare. In his excellent book *Beyond War: The Human Potential for Peace*, Douglas Fry lists 70 non-warring societies from every part of the globe. Studies have found the majority of human societies to have no warfare or a very mild form of it. (Of course all warfare prior to the past century could be re-classified as relatively very mild.) Australia did not know warfare until the Europeans came. Neither did most of the peoples of the Arctic, the Great Basin, or Northeast Mexico.

Many non-warring societies are simple, nomadic, egalitarian, hunter-gatherer cultures. Some are isolated from potential enemies, which is not surprising given the likelihood that one group will take up war in defense against another that threatens it. Some are less isolated but run from other groups that make war rather than engage them. These societies are not always in places that lack major predatory animals. They are groups of people who may have to defend against animal attack and who often hunt for food. They may also witness individual acts of violence, feuding, or executions, while nonetheless avoiding war. Some cultures discourage heated emotions and aggression of any sort. They often hold all sorts of false beliefs that discourage violence, such as that spanking a child will kill it. Yet these beliefs seem to produce no worse lives than, for example, the false belief that spanking benefits children.

Anthropologists have tended to imagine warfare as something that existed in some form for all the millions of years of human evolution. But "imagine" is the key word. Wounded Australopithecine bones thought to show war injuries actually show the tooth marks of leopards. The Walls of Jericho were apparently built to protect against flooding, not warfare. There is, in fact, no evidence of warfare older than 10,000 years, and there would be, because war leaves its mark in wounds and weapons. This suggests that of the 50,000 years modern Homo sapiens have existed, 40,000 saw no warfare, and that millions of years of prior ancestry were also war-free. Or, as an anthropologist put it, "People have lived in hunter-gatherer bands for 99.87 percent of human existence."[1] War arises in some, but not all, complex, sedentary societies, and tends to grow along with their complexity. This fact makes it unlikely war could be found more than 12,500 years ago.

One could argue that individual killings out of jealous rage were the equivalent of war for small groups. But they are very different from organized warfare in which violence is directed anonymously against members of another group. In the world of small non-agricultural bands, family ties on one's mother or father or spouse's side connected one to other bands. In the newer world of patrilineal clans, on the other hand, one finds the precursor to nationalism: attacks on any member of another clan that has injured any member of your own.[2]

A more appropriate candidate for precursor to war than individual human violence may be group violence directed against large animals. But that, too, is very different from war as we know it. Even in our war-crazed culture, most people are very resistant to killing humans but not to killing other animals. Group hunting of ferocious animals doesn't go very far back in human history either. As Barbara Ehrenreich argues, the bulk of the time our ancestors spent evolving they spent evolving not as predators, but as prey.[3]

So, no matter how violent chimpanzees can be, or how peaceful bonobos, imagining ancient common ancestors of primates who thirsted for war is nothing more than imagining. A search for alternatives to that story can be more concrete, given the existence today and in recorded history of hunter-gatherer societies. Some of these cultures have found a wide variety of means of avoiding and resolving disputes that do not include war. That people everywhere are skilled at cooperation and find cooperation more pleasurable than war doesn't make the news precisely because we all know it already. And yet we hear a lot about "man the warrior" and rarely see cooperation identified as a central or essential trait of our species.

Warfare as we have known it in recent millennia has developed alongside other societal changes. But did most relatively recent people in complex and stable societies engage in something resembling warfare or not? Some ancient societies have not been shown to have engaged in warfare, so it is likely they lived without it. And, of course, most of us, even in the most militaristic states, live without any direct connection to war, which would seem to suggest that a whole society could do the same. The emotional drives supporting war, the collective thrill of victory and so forth, may be culturally learned, not inevitable, since some cultures appear too distant in outlook to appreciate them at all. Kirk Endicott recounts, "I once asked a Batek man why their ancestors had not shot the Malay slave-raiders...with poisoned blowpipe darts [used for hunting animals]. His shocked answer was: 'Because it would kill them!'"[4]

Everybody Does It

Anthropologists often focus on non-industrialized cultures, but can techno-logically advanced nations also live without war? Let's assume that Switzerland is a fluke of geopolitical strategy. There are many other nations to consider. In fact, most nations of the world, for one reason or another, including those that fight horrible lengthy wars when attacked, do not initiate warfare. Iran, that terrible demonic threat in U.S. "news" media, has not attacked another country in centuries. The last time Sweden launched or even participated in a war was a skirmish with Norway in 1814. To his credit, Douglas Fry notes the peaceful nature of some modern nations, including Iceland, which has been at peace for 700 years and Costa Rica, which abolished its military after World War II.[5]

The Global Peace Index annually ranks the world's most peaceful na-tions, including domestic factors in the calculation as well as foreign war making.[6] Here are the top 20 nations as of 2010:

1.	New Zealand	11.	Slovenia
2.	Iceland	12.	Czech Republic
3.	Japan	13.	Portugal
4.	Austria	14.	Canada
5.	Norway	15.	Qatar
6.	Ireland	16.	Germany
7.	Denmark	17.	Belgium
8.	Luxembourg	18.	Switzerland
9.	Finland	19.	Australia
10.	Sweden	20.	Hungary

One explanation for some nations' failure to make war is that they would like to but haven't had an opportunity to launch any wars they could plausibly win. This at least suggests a degree of rationality in war-making decisions. If all nations knew they couldn't win any wars, would there be no more wars?

Another explanation is that countries don't launch wars because they don't have to, since the cops of the world are looking out for them and main-taining a Pax Americana. Costa Rica, for example, has accepted a U.S. military presence. This would be an even more encouraging explanation, suggesting that nations do not want to begin wars if they don't have to.

In fact, nobody can even imagine a war breaking out between nations in the European Union (the birthplace of the worst wars in world history) or between states in the United States. The change in Europe is incredible. After centuries of fighting, it has found peace. And peace within the United States is so secure it seems ludicrous even to notice it. But it should be appreciated and understood. Does Ohio refrain from attacking Indiana because the feds would punish Ohio, or because Ohio is certain that Indiana will never attack *it*, or because Ohioans' overpowering war-lust is satisfied by wars with places like Iraq and Afghanistan, or because Buckeyes actually have better things to do than engage in mass murder? The best answer, I think, is the last one, but the power of the federal government is a necessity and something we may have to create at an international level before we have secure and unquestionable international peace.

A crucial test, it seems to me, is whether nations leap at the chance to join war-bound "coalitions" dominated by the United States. If countries refrain from war purely because they can't win any, shouldn't they leap at the chance to participate as junior partners in wars against weak impoverished nations with valuable resources to plunder? Yet they do not.

In the case of the 2003 attack on Iraq, the Bush-Cheney gang bribed and threatened until 49 countries had supposedly agreed to put their names down as the "coalition of the willing." Many other countries, large and small, refused. Of the 49 on the list, one denied any knowledge of being on it, one had its name removed, and another refused to assist with the war in any way. Only four countries participated in the invasion, 33 in the occupation. Six of the countries in this military coalition actually had no militaries whatsoever. Many of the countries apparently joined in exchange for large amounts of foreign aid, which tells us something else about U.S. generosity when it comes to charity abroad. The 33 token participants in the occupation quickly began pulling out as carelessly as they had been careful getting in, to the point where by 2009 only the United States remained.

We also appear perfectly capable of limiting war, raising the question of why we can't limit it a bit more and a bit more until it is gone. The ancient Greeks chose not to take up the bow and arrow for 400 years after the Persians had shown them—in fact, made them feel—what that weapon could do. When the Portuguese brought firearms to Japan in the 1500s, the Japanese banned them, just as elite warriors did in Egypt and Italy as well. The Chinese, who had invented so-called gunpowder in the first place, had chosen not to use it for war. King Wu of Chou, the first ruler of the Zhou Dynasty, after winning a war, set free the horses, dispersed the oxen, and had the chariots and coats of mail smeared with the blood of cattle yet retained them in the arsenal to show that they would not be used again. The shields and swords were turned upside down and wrapped in tiger skins. The King disbanded the army, turned his generals into princes, and commanded them to seal up their bows and arrows in their quivers.

After poisonous gases became weapons during World War I, the world mostly banned them. Nuclear bombs were shown to be wonderful tools from the perspective of war making 65 years ago, but they have not been used since, except in depleted uranium. Most of the world's nations have banned land mines and cluster bombs, even though the United States has refused to join them.

Do deep drives urge us toward war? In some human cultures they certainly do, but there's no reason those cultures cannot be changed. The changes just might need to be deeper and broader than an amendment to the Constitution.

If It Looks Avoidable and Sounds Avoidable...

Another reason to doubt that any particular war is unavoidable is the history of accidents, stupid mistakes, petty rivalries, scheming bureaucrats, and tragic-comic errors through which our governments blunder into each war, while on other occasions stumbling right up to the edge without going over. It's hard to discern rational competition among imperial nations—or, for that matter, ineluctable forces of overpopulation and innate aggression—when looking at how wars actually come to be. As we'll see in Chapter 6, war makers deal in financial interests, industry pressures, electoral calculations, and pure ignorance, all factors that appear susceptible to change or elimination.

War may dominate human history, and certainly our history books pretend there's been nothing but war, but warfare has not been constant. It's ebbed and flowed. Germany and Japan, such eager war makers 75 years ago, are now far more interested in peace than is the United States. The Viking nations of Scandinavia don't seem interested in waging war on anyone. Groups like the Amish within the United States avoid participation in war, and their members have done so at great cost when forced to resist drafts into non-combat service, as during World War II. Seventh Day Adventists have refused to participate in war, and have been used in tests of nuclear radiation instead. If we can avoid wars sometimes, and if some of us can avoid wars all the time, why can't we collectively do better?

Peaceful societies use wise forms of conflict resolution that repair, restore, and respect, rather than just punishing. Diplomacy, aid, and friendship are proven alternatives to war in the modern world. In December 1916 and January 1917, President Woodrow Wilson did something very appropriate. He asked the Germans and the Allies to clear the air by stating their aims and interests. He proposed to serve as a mediator, a proposal the British and the Austro-Hungarians accepted. The Germans did not accept Wilson as an honest mediator, for the understandable reason that he had been assisting the British war effort. Imagine for a minute, however, if things had gone only a little differently, if diplomacy had been used successfully a few years earlier, and war had been avoided, sparing some 16 million lives. Our genetic makeup wouldn't have been altered. We'd still have been the same creatures we are, capable of war or peace, whichever we choose.

War may not have been the first and only option President Wilson considered in 1916, but that doesn't mean he saved it for last. In many cases governments claim that war will only be a last resort, even while secretly planning to launch a war. President George W. Bush planned to attack Iraq for many months while pretending that war would only be a last resort and was something he was working hard to avoid. Bush kept up that pretense at a press conference on January 31, 2003, the same day on which he had just proposed to Prime Minister Tony Blair that one way they could gin up an excuse for war might be to paint planes with UN colors and try to get them shot at. For years, as the war on Iraq went on, pundits urged the necessity of swiftly launching a war against Iran as well. For several years, such a war was not launched, and yet no dire consequences seemed to follow from that restraint.

An earlier instance of restraint toward Iraq had also avoided, rather than created, disaster. In November 1998, President Clinton scheduled air attacks against Iraq, but then Saddam Hussein promised complete cooperation with UN weapons inspectors. Clinton called off the assault. Media pundits, as Norman Solomon recounts, were quite disappointed, denouncing Clinton's refusal to go to war simply because the justification for the war had been taken away—a mistake Clinton's successor would not make. If Clinton *had* gone to war his actions would not have been unavoidable; they would have been criminal.[7]

The Good War

Any argument against any war for the past few decades has been met with the following rebuttal: If you oppose this war, you must oppose all wars; if you oppose all wars you must oppose World War II; World War II was a good war; therefore you are wrong; and if you are wrong this current war must be right. (The phrase "the good war" really caught on as a description of World War II during the war on Vietnam, not during World War II itself.) This argument is made not only in the United States but also in Britain and Russia. The glaring fallaciousness of this rebuttal is no deterrent to its use. Demonstrating that World War II was not a good war might be. The essence of World War II's goodness has always included its necessity. World War II, we've all been told, simply could not have been avoided.

But World War II was not a good war, not even from the perspective of the Allies or that of the United States. As we saw in Chapter 1, it was not fought to save the Jews, and it did not save them. Refugees were turned away and abandoned. Plans to ship Jews out of Germany were frustrated by Britain's blockade. As we saw in Chapter 2, this war was not fought in self-defense. It was also not fought with any restraint or concern for civilian life. It was not fought against racism by a nation imprisoning Japanese Americans and segregating African-American soldiers. It was not fought against imperialism by the world's leading and most up-and-coming imperialists. Britain fought because Germany invaded Poland. The United States fought in Europe because Britain was at war with Germany, although the United States did not fully enter the war until its fleet was attacked by the Japanese in the Pacific. That Japanese attack was, as we have seen, perfectly avoidable and aggressively provoked. The war with Germany that arrived immediately after meant a full commitment to a war in which the United States had long been assisting England and China.

The more months and years and decades we imagine going back in time to fix the problem, the simpler and easier we can imagine it would have been to prevent Germany from attacking Poland. Even most supporters of World War II as a "good war" agree that the Allies' actions following World War I helped bring on the second war. On September 22, 1933, David Lloyd George, who had been the prime minister of England during World War I, gave a speech counseling against the overthrow of Nazism in Germany, because the result might be something worse: "extreme communism."

In 1939, when Italy tried to open negotiations with Britain on behalf of Germany, Churchill shut them down cold: "If Ciano realises [sic] our inflexible purpose he will be less likely to toy with the idea of an Italian mediation."[8] Churchill's inflexible purpose was to go to war. When Hitler, having invaded Poland, proposed peace with Britain and France and asked for their help in expelling Germany's Jews, Prime Minister Neville Chamberlain insisted on war.

Of course, Hitler was not particularly trustworthy. But what if the Jews had been spared, Poland had been occupied, and peace had been maintained between the Allies and Germany for some minutes, hours, days, weeks, months, or years? The war could have begun whenever it began, with no harm done and some moments of peace gained. And every moment of peace gained could have been used to attempt to negotiate a more permanent peace, as well as independence for Poland. In May 1940, Chamberlain and Lord Halifax both favored peace negotiations with Germany, but Prime Minister Churchill refused. In July 1940, Hitler gave another speech proposing peace with England. Churchill was not interested.

Even if we pretend that the Nazi invasion of Poland was truly unavoidable and assume that a Nazi attack on England was irrevocably planned, why was immediate war the answer? And once other nations had begun it, why did the United States have to join in? Napoleon had invaded lots of European countries without the U.S. president's launching a massive PR campaign to demand that we join the fight and make the world safe for democracy, as Wilson did for World War I, and as Roosevelt reprised for World War II.

World War II killed 70 million people, and that sort of outcome could be more or less foreseen. What did we imagine was worse than that? What could we have been preventing? The United States took no interest in the holocaust and did not prevent it. And the holocaust, of Jews and non-Jews, only killed a total of some 11 million people. There were resisters in Germany. Hitler, if he stayed in power, wasn't going to live forever or necessarily commit suicide by imperial war if he saw other options. Aiding the people in the territories Germany had occupied would have been easy enough. The U.S. policy was instead to blockade and starve them, which took great effort and had hideous results.

The possibility of Hitler or his heirs consolidating power, holding onto it, and attacking the United States seems extremely remote. The United States had to go to enormous lengths to provoke Japan into attacking it. Hitler was going to be lucky to hold onto his sanity, much less a global empire. But suppose that Germany eventually had brought the war to our shores. Is it conceivable that any American would not have then fought 20 times harder and won a truly defensive war more quickly? Or perhaps the Cold War would have been waged in opposition to Germany rather than the Soviet Union. The Soviet empire ended without war; why could a German empire not have done the same? Who knows? What we do know is the unmatchable horror of what did happen.

The United States and its allies engaged in the indiscriminate mass-slaughter of German, French, and Japanese civilians from the air, developed the deadliest weapons anyone had ever seen, destroyed the concept of limited warfare, and transformed war into an adventure that victimizes civilians more than soldiers. In the United States people invented the idea of permanent war, gave near-total war-making powers to presidents, created secret agencies with the power to engage in warfare with no oversight, and built a war economy that would require wars from which to profit.

World War II and the new practice of total war brought torture back from the Middle Ages; developed chemical, biological, and nuclear weapons for current and future use, including napalm and Agent Orange; and launched programs of human experimentation in the United States. Winston Churchill, who drove the agenda of the Allies as much as anyone else, had earlier written, "I am strongly in favor of using poisoned gas against uncivilized tribes."[9] Wherever you peer too closely at the goals and conduct of the "good war" that's what you tend to see: Churchillian eagerness to exterminate enemies en masse.

If World War II was a good war, I'd really hate to see a bad one. If World War II was a good war, why did President Franklin Roosevelt have to lie us into it? On September 4, 1941, Roosevelt gave a "fireside chat" radio address in which he claimed that a German submarine, completely unprovoked, had attacked the U.S. destroyer *Greer*, which—despite being called a destroyer—had been harmlessly delivering mail.

Really? The Senate Naval Affairs Committee questioned Admiral Harold Stark, Chief of Naval Operations, who said the *Greer* had been tracking the German submarine and relaying its location to a British airplane, which had dropped depth charges on the submarine's location without success. The *Greer* had continued tracking the submarine for hours before the submarine turned and fired torpedoes.

A month and a half later, Roosevelt told a similar tall tale about the *USS Kearny*. And then he really piled on. Roosevelt claimed to have in his possession a secret map produced by Hitler's government that showed plans for a Nazi conquest of South America. The Nazi government denounced this as a lie, blaming of course a Jewish conspiracy. The map, which Roosevelt refused to show the public, in fact actually showed routes in South America flown by American airplanes, with notations in German describing the distribution of aviation fuel. It was a British forgery, and apparently of about the same quality as the forgeries President George W. Bush would later use to show that Iraq had been trying to purchase uranium.[10]

Roosevelt also claimed to have come into possession of a secret plan produced by the Nazis for the replacement of all religions with Nazism: "The clergy are to be forever silenced under penalty of the concentration camps, where even now so many fearless men are being tortured because they have placed God above Hitler."[11]

Such a plan sounded like something Hitler would indeed draw up had Hitler not himself been an adherent of Christianity, but Roosevelt of course had no such document.

Why were these lies necessary? Are good wars only recognizable after the fact? Do good people at the time have to be deceived into them? And if Roosevelt knew what was happening in the concentration camps, why wouldn't the truth have been sufficient?

If World War II was a good war, why did the United States have to wait until its imperial outpost in the middle of the Pacific was attacked? If the war was aimed at opposing atrocities, there had been many reported, going back to the bombing of Guernica. Innocent people were under attack in Europe. If the war had something to do with that, why did the United States' open participation have to wait until Japan attacked and Germany declared war?

If World War II was a good war, why did Americans have to be drafted to fight in it? The draft came before Pearl Harbor, and many soldiers deserted, especially when their length of "service" was extended beyond 12 months. Thousands volunteered after Pearl Harbor, but the draft was still the primary means of producing cannon fodder. During the course of the war, 21,049 soldiers were sentenced for desertion and 49 were given death sentences. Another 12,000 were classified as conscientious objectors.[12]

If World War II was a good war, why did 80 percent of the Americans who finally made it into combat choose not to fire their weapons at the enemies? General S. L. A. Marshall's research has been widely cited and debated, and repeatedly confirmed in its rough conclusions by numerous studies of other wars. Marshall, himself very much a supporter of militarism, interviewed U.S. soldiers in World War II and was surprised to discover that only 15 to 20 percent of them, when deployed along a line of fire, actually fired their weapons at the enemy. Prior to this groundbreaking research it had been widely assumed that most soldiers performed this basic function as commanded.

There is good evidence that the behavior Marshall first identified was the norm in the ranks of the Germans, British, French, and so forth, and had been the norm in previous wars as well. The problem—for those who see this encouraging and life-saving characteristic as a problem—was that about 98 percent of people are very resistant to killing other human beings. You can show them how to use a gun and tell them to go shoot it, but in the moment of combat many of them will aim for the sky, drop in the dirt, assist a buddy with his weapon, or suddenly discover that an important message needs to be conveyed along the line. They're not scared of being shot. At least that's not the most powerful force at play. They're horrified of committing murder.

Coming out of World War II with the U.S. military's new understanding of what happens in the heat of battle, training techniques changed. Soldiers would no longer be taught to fire. They would be conditioned to kill without thinking. Bull's-eye targets would be replaced with targets resembling human beings. Soldiers would be drilled to the point where, under pressure, they would instinctively react by committing murder. Here's a chant used in basic training at the time of the war on Iraq that may have helped get U.S. soldiers into the proper frame of mind to kill:

> We went to the market where all the hadji shop,
> pulled out our machetes and we began to chop,
> We went to the playground where all the hadji play,
> pulled out our machine guns and we began to spray,
> We went to the mosque where all the hadji pray,
> threw in a hand grenade and blew them all away.[13]

These new techniques have been so successful that in the Vietnam War and other wars since, nearly all U.S. soldiers have shot to kill, and huge numbers of them have suffered the psychological damage that comes from having done so.

The training that our children are receiving as they zap the enemy dead time after time in video games may be better war training than what Uncle Sam provided the "greatest generation." Children playing video games that simulate murder may, in fact, be being trained to become our future homeless veterans reliving their glory days on park benches.

Which brings me back to this question: If World War II was a good war, why did soldiers who hadn't been preconditioned as sociopathic lab rats not participate? Why did they just take up space, wear the uniforms, eat the grub, miss their families, and lose their limbs, but not actually do what they were there to do, not actually contribute to the cause even as much as the people who stayed home and grew tomatoes? Could it be that, for healthy well-adjusted people, even good wars are just not good?

If World War II was a good war, why do we hide it? Shouldn't we want to look at it, if it was good? Admiral Gene Larocque recalled in 1985:

> World War II has warped our view of how we look at things today. We see things in terms of that war, which in a sense was a good war. But the twisted memory of it encourages the men of my generation to be willing, almost eager, to use military force anywhere in the world.
>
> For about 20 years after the war, I couldn't look at any film on World War II. It brought back memories that I didn't want to keep around. I hated to see how they glorified war. In all those films, people get blown up with their clothes and fall gracefully to the ground. You don't see anybody being blown apart.[14]

Betty Basye Hutchinson, who cared for World War II veterans in Pasadena, California, as a nurse, remembers 1946:

> All my friends were still there, undergoing surgery. Especially Bill. I would walk him in downtown Pasadena—I'll never forget this. Half his face completely gone, right? Downtown Pasadena after the war was a very elite community. Nicely dressed women, absolutely staring, just standing there staring. He was aware of this terrible stare. People just looking right at you and wondering: What is this? I was going to cuss her out, but I moved him away. It's like the war hadn't come to Pasadena until we came there. Oh it had a big impact on the community. In the Pasadena paper came some letters to the editor: Why can't they be kept on their own grounds and off the streets.[15]

Native Nazism

A few other things Americans are loathe to recall are the inspiration our own country offered to Hitler, the financial support our corporations offered him, and the fascist coup plotted by our own respected business leaders. If World War II was an unavoidable clash between good and evil, what are we to think of American contributions to and sympathies with the evil side?

Adolf Hitler grew up playing "cowboys and Indians." He grew up to praise the U.S. slaughter of native peoples, and the forced marches to reservations. Hitler's concentration camps were at first thought of in terms of American Indian reservations, although other models for them may have included the British camps in South Africa during the 1899-1902 Boer War, or the camps used by Spain and the United States in the Philippines.

The pseudo-scientific language in which Hitler couched his racism, and the eugenic schemes for purifying a Nordic race, right down to the method of ushering undesirables into gas chambers, were also U.S.-inspired. Edwin Black wrote in 2003:

> Eugenics was the racist pseudoscience determined to wipe away all human beings deemed "unfit," preserving only those who conformed to a Nordic stereotype. Elements of the philosophy were enshrined as national policy by forced sterilization and segregation laws, as well as marriage restrictions, enacted in twenty-seven states.... Ultimately, eugenics practitioners coercively sterilized some 60,000 Americans, barred the marriage of thousands, forcibly segregated thousands in "colonies," and persecuted untold numbers in ways we are just learning....
>
> Eugenics would have been so much bizarre parlor talk had it not been for extensive financing by corporate philanthropies, specifically the Carnegie Institution, the Rockefeller Foundation and the Harriman railroad fortune.... The Harriman railroad fortune paid local charities, such as the New York Bureau of Industries and Immigration, to seek out Jewish, Italian and other immigrants in New York and other crowded cities and subject them to deportation, trumped up confinement, or forced sterilization. The Rockefeller Foundation helped found the German eugenics program and even funded the program that Josef Mengele worked in before he went to Auschwitz....
>
> The most commonly suggested method of eugenicide in America was a "lethal chamber" or public locally operated gas chambers.... Eugenic breeders believed American society was not ready to implement an organized lethal solution. But many mental institutions and doctors practiced improvised medical lethality and passive euthanasia on their own. [16]

The U.S. Supreme Court endorsed eugenics in a 1927 ruling in which Justice Oliver Wendell Holmes wrote, "It is better for all the world, if instead of waiting to execute degenerate offspring for crime, or to let them starve for their imbecility, society can prevent those who are manifestly unfit from continuing their kind.... Three generations of imbeciles are enough."[17] Nazis would quote Holmes in their own defense at the war crimes trials. Hitler, two decades earlier, in his book *Mein Kampf* praised American eugenics. Hitler even wrote a fan letter telling American eugenicist Madison Grant that he considered his book "the bible." Rockefeller gave $410,000, almost $4 million in today's money, to German eugenics "researchers."

Britain may want to claim some credit here, as well. In 1910, Home Secretary Winston Churchill proposed sterilizing 100,000 "mental degenerates" and confining tens of thousands more in state-run labor camps. This plan, not executed, would have supposedly saved the British from racial decline.[18]

Following World War I, Hitler and his cronies, including propaganda minister Joseph Goebbels, admired and studied George Creel's Committee on Public Information (CPI), as well as British war propaganda. They learned from the CPI's use of posters, film, and news media. One of Goebbels's favorite books on propaganda was Edward Bernays's *Crystallizing Public Opinion*, which may have helped inspire the naming of a night of anti-Jewish rioting "Kristallnacht."

Prescott Sheldon Bush's early business efforts, like those of his grandson George W. Bush, tended to fail. He married the daughter of a very rich man named George Herbert Walker who installed Prescott Bush as an executive in Thyssen and Flick. From then on, Prescott's business dealings went better, and he entered politics. The Thyssen in the firm's name was a German named Fritz Thyssen, a major financial backer of Hitler referred to in the *New York Herald-Tribune* as "Hitler's Angel."

Wall Street corporations viewed the Nazis, much as Lloyd George did, as enemies of communism. American investment in Germany increased 48.5 percent between 1929 and 1940 even as it declined sharply everywhere else in continental Europe.[19] Major investors included Ford, General Motors, General Electric, Standard Oil, Texaco, International Harvester, ITT, and IBM. Bonds were sold in New York in the 1930s that financed the Aryanization of German companies and real estate stolen from Jews. Many companies continued doing business with Germany through the war, even if it meant benefitting from concentration-camp labor. IBM even provided the Hollerith Machines used to keep track of Jews and others to be murdered, while ITT created the Nazis' communications system as well as bomb parts and then collected $27 million from the U.S. government for war damage to its German factories.

U.S. pilots were instructed not to bomb factories in Germany that were owned by U.S. companies. When Cologne was leveled, its Ford plant, which provided military equipment for the Nazis, was spared and even used as an air raid shelter. Henry Ford had been funding the Nazis' anti-Semitic propaganda since the 1920s. His German plants fired all employees with Jewish ancestry in 1935, before the Nazis required it. In 1938, Hitler awarded Ford the Grand Cross of the Supreme Order of the German Eagle, an honor only three people had previously received, one of them being Benito Mussolini. Hitler's loyal colleague and leader of the Nazi Party in Vienna, Baldur von Schirach, had an American mother who said her son had discovered anti-Semitism by reading Henry Ford's *The Eternal Jew*.

The companies Prescott Bush profited from included one engaged in mining operations in Poland using slave labor from Auschwitz. Two former slave laborers later sued the U.S. government and Bush's heirs for $40 billion, but the suit was dismissed by a U.S. court on the grounds of state sovereignty.

Until the United States entered World War II it was legal for Americans to do business with Germany, but in late 1942 Prescott Bush's business interests were seized under the Trading with the Enemy Act. Among those businesses involved was the Hamburg America Lines, for which Prescott Bush served as a manager. A congressional committee found that Hamburg America Lines had offered free passage to Germany for journalists willing to write favorably about the Nazis, and had brought Nazi sympathizers to the United States.

The McCormack-Dickstein Committee was established to investigate a homegrown American fascist plot hatched in 1933. The plan was to engage a half million World War I veterans, angry over not being paid their promised bonuses, to oust President Roosevelt and install a government modeled on Hitler and Mussolini's. The plotters included the owners of Heinz, Birds Eye, Goodtea, and Maxwell House. They made the mistake of asking Smedley Butler to lead the coup, something a reader of this book will realize Butler was unlikely to go along with. In fact, Butler ratted them out to Congress. His account was corroborated in part by a number of witnesses, and the committee concluded that the plot was real. But the names of the wealthy backers of the plot were blacked out in the committee's records, and nobody was prosecuted. President Roosevelt had reportedly cut a deal. He would refrain from prosecuting some of the wealthiest men in America for treason. They would agree to end Wall Street's opposition to his New Deal programs.

A very powerful Wall Street firm at the time, heavily invested in Germany, was Sullivan and Cromwell, home to John Foster Dulles and Allen Dulles, two brothers who boycotted their own sister's wedding because she married a Jew. John Foster Dulles would serve as secretary of state for President Eisenhower, intensify the Cold War, and get a Washington airport named after him. Allen, whom we encountered in Chapter 2, would be Swiss director of the Office of Strategic Services during the war and later the first civilian director of Central Intelligence from 1953 to 1961. J.F. Dulles, during the pre-war period, would begin his letters to German clients with the words "Heil Hitler." In 1939, he told the Economic Club of New York, "We have to welcome and nurture the desire of the new Germany to find for her energies a new outlet."[20]

Allen Dulles was an originator of the idea of criminal immunity for multinational corporations, which was necessitated by U.S. corporations' aid to Nazi Germany. In September 1942, A. Dulles called the Nazi holocaust "a wild rumor, inspired by Jewish fears."[21] A. Dulles signed off on a list of German corporate executives to be spared prosecution for their collaboration in war crimes, on the grounds that they would be helpful in rebuilding Germany. Mickey Z. in his excellent book *There Is No Good War: The Myths of World War II* calls this "Dulles' List" and contrasts it with "Schindler's List," a list of Jews one German executive sought to save from genocide, which was the focus of a 1982 book and a 1993 Hollywood movie.

None of these connections between Nazism and the United States make Nazism any less evil, or U.S. opposition to it any less noble. Despite the efforts of some of the wealthiest in the United States, the urgings of radio hosts like Father Coughlin and celebrities like Charles Lindberg, the organizing of groups like the Ku Klux Klan, the National Gentile League, the Christian Mobilizers, the German-American Bund, the Silver Shirts, and the American Liberty League, Nazism never took hold in the United States, whereas the mission of destroying it through warfare did. But for a "good war" to truly have been unavoidable, ought we not to have been completely refraining from assisting the other side?

Well, What Would You Suggest?

The fact is that other actions by the United States and the powerful and wealthy within it, from the end of World War I until the start of World War II could have changed the course of events. Diplomacy, aid, friendship, and honest negotiations could have prevented war. Alertness to the danger of war as a greater threat than a government leaning toward communism would have helped. Of course, greater resistance to Nazism by the German people could also have made the difference, a lesson Germany seems actually to have learned. In 2010 their president was forced out for announcing that war in Afghanistan could be economically profitable for Germany. In the United States, such comments can win you votes.

Could the German people, the German Jews, the Poles, the French, and the Brits have used nonviolent resistance? Gandhi urged them to do so, openly stating that thousands might have to die and that success would come very slowly. At what stage might what degree of such incredibly brave and selfless action have succeeded? Those who engaged in it would never have known, and we will never know. But we know that India won its independence, as Poland would later win its from the Soviet Union, as South Africa would later end apartheid and the United States end Jim Crow, as the Philippines would restore democracy and remove U.S. bases, as El Salvador would remove a dictator, and as people would achieve large and lasting victories the world over without war and without the damaging effects of the sort that World War II left behind, from which we have yet to—and may never—recover.

We also know that the people of Denmark saved most Danish Jews from the Nazis, sabotaged Nazi war efforts, went on strike, publicly protested, and refused to submit to the German occupation. Likewise, many in the occupied Netherlands resisted. We also know that in 1943 a nonviolent protest in Berlin led by non-Jewish women whose Jewish husbands had been imprisoned, successfully demanded their release, forced a reversal in Nazi policy, and saved their husbands' lives. A month later, the Nazis released inter-married Jews in France as well.

What if that protest in the heart of Berlin, which was being joined by Germans of all backgrounds, had grown much larger? What if wealthy Americans during the preceding decades had funded German schools of nonviolent action rather than German schools of eugenics? There is no way of knowing what was possible. One simply had to try. When a German soldier tried to tell the king of Denmark that a swastika would be raised over Amalienborg Castle, the king objected: "If this happens, a Danish soldier will go and take it down." "That Danish soldier will be shot," replied the German. "That Danish soldier will be myself," said the king. The swastika never flew.[22]

If we begin to doubt the goodness and justness of World War II, we open ourselves up to similar doubts about all other wars. Would a Korean War have been needed if we hadn't sliced the country in half? Was the Vietnam War needed to prevent the domino-falling that did not actually happen when the United States was defeated there? And so on.

"Just war" theorists maintain that some wars are morally required—not just defensive wars, but humanitarian wars fought for good motives and with restrained tactics. Thus, a week before the 2003 assault on Baghdad, just war theorist Michael Walzer argued in the *New York Times* for tighter containment of Iraq through what he termed a "little war," which would have included extending the no-flight zones to cover the entire nation, imposing tougher sanctions, sanctioning other nations that did not cooperate, sending in more inspectors, flying unannounced surveillance flights, and pressuring the French to send in troops.[23] Indeed this plan would have been better than what was done. But it writes the Iraqis completely out of the picture, ignores their claims of not possessing weapons, ignores the French claims of not believing Bush's lies about weapons, ignores the history of the United States' sending in spies along with weapons inspectors, and appears oblivious to the likelihood that greater restrictions and suffering, in combination with a greater troop presence, could lead to a larger war. The just course of action cannot, in fact, be found by devising the most restrained form of aggressive warfare. The just course of action is whatever policy is most likely to avoid warfare.

Making war is always a choice, just as maintaining policies that make war more likely is optional and can be changed. We are told that there is no choice, that there is pressure to act immediately. We feel a sudden desire to be involved and to *do something*. Our options seem limited to doing something to support a war or doing nothing at all. There's an intense thrill of excitement, the romance of the crisis, and the opportunity to act collectively in a manner we're told is brave and courageous, even if the riskiest thing we do is hang up a flag at a busy intersection. Some people only understand violence, we're told. Some problems are, regrettably perhaps, past the point where anything other than massive levels of violence can do any good; no other tools exist.

This is just not so, and this belief does immense damage. War is a meme, a contagious idea, that serves its own ends. War excitement keeps war alive. It does no good for human beings.

One might argue that war has been made unavoidable by a war economy that depends on it, a communications system that favors it, and a corrupt system of government of, by, and for the war profiteers. But that is a lesser-grade unavoidability. That requires reforming our government in the manner described in my earlier book *Daybreak*, at which point war loses its status of unavoidability and becomes avoidable.

One might argue that war is unavoidable because it is not subject to rational discussion. War has always been around and always will be. Like your appendix, your earlobes, or nipples on men, it may not serve any purpose, but it is a part of us that can't be wished away. But the age of something doesn't make it permanent; it just makes it old.

"War is inevitable" is not an argument for war so much as a sigh of despair. If you were here and heaved such a sigh, I'd shake you by the shoulders, throw cold water on your face, and shout, "What's the point of living if you aren't going to try to make life better?" Since you're not here, there's little I can say.

Except this: Even if you believe that war, in a general sense, simply must go on, you still have no basis not to join in the opposition to any particular war. Even if you believe some past war was justified, you still have no basis not to oppose the war being planned right here today. And one day, after we oppose every particular potential war, warfare will be over. Whether or not that was possible.

5

WARRIORS
ARE NOT HEROES

Pericles honored those who had died in war on the side of Athens:

> I have dwelt upon the greatness of Athens because I want to show you that we are contending for a higher prize than those who enjoy none of these privileges, and to establish by manifest proof the merit of these men whom I am now commemorating. Their loftiest praise has been already spoken. For in magnifying the city I have magnified them, and men like them whose virtues made her glorious. And of how few Hellenes can it be said as of them, that their deeds when weighed in the balance have been found equal to their fame! I believe that a death such as theirs has been the true measure of a man's worth; it may be the first revelation of his virtues, but is at any rate their final seal. For even those who come short in other ways may justly plead the valor with which they have fought for their country; they have blotted out the evil with the good, and have benefited the state more by their public services than they have injured her by their private actions.
>
> None of these men were enervated by wealth or hesitated to resign the pleasures of life; none of them put off the evil day in the hope, natural to poverty, that a man, though poor, may one day become rich. But, deeming that the punishment of their enemies was sweeter than any of these things, and that they could fall in no nobler cause, they determined at the hazard of their lives to be honorably avenged, and to leave the rest. They resigned to hope their unknown chance of happiness; but in the face of death they resolved to rely upon themselves alone. And when the moment came they were minded to resist and suffer, rather than to fly and save their lives; they ran away from the word of dishonor, but on the battlefield their feet stood fast, and in an instant, at the height

of their fortune, they passed away from the scene, not of their fear, but of their glory.[1]

Abraham Lincoln honored those who had died in war on the side of the North:

> Four score and seven years ago our fathers brought forth on this continent, a new nation, conceived in Liberty, and dedicated to the proposition that all men are created equal. Now we are engaged in a great civil war, testing whether that nation, or any nation so conceived and so dedicated, can long endure. We are met on a great battle-field of that war. We have come to dedicate a portion of that field, as a final resting place for those who here gave their lives that that nation might live. It is altogether fitting and proper that we should do this.
>
> But, in a larger sense, we can not dedicate—we can not consecrate—we can not hallow—this ground. The brave men, living and dead, who struggled here, have consecrated it, far above our poor power to add or detract. The world will little note, nor long remember what we say here, but it can never forget what they did here. It is for us the living, rather, to be dedicated here to the unfinished work which they who fought here have thus far so nobly advanced. It is rather for us to be here dedicated to the great task remaining before us—that from these honored dead we take increased devotion to that cause for which they gave the last full measure of devotion—that we here highly resolve that these dead shall not have died in vain—that this nation, under God, shall have a new birth of freedom—and that government of the people, by the people, for the people, shall not perish from the earth.[2]

Even though presidents don't say these things anymore, and if they can help it don't talk about the dead at all, the same message goes without saying today. Soldiers are praised to the skies, and the part about their risking their lives is understood without being mentioned. Generals are so effusively praised that it's not uncommon for them to get the impression they run the government. Presidents much prefer being commander-in-chief to being chief executive. The former can be treated almost as a deity, while the latter is a well-known liar and cheat.

But the prestige of the generals and the presidents comes from their closeness to the unknown yet glorious troops. When the bigwigs don't want their policies questioned, they need merely suggest that such questioning constitutes criticism of the troops or expression of doubt regarding the invincibility of the troops. In fact, wars themselves do very well to associate themselves with soldiers. The soldiers' glory may all derive from the possibility that they will be killed in a war, but the war itself is only glorious because of the presence of the sainted troops—not actual particular troops, but the abstract heroic givers of the ultimate sacrifice pre-honored by the Tomb of the Unknown Soldier.

As long as the greatest honor one can aspire to is to be shipped off and killed in somebody's war, there will be wars. President John F. Kennedy wrote in a letter to a friend something he would never have put in a speech: "War will exist until the distant day when the conscientious objector enjoys the same reputation and prestige as the warrior does today."[3, 4] I would tweak that statement a little. It should include those refusing to participate in a war whether or not they are granted the status of "conscientious objector." And it should include those resisting the war nonviolently outside of the military as well, including by traveling to the expected sites of bombings in order to serve as "human shields."

When President Barack Obama was given a Nobel Peace Prize and re- marked that other people were more deserving, I immediately thought of sev- eral. Some of the bravest people I know or have heard of have refused to take part in current wars or tried to place their bodies into the gears of the war machine. If they enjoyed the same reputation and prestige as the warriors, we would all hear about them. If they were so honored, some of them would be permitted to speak through our television stations and newspapers, and before long war would, indeed, no longer exist.

What Is a Hero?

Let's look more closely at the myth of military heroism handed down to us by Pericles and Lincoln. Random House defines a hero as follows (and defines heroine the same way, substituting "woman" for "man"):

> 1. a man of distinguished courage or ability, admired for his brave deeds and noble qualities.
>
> 2. a person who, in the opinion of others, has heroic qualities or has per- formed a heroic act and is regarded as a model or ideal: *He was a local hero when he saved the drowning child.*
>
> [...]
>
> 4. Classical Mythology.
>   a. a being of godlike prowess and beneficence who often came to be honored as a divinity.

Courage *or ability*. Brave deeds *and noble qualities*. There is something more here than merely courage and bravery, merely facing up to fear and dan- ger. But what? A hero is *regarded as a model or ideal*. Clearly someone who bravely jumped out a 20-story window would not meet that definition, even if their bravery was as brave as brave could be. Clearly heroism must require bravery of a sort that people regard as a model for themselves and others. It must include prowess *and beneficence*. That is, the bravery can't just be bravery; it must also be good and kind. Jumping out a window does not qualify. The question, then, is whether killing and dying in wars should qualify as good and kind. Nobody doubts that it's courageous and brave.

If you look up "bravery" in the dictionary, by the way, you'll find "courage" and "valor." Ambrose Bierce's *Devil's Dictionary* defines "valor" as:

A soldierly compound of vanity, duty, and the gambler's hope.

"Why have you halted?" roared the commander of a division at Chickamauga, who had ordered a charge: "move forward, sir, at once."

"General," said the commander of the delinquent brigade, "I am persuaded that any further display of valor by my troops will bring them into collision with the enemy."[5]

But would such valor be good and kind or destructive and foolhardy? Bierce had himself been a Union soldier at Chickamauga and had come away disgusted. Many years later, when it had become possible to publish stories about the Civil War that didn't glow with the holy glory of militarism, Bierce published a story called "Chickamauga" in 1889 in the *San Francisco Examiner* that makes participating in such a battle appear the most grotesquely evil and horrifying deed one could ever do. Many soldiers have since told similar tales.

It's curious that war, something consistently recounted as ugly and horrible, should qualify its participants for glory. Of course, the glory doesn't last. Mentally disturbed veterans are kicked aside in our society. In fact, in dozens of cases documented between 2007 and 2010, soldiers who had been deemed physically and psychologically fit were welcomed into the military, performed "honorably," and had no recorded history of psychological problems. Then, upon being wounded, the same formerly healthy soldiers were diagnosed with a pre-existing personality disorder, discharged, and denied treatment for their wounds. One soldier was locked in a closet until he agreed to sign a statement that he had a pre-existing disorder—a procedure the Chairman of the House Veterans Affairs Committee called "torture."[6]

Active duty troops, the real ones, are not treated by the military or society with particular reverence or respect. But the mythical, generic "troop" is a secular saint purely because of his or her willingness to rush off and die in the very same sort of mindless, murderous orgy ants regularly engage in. Yes, ants. Those teeny little pests with brains the size of...well, the size of something smaller than an ant: they wage war. And they're better at it than we are.

Are Ants Heroes Too?

Ants wage long and complex wars with extensive organization and unmatched determination, or what we might call "valor." They are absolutely loyal to the cause in a way that no patriotic humans can match: "It'd be like having an American flag tattooed to you at birth," ecologist and photojournalist Mark Moffett told *Wired* magazine. Ants will kill other ants without flinching. Ants will make the "ultimate sacrifice" with no hesitation. Ants will proceed with their mission rather than stop to help a wounded warrior.

The ants who go to the front, where they kill and die first, are the smallest and weakest ones. They are sacrificed as part of a winning strategy. "In some ant armies, there can be millions of expendable troops sweeping forward in a dense swarm that's up to 100 feet wide." In one of Moffett's photos, which shows "the marauder ant in Malaysia, several of the weak ants are being sliced in half by a larger enemy termite with black, scissor-like jaws." What would Pericles say at their funeral?

"According to Moffett, we might actually learn a thing or two from how ants wage war. For one, ant armies operate with precise organization despite a lack of central command." And no wars would be complete without some lying: "Like humans, ants can try to outwit foes with cheats and lies." In another photo, "two ants face off in an effort to prove their superiority—which, in this ant species, is designated by physical height. But the wily ant on the right is standing on a pebble to gain a solid inch over his nemesis."[7] Would honest Abe approve?

In fact, ants are such dedicated warriors that they can even fight civil wars that make that little skirmish between the North and South look like touch football. A parasitic wasp, *Ichneumon eumerus*, can dose an ant nest with a chemical secretion that causes the ants to fight a civil war, half the nest against the other half.[8] Imagine if we had such a drug for humans, a sort of a prescription-strength Fox News. If we dosed the nation, would all the resulting warriors be heroes or just half of them? Are the ants heroes? And if they are not, is it because of what they are doing or purely because of what they are thinking about what they are doing? And what if the drug makes them think they are risking their lives for the benefit of future life on earth or to keep the anthill safe for democracy?

Bravery Plus

Soldiers are generally lied to, as the whole society is lied to, and—in addition—as only military recruiters can lie to you. Soldiers often believe they are on a noble mission. And they can be very brave. But so can police officers and fire fighters in quite similar ways, for worthwhile ends but much less glory and hoo-ha. What is the good of being courageous for a destructive project? If you mistakenly believe you are doing something valuable, your bravery might—I think—be tragic. And it might be bravery worth emulating in other circumstances. But you yourself would hardly be a model or an ideal. Your actions would not have been good and kind. In fact, in a common but completely nonsensical pattern of speech, you could end up being denounced as a "coward."

When terrorists flew airplanes into buildings on September 11, 2001, they may have been cruel, murderous, sick, despicable, criminal, insane, or blood-thirsty, but what they were usually called on U.S. television was "cowards." It was hard not to be struck, in fact, by their bravery, which is probably why so many commentators instantly reached for the opposite description. "Bravery" is understood to be a good thing, so mass murder can't be bravery, so therefore it was cowardice. I'm guessing this was the thought process. One television host didn't play along.

"We have been the cowards," said Bill Maher, agreeing with a guest who had said the 9/11 murderers were not cowards. "Lobbing cruise missiles from two thousand miles away. That's cowardly. Staying in the airplane when it hits the building. Say what you want about it. Not cowardly. You're right."[9] Maher was not defending the murders. He was merely defending the English language. He lost his job anyway.

The problem that I think Maher identified is that we've glorified bravery for its own sake without stopping to realize that we don't really mean that. The drill sergeant means it. The military wants soldiers as brave as ants, soldiers who will follow orders, even orders likely to get them killed, without stopping to think anything over for themselves, without pausing for even a second to wonder whether the orders are admirable or evil. We'd be lost without bravery. We need it to confront all kinds of unavoidable dangers, but mindless bravery is useless or worse, and certainly not heroic. What we need is something more like honor. Our model and ideal person should be someone who is willing to take risks when required for what he or she has carefully determined to be a good means to a good end. Our goal should not be embarrassing the rest of the world's primates, even violent chimpanzees, through our mindless imitation of little bugs. "The 'heroes,'" wrote Norman Thomas, "whether of the victorious or the vanquished nation, have been disciplined in the acceptance of violence and a kind of blind obedience to leaders. In war there is no choice between complete obedience and mutiny. Yet a decent civilization depends on the capacity of men [and women] to govern themselves by processes under which loyalty is consistent with constructive criticism."[10]

There are good things about soldiering: courage and selflessness, group solidarity, sacrifice, and support for one's buddies, and—at least in one's imagination—for the greater world; physical and mental challenges; and adrenaline. But the whole endeavor brings out the best for the worst by using the noblest traits of character to serve the vilest ends. Other aspects of military life are obedience, cruelty, vengefulness, sadism, racism, fear, terror, injury, trauma, anguish, and death. And the greatest of these is the obedience, because it can lead to all the others. The military conditions its recruits to believe that obedience is part of trust, and that by trusting superiors you can receive proper preparation, perform better as a unit, and stay safe. "Let go of that rope now!" and someone catches you. At least in training. Someone is screaming one inch from your nose: "I'll wipe the floor with your sorry ass, soldier!" Yet you survive. At least in training.

Following orders in a war, and facing enemies that want you dead, actually tends to get you killed, even if you've been conditioned to behave as if it didn't. It still will. And your loved ones will be devastated. But the military will roll right along without you, having put a little more cash into the pockets of weapons makers, and having made millions of people a little more likely to join anti-American terrorist groups. And if your modern-day soldier job is to blast distant strangers to bits without directly risking your own life at all, don't kid yourself that you'll be able to live peacefully with what you've done, or that anybody's going to think you're a hero. That's not heroic; it's neither brave nor good, much less both.

A Service Industry

On June 16, 2010, Congresswoman Chellie Pingree of Maine, who, unlike most of her colleagues, was listening to her constituents and opposing further funding of the wars, questioned Gen. David Petraeus in a House Armed Services Committee hearing as follows:

> Thank you...General Petraeus for being with us today and for your great service to this country. We greatly appreciate that, and I want to say at the offset (*sic*) how much I appreciate the hard work and sacrifice of our troops, particularly representing the state of Maine where we have a high proportion of people who have served in the military, um, we're grateful for their work and their sacrifice and, uh, the sacrifice of their families....
>
> I disagree with you basically on the premise that our continued military presence in Afghanistan actually strengthens our national security. Since the surge of troops in southern and eastern Afghanistan started, we have seen only increased levels of violence, coupled with an

incompetent and corrupt Afghan government. I am of the belief that continuing with this surge and increasing the level of American forces will have the same result: more American lives lost, and we will be no closer to success. In my opinion the American people remain skeptical that continuing to put their sons and daughters in harm's way in Afghanistan is worth the price being paid, and I think they have good reason to feel that way. It seems that increased military operations in southern and eastern Afghanistan have resulted in increased instability, increased violence, and more civilian casualties....[11]

This and more was all part of the congresswoman's opening question, congressional questioning often being more about speaking for one's allotted five minutes than allowing the witness to speak. Pingree went on to recount evidence that when U.S. forces pull out of areas in Afghanistan, local leaders can be better able to oppose the Taliban—its chief recruiting tool having been the U.S. occupation. She quoted the Russian ambassador who was familiar with the Soviet Union's earlier occupation of Afghanistan as saying that the United States had by now made all the same mistakes and was moving on to making new ones. After Petraeus expressed his complete disagreement, without actually providing any new information, Pingree interrupted:

> In the interest of time, and I know I'm going to run out here, I'll just say I appreciate and I appreciated from the start that you and I disagree. I wanted to put the sentiment out there that I do think increasingly the American public is concerned about the expense, the loss of lives, and I think all of us are concerned with our lack of success, but thank you very much for your service.

At that point, Petraeus jumped in to explain that he wanted to get out of Afghanistan, that he shared all of Pingree's concerns, but that he believed what he was doing actually was improving national security. The reason "we" were in Afghanistan was "very clear," he said, without explaining what it was. Pingree said: "I'll just say again: I appreciate your service. We have a strategic disagreement here."

Pingree's "questioning" was the closest thing we ever see in Congress— and it's very rare—to an articulation of the view of the majority of the public. And it wasn't just talk. Pingree followed up by voting against the funding of an escalation in Afghanistan. But I've quoted this exchange in order to point out something else. While accusing Gen. Petraeus of causing young American men and women to be killed for no good reason, causing Afghan civilians to be killed for no good reason, destabilizing Afghanistan and making us less rather than more secure, Congresswoman Pingree managed to thank the general three times for this "service." Huh?

Let's correct a deep misunderstanding. War is not a service. Taking my tax dollars, and in return killing innocent people and endangering my family with the possible blowback is just not a service. I don't feel served by such action. I don't ask for it. I'm not mailing an extra check to Washington as a tip to express my gratitude. If you want to serve humanity, there are many wiser career moves than joining the death machine—and as a bonus you get to stay alive and have your services appreciated. Therefore I will not call what the Department of War does "service" or the people who do it "service men and women" or the committees that purport to oversee what actually they rubberstamp "armed services" committees. What we need are unarmed services committees, and we need them with the reputation and prestige that Kennedy wrote about. A Department of Defense limited to actual defense would be a different story.

About Being Dead

During recent wars, presidents have tended not to go near any battlefields, if there are any battlefields, even after the fact as Lincoln did, or even to attend military funerals back home, or even to allow cameras to film the bodies returning in boxes (something forbidden during George W. Bush's presidency), or even to give speeches that mention the dead. There are endless speeches about the noble causes of the wars and even the bravery of the troops. The topic of dying, however, is for some reason regularly evaded.[12]

Franklin Roosevelt once said on the radio, "Eleven brave and loyal men of our Navy were killed by the Nazis." Roosevelt was pretending a German submarine had attacked the USS Kearny unprovoked and with no warning. In reality the sailors may have been extremely brave, but in Roosevelt's tall tale, they would have actually been innocent unsuspecting bystanders attacked while minding their own business on a merchant ship. How much bravery and loyalty would that have required?

To his credit, in an unusual acknowledgment of what war involves, Roosevelt later said of the coming war: "The casualty lists of soldiers will undoubtedly be large. I deeply feel the anxiety of all families of the men in our armed forces and the relatives of the people in cities which have been bombed." FDR did not, however, attend soldiers' funerals. Lyndon Johnson avoided the topic of war dead, and attended only two funerals out of the tens of thousands of soldiers he'd ordered to their deaths. Nixon and both presidents Bush collectively attended a grand total of zero funerals of the soldiers they sent to die.

And, needless to say, presidents never honor the non-American victims of their wars. If "liberating" a country requires "sacrificing" a few thousand

Americans and a few hundred thousand natives, why aren't all of those people mourned? Even if you think the war was justified and accomplished some mysterious good, doesn't honesty require recognizing who has died?

President Ronald Reagan visited a cemetery of German war dead from World War II. His itinerary was the result of negotiations with Germany's president who was aware that Reagan might visit the site of a former concentration camp as well. Reagan remarked, prior to the trip, "There's nothing wrong with visiting that cemetery where those young men are victims of Nazism also....They were victims, just as surely as the victims in the concentration camps." Were they? Were Nazi soldiers killed in the war victims? Does it depend on whether they believed they were doing something good? Does it depend on how old they were and what lies were told them? Does it depend whether they were employed on a battlefield or in a concentration camp?

And what about American war dead? Are a million Iraqis collateral damage and 4,000 Americans heroic casualties? Or are all 1,004,000 victims? Or are those who were attacked victims and those who did the attacking murderers? I think there's actually room for some subtlety here, and that any such question is best answered in terms of a particular individual, and that even then there can be more than one answer. But I think the legal answer—that those participating in an aggressive war are murderers, and the other side their victims—gets at an important part of the moral answer. And I think it's an answer that becomes more correct and complete the more people become aware of it.

President George W. Bush, together with a visiting foreign head of state, held a press conference at the enormous house he called his "ranch" in Crawford, Texas, on August 4, 2005. He was asked about 14 marines from Brook Park, Ohio, who had just been killed by a roadside bomb in Iraq. Bush replied, "The people of Brook Park and the family members of those who lost their life, I hope they can take comfort in the fact that millions of their fellow citizens pray for them. I hope they also take comfort in the understanding that the sacrifice was made in a noble cause."

Two days later, Cindy Sheehan, the mother of a U.S. soldier killed in Iraq in 2004, camped out near a gate to Bush's property in an effort to ask him what in the world the noble cause was. Thousands of people joined her, including members of Veterans for Peace at whose conference she had been speaking just before heading to Crawford. The media gave the story lots of attention for weeks, but Bush never answered the question.

Most presidents do visit the Tomb of the Unknown Soldier. But the soldiers who died at Gettysburg are not remembered. We remember that the North won the war, but we have no individual or collective memory of each soldier who was part of that victory. Soldiers are almost all unknown, and the Tomb of the Unknown represents them all. This is an aspect of war that was present even when Pericles spoke, but was perhaps less present during the knightly battles and crusades of the Middle Ages, or in Japan during the age of the samurai. When war is waged with swords and armor—expensive equipment suited only to elite killers who specialize in killing and nothing else—those warriors may risk their lives for their own personal glory.

The Swords and Horses Are Only in the Recruiting Ads

When "noble" referred to those inheriting wealth as well as the characteristics expected of them, each soldier was at least slightly more than a cog in a war machine. That changed with guns, and with the tactics Americans learned from the natives and employed against the British. Now, any poor man could be a war hero, and he would be given a medal or a stripe in place of nobility. "A soldier will fight long and hard for a bit of colored ribbon," remarked Napoleon Bonaparte.[13] In the French Revolution, you didn't need a family crest; you could fight and die for a national flag. By the time of Napoleon and of the U.S. Civil War, you didn't even need daring or ingenuity to be an ideal warrior. You just had to take your place in a long line, stand there, and sometimes pretend to shoot your gun.

Cynthia Wachtell's book *War No More: The Antiwar Impulse in American Literature 1861-1914* tells a story of opposition to war overcoming self-deceptions, self-censorship, the censorship of the publishing industry, and public unpopularity, and establishing itself as a constant thread and genre of U.S. literature (and cinema) ever since. It's a story, in large part, of people clinging to old ideas of warrior nobility and finally beginning to let them go.

In the years leading up to and including the Civil War, war—almost by definition—could not be opposed in literature. Under the heavy influence of Sir Walter Scott, war was presented as an idealized and romantic endeavor. Death was painted with soft tones of desirable sleep, natural beauty, and chivalric glory. Wounds and injuries did not appear. Fear, frustration, stupidity, resentment and other characteristics so central to actual war did not exist in its fictionalized form.

"Sir Walter had so large a hand in making Southern character, as it existed before the war," remarked Mark Twain, "that he is in great measure responsible for the war." Northern character bore a striking resemblance to the Southern variety. "If the North and South could agree on little else during the war years," Wachtell writes, "they were in easy agreement about their literary preferences. Whether their allegiance was to the Confederacy or the Union, readers wanted to be reassured that their sons, brothers, and fathers were playing parts in a noble endeavor that was favored by God. Popular wartime writers drew on a shared vocabulary of highly sentimentalized expressions of pain, sorrow, and sacrifice. Less rosy and idealized interpretations of the war were unwelcome."[14]

Glorification of war was dominant through what Phillip Knightley calls the "golden age" for war correspondents, 1865-1914: "To readers in London or New York, distant battles in strange places must have seemed unreal, and the Golden Age style of war reporting—where guns flash, cannons thunder, the struggle rages, the general is brave, the soldiers are gallant, and their bayonets make short work of the enemy—only added to the illusion that it was all a thrilling adventure story."[15]

We're still living off this antiquated pro-war literature today. It roams the land like a zombie, just as surely as do creationism, global-warming denial, and racism. It shapes Congress members' servile reverence for David Petraeus as surely as it would if he fought with a sword and a horse rather than a desk and a television studio. And it is just as deadly and pointless as it was when the soldiers of World War I marched off to die in the fields for it:

> Both sides recalled ancient glories, using the symbol of the warrior knight to portray battle as an exercise in manly honor and aristocratic leadership, while using modern technology to fight a war of attrition. At the Battle of the Somme, begun in July 1916, British forces bombarded enemy lines for eight days and then advanced from the trenches shoulder to shoulder. German machine gunners killed 20,000 of them the first day. After four months the German forces had fallen back a few miles at a cost of 600,000 Allied dead and 750,000 German dead. In contrast to the colonial conflicts familiar to all the imperial powers involved, the death toll on both sides was appallingly high.[16]

Because war makers lie throughout the course of wars, just as they do prior to launching them, the people of Britain, France, Germany, and later the United States, were not remotely aware of the full extent of the casualties as World War I played out. Had they been, they might have stopped it.[17]

War Is for the Poor

Even to say that we've democratized war is to put a pleasant spin on things, and not just because war decisions are still made by an unaccountable elite. Since the Vietnam War, the United States has dropped all pretense of a military draft equally applied to all. Instead we spend billions of dollars on recruitment, increase military pay, and offer signing bonuses until enough people "voluntarily" join by signing contracts that allow the military to change the terms at will.

If more troops are needed, just extend the contracts of the ones you've got. Need more still? Federalize the National Guard and send kids off to war who signed up thinking they'd be helping hurricane victims. Still not enough? Hire contractors for transportation, cooking, cleaning, and construction. Let the soldiers be pure soldiers whose only job is to kill, just like the knights of old. Boom, you've instantly doubled the size of your force, and nobody's noticed except the profiteers.

Still need more killers? Hire mercenaries. Hire foreign mercenaries. Not enough? Spend trillions of dollars on technology to maximize the power of each person. Use unmanned aircraft so nobody gets hurt. Promise immigrants they'll be citizens if they join. Change the standards for enlistment: take 'em older, fatter, in worse health, with less education, with criminal records. Make high schools give recruiters aptitude test results and students' contact information, and promise students they can pursue their chosen field within the wonderful world of death, and that you'll send them to college if they live—hey, just promising it costs you nothing. If they're resistant, you started too late. Put military video games in shopping malls. Send uniformed generals into kindergartens to warm the children up to the idea of truly and properly swearing allegiance to that flag. Spend 10 times the money on recruiting each new soldier as we spend educating each child. Do anything, anything, anything other than starting a draft.

But there's a name for this practice of avoiding a traditional draft. It's called a poverty draft. Because people tend not to want to participate in wars, those who have other career options tend to choose those other options. Those who see the military as one of their only choices, their only shot at a college education, or their only way to escape their troubled lives are more likely to enlist. According to the Not Your Soldier Project:

> The majority of military recruits come from below-median income neighborhoods.
>
> In 2004, 71 percent of black recruits, 65 percent of Latino recruits, and 58 percent of white recruits came from below-median income neighborhoods.
>
> The percentage of recruits who were regular high school graduates dropped from 86 percent in 2004 to 73 percent in 2006.
>
> [The recruiters] never mention that the college money is difficult to come by—only 16 percent of enlisted personnel who completed four years of military duty ever received money for schooling. They don't say that the job skills they promise won't transfer into the real world. Only 12 percent of male veterans and 6 percent of female veterans use skills

learned in the military in their current jobs. And of course, they down-play the risk of being killed while on duty.[18]

An Associated Press analysis in 2007 found that of all the U.S. troops thus far killed in Iraq, almost three-quarters of them had come from towns with a per-capita income level below the U.S. national average, and a majority of them from towns with more than the average number of people in poverty. The U.S. military has recruitment programs that focus on poor neighbor-hoods, including the Army GED Plus Enlistment Program that signs up re-cruits who haven't graduated from high school. Recruiters make their pitches to community college students, suggesting the military as their only real op-tion: "This place is a dead end. I can offer you more."

Jorge Mariscal highlights "the tragic example of Sgt. Paul Cortez, who... joined the Army, and was sent to Iraq. On March 12, 2006, he participated in the gang rape of a 14-year-old Iraqi girl and the murder of her and her entire family." A former classmate said "He would never do something like that.... That's not him."

Let us accept the claim that "that's not him." Nevertheless, because of a series of unspeakable and unpardonable events within the context of an ille-gal and immoral war, "that" is what he became. On February 21, 2007, Cortez pled guilty to the rape and four counts of felony murder. He was convicted a few days later, sentenced to life in prison and a lifetime in his own personal hell.[19]

In a 2010 book called *The Casualty Gap*, Douglas Kriner and Francis Shen look at the data from World War II, Korea, Vietnam, and Iraq. They found that only in World War II was a fair draft employed, while the other three wars drew disproportionately from poorer and less educated Americans, opening a "casualty gap" that grew dramatically larger in Korea, again in Vietnam, and yet again in the war on Iraq as the military shifted from conscription to "volunteer." The authors also cite a survey showing that as Americans become aware of this casualty gap, they become less supportive of wars.[20]

The transition from war primarily by the rich to war primarily by the poor has been a very gradual one and is far from complete. For one thing, those in the highest positions of power in the military are more likely to have come from privileged backgrounds. And regardless of their background, top officers are the least likely to see dangerous combat. Leading the troops into battle is not how it works anymore, except in our imaginations. Both presi-dents Bush saw their approval ratings soar in public opinion polls when they fought wars—at least at first when the wars were still new and magnificent. Never mind that these presidents fought their wars from the air-conditioned Oval Office. One result of this is that those making the decisions upon which the most lives hang are the least likely to see war death up close, or to have ever seen it.

The Air-Conditioned Nightmare

The first President Bush had seen World War II from an airplane, already a distance away from the dying, although not as far away as Reagan who had avoided going to war. Just as thinking of enemies as subhuman makes it easier to kill them, bombing them from high in the sky is much easier psychologically than participating in a knife fight or shooting a traitor standing blindfolded beside a wall. Presidents Clinton and Bush Jr. avoided the Vietnam War, Clinton through educational privilege, Bush through being the son of his father. President Obama never went to war. Vice Presidents Dan Quayle, Dick Cheney, and Joe Biden, like Clinton and Bush Jr., dodged the draft. Vice President Al Gore went to the Vietnam War briefly, but as an army journalist, not a soldier who saw combat.

Rarely does someone deciding that thousands must die have the experience of having seen it happen. On August 15, 1941, the Nazis had already killed a lot of people. But Heinrich Himmler, one of the top military bigwigs in the country who would oversee the murder of some 11 million Jews, Gypsies, communists, homosexuals, and the mentally and physically disabled, had never seen anyone die. He asked to watch a shooting in Minsk. Jews were told to jump into a ditch where they were shot and covered with dirt. Then more were told to jump in. They were shot and covered. Himmler stood right at the edge watching, until something from someone's head splashed onto his coat. He turned pale and turned away. The local commander said to him:

"Look at the eyes of the men in this Kommando. What kind of followers are we training here? Either neurotics or savages!"[21] Himmler told them to do their duty even if it was hard. He returned to doing his from the comfort of a desk.

Shalt Thou Kill or Not?

Killing sounds a lot easier than it is. Throughout history, men have risked their own lives to avoid having to take part in wars:

> Men have fled their homelands, served lengthy prison terms, hacked off limbs, shot off feet or index fingers, feigned illness or insanity, or, if they could afford to, paid surrogates to fight in their stead. "Some draw their teeth, some blind themselves, and others maim themselves, on their way to us," the governor of Egypt complained of his peasant recruits in the early nineteenth century. So unreliable was the rank and file of the

eighteenth-century Prussian army that military manuals forbade camping near a woods or forest. The troops would simply melt away into the trees.[22]

Although killing non-human animals comes easily to most people, killing one's fellow human beings is so radically outside the normal focus of one's life which involves co-existing with people that many cultures have developed rituals to transform a normal person into a warrior, and sometimes back again following a war. The ancient Greeks, Aztecs, Chinese, Yanomamo Indians, and Scythians also used alcohol or other drugs to facilitate killing.[23]

Very few people kill outside of the military, and most of them are extremely disturbed individuals. James Gilligan, in his book *Violence: Reflections on a National Epidemic*, diagnosed the root cause of murderous or suicidal violence as deep shame and humiliation, a desperate need for respect and status (and, fundamentally love and care) so intense that only killing (oneself and/or others) could ease the pain—or, rather, the lack of feeling. When a person becomes so ashamed of his needs (and of being ashamed), Gilligan writes, and when he sees no nonviolent solutions, and when he lacks the ability to feel love or guilt or fear, the result can be violence. But what if violence is the start? What if you condition healthy people to kill without thought? Can the result be a mental state resembling that of the person who's internally driven to kill?

The choice to engage in violence outside of war is not a rational one, and often involves magical thinking, as Gilligan explains by analyzing the meaning of crimes in which murderers have mutilated their victims' bodies or their own. "I am convinced," he writes, "that violent behavior, even at its most apparently senseless, incomprehensible, and psychotic, is an understandable response to an identifiable, specifiable set of conditions; and that even when it seems motivated by 'rational' self-interest, it is the end product of a series of irrational, self-destructive, and unconscious motives that can be studied, identified, and understood."[24]

The mutilation of bodies, whatever drives it in each case, is a fairly common practice in war, although engaged in mostly by people who were not inclined to murderous violence prior to joining the military. Numerous war trophy photos from the war on Iraq show corpses and body parts mutilated and displayed in close-up, laid out on a platter as if for cannibals. Many of these images were sent by American soldiers to a website that marketed pornography. Presumably, these images were viewed as war pornography. Presumably, they were created by people who had come to love war—not by the Himmlers or the Dick Cheneys who enjoy sending others, but by people who actually enjoyed being there, people who signed up for college money or adventure and were trained as sociopathic killers.

On June 9, 2006, the U.S. military killed Abu Musab al-Zarqawi, took a photo of his dead head, blew it up to enormous proportions, and displayed it in a frame at a press conference. From the way it was framed, the head could have been connected to a body or not. Presumably this was meant to be not only proof of his death, but a kind of revenge for al-Zarqawi's beheading of Americans.

Gilligan's understanding of what motivates violence comes from working in prisons and mental health institutions, not from participating in war, and not from watching the news. He suggests that the obvious explanation for violence is usually wrong:

> Some people think that armed robbers commit their crimes in order to get money. And of course, sometimes, that is how they rationalize their behavior. But when you sit down and talk with people who repeatedly commit such crimes, what you hear is, "I never got so much respect before in my life as I did when I first pointed a gun at somebody," or, "You wouldn't believe how much respect you get when you have a gun pointed at some dude's face." For men who have lived for a lifetime on a diet of contempt and disdain, the temptation to gain instant respect in this way can be worth far more than the cost of going to prison, or even of dying.[25]

While violence, at least in the civilian world, may be irrational, Gilligan suggests clear ways in which it can be prevented or encouraged. If you wanted to increase violence, he writes, you would take the following steps that the United States has taken: Punish more and more people more and more harshly; ban drugs that inhibit violence and legalize and advertise those that stimulate it; use taxes and economic policies to widen disparities in wealth and income; deny the poor education; perpetuate racism; produce entertainment that glorifies violence; make lethal weapons readily available; maximize the polarization of social roles of men and women; encourage prejudice against homosexuality; use violence to punish children in school and at home; and keep unemployment sufficiently high. And why would you do that or tolerate it? Possibly because most victims of violence are poor, and the poor tend to organize and demand their rights better when they aren't terrorized by crime.

Gilligan looks at violent crimes, especially murder, and then turns his attention to our system of violent punishment, including the death penalty, prison rape, and solitary confinement. He views retributive punishment as the same sort of irrational violence as the crimes it is punishing. He sees structural violence and poverty as doing the most damage, but he does not address the subject of war. In scattered references Gilligan makes clear that he lumps war into his theory of violence, and yet in one place he opposes ending wars, and nowhere does he explain how his theory can be coherently applied.

Wars are created by governments, just like our criminal justice system. Do they have similar roots? Do soldiers and mercenaries and contractors and bureaucrats feel shame and humiliation? Do war propaganda and military training produce the idea that the enemy has disrespected the warrior who must now kill to recover his honor? Or is the humiliation of the drill sergeant intended to produce a reaction redirected against the enemy? What about the Congress members and presidents, the generals and weapons corporation CEOs, and the corporate media—those who actually decide to have a war and make it happen? Don't they have a high degree of status and respect already, even if they may have gone into politics because of their exceptional desire for such attention? Aren't there more mundane motivations, like financial profit, campaign financing, and vote winning at work here, even if the writings of the Project for the New American Century have a lot to say about boldness and dominance and control?

And what about the public at large, including all those nonviolent war supporters? Common slogans and bumper stickers include: "These colors don't run," "Proud to be an American," "Never back down," "Don't cut and run." Nothing could be more irrational or symbolic than a war on a tactic or an emotion, as in the "global war on terrorism," which was launched as revenge, even though the primary people against whom the revenge was desired were already dead. Do people think their pride and self-worth depend on the vengeance to be found in bombing Afghanistan until there's nobody left resisting U.S. dominance? If so, it will not a bit of good to explain to them that such actions actually make us less safe. But what if people who crave respect find out that such behavior makes their country despised or a laughingstock, or that the government is playing them for fools, that Europeans have a higher standard of living as a result of not putting all their money into wars, or that a puppet president like Afghanistan's Hamid Karzai has been making off with suitcases of American money?

Regardless, other research finds that only about two percent of people actually enjoy killing, and they are extremely mentally disturbed. The purpose of military training is to make normal people, including normal war supporters, into sociopaths, at least in the context of war, to get them to do in war what would be viewed as the single worst thing they could do at any other time or place. The way people can be predictably trained to kill in war is to simulate killing in training. Recruits who stab dummies to death, chant "Blood makes the grass grow!" and shoot target practice with human-looking targets, will kill in battle when they're scared out of their minds. They won't need their minds. Their reflexes will take over. "The only thing that has any hope of influencing the midbrain," writes Dave Grossman, "is also the only thing that influences a dog: classical and operant conditioning."

That is what is used when training firefighters and airline pilots to react to emergency situations: precise replication of the stimulus that they will face (in a flame house or a flight simulator) and then extensive shaping of the desired response to that stimulus. Stimulus-response, stimulus-response, stimulus-response. In the crisis, when these individuals are scared out of their wits, they react properly and they save lives.... We do not *tell* school children what they should do in case of fire, we *condition* them; and when they are frightened, they do the right thing.[26]

It is only through intense and well-designed conditioning that most people can be brought to kill. As Grossman and others have documented, "throughout history the majority of men on the battlefield would not attempt to kill the enemy, even to save their own lives or the lives of their friends."[27] We've changed that.

Grossman believes that phony violence in movies, video games, and the rest of our culture is a major contributor to actual violence in society and he condemns it, even while advising on better ways in which the military can create wartime killers. While Grossman is in the business of counseling soldiers traumatized by having killed, he assists in producing more killing. I don't think his motivations are as awful as that sounds. I think he simply believes killing is transformed into a force for good by a declaration of war by his country. At the same time he advocates for reducing simulations of violence in the media and in children's games. Nowhere in *On Killing* does he address the awkward fact that violent media powerful enough to drive non-war violence must also make the work of military recruiters and trainers easier.

In 2010, protests by peace activists forced the Army to close down something it had called the Army Experience Center, which had been located in a Pennsylvania shopping mall. At the center, kids had played war-simulating video games that included the use of real military weapons hooked up to video screens. Recruiters offered helpful tips. The Army did this for children too young to legally be recruited, clearly believing that it would boost recruitment later on. Of course, other ways we teach children that violence can be good and useful include the continued use of war itself and the use of state executions in our criminal justice system.

In August 2010, a judge in Alabama tried a man for the crime of threatening on Facebook to commit mass murder similar to a shooting spree that killed 32 people at Virginia Tech. The sentence? The man had to join the military. The Army said it would take him after he was off probation. "Military is a good, good thing for you," the judge told him. "I'd say it's an appropriate outcome," the man's lawyer agreed.[28]

If there is a connection between violence outside of war and inside it, if the two are not completely unrelated activities, one might expect to see above-average rates of violence from veterans of war, especially from those who have engaged in face-to-face combat on the ground. In 2007, the Bureau of Justice Statistics released a report, using 2004 data, on veterans in prison, announcing, "Among adult males in the U.S. population in 2004, veterans were half as likely as non-veterans to be in prison (630 prisoners per 100,000 veterans, compared to 1,390 prisoners per 100,000 non-veteran U.S. residents)."

That seems significant, and I've seen it quoted without what came next:

The difference is largely explained by age. Two-thirds of male veterans in the U.S. population were at least 55 years old, compared to 17 percent of non-veteran men. The incarceration rate of these older male veterans (182 per 100,000) was far lower than for those under age 55 (1,483 per 100,000).[29]

But this doesn't tell us whether veterans are more or less likely to be incarcerated, much less violent. The report tells us that more of those veterans who are incarcerated have been convicted of violent crimes than is the case for incarcerated non-veterans, and that only a minority of those veterans who are incarcerated have been in combat. But it does not tell us whether men or women who have been in combat are more or less likely to commit violent crimes than others in their same age group.

If crime statistics did show an increased rate of violent crime by war veterans, no politician who wanted to remain a politician for long would be eager to publish them. In April 2009, newspapers reported that the FBI and the Department of Homeland Security had been advising their employees who were looking into white supremacists and "militia/sovereign-citizen extremist groups" to focus on veterans from Iraq and Afghanistan. The resulting storm of indignation could not have been more volcanic had the FBI advised focusing on white people as suspected members of such groups!

Of course it seems unfair to send people off to do a horrible job and then hold a prejudice against them when they get back. Veterans' groups are dedicated to fighting such prejudices. But group statistics should not be treated as grounds for unfair treatment of individuals. If sending people to war makes them statistically more likely to be dangerous we ought to know that, since sending people to war is something we can choose to stop doing. Nobody will be at any risk of treating veterans unfairly when we have no more veterans.

On July 28, 2009, the *Washington Post* ran an article that began:

Soldiers returning from Iraq after serving with a Fort Carson, Colo., combat brigade have exhibited an exceptionally high rate of criminal behavior...carrying out a string of killings and other offenses that the ex-soldiers attribute to lax discipline and episodes of indiscriminate killing during their grueling deployment.[30]

Crimes these soldiers had committed in Iraq included killing civilians at random—in some cases at point-blank range—using banned stun guns on captives, pushing people off bridges, loading weapons with illegal hollow-point bullets, abusing drugs, and mutilating the bodies of Iraqis. Crimes they had committed upon returning home included rape, domestic abuse, shootings, stabbings, kidnappings, and suicides.

We can't extrapolate to the whole military from a case involving 10 veterans, but it is suggestive that the military itself believed that problems typical of the current war experience "may have increased the risks" of veterans committing murder back in the civilian world where murder is no longer admirable.

Numerous studies conclude that veterans suffering from post-traumatic stress disorder (PTSD) are significantly more likely to commit acts of violence than veterans not suffering from PTSD. Of course, those suffering PTSD are also more likely to be those who saw a lot of combat. Unless non-suffering veterans have lower rates of violence than civilians, veterans on average must have higher.

While statistics on murder seem hard to come by, those on suicide are more readily available. At the time of this writing, the U.S. military was losing more lives to suicide than to combat, and those troops who had seen combat were committing suicide at a higher rate than those who hadn't. The Army put the suicide rate for active duty soldiers at 20.2 per 100,000, higher than the U.S. average even when adjusted for gender and age. And the Veterans Administration in 2007 put the suicide rate for U.S. veterans who had left the military at a stunning 56.8 per 100,000, higher than the average suicide rate in any nation on earth, and higher than the average suicide rate for males anywhere outside of Belarus—the same place where Himmler observed mass murder. *Time* magazine noted on April 13, 2010, that—despite the military's reluctance to admit it—one contributing factor, amazingly enough, was probably war:

> The experience of combat itself may also play a role. "Combat increases fearlessness about death and the capability for suicide," said Craig Bryan, a University of Texas psychologist, briefing Pentagon officials in January. The combination of combat exposure and ready access to guns can be lethal to anyone contemplating suicide. [31]

Bryan described the dilemma the U.S. military is in, as it conditions its members to ignore pain and suffering, it is also conditioning them to be more likely to commit suicide. To reduce that result would require reducing its primary mission.

Another contributing factor could be the lack of any clear understanding as to what a war is for. Soldiers in a war like the war on Afghanistan have no good basis to believe the horrors they're facing and committing are justified by something more important. When the president's representative to Afghanistan can't communicate the purpose of the war to senators, how can soldiers be expected to know? And how can one live with having killed without knowing what it was for?

Veterans Not So Glorious

Of course, most veterans who run into hard times do not commit suicide. In fact, veterans in the United States—all those "support the troops" speeches by the rich and powerful notwithstanding—are very disproportionately likely to be homeless. The military does not, of course, put the same focus on helping warriors become non-warriors that it put on their previous transformation. And society does not wholeheartedly encourage veterans to believe their actions were justified.

Vietnam War veterans were welcomed back with a good deal of scorn and contempt, which affected their mental state horribly. Veterans of the wars on Iraq and Afghanistan have often been welcomed home with the question "Do you mean that war is still going on?" That question may not be as damaging as telling someone they've committed murder, but it's a long way from emphasizing the supreme importance and value of what they've done.

Saying what may be most helpful to veterans' mental health is, all else equal, something I'd like to do. But it is not what I am doing in this book. If we are going to get beyond war it will be through developing a culture of greater kindness that shuns cruelty, revenge, and violence. The people primarily responsible for wars are the ones at the top, those discussed in Chapter 6. Punishing their crimes would deter war in the future. Punishing veterans would not deter war in the least. But the message that needs to permeate our society is not one of praise and gratitude for the worst crimes we produce.

The solution, I think, is not to praise or punish veterans, but to show them kindness while speaking the truth required to stop producing more of them. Veterans and non-veterans alike could have free and top-quality mental healthcare, standard healthcare, educational opportunities, job opportunities, childcare, vacations, guaranteed employment, and retirement if we stopped dumping all of our resources into wars. Providing veterans with those basic components of a happy, healthy civilian life would probably more than balance out any discomfort they feel at hearing criticism of war.

Matthis Chiroux is a U.S. soldier who refused to deploy to Iraq. He says that he was stationed in Germany and made friends with a lot of Germans, some of whom told him that what his country was doing in Iraq and Afghanistan was genocide. Chiroux says that this deeply offended him, but that he thought about it and acted on it, and it may very well have saved his life. He is now grateful, he says, to some courageous Germans who were willing to offend him. Here's to offending people!

I've met a number of veterans of the wars on Iraq and Afghanistan who have found some comfort and relief in becoming vocal opponents of the very wars they fought in and, in some cases, becoming resisters who refuse to fight anymore. Veterans, and even active duty troops, need not be enemies of peace activists. As Captain Paul Chappell points out in his book *The End of War*, there's always a large gap between stereotypes. Soldiers who take sadistic joy in slaughtering innocents and peace activists who spit on veterans are miles apart (or perhaps a little closer than they think), but the average participant and opponent of war are much closer together and have much more in common than that which separates them. A significant percentage of Americans, and even a significant percentage of peace activists, work for weapons makers and other suppliers of the war industry.

While soldiers find it easier to kill from a distance with drones or using heat sensors and night vision, playing a video-game war in which they don't have to see their victims, the politicians who send them into war are even a further step removed and have an even easier time avoiding feelings of responsibility. How else can we understand a situation in which hundreds of members of the House of Representatives are "opponents" and "critics" of wars yet keep funding them? And the rest of us civilians are yet another step removed again.

Soldiers have long found it easier to kill using a piece of equipment requiring more than one person to operate it, diffusing the responsibility. We think in just the same way. There are hundreds of millions of people failing to take drastic measures to stop these wars, so surely I can't be blamed for the same failure, right? The least I can do, while pushing myself toward stronger opposition, is to sympathize with people who in many cases went into the military in the absence of other options that I had, and to honor above all those who find the courage and heroism within the military to lay down their weapons and refuse to do what they're told, or at least find the wisdom to speak out in later regret about what they've done.

Soldiers' Stories

The lies that have been told to launch wars have always included dramatic stories, and since the creation of the cinema, stories of heroic warriors have been found there. The Committee on Public Information produced feature-length films as well as giving those four-minute speeches when reels were changed.

> In *The Unbeliever* (1918), made with the cooperation of the U.S. Marine Corps, the rich and powerful Phil learns that "class pride is junk" as he watches his chauffeur die in battle, finds faith after seeing an image of Christ walking across the battlefield, and falls in love with a beautiful Belgian girl who barely escapes rape by a German officer.[32]

D.W. Griffith's 1915 film *The Birth of a Nation* about the Civil War and reconstruction helped launch a domestic war on black people, but his *Hearts of the World* in 1918, made with military assistance, taught Americans that World War I was about heroically rescuing the innocent from the clutches of evil ones.

For World War II, the Office of War Information suggested messages, reviewed scripts, and asked that objectionable scenes be cut, taking over the film industry to promote war. The Army also hired Frank Capra to produce seven pro-war films. This practice has, of course, continued to the current day with Hollywood blockbusters being regularly produced with assistance from the U.S. military. The troops in these stories are depicted as heroes.

During real wars, the military loves to tell the dramatic stories of real-life heroes, too. Nothing's better for recruitment. Just a couple of weeks into the war on Iraq, the U.S. media, at the prompting of the military and the White House, began giving saturation coverage to the story of a female soldier named Jessica Lynch who had supposedly been captured during a hostile exchange and then dramatically rescued. She was both the heroine and the damsel in distress. The Pentagon falsely claimed Lynch had stab and bullet wounds, and that she had been slapped about on her hospital bed and interrogated. Lynch denied the whole story and complained that the military had used her. On April 24, 2007, Lynch testified before the House Committee on Oversight and Government Reform: "[Right after my capture], tales of great heroism were being told. My parent's home in Wirt County was under siege of the media all repeating the story of the little girl Rambo from the hills who went down fighting. It was not true....I am still confused as to why they chose to lie."[33]

One soldier involved in the operation who knew the stories were false and who commented at the time that the military was "making a movie" was Pat Tillman. He had been a football star and had famously given up a multi-million dollar football contract in order to join the military and do his patriotic duty to protect the country from evil terrorists. He was the most famous actual troop in the U.S. military, and television pundit Ann Coulter called him "an American original—virtuous, pure, and masculine like only an American male can be."[34]

Except that he came to no longer believe the stories that had led him to enlist, and Ann Coulter stopped praising him. On September 25, 2005, the *San Francisco Chronicle* reported that Tillman had become critical of the Iraq war and had scheduled a meeting with the prominent war critic Noam Chomsky to take place when he returned from Afghanistan, all information that Tillman's mother and Chomsky later confirmed. Tillman couldn't confirm it because he had died in Afghanistan in 2004 from three bullets to the forehead at short range, bullets shot by an American.

The White House and the military knew Tillman had died from so-called friendly fire, but they falsely told the media he'd died in a hostile exchange. Senior army commanders knew the facts and yet approved awarding Tillman a Silver Star, a Purple Heart, and a posthumous promotion, all based on his having died fighting the enemy.

Dramatic stories that challenge the idea of heroic warriors are told as well. Karen Malpede's play *Prophecy* depicts a suicidal veteran of the war on Iraq. Films like *In the Valley of Ellah* convey the damage that war does to soldiers, and give expression to their belief that what they've done is the opposite of heroic. *Green Zone* depicts a soldier realizing a bit late that the war on Iraq was based on lies.

But there is no need to turn to fiction or to fabricate stories that show soldiers as they really are. All that's required is talking to them. Many, of course, still support wars after having been in them. Even more support the general idea of war and have pride in what they've done, even if they have criticisms of the particular war they were part of. But some become outspoken opponents of wars, recounting their experiences in order to dispel mythologies. Members of Iraq Veterans Against the War gathered near Washington in March 2008 for an event they called "Winter Soldier." They spoke these words:[35]

> He watched the commander who had given us the order to shoot anyone on the street shoot two old ladies that were walking and carrying vegetables. He said that the commander had told him to shoot the women, and when he refused, the commander shot them. So, when this marine started shooting at people in cars that nobody else felt were threatening, he was following his commander's example.
>
> —Jason Wayne Lemieux

> I remember one woman walking by. She was carrying a huge bag, and she looked like she was heading toward us, so we lit her up with the Mark 19, which is an automatic grenade launcher, and when the dust

settled, we realized that the bag was full of groceries. She had been trying to bring us food and we blew her to pieces.... Something else we
were encouraged to do, almost with a wink and a nudge, was to carry
drop weapons, or by my third tour, drop shovels. We would carry these
weapons or shovels with us because if we accidentally shot a civilian,
we could just toss the weapon on the body, and make them look like an
insurgent.

—Jason Washburn

I want to start by showing you a video of the Executive Officer of Kilo
Company. We had gotten into a two-hour long firefight, and it was over
for quite some time, but he still felt the need to drop a five-hundred
pound laser-guided missile on northern Ramadi.

[The video shows the officer gloating after the missile strike: "I
think I just killed half of the population of northern Ramadi!"]

On April 18, 2006, I had my first confirmed kill. He was an innocent man. I don't know his name. I call him 'the Fat Man.' During the
incident, he walked back to his house, and I shot him in front of his
friend and father. The first round didn't kill him after I'd hit him in the
neck. Afterwards, he started screaming and looked right into my eyes.
I looked at my friend I was on post with, and I said 'Well, I can't let that
happen.' I took another shot and took him out. The rest of his family
carried him away. It took seven Iraqis to carry his body.

We were all congratulated after we had our first kills, and that happened to have been mine. My company commander personally congratulated me. This is the same individual who stated that whoever gets their
first kill by stabbing them to death would get a four-day pass when we
returned from Iraq.... I am sorry for the hate and destruction that I have
inflicted on innocent people....I am no longer the monster I once was.

—Jon Michael Turner

There were many more stories like these, and what seemed heroic was the
telling of them, not what they told. We don't usually get to hear what soldiers
think. As much as the general public is ignored in Washington, soldiers are
even more ignored. Rarely do we even see polls of what troops believe. But
in 2006, while presidents and Congress members were talking up the war
"for the troops" a survey found that 72 percent of U.S. troops in Iraq wanted
the war ended before 2007. An even higher percentage, 85 percent, falsely
believed the war was "to retaliate for Saddam's role in the 9-11 attacks." Of
course Saddam Hussein had no role in those attacks. And 77 percent believed
a major reason for the war was "to stop Saddam from protecting al Qaeda in
Iraq."[36] Of course there was no al Qaeda in Iraq until the war created it. These

soldiers believed the war lies, and they still wanted the war ended. But most of them did not lay down their weapons.

Does their participation in an aggressive war get a pass because they were lied to? Well, it certainly puts even more blame on the top decision makers who need to be held accountable. But more important than answering that question, I think, is preventing future lies to future potential warriors. It is toward that end that the truth about past wars should be brought out. The truth is this: war has not been and cannot be a service. It is not heroic. It is shameful. Part of recognizing these facts will involve stripping away the aura of heroism from soldiers. When politicians stop falsely pretending to have fought in wars—a rather common practice, and something a senatorial candidate was caught doing in 2010—and start falsely pretending not to have done so, we'll know we're making progress.

Another sign of progress looks like this:

> On July 30, [2010], approximately 30 active-duty soldiers, veterans, military families, and supporters held a rally outside the gates of Fort Hood [from which soldiers already suffering PTSD have been sent back to war] with a large banner directed at Colonel Allen, commander of 3rd ACR [Armored Cavalry Regiment], which read 'Col. Allen...Do Not Deploy Wounded Soldiers!' Demonstrators also carried placards that read:
>
> "Tell the brass: Kiss my ass!"
>
> and
>
> "They lie, we die!"
>
> The demonstration was at a main entry point for the base, so thousands of active-duty GIs and their families passed by the demonstration. Many also joined after seeing the demonstration. Fort Hood Military Police sent vehicles and troops to intimidate the demonstrators, fearing a growing movement.[37]

6

WAR MAKERS DO NOT HAVE NOBLE MOTIVES

Many discussions of lies that launch wars quickly come around to the question "Well then why *did* they want the war?" There is usually more than one single motive involved, but the motives are not terribly hard to find.

Unlike many soldiers who have been lied to, most of the key war deciders, the masters of war who determine whether or not wars happen, do not in any sense have noble motives for what they do. Though noble motives can be found in the reasoning of some of those involved, even in some of those at the highest levels of decision making, it is very doubtful that such noble intentions alone would ever generate wars.

Economic and imperial motives have been offered by presidents and Congress members for most major U.S. wars, but they have not been endlessly hyped and dramatized as have other alleged motivations. War with Japan was largely about the economic value of Asia, but fending off the evil Japanese emperor made a better poster. The Project for the New American Century, a think tank pushing for war on Iraq, made its motives clear a dozen years before it got its war—motives that included U.S. military dominance of the globe with more and larger bases in key regions of "American interest." That goal was not repeated as often or as shrilly as "WMD," "terrorism," "evildoer," or "spreading democracy."

The most important motivations for wars are the least talked about, and the least important or completely fraudulent motivations are the most discussed. The important motivations, the things the war masters mostly discuss in private, include electoral calculations, control of natural resources, intimidation of other countries, domination of geographic regions, financial profits for friends and campaign funders, the opening up of consumer markets, and prospects for testing new weapons.

If politicians were honest, electoral calculations would deserve to be openly discussed and would constitute no ground for shame or secrecy. Elected officials ought to do what will get them reelected, within the structure of laws that have been democratically established. But our conception of democracy has become so twisted that reelection as a motivation for action is hidden away alongside profiteering. This is true for all areas of government work; the election process is so corrupt that the public is viewed as yet another corrupting influence. When it comes to war, this sense is heightened by politicians' awareness that wars are marketed with lies.

In Their Own Words

The Project for the New American Century (PNAC) was a think tank from 1997 to 2006 in Washington (later revived in 2009). Seventeen members of PNAC served in high positions in the George W. Bush administration, including vice president, chief of staff to the vice president, special assistant to the president, deputy secretary of "defense," ambassador to Afghanistan and Iraq, deputy secretary of state, and under secretary of state.

One individual who was part of PNAC and later of the Bush administration, Richard Perle, together with another Bush bureaucrat-to-be Douglas Feith, had worked for Israeli Likud leader Benjamin Netanyahu in 1996 and produced a paper called *A Clean Break: A New Strategy for Securing the Realm*. The realm was Israel, and the strategy advocated was hyper-militarized nationalism and the violent removal of regional foreign leaders, including Saddam Hussein.

In 1998, PNAC published an open letter to President Bill Clinton urging him to adopt the goal of regime change for Iraq, which he did. That letter included this: "[I]f Saddam does acquire the capability to deliver weapons of mass destruction, as he is almost certain to do if we continue along the present course, the safety of American troops in the region, of our friends and allies like Israel and the moderate Arab states, and a significant portion of the world's supply of oil will all be put at hazard."[1]

In 2000, PNAC published a paper titled *Rebuilding America's Defenses*. The goals set forth in this paper fit much more coherently with the actual behavior of the masters of war than do any notions of "spreading democracy" or "standing up to tyranny." When Iraq attacks Iran the United States helps out. When it attacks Kuwait the United States steps in. When it does nothing the United States bombs it. This behavior makes no sense in terms of the fictional stories we're told, but makes perfect sense in terms of these goals from PNAC:

- maintaining U.S. preeminence.
- precluding the rise of a great power rival.

- shaping the international security order in line with American principles and interests.

PNAC determined that the U.S. government would need to "fight and decisively win multiple, simultaneous major theater wars" and "perform the 'constabulary' duties associated with shaping the security environment in critical regions." In the same 2000 paper, PNAC wrote:

> While the unresolved conflict with Iraq provides the immediate justification, the need for a substantial American force presence in the Gulf transcends the issue of the regime of Saddam Hussein. The placement of U.S. bases has yet to reflect these realities.... From an American perspective, the value of such bases would endure even should Saddam pass from the scene. Over the long term, Iran may well prove as large a threat to U.S. interests in the Gulf as Iraq has. And even should U.S.-Iranian relations improve, retaining forward-based forces in the region would still be an essential element in U.S. security strategy....[2]

These papers were published and widely available years before the invasion of Iraq, and yet to suggest that U.S. forces would try to stay and build permanent bases in Iraq even after killing Saddam Hussein was scandalous in the halls of Congress or the corporate media. To suggest that the war on Iraq had anything to do with imperial U.S. bases or oil or Israel, much less that Hussein did not as yet have weapons, was heretical. Even worse was to suggest that those bases might be used to launch attacks on other countries, in line with PNAC's goal of "maintaining U.S. preeminence." And yet supreme allied commander of NATO for Europe from 1997 to 2000 Wesley Clark claims that in 2001, Secretary of War Donald Rumsfeld put out a memo proposing to take over seven countries in five years: Iraq, Syria, Lebanon, Libya, Somalia, Sudan, and Iran.

The basic outline of this plan was confirmed by none other than former British prime minister Tony Blair, who in 2010 pinned it on former vice president Dick Cheney:

> Cheney wanted forcible "regime change" in all Middle Eastern countries that he considered hostile to U.S. interests, according to Blair. "He would have worked through the whole lot, Iraq, Syria, Iran, dealing with all their surrogates in the course of it—Hezbollah, Hamas, etc.," Blair wrote. "In other words, he [Cheney] thought the world had to be made anew, and that after 11 September, it had to be done by force and with urgency. So he was for hard, hard power. No ifs, no buts, no maybes."[3]

Crazy? Sure! But that's what succeeds in Washington. As each of those invasions happened, new excuses would have been made public for each. But the underlying reasons would have remained those quoted above.

Conspiracy Theories

Part of the ethos of "toughness" required of U.S. war makers has been a habit of thought that detects a major, global, and demonic enemy behind every shadow. For decades the enemy was the Soviet Union and the threat of global communism. But the Soviet Union never had the global military presence of the United States or the same interest in empire building. Its weapons and threats and aggressions were constantly exaggerated, and its presence was detected anytime a small, poor nation put up resistance to U.S. dominance. Koreans and Vietnamese, Africans and South Americans couldn't possibly have their own sovereign interests, it was assumed. If they were refusing our unsolicited guidance, somebody had to be putting them up to it.

A commission created by President Reagan called the Commission on Integrated Long-Term Strategy proposed more small wars in Asia, Africa, and Latin America. Concerns included "U.S. access to critical regions," "American credibility among allies and friends," "American self-confidence," and "America's ability to defend its interests in the most vital regions, such as the Persian Gulf, the Mediterranean, and the Western Pacific."

But what should the public be told our interests were being defended against? Why, an evil empire, of course! During the so-called Cold War, the communist conspiracy justification was so common that some very intelligent people believed U.S. war making couldn't go on without it. Here's Richard Barnet:

> The myth of monolithic Communism—that all activities of people everywhere who call themselves Communists or whom J. Edgar Hoover calls Communists are planned and controlled in the Kremlin—is essential to the ideology of the national security bureaucracy. Without it the President and his advisers would have a harder time identifying the enemy. They certainly could not find opponents worthy of the "defense" efforts of the mightiest military power in the history of the world.[4]

Ha! My apologies if you had any drink in your mouth and sprayed it on your clothing as you read that. As if the wars will not go on! As if the wars were not the reason for the communist threat, rather than the other way around! Writing in 1992, John Quigley could see this clearly:

> [T]he political reform that swept eastern Europe in 1989-90 left the cold war on the ash heap of history. Even so, our military interventions did not end. In 1989, we intervened to support a government in the

Philippines and to overthrow one in Panama. In 1990, we sent a massive force to the Persian Gulf.... The continuation of military interventions is not, however, surprising, because the aim all along...has been less to fight communism than to maintain our own control.[5]

The threat of the Soviet Union or communism was, within a dozen years replaced with the threat of al Qaeda or terrorism. Wars against an empire and an ideology would become wars against a small terrorist group and a tactic. The change had some advantages. While the Soviet Union could publicly collapse, a secretive and widely dispersed collection of terrorist cells to which we could apply the name al Qaeda could never be proven to have gone away. An ideology could fall out of favor, but anywhere the U.S. government fought wars or imposed unwelcome control, people would fight back, and their fighting would be "terrorism" because it was directed against the U.S. government. This was a new justification for never-ending war. But the motivation was the war, not the crusade to eliminate terrorism, a crusade which would, of course, produce more terrorism.

The motivation was U.S. control over areas of "vital interest," namely profitable natural resources and markets and strategic positions for military bases from which to extend power over yet more resources and markets, and from which to deny any imaginable "rivals" anything resembling "American self-confidence." This is, of course, aided and abetted by the motivations of those who profit financially from the war making itself.

For Money and Markets

Economic motivations for wars are not exactly news. The most famous lines from Smedley Butler are not actually in his book *War Is A Racket*, but in a 1935 issue of the socialist newspaper *Common Sense*, where he wrote:

> I spent 33 years and four months in active military service and during that period I spent most of my time as a high class muscle man for Big Business, for Wall Street and the bankers. In short, I was a racketeer, a gangster for capitalism. I helped make Mexico and especially Tampico safe for American oil interests in 1914. I helped make Haiti and Cuba a decent place for the National City Bank boys to collect revenues in. I helped in the raping of half a dozen Central American republics for the benefit of Wall Street. I helped purify Nicaragua for the International Banking House of Brown Brothers in 1902-1912. I brought light to the Dominican Republic for the American sugar interests in 1916. I helped make Honduras right for the American fruit companies in 1903. In China in 1927 I helped see to it that Standard Oil went on its way unmolested. Looking back on it, I might have given Al Capone a few hints. The

best he could do was to operate his racket in three districts. I operated on three continents.[6]

This explanation of motives for wars was not usually presented in Butler's colorful language, but it wasn't secret either. In fact, war propagandists have long argued for portraying wars as beneficial to big business whether or not they actually would be:

> For the sake of the business men the war must appear as a profitable enterprise. L.G. Chiozza, Money, M.P., published a statement in the London *Daily Chronicle* for August 10th, 1914, which is a pattern for this sort of thing. He wrote: "Our chief competitor both in Europe and outside it will be unable to trade, and at the conclusion of the War the unmistakable antagonism which German aggression is everywhere arousing will help us to keep the trade and shipping we will win from her."[7]

To Carl von Clausewitz, who died in 1831, war was "a continuation of political relations, a carrying out of the same by other means."[8] That sounds about right, as long as we understand that war makers often have a preference for the means of war even when other means might achieve the same results. In an August 31, 2010, Oval Office speech praising the wars in Iraq and Afghanistan, President Obama exclaimed: "New markets for our goods stretch from Asia to the Americas!" In 1963, John Quigley, not yet an analyst of war lies, was a marine assigned to lecture his unit on world affairs. When one of his students objected to the idea of fighting in Vietnam, Quigley "explained patiently that there was oil underneath Vietnam's continental shelf, that Vietnam's large population was an important market for our products, and that Vietnam commanded the sea route from the Middle East to the Far East."[9]

But let's start at the beginning. Before he became president, William McKinley said, "We want a foreign market for our surplus products." As president, he told Governor Robert LaFollette of Wisconsin he wanted "to attain U.S. supremacy in world markets." When Cuba was in danger of achieving its independence from Spain without assistance, McKinley persuaded Congress not to recognize the revolutionary government. After all, his goal was not Cuban independence, or Puerto Rican or Filipino independence. When he took over the Philippines, McKinley thought he was advancing the goal of "supremacy in world markets." When the people of the Philippines fought back, he called it an "insurrection." He described the war as a humanitarian mission for the Filipinos' own good.[10] McKinley pioneered by saying first what later presidents would say as a matter of routine when engaged in wars for resources or markets.

A month before the United States entered World War I, on March 5, 1917, the U.S. ambassador to Great Britain, Walter Hines Page, sent a cable to President Woodrow Wilson, reading in part:

> The pressure of this approaching crisis, I am certain, has gone beyond the ability of the Morgan financial agency for the British and French governments. The financial necessities of the Allies are too great and urgent for any private agency to handle, for every such agency has to encounter business rivalries and sectional antagonism. It is not improbable that the only way of maintaining our present preeminent trade position and averting a panic is by declaring war on Germany.[11]

When peace had been made with Germany ending World War I, President Wilson kept U.S. troops in Russia to fight the Soviets, despite earlier claims that U.S. troops were in Russia in order to defeat Germany and intercept supplies bound for Germany. Senator Hiram Johnson (P-CA) had famously said of the launching of the war: "The first casualty when war comes, is truth." He now had something to say about the failure to end the war when the peace treaty had been signed. Johnson denounced the ongoing fighting in Russia and quoted from the *Chicago Tribune* when it claimed that the goal was to help Europe collect Russia's debt.[12]

In 1935, considering the brewing financial interest in war with Japan, Norman Thomas pointed out that, at least from a national perspective, if not from the perspective of particular profiteers, it made no sense: "Our whole trade with Japan, China, and the Philippines in 1933 amounted to 525 million dollars or enough to have carried on the First World War for less than two and one-half days!"[13] Yes, he called it the "first" world war, because he saw what was coming.

One year before the attack on Pearl Harbor, a State Department memo on Japanese expansionism said not a word about independence for China. But it did say, "[O]ur general diplomatic and strategic position would be considerably weakened—by our loss of Chinese, Indian, and South Seas markets (and by our loss of much of the Japanese market for our goods, as Japan would become more and more self-sufficient) as well as by insurmountable restrictions upon our access to rubber, tin, jute, and other vital materials of the Asian and Oceanic regions."[14]

During World War II, Secretary of State Cordell Hull chaired a State Department subcommittee on political problems, which decided to handle perceived public fears that the United States would try to oversee and police the entire globe. The fears would be calmed by convincing the public that U.S. goals were to prevent another war and to provide "free access" to other people's resources. The words of the Atlantic Charter ("equal access") became "free access," meaning access for the United States, but not necessarily for anybody else.[15]

During the Cold War, the stated reasons for wars changed more than the real ones, as fighting communism gave cover for killing people to win markets, foreign labor, and resources. The U.S. government said it was fighting for democracy, but it backed dictators like Anastasio Somoza in Nicaragua, Fulgencio Batista in Cuba, and Rafael Trujillo in the Dominican Republic. The result was a bad name for the United States, and the empowering of leftist governments in reaction to U.S. interference. Senator Frank Church (D-ID) concluded that the U.S. government had "lost, or grievously impaired, the good name and reputation of the United States."[16]

Even if war makers did not have economic motives, it would still be impossible for corporations not to see economic gains as fortuitous byproducts of wars. As George McGovern and William Polk noted in 2006: "In 2002, just before the American invasion [of Iraq], only one of the world's ten most profitable corporations was in the oil and gas field; in 2005 four of the ten were. They were Exxon-Mobil and Chevron Texaco (American) and Shell and BP (British). The Iraq war doubled the price of crude; it would go up another 50 percent during the first months of 2006."[17]

For the Profits

Profiting from the waging of war has been a common part of U.S. wars since at least the Civil War. During the 2003 war on Iraq, Vice President Cheney directed massive no-bid contracts to a company, Halliburton, from which he was still receiving compensation, and profited from the same illegal war he defrauded the American public into launching. British prime minister Tony Blair was a little more circumspect in his war profiteering. The Stop the War Coalition kept up with him, however, writing in 2010:

> [Blair] earns £2 million a year for one day a month's work, from the US investment bank J P Morgan, who just happen to be making huge profits from financing "reconstruction" projects in Iraq. There's no end of gratitude for Blair's services to the oil industry, the Iraq invasion so clearly being aimed at controlling the world's second largest oil reserves. The Kuwaiti Royal Family paid him around a million to produce a report on Kuwait's future, and business deals though a consultancy he has set up to advise other countries in the Middle East are projected to earn around £5 million a year. Just in case he runs short, he has signed up with the South Korean oil firm UI Energy Corporation, which has extensive interests in Iraq and which some estimates say will eventually net him £20 million.[18]

For Money and Class

Another economic motivation for war that is often overlooked is the advantage war presents for a privileged class of people who are concerned that those denied a fair share of the nation's wealth might rebel. In 1916 in the United States, socialism was gaining in popularity, while any sign of class struggle in Europe had been silenced by World War I. Senator James Wadsworth (R-NY) proposed compulsory military training out of fear that "these people of ours shall be divided into classes."[19] The poverty draft may serve a similar function today. The American Revolution may have as well. World War II put a stop to depression-era radicalism that saw the Congress of Industrial Organizations (CIO) organizing black and white workers together.

World War II soldiers took their orders from Douglas MacArthur, Dwight Eisenhower, and George Patton, men who in 1932 had led the military's assault on the "Bonus Army," World War I veterans camped out in Washington, pleading to be paid the bonuses they'd been promised. This was a struggle that looked like a failure until World War II veterans were given the GI Bill of Rights.

McCarthyism led many struggling for the rights of working people to place militarism ahead of their own struggles for the latter half of the twentieth century. Barbara Ehrenreich wrote in 1997: "Americans credited the Gulf War with 'bringing us together.' Serbian and Croatian leaders solved their people's post-communist economic discontents with an orgy of nationalist violence."[20]

I was working for low-income community groups on September 11, 2001, and I recall how all talk of a better minimum wage or more affordable housing went away in Washington when the war trumpets sounded.

For Oil

A major motivation for wars is the seizing of control over other nations' resources. World War I made clear to war makers the importance of oil to fueling the wars themselves, as well as to fueling an industrial economy, and from that point forward a major motivation for war has been the conquest of nations that have supplies of oil. In 1940 the United States produced a majority (63 percent) of the world's oil, but in 1943 Secretary of the Interior Harold Ickes said, "If there should be a World War III, it would have to be fought with someone else's petroleum, because the United States wouldn't have it."[21]

President Jimmy Carter decreed in his last State of the Union address: "An attempt by any outside force to gain control of the Persian Gulf region will be regarded as an assault on the vital interests of the United States of

America, and such an assault will be repelled by any means necessary, including military force."[22]

Whether or not the first Gulf War was fought for oil, President George H. W. Bush said it was. He warned that Iraq would control too much of the world's oil if it invaded Saudi Arabia. The U.S. public denounced "blood for oil" and Bush quickly changed his tune. His son, attacking the same country a dozen years later, would allow his vice president to plan the war in secret meetings with oil executives, and would work hard to impose a "hydrocarbons law" on Iraq to benefit foreign oil companies, but he would not try to publicly sell the war as a mission to steal Iraqi oil. Or at least, that was not the primary focus of the sales pitch. There *was* a September 15, 2002, *Washington Post* headline that read "In Iraqi War Scenario, Oil Is Key Issue; U.S. Drillers Eye Huge Petroleum Pool."

Africom, the U.S. military's command structure for that seldom discussed chunk of land larger than all of North America, the African continent, was created by President George W. Bush in 2007. It had been envisioned a few years earlier, however, by the African Oil Policy Initiative Group (including representatives of the White House, Congress, and the oil corporations) as a structure "which could produce significant dividends in the protection of U.S. investments."[23] According to Gen. Charles Wald, deputy commander of U.S. forces in Europe: "A key mission for U.S. forces [in Africa] would be to insure that Nigeria's oilfields, which in the future could account for as much as 25 percent of all U.S. oil imports, are secure."[24] I wonder what he means by "secure." Somehow I doubt his concern is to boost the oilfields' self-confidence.

U.S. involvement in Yugoslavia in the 1990s was not unrelated to lead, zinc, cadmium, gold, and silver mines, cheap labor, and a deregulated market. In 1996, U.S. Secretary of Commerce Ron Brown died in a plane crash in Croatia along with top executives for Boeing, Bechtel, AT&T, Northwest Airlines, and several other corporations that were lining up government contracts for "reconstruction."[25] Enron, the famously corrupt corporation that would implode in 2001, was a part of so many such trips that it issued a press release to state that none of its people had been on this one. Enron gave $100,000 to the Democratic National Committee in 1997, six days before accompanying new commerce secretary Mickey Kantor to Bosnia and Croatia and signing a deal to build a $100 million power plant.[26] The annexation of Kosovo, Nicolas Davies writes in *Blood on Our Hands*:

> [D]id succeed in creating a small militarized buffer state between Yugoslavia and the projected route of the AMBO oil pipeline through Bulgaria, Macedonia, and Albania. This pipeline is being built, with U.S. government support, to provide the United States and Western

Europe with access to oil from the Caspian Sea.... Energy Secretary Bill Richardson explained the underlying strategy in 1998. "This is about America's energy security," he explained. "It's very important to us that both the pipeline map and the politics come out right."[27]

Longtime master of war Zbigniew Brzezinski spoke at a RAND Corporation forum on Afghanistan in a Senate caucus room in October 2009. His first statement was that "withdrawal from Afghanistan in the near future is a No-No." He offered no reasons why and suggested that his other statements would be more controversial.

During a subsequent question-and-answer period, I asked Brzezinski why such a statement should be considered uncontroversial when approximately half of Americans at that time opposed the occupation of Afghanistan. I asked how he would respond to the arguments of a U.S. diplomat who had just resigned in protest. Brzezinski responded that a lot of people are weak and don't know any better, and they should be ignored. Brzezinski said one of the main goals for the war on Afghanistan was to build a north-south gas pipeline to the Indian Ocean. This didn't noticeably shock anyone in the room.

In June 2010, a military-connected public relations firm persuaded the *New York Times* to run a front-page story proclaiming the discovery of vast mineral wealth in Afghanistan. Most of the claims were dubious, and those that were solid were not new. But the story had been planted at a time when senators and Congress members were beginning to turn ever so slightly against the war. Apparently the White House or the Pentagon believed the possibility of stealing Afghans' lithium would generate more war support in Congress.

For Empire

Fighting for territory, whatever rocks may lie beneath it, is a venerable motivation for war. Up through World War I and including it, empires battled each other for various territories and colonies. In the case of World War I there were Alsace-Lorraine, the Balkans, Africa, and the Middle East. Wars are also fought to assert influence rather than ownership in regions of the globe. The U.S. bombing of Yugoslavia in the 1990s may have involved a desire to keep Europe subordinate to the United States through NATO, an organization that was in danger of losing its reason to exist.[28] A war can also be fought for the purpose of weakening another nation without occupying it. National Security Advisor Brent Scowcroft said one purpose of the Gulf War was to leave Iraq with "no offensive capability."[29] The United States' success in this regard came in handy when it attacked Iraq again in 2003.

The *Economist* was concerned to keep the war on Afghanistan going in 2007: "Defeat would be a body blow not only to the Afghans, but to the NATO alliance."[30] The British Pakistani historian Tariq Ali commented:

> As ever, geopolitics prevails over Afghan interests in the calculus of the big powers. The basing agreement signed by the U.S. with its appointee in Kabul in May 2005 gives the Pentagon the right to maintain a massive military presence in Afghanistan in perpetuity, potentially including nuclear missiles. That Washington is not seeking permanent bases in this fraught and inhospitable terrain simply for the sake of "democratization and good governance" was made clear by NATO's Secretary-General Jaap de Hoop Scheffer at the Brookings Institution in February 2009: a permanent NATO presence in a country that borders the ex-Soviet republics, China, Iran, and Pakistan was too good to miss.[31]

For the Guns

Another motivation for wars is the justification they provide for maintaining a large military and producing more weapons. This may have been a key motivation for various U.S. military actions following the Cold War. Talk of a peace dividend faded as wars and interventions proliferated. Wars also appear to be fought on occasion in a manner that allows the use of particular weapons even though the strategy makes no sense as a means to victory. In 1964, for example, U.S. war makers decided to bomb North Vietnam even though their intelligence told them the resistance in the South was home grown.

Why? Possibly because bombs were what they had to work with and—for whatever other reasons—they wanted war. As we've seen above, nuclear bombs were dropped unnecessarily on Japan, the second one even more unnecessarily than the first. That second one was a different type of bomb, a plutonium bomb, and the Pentagon wanted to see it tested. World War II in Europe had drawn to a close with a completely unnecessary U.S. bombing of the French town of Royan—again despite the French being U.S. *allies*. This bombing was an early use of napalm on human beings, and the Pentagon apparently wanted to see what it would do.[32]

Machismo

But men cannot live by bread alone. Wars fought against a global menace (communism, terrorism, or another) are also wars fought to display one's prowess to bystanders, thus preventing the toppling of dominoes—a danger that can always be precipitated by a loss of "credibility." Remarkably, in war-mongerspeak "credibility" is a synonym for "bellicosity," not "honesty." Thus, nonviolent approaches to the world lack not only violence but also "credibility." There is something indecent about them. According to Richard Barnet, "Military officers in the [Lyndon] Johnson Administration consistently argued the risks of defeat and humiliation were greater than the risks of mining Haiphong, obliterating Hanoi, or bombing 'selected targets' in China."[33] They knew the world would be outraged by such actions, but somehow there is nothing *humiliating* about the prospect of being ostracized as murderous madmen. Only softness can be humiliating.

One of the most dramatic news stories that came out of Daniel Ellsberg's release of the Pentagon Papers was the news that 70 percent of the motivation of the people behind the war on Vietnam was "to save face." It wasn't to keep the communists out of Peoria or to teach the Vietnamese democracy or anything so grand. It was to protect the image, or perhaps the self-image, of the war makers themselves. Assistant Secretary of "Defense" John McNaughton's March 24, 1965, memo said U.S. goals in horrifically bombing the people of Vietnam were 70 percent "to avoid a humiliating U.S. defeat (to our reputation as guarantor)," 20 percent to keep territory out of Chinese hands, and 10 percent to permit people a "better, freer way of life."

McNaughton was concerned that other nations, wondering whether or not the United States would have the toughness to bomb the hell out of them too, might ask questions like: "Is the U.S. hobbled by restraints which might be relevant in future cases (fear of illegality, of U.N., of neutral reaction, of domestic pressures, of U.S. losses, of deploying U.S. ground forces in Asia, of war with China or Russia, of use of nuclear weapons, etc.)?"[34] That's a lot to prove you're not afraid of. But then the U.S. military did drop a lot of bombs on Vietnam trying to prove it, over seven million tons, as compared to the two million dropped in World War II. Ralph Stavins argues in *Washington Plans an Aggressive War* that John McNaughton and William Bundy understood that only withdrawal from Vietnam made sense, but backed escalation out of fear of seeming personally weak.[35]

In 1975, after defeat in Vietnam, the masters of war were even touchier about their machismo than usual. When the Khmer Rouge seized a U.S.-registered merchant vessel, President Gerald Ford demanded the release of the ship and its crew. The Khmer Rouge complied. But U.S. jet fighters went ahead and bombed Cambodia as a means of showing that, as the White House put it, the United States "still stood ready to meet force with force to protect its interests."[36]

Such displays of toughness are understood in Washington, to not only advance careers but also to enhance reputations in perpetuity. Presidents have long believed they could not be remembered as great presidents without wars. Theodore Roosevelt wrote to a friend in 1897, "In strict confidence...I should welcome almost any war, for I think this country needs one."[37]

According to novelist and author Gore Vidal, President John Kennedy told him that a president needed a war for greatness and that without the Civil War Abraham Lincoln would have been just another railroad lawyer. According to Mickey Herskowitz, who had worked with George W. Bush in 1999 on the latter's "autobiography," Bush wanted a war before becoming president.[38]

One disturbing thing about all this longing for war is that, while many of the motivations seem base, greedy, foolish, and despicable, some of them seem very personal and psychological. Perhaps it's "rational" to want world markets to buy U.S. products and to produce them more cheaply, but why must the United States have *supremacy* in world markets?" Why do we collectively need "self-confidence?" Isn't that something each individual person finds on their own? Why the emphasis on "preeminence"? Why is there so little talk in the back rooms about being protected from foreign threats and so much about dominating foreigners with our superiority and fearsome "credibility"? Is war about being respected?

When you combine the illogic of these motivations for war with the fact that wars so often fail on their own terms and yet are repeated time and time again, it becomes possible to doubt that the masters of war are always masters of their own consciousness. The United States did not conquer Korea or Vietnam or Iraq or Afghanistan. Historically, empires have not lasted. In a rational world we would skip the wars and go straight to the peace negotiations that follow them. Yet, so often, we do not.

During the war on Vietnam, the United States apparently began the air war, began the ground war, and proceeded with each step of escalation because the war planners couldn't think of anything else to do other than ending the war, and despite their high confidence that what they were doing would not work. After a lengthy period during which these expectations were fulfilled, they did what they could have done from the start and ended the war.

Are These People Crazy?

As we saw in Chapter 2, war makers debate what purpose the public should be told a war is serving. But they also debate what purpose to tell themselves a war is serving. According to Pentagon historians, by June 26, 1966, "the strategy was finished," for Vietnam, "and the debate from then on centered on how much force and to what end."[39] To what end? An excellent question.

This was an internal debate that assumed the war would go forward and that sought to settle on a reason why. Picking a reason to tell the public was a separate step beyond that one.

President George W. Bush at times suggested that the war on Iraq was revenge for Saddam Hussein's alleged (and likely fictitious) role in an assassination attempt against Bush's father,[40] and at other times Bush the lesser revealed that God had told him what to do.[41] After bombing Vietnam, Lyndon Johnson supposedly gloated, "I didn't just screw Ho Chi Minh, I cut his pecker off." Bill Clinton in 1993, according to George Stephanopoulos, remarked about Somalia: "We're not inflicting pain on these fuckers. When people kill us, they should be killed in greater numbers. I believe in killing people who try to hurt you. And I can't believe we're being pushed around by these two-bit pricks."[42] In May 2003, *New York Times* columnist Tom Friedman said on the *Charlie Rose Show* on PBS, that the purpose of the Iraq war was to send U.S. troops door-to-door in Iraq to say, "Suck on this."

Are these people serious, crazy, obsessed with their penises, or drugged? The answers seem to be: yes, yes, of course, and they've all drunk alcohol as needed. During the 1968 presidential campaign, Richard Nixon told his aide Bob Haldeman that he would force the Vietnamese to surrender by acting crazy (this while successfully running for president, whatever that may say of our electorate):"[The North Vietnamese will] believe any threat of force that Nixon makes, because it's Nixon.... I call it the Madman Theory, Bob. I want the North Vietnamese to believe I've reached the point where I might do *anything* to stop the war."[43]

One of Nixon's madman ideas was to drop nukes, but another was saturation bombing of Hanoi and Haiphong. Whether he'd been pretending to be crazy or not, Nixon actually did this, dropping 36 thousand tons on two cities in 12 days before agreeing to the same terms that had been offered prior to that fit of mass murder. If there was a point to this, it may have been the same one that later motivated "surge" escalations in Iraq and Afghanistan—the desire to look tough before leaving, thus transforming defeat into a vague claim of having "finished the job." But maybe there was no point.

In Chapter 5 we looked at the irrationality of violence outside of wars. Can the making of wars perhaps be equally irrational? Just as someone may rob a store because they need food but also be driven by an insane need to murder the clerk, can the masters of war fight for bases and oil wells but also be driven by what Dr. Martin Luther King, Jr. called the madness of militarism?

If Barbara Ehrenreich is right to trace the pre-history of war-lust to humans as the prey of larger animals, to hunting bands turning the tables on those predators, and to early religions of animal worship, animal sacrifice, and human sacrifice, war may lose some of its glory and pride but become more easily understandable. Even those who defend current practices of torture, even torture for the sake of extracting false grounds for war, cannot explain why the U.S. government tortures people *to death*.

Is this part of the spectacle of war that is older than our history? Are the warmongers proving to themselves the ultimate importance of their cause by mutilating their enemy? Are they reveling in fear and horror of the great forces of evil that were once leopards and are now Muslims, and glorying in the courage and sacrifice needed for the good to triumph? Is war, in fact, the current form of human "sacrifice," a word we still use without recalling its long history or pre-history? Were the first sacrifices simply humans lost to predators? Did their survivors comfort themselves by describing their family members as voluntary offerings? Have we been lying about life and death *that long*? And are war stories the current version of that same lie?

Konrad Lorenz noted a half century ago the psychological similarity between religious awe and the arousal experienced by an animal facing mortal danger. "What is known in German as the *heiliger Schauer*, or 'holy shiver' of awe, may be a 'vestige,' he suggested, of the widespread and entirely unconscious defensive response which causes an animal's fur to stand on end, thus increasing its apparent size." Lorenz believed that "to the humble seeker of biological truth there cannot be the slightest doubt that human militant enthusiasm evolved out of a communal defense response of our prehuman ancestors."[44] It was thrilling to band together and fight off a vicious lion or bear. The lions and bears are mostly gone, but the longing for that thrill is not. As we saw in Chapter 4, many human cultures do not tap into that longing and do not engage in war. Ours, thus far, is one that still does.

When faced with danger or even the sight of bloodshed, a person's heart and breathing increase, blood is drawn away from the skin and viscera, the pupils dilate, the bronchi distend, the liver releases glucose to the muscles, and blood clotting speeds up. This may be terrifying or exhilarating, and no doubt the culture of each person has an impact on how it is perceived. In some cultures such sensations are avoided at all cost. In ours, this phenomenon contributes to the motto of nightly news shows: "If it bleeds, it leads." And even more exciting than witnessing or facing danger is joining together as a group to confront and conquer it.

I don't doubt that crazed longings drive the masters of war, but once they have adopted the attitude of sociopaths, their statements sound cool and calculating. Harry Truman spoke in the Senate on June 23, 1941: "If we see that Germany is winning we ought to help Russia, and if Russia is winning we ought to help Germany, and that way let them kill as many as possible, although I don't want to see Hitler victorious under any circumstances."[45] Because that Hitler had no morals.

Spreading Democracy and Manure

The masters of war tell their lies to win public support, but keep their wars going for many years in the face of strong public opposition. In 1963 and 1964 as the war makers were trying to figure out how to escalate the war in Vietnam, the Sullivan Task Force analyzed the matter; war games conducted by the Joint Chiefs of Staff and known as the Sigma Games put the war makers through possible scenarios; and the United States Information Agency measured world and congressional opinion only to learn that the world would oppose an escalation but Congress would go along with anything. Yet, "conspicuously absent from these surveys was any study of American public opinion; the war makers were not interested in the views of the nation."[46]

It turned out, however, that the nation was interested in the views of the war makers. The result was President Lyndon Johnson's decision, similar to Polk and Truman's earlier decisions, not to run for reelection. And yet the war rolled on and escalated at the command of President Nixon.

Truman had a 54 percent approval rating until he went to war on Korea and then it dropped into the 20s. Lyndon Johnson's went from 74 to 42 percent. George W. Bush's approval rating fell from 90 percent to lower than Truman's. In the 2006 congressional elections, the voters gave a huge victory to the Democrats over the Republicans, and every media outlet in the country said that exit polls were finding that the number one motivation of voters was opposition to the war in Iraq. The Democrats took over the Congress and proceeded to immediately escalate that war. Similar elections in 2008 also failed to end the wars in Iraq and Afghanistan. Opinion polls in between elections likewise seem not to immediately influence the conduct of those making wars. By 2010 the war on Iraq had been scaled back, but the war on Afghanistan and the drone bombing of Pakistan escalated.

For decades, the U.S. public has largely gone along with wars if they are short. If they drag on, they may stay popular, like World War II, or become unpopular, like Korea and Vietnam, depending on whether the public believes the government's arguments for why the war is necessary. Most wars, including the 1990 Persian Gulf War, have been kept short enough that the public didn't mind the ludicrous rationales.

The wars in Afghanistan and Iraq that began in 2001 and 2003, in contrast, dragged on for several years without any plausible justification. The public turned against these wars, but elected officials appeared not to care. Both President George W. Bush and Congress hit all-time record lows in presidential and congressional approval ratings. Barack Obama's 2008 presidential campaign used the theme of "Change," as did most congressional campaigns in 2008 and 2010. Any actual change, however, was fairly superficial.

When they think it will work, even temporarily, war makers will simply lie and tell the public that a war isn't happening at all. The United States arms other nations and assists in their wars. U.S. funding, weapons, and/or troops have taken part in wars in places like Indonesia, Angola, Cambodia, Nicaragua, and El Salvador, while U.S. presidents claimed otherwise or just said nothing. Records released in 2000 revealed that unbeknownst to the American public, the United States had begun massive bombing of Cambodia in 1965, not 1970, dropping 2.76 million tons between 1965 and 1973, and contributing to the rise of the Khmer Rouge.[47] When President Reagan fueled war in Nicaragua, despite Congress having forbidden it, a scandal played out in 1986 that acquired the name "Iran-Contra," because Reagan was illegally selling weapons to Iran in order to fund the Nicaraguan war. The public was fairly forgiving, and the Congress and the media were overwhelmingly forgiving, of the crimes uncovered.

So Many Secrets

The masters of war fear, above all, two things: transparency and peace. They do not want the public to find out what they are doing or why. And they do not want peace to get in the way of their doing it.

Richard Nixon believed the "most dangerous man in America" was Daniel Ellsberg, the man who had leaked the Pentagon Papers and exposed decades of war lies by Eisenhower, Kennedy, and Johnson. When Ambassador Joseph Wilson, in 2003, published a column in the *New York Times* debunking some of the Iraq war lies, the Bush White House retaliated by exposing the identity of his wife as an undercover agent, placing her life at risk. In 2010, President Obama's Justice Department charged Private First Class Bradley Manning (later Chelsea Manning) with crimes carrying a maximum penalty of 52 years in prison. Manning was charged with leaking to the public a video of an apparent murder of civilians by a U.S. helicopter crew in Iraq and information on the planning of the war on Afghanistan.

Peace offers have been rejected and hushed up prior to or during World War II, Korea, Afghanistan, Iraq, and many other wars. In Vietnam, peace settlements were proposed by the Vietnamese, the Soviets, and the French, but rejected and sabotaged by the United States. The last thing you want when trying to start or continue a war—and when trying to sell it as a reluctant action of last resort—is for word to leak out that the other side is proposing peace talks.

Make Sure Americans Die

If you can start a war and claim aggression from the other side, nobody will hear their cries for peace. But you will have to make sure that some Americans die. Then a war can be not only begun but also continued indefinitely so that those already killed shall not have died in vain. President Polk knew this in the case of Mexico. So did those war propagandists who "remembered the *Maine*." As Richard Barnet explains, in the context of Vietnam: "The sacrifice of American lives is a crucial step in the ritual of commitment. Thus William P. Bundy stressed in working papers the importance of 'spilling American blood' not only to whip up the public to support a war that could touch their emotions in no other way, but also to trap the President."[48]

Who was William P. Bundy? He was in the CIA and became an advisor to Presidents Kennedy and Johnson. He was exactly the kind of bureaucrat who succeeds in Washington. In fact he was considered a "dove" by the standards of those in power, people like his brother McGeorge Bundy, national security advisor to Kennedy and Johnson, or William Bundy's father-in-law Dean Acheson, secretary of state for Truman. The war makers do what they do, because only aggressive war makers advance through the ranks and keep their jobs as high-level advisors in the U.S. government. While resisting militarism is a good way to derail your career, no one seems to have ever heard of a DC bureaucrat being sidelined for excessive warmongering. Pro-war counsel may be rejected, but is always considered respectable and important.

One can become known as soft without recommending any course of action whatsoever. All that is required is that one question information that is being used to justify hard policies. We saw this in the run-up to the 2003 invasion of Iraq, as bureaucrats learned that information disproving claims about weapons in Iraq was not welcome and would not advance their careers. Similarly, State Department employees in the late 1940s who knew anything about China and dared to point out Mao's popularity (not to approve it, just to recognize it) were branded as disloyal and their careers were derailed.[49] War makers find it easier to lie if they arrange to be lied to themselves.

Catapulting the Propaganda

The dishonesty of war makers can be found in the contrast between what they say publicly and what they actually do, including what they say in private. But it is also evident in the very nature of their public statements, which are designed to manipulate emotions.

The Institute for Propaganda Analysis, which existed from 1937 to 1942, identified seven useful techniques for tricking people into doing what you want them to do:

1. Name-calling (an example would be "terrorist").
2. Glittering generalities (if you say you're spreading democracy and then explain that you're using bombs, people will have already agreed with you before they hear about the bombs).
3. Transfer (if you tell people that God or their nation or science approves, they may want to as well).
4. Testimonial (putting a statement in the mouth of a respected authority).
5. Plain folks (think millionaire politicians chopping wood or calling their gargantuan house a "ranch").
6. Card stacking (slanting the evidence).
7. Bandwagon (everyone else is doing it, don't be left out).[50]

There are many more. Prominent among them is simply the use of fear: *We can go to war or die horrible deaths at the hands of fiendish beasts, but it's your choice, entirely up to you, no pressure, except that our executioners will be here by next week if you don't hurry it up!*

The technique of testimonial is used in combination with fear. Great authorities should be deferred to, not just because it's easier, but also because they will save you from danger if you obey them, and you can start obeying them by believing them. Think of the people in the Milgram experiment willing to administer electric shocks to what they believed was the point of murder if an authority figure told them to do so. Think of George W. Bush's popularity shooting from 55 percent to 90 percent approval purely because he was the nation's president when airplanes flew into buildings in 2001 and he let out a war whoop or two. The mayor of New York City at the time, Rudy Giuliani, went through a similar transformation. Bush (and Obama) didn't include 9/11 in their war speeches for no reason.

Those who constitute the real driving force behind a war know exactly what they are lying about and why. Members of a committee like the White House Iraq Group, whose task was to market a war on Iraq to the public, carefully choose the most effective lies and set them on their course through the welcoming ears and mouths of politicians and pundits. Machiavelli told tyrants that they must lie to be great, and would-be great ones have been heeding his advice for centuries.

Arthur Bullard, a liberal reporter who urged Woodrow Wilson, to employ dishonesty rather than censorship, argued that "Truth and falsehood are arbitrary terms.... There is nothing in experience to tell us that one is always preferable to the other.... There are lifeless truths and vital lies.... The force of an idea lies in its inspirational value. It matters very little whether it is true or false."[51]

A Senate committee report in 1954 advised: "We are facing an implacable enemy whose avowed objective is world domination by whatever means and at whatever cost. There are no rules in such a game. Hitherto acceptable norms of human conduct do not apply."[52]

Philosophy professor Leo Strauss, an influence on neoconservatives associated with PNAC, backed the idea of the "noble lie," of the need for a wise elite to lie to the general public for its own good. The trouble with such theories is that, in practice, when we find out we've been lied to we're not just irrationally more angry about the lies than grateful for all the good they've done us, we're justifiably outraged because they've never done us any good.

7

WARS ARE NOT PROLONGED
FOR THE GOOD OF SOLDIERS

We learn a lot about the real motives for wars when whistleblowers leak the minutes of secret meetings, or when congressional committees publish the records of hearings decades later. War planners write books. They make movies. They face investigations. Eventually the beans tend to get spilled. But I have never ever, not even once, heard of a private meeting in which top war makers discussed the need to keep a war going in order to benefit the soldiers fighting in it.

The reason this is remarkable is that you almost never hear a war planner speak *in public* about the reasons for keeping a war going without claiming that it must be done for the troops, to support the troops, in order not to let the troops down, or so that those troops already dead will not have died in vain. Of course, if they died in an illegal, immoral, destructive action, or simply a hopeless war that must be lost sooner or later, it's unclear how piling on more corpses will honor their memories. But this is not about logic.

The idea is that the men and women risking their lives, supposedly on our behalf, should always have our support—even if we view what they're doing as mass murder. Peace activists, in contrast to war planners, say the very same thing about this in private that they say in public: we want to support those troops by not giving them illegal orders, not coercing them to commit atrocities, not sending them away from their families to risk their lives and bodies and mental well-being.

War makers' private discussions about whether and why to keep a war going deal with all the motives discussed in Chapter 6. They only touch on the topic of troops when considering how many of them there are or how long their contracts can be extended before they start killing their commanders. In public, it's a very different story, one often told with smartly uniformed troops positioned as a backdrop. The wars are all about the troops and in fact must be extended for the benefit of the troops. Anything else would offend and disappoint the troops who have devoted themselves to the war.

Our wars employ more contractors and mercenaries now than troops. When mercenaries are killed and their bodies publicly displayed, the U.S. military will gladly destroy a city in retaliation, as in Fallujah, Iraq. But war propagandists never mention the contractors or the mercenaries. It's always the troops, the ones doing the killing, and the ones drawn from the general population of just plain folks, even though the troops are being paid, just like the mercenaries, only less.

Why All the Troop Talk?

The purpose of making a war be about the people (or some of the people) fighting it is to maneuver the public into believing that the only way to oppose the war would be to sign on as an enemy of the young men and women fighting in it on our nation's side. Of course, this makes no sense at all. The war has some purpose or purposes other than indulging (or, more accurately, abusing) the troops. When people oppose a war, they do not do so by taking the position of the opposite side. They oppose the war in its entirety. But illogic never slowed down a war maker. "There will be some nervous Nellies," said Lyndon Johnson on May 17, 1966, "and some who will become frustrated and bothered and break ranks under the strain. And some will turn on their leaders and on their country and on our fighting men."[1]

Try to follow the logic: Troops are brave. Troops are the war. Therefore the war is brave. Therefore anyone opposing the war is cowardly and weak, a nervous Nelly. Anyone opposing a war is a bad troop who has turned against his or her commander-in-chief, country, and the other troops—the good troops. Never mind if the war is destroying the country, bankrupting the economy, endangering us all, and eating out the nation's soul. The war *is* the country, the whole country has a wartime leader, and the whole country must obey rather than think. After all, this is a war to spread *democracy*. On August 31, 2010, President Obama said in an Oval Office speech: "This afternoon, I spoke to former President George W. Bush. It's well known that he and I disagreed about the war [on Iraq] from its outset. Yet no one can doubt President Bush's support for our troops, or his love of country and commitment to our security."

What can this mean? Never mind that Obama voted repeatedly to fund the war as a senator and insisted on keeping it going as president. Never mind that, in this same speech, he embraced a whole series of lies that had launched and prolonged the war, and then pivoted to use those same lies to support an escalated war in Afghanistan. Let's suppose that Obama really did "disagree about the war" with Bush. He must have thought the war was bad for our country and our security and the troops. If he'd thought the war was good for those things, he'd have had to agree with Bush. So, at best, Obama is saying that despite his love (never respect or concern; with troops it's always *love*) for the troops and so forth, Bush did them and the rest of us wrong unintentionally. The war was the biggest accidental blunder of the century. But no big deal. These things happen.

Because Obama's speech was about war, he spent a big chunk of it, as is required, praising the troops: "[O]ur troops fought block by block to help Iraq seize the chance for a better future. They shifted tactics to protect the Iraqi people," etc. True humanitarians. And it will no doubt be for their benefit that the war on Afghanistan and other wars drag on in the future, if we don't put an end to the madness of militarism.

You're for the War or Against the Troops

The media watch group Fairness and Accuracy in Reporting (FAIR) noticed in March, 2003, as the war on Iraq began, that media outlets were doing something peculiar to the English language. The Associated Press and other outlets were using "pro-war" and "pro-troops" interchangeably. We were being offered the choices of being pro-troop or antiwar, with the latter apparently necessitating that we also be anti-troop. The day before the U.S. attack on Baghdad, FAIR noted, the Associated Press published this headline: "Anti-War, Pro-Troops Rallies Take to Streets as War Rages."

Another story (3/22/03), about pro- and anti-war activities, was labeled *Weekend Brings More Demonstrations—Opposing War, Supporting Troops.* The clear implication is that those who call for an end to the invasion of Iraq are opposed to U.S. troops, as in the story *Protesters Rally Against War; Others Support Troops* (3/24/03).[2]

This media practice does not outright call one side of a debate "anti-troop," but neither does it call one side "pro-war," despite that side's clear purpose of promoting war. Just as those defending the right to abortion don't want to be called pro-abortion, war supporters don't want to be called pro-war. War is an unavoidable necessity, they think, and a means toward achieving peace; our role in it is to cheer for the troops. But war proponents are not defending their nation's right to wage war if needed, which would be a better analogy with abortion rights. They're cheering for a specific war, and that specific war is always a fraudulent and criminal enterprise. Those two facts should disqualify war proponents from hiding behind the label "pro-troops" and using it to slander war opponents, although if they'd like to start using the label "anti-peace" I wouldn't protest.

One of the most inconvenient pieces of information for campaigns to prolong war to "support the troops" is anything telling us what the troops currently engaged in the war actually think of it. What if we were to "support the troops" by doing what the troops wanted? That's a very dangerous idea to start floating around. Troops are not supposed to have thoughts. They're supposed to obey orders. So supporting what they're doing actually means supporting what the president or the generals have ordered them to do. Taking too much interest in what the troops themselves actually think could be very risky for the future stability of this rhetorical house of cards.

A U.S. pollster, as we noted in Chapter 5, was able to poll U.S. troops in Iraq in 2006, and found that 72 percent of those polled wanted the war to be ended in 2006. For those in the Army, 70 percent wanted that 2006 ending date, but in the Marines only 58 percent did. In the reserves and National Guard, however, the numbers were 89 and 82 percent, respectively.[3] Since wars are fought to "support the troops" shouldn't the war have ended? And shouldn't the troops, revealed in the poll to be badly misinformed, have been told the available facts about what the war was and was not for?

Of course not. Their role was to obey orders, and if lying to them helped get them to obey orders, then that was best for all of us. We never said we trusted or respected them, only that we loved them. Perhaps it would be more accurate for people to say that they love the fact that it is the troops out there willing to stupidly kill and die for someone else's greed or power mania, and not the rest of us. Better you than me. Love ya! Ciao!

The funny thing about our love for the troops is how little the troops get out of it. They don't get their wishes regarding military policy. They don't even get armor that would protect them in war as long as there are war-profiteering CEOs that need the money more desperately. And they don't even sign meaningful contracts with the government that have terms the troops can enforce. When a troop's time in war is done, if the military wants him or her to stay longer, it "stop losses" them and sends them right back into a war, regardless of the terms in the contract. And—this will come as a surprise to anyone who watches congressional debates over war funding—whenever our representatives vote another hundred billion dollars to "fund the troops," the troops don't get the money. Usually the money is about a million dollars per troop. If the government actually offered the troops their share of that supportive funding and gave them the option of contributing their shares to the war effort and staying in the fight, if they so chose, do you think the armed forces might experience a wee little reduction in numbers?

Just Send More of Them

The fact is that the last thing war makers care about—albeit the first thing they talk about—is the troops. There's not a politician alive in the United States who hasn't uttered the phrase "support the troops." Some push the idea to the point of requiring the slaughter of more troops, and the use of troops in the slaughter of more non-Americans. When the parents and loved ones of those troops already dead denounce the war that has harmed them and call for its termination, war supporters accuse them of failing to honor the memory of their dead. If those already dead died for a good cause, then it ought to be more persuasive to simply mention that good cause. Yet, when Cindy Sheehan asked George W. Bush what good cause her son had died for, neither Bush nor anyone else was ever able to provide an answer. Instead, all we heard was the need for more to die *because some already had.*

Even more frequently we're told that a war must be continued simply because there are troops currently fighting in it. This sounds sadistic at first. We know that war damages many of its participants horribly. Does it really make sense to continue a war *because* there are soldiers in the war? Shouldn't there be some other reason? And yet that's what happens. Wars are continued when Congress funds them. And even many professed "opponents" of wars in Congress fund them to "support the troops," thus prolonging what they claim to oppose. In 1968, the chairman of the House Appropriations Committee, George Mahon (D-TX) said voting to fund the war on Vietnam was no measure of whether or not one supported the war on Vietnam. Such a vote, he said, "does not involve a test as to one's basic views with respect to the war in Vietnam. The question here is that they are there, regardless of our views otherwise."[4]

Now, the "they are there, regardless" argument—which seems to never grow stale—is an odd one to say the least, since if the war were not funded the troops would have to be brought home, and then they would not be there. To get out of this logical cul-de-sac, war supporters invent scenarios in which Congress stops funding wars, but the wars continue, only this time without ammunition or other supplies. Or, in another variation, by defunding a war Congress denies the Pentagon the funding to withdraw the troops, and they are simply left behind in whatever little country they've been terrorizing.

Nothing resembling these scenarios has happened in the real world. The cost of shipping troops and equipment home or to the nearest imperial outpost is negligible to the Pentagon, which routinely "misplaces" greater sums of cash. But, purely to get around this nonsense, antiwar Congress members including Barbara Lee (D-CA), during the wars on Iraq and Afghanistan, began introducing bills to defund the war and to provide new funds purely for the withdrawal. War supporters nonetheless denounced such proposals as...guess what? Failures to support the troops.

The chairman of the house appropriations committee from 2007 through 2010 was David Obey (D-WI). When the mother of a soldier being sent to Iraq for the third time and being denied needed medical care asked him to stop funding the war in 2007 with a "supplemental" spending bill, Congressman Obey screamed at her, saying among other things:

> We're trying to use the supplemental to end the war, but you can't end the war by going against the supplemental. It's time these idiot liberals understand that. There's a big difference between funding the troops and ending the war. I'm not gonna deny body armor. I'm not gonna deny funding for veterans' hospitals, defense hospitals, so you can help people with medical problems, that's what you're gonna do if you're going against the bill.[5]

Congress had funded the war on Iraq for years without providing troops with adequate body armor. But funding for body armor was now in a bill to prolong the war. And funding for veterans' care, which could have been provided in a separate bill, was packaged into this one. Why? Precisely so that people like Obey could more easily claim that the war funding was for the benefit of the troops. Of course it's still a transparent reversal of the facts to say that you can't end the war by ceasing to fund it. And if the troops came home, they wouldn't need body armor. But Obey had completely internalized the crazy propaganda of war promotion. He seemed to actually believe that the only way to end a war was to pass a bill to fund it but to include in the bill some minor and rhetorical antiwar gestures.

On July 27, 2010, having failed for another three-and-a-half years to end the wars by funding them, Obey brought to the House floor a bill to fund an escalation of the war on Afghanistan, specifically to send 30,000 more troops plus corresponding contractors into that hell. Obey announced that his conscience was telling him to vote no on the bill because it was a bill that would just help recruit people who want to attack Americans. On the other hand, Obey said, it was his duty as committee chair (apparently a higher duty than the one to his conscience) to bring the bill to the floor. Even though it would encourage attacks on Americans? *Isn't that treason?*

Obey proceeded to speak against the bill he was bringing to the floor. Knowing it would safely pass, he voted against it. One could imagine, with a few more years of awakening, David Obey reaching the point of actually trying to stop funding a war he "opposes," except that Obey had already announced his plan to retire at the end of 2010. He ended his career in Congress on that high note of hypocrisy because war propaganda, most of it about troops, has persuaded legislators that they can be "critics" and "opponents" of a war while funding it.

You Can Check Out Anytime You Like, But You Can Never Leave

You might imagine from the efforts Congress goes to in avoiding and recklessly rushing through debates on whether to initially launch wars that such decisions are of minor importance, that a war can be easily ended at any point once it has begun. But the logic of continuing wars as long as there are soldiers involved in them means that wars can never be ended, at least not until the commander-in-chief sees fit. This is not brand new, and goes back as many war lies do, at least as far as the first U.S. invasion of the Philippines. The editors of *Harpers Weekly* opposed that invasion. "Echoing the president, however, they concluded that once the country was at war, everyone must pull together to support the troops."[6]

This truly bizarre idea has penetrated U.S. thinking so deeply, in fact, that even liberal commentators have fantasized that they've seen it enshrined in the U.S. Constitution. Here's Ralph Stavins, speaking of the war on Vietnam: "Once the blood of a single American soldier had been spilled, the President would assume the role of Commander in Chief and would be obliged to discharge his constitutional duty to protect the troops in the field. This obligation made it unlikely that troops would be removed and far more likely that additional troops would be sent over."[7] The trouble with this is not just that the clearest way to protect troops is to bring them home, but also that the president's constitutional obligation to protect the troops in the field doesn't exist in the Constitution.

"Supporting the troops" is often expanded from meaning that we need to keep troops in a war longer to meaning that we also need to communicate to them our appreciation for the war, even if we oppose it. This could mean anything from not prosecuting atrocities, pretending the atrocities are extreme exceptions, pretending the war has succeeded or met some of its goals or that it had different goals more easily met, or sending letters and gifts to troops and thanking them for their "service."

"When the war begins, if the war begins," said John Kerry (D-MA) just before the 2003 invasion of Iraq, "I support the troops and I support the United States of America winning as rapidly as possible. When the troops are in the field and fighting—if they're in the field and fighting—remembering what it's like to be those troops—I think they need a unified America that is prepared to win." Kerry's fellow presidential candidate Howard Dean called Bush's foreign policy "ghastly" and "appalling" and loudly, if inconsistently, opposed attacking Iraq. But he stressed that if Bush started a war, "Of course I'll support the troops."[8] I'm sure troops would like to believe everyone back home supports what they're doing, but don't they have other things to worry about during a war? And wouldn't some of them like to know that some of us are checking up on whether they've been sent to risk their lives for a good reason or not? Wouldn't they feel more secure in their mission, knowing that a check on recklessly turning them into cannon fodder was alive and active?

In August 2010 I compiled a list of about 100 congressional challengers, from every political party, who swore to me that they would not vote a dime for the wars in Iraq or Afghanistan. One Independent Green Party candidate in Virginia refused to sign on, pointing out to me that if he did, his Republican opponent would accuse him of not supporting the troops. I pointed out to him that a majority of the voters in his district wanted the war ended and that he could accuse war supporters of subjecting troops to illegal orders and endangering their lives for no good reason, in fact for a bad reason. While this candidate still did not sign on, preferring to represent his opponent rather than the people of his district, he expressed surprise and approval for what I told him, which was apparently news to him.

That's typical. Atypical are congress members like Alan Grayson (D-FL). In 2010 he was perhaps the most vocal opponent of the war on Afghanistan, urging the public to lobby his colleagues to vote against funding bills. This led to predictable attacks from his opponents in the coming election—as well as more corporate spending against him than any other candidate. On August 17, 2010, Grayson sent out this email:

> I've been introducing you to my opponents. On Friday, it was Dan Fanelli, the racist. Yesterday, it was Bruce O'Donoghue, the tax cheat. And today, it's Kurt Kelly, the warmonger.
>
> In Congress, I am one of the most outspoken opponents of the wars in Iraq and Afghanistan. Before I was elected, I spent years prosecuting war profiteers. So I know what I'm talking about.
>
> Unlike chickenhawk Kurt Kelly. On Fox News (where else?) Kelly said this about me: "He put our soldiers, and our men and women in the military in harm's way, and maybe he wants them to die."
>
> Yes, Kurt. I do want them to die: of old age, at home in bed, surrounded by their loved ones, after enjoying many Thanksgiving turkeys between now and then. And you want them to die: in a scorching desert, 8000 miles from home, alone, screaming for help, with a leg blown off and their guts hanging out of their stomachs, bleeding to death.

Grayson has a point. Those who fail to "support the troops" can't very well be accused of putting the troops at risk, since "supporting the troops" consists precisely of leaving the troops at risk. But warmongers like to believe that opposing a war is the equivalent of siding with an enemy.

Only the Enemy Opposes a War

Imagine an atheist's position on a debate over whether God is a holy trinity or just a single being. If the atheist opposes the holy trinity position, he's quickly accused of backing the single being, and vice versa, by those who can't wrap their minds around the possibility of honestly not wanting to take one side or the other. To those for whom opposition to a war's existence is incomprehensible, failure to cheer for the red, white, and blue must equate with cheering for some other flag. And to those marketing the war to these people, waving an American flag is enough to nudge them to this conclusion.

In 1990, Chris Wallace of ABC News asked the former commander of the war on Vietnam, William Westmoreland, the following question: "It's become almost a truism by now that you didn't lose the Vietnam War so much in the jungles there as you did in the streets in the United States. How worried should the president and the Pentagon be now about this new peace movement?"[9] With that kind of question, who needs answers? The war has already been sold before you open your mouth.

When Congressmen Jim McDermott (D-WA) and David Bonior (D-MI) questioned the Iraq war lies in 2002, *Washington Post* columnist George Will wrote, "Saddam Hussein finds American collaborators among senior congressional Democrats."[10] These war pitchers were equating criticizing a war with fighting a war—on the side of the enemy! Thus, ending a war because we the people are against it is the same thing as losing a war to the enemy. Wars can neither be lost nor ended. They must simply be continued indefinitely for the good of the troops.

And when the war makers want to escalate a war, they pitch that idea as a means toward ending the war, as we'll see in Chapter 9. But when it comes time to demand the funding and force Congressman Obey to reject his conscience, then the escalation is disguised as a mere continuation. It's easier to fund a war on behalf of the troops out there in harm's way if nobody knows that what you're funding is actually the shipping of another 30,000 troops to join the ones already deployed, in which case rejecting the funding couldn't conceivably strand any troops without bullets; it would just mean not sending more troops to join them.

At the end of 2009 and the beginning of 2010, we had a good democratic debate over whether to escalate the war in Afghanistan, a debate in the corporate media between the commander-in-chief and his generals. Congress and the public were largely left out. In 2009 President Obama had already launched a similar escalation with no debate at all. For this second round, once the president had caved in to the generals, one of whom he would later fire for a seemingly much more minor act of insubordination, the media ended the story, conducted no more polls, and considered the escalation done. In fact, the president went ahead and started sending the troops. And Congress members who had sworn they opposed the escalation began talking about the need to fund the "troops in the field." By the time six months had gone by, it was possible to make the vote on the funding a big story without mentioning that it was for an escalation at all.

Just as escalations can be described as support-the-troop continuations, war continuations can be disguised as withdrawals. On May 1, 2003, and August 31, 2010, Presidents Bush and Obama declared the war on Iraq, or the "combat mission," over. In each case, the war went on. But the war became ever more purely about the troops as it shed any pretenses of having some purpose other than prolonging its own existence.

Support the Veterans?

As we saw in Chapter 5, no matter how much government officials talk about the troops as their motivation for action, they fail to take action to care for veterans who've already been deployed. War veterans are abandoned rather than supported. They need to be treated with respect and to be respectfully told that we disagree with what they did, and they need to be provided healthcare and education. Until we can do that for every living veteran, what business do we have creating more of them? Our goal, in fact, should be to put the Veterans Administration out of operation by ceasing to manufacture veterans.

Until that time, young men and women should be told that war is not a smart career move. Yellow ribbons and speeches won't pay your bills or make your life fulfilling. As we saw in Chapter 5, war is not a good way to be heroic. Why not serve as a member of an emergency rescue crew, a firefighter, a labor organizer, a nonviolent activist? There are many ways to be heroic and take risks without murdering families. Think of the Iraqi oil workers who blocked privatization and formed a labor union in the face of U.S. attacks in 2003. Picture them ripping off their shirts and saying, "Go ahead and shoot." They were taking risks for their nation's independence. Isn't that heroic?

I understand the desire to support those making sacrifices supposedly for us, and those who already have made the "ultimate sacrifice," but our alternatives are not cheering for more war or joining the enemy, creating more veterans or abusing the ones we have. There are other options. That we don't think so is purely the result of our televisions spouting nonsense with great frequency for so long it begins to smell sensible. Comedian Bill Maher expressed his frustration on television this way:

> For the longest time, every Republican election has been based on some sentimental bullshit: the flag, or the flag pin, or the Pledge, or the, "It's morning in America." Bill Clinton got a blowjob in the Oval Office. And the Dixie Chicks insulted President Bush on foreign soil. And when that happens, it hurts the feelings of our troops. And then Tinkerbell's light goes out and she dies. Yes, yes, the love of our troops, the ultimate in fake patriotism. Are you kidding? The troops, we pay them like shit, we fuck them and trick them on deployment, we nickel and dime them on medical care when they get home, not to mention the stupid wars that we send them to. Yeah, we love the troops the way Michael Vick loves dogs. You know how I would feel supported if I was a troop overseas? If the people back home were clamoring to get me out of these pointless errands. That's how I would feel supported. But, you know, don't hold your breath on that one fellas because, you know, when America invades a country, we love you long time. Seriously, we never leave, we leave like Irish relatives: not at all.[11]

If we all purged ourselves, as Maher has, of the "support-the-troops" propaganda, we wouldn't have to say "Support the Troops, Bring Them Home." We could skip half of that and jump ahead to "Bring them home and prosecute the criminals who sent them." It should go without saying that we wish the troops well. That's one of the main reasons we don't want them pointlessly killing and dying!

But we do not actually approve of what they are doing. Our praise is reserved for those soldiers who refuse illegal orders and nonviolently resist. And we approve of the work being done courageously and with great dedication by Americans in hundreds of professions other than war. We ought to say we support *them* once in a while. We all fail to do that, and fortunately we don't accuse each other of wanting all those people dead, the way we do if someone fails to say, "I support the troops."

Support the Mass Murder?

Blogger John Caruso collected a list of news items reporting things he especially did not support, things that get brushed aside as too inconvenient when we delude ourselves into believing that wars are fought on behalf of the soldiers fighting them. Here's part of the list:

From the *New York Times*:
> "We had a great day," Sergeant Schrumpf said. "We killed a lot of people."

But more than once, Sergeant Schrumpf said, he faced a different choice: one Iraqi soldier standing among two or three civilians. He recalled one such incident, in which he and other men in his unit opened fire. He recalled watching one of the women standing near the Iraqi soldier go down.

"I'm sorry," the sergeant said. "But the chick was in the way."

From *Newsday*:

"Raghead, raghead, can't you see? This old war ain't—to me," sang Lance Cpl. Christopher Akins, 21, of Louisville, Ky., sweat running down his face in rivulets as he dug a fighting trench one recent afternoon under a blazing sun.

Asked whom he considered a raghead, Akins said: "Anybody who actively opposes the United States of America's way...If a little kid actively opposes my way of life, I'd call him a raghead, too."

From the *Las Vegas Review-Journal*:

The 20-year veteran of the Marine Corps said he found the soldier after dark inside a nearby home with the grenade launcher next to him. Covarrubias said he ordered the man to stop and turn around.

"I went behind him and shot him in the back of the head," Covarrubias said. "Twice."

Did he feel any remorse for executing a man who'd surrendered to him? No; in fact, he'd taken the man's ID card off of his dead body to keep as a souvenir.

From the *Los Angeles Times*:

"I enjoy killing Iraqis," says Staff Sgt. William Deaton, 30, who killed a hostile fighter the night before. Deaton has lost a good friend in Iraq. "I just feel rage, hate when I'm out there. I feel like I carry it all the time. We talk about it. We all feel the same way."[12]

8

WARS ARE NOT
FOUGHT ON BATTLEFIELDS

We talk of sending soldiers off to fight on battlefields. The word "battlefield" appears in millions, possibly billions, of news stories about our wars. And the term conveys to many of us a location in which soldiers fight other soldiers. We don't think of certain things being found in a battlefield. We don't imagine whole families, or picnics, or wedding parties, for example, as being found on a battlefield—or grocery stores or churches. We don't picture schools or playgrounds or grandparents in the middle of an active battlefield. We visualize something similar to Gettysburg or World War I France: a field with a battle on it. Maybe it's in the jungle or the mountains or the desert of some distant land that U.S. troops are "defending," but it's some sort of a field with a battle on it. What else could a battlefield be?

At first glance, our battlefields do not appear to be where we live and work and play as civilians, as long as "we" is understood to mean Americans. Wars don't happen in the United States. But for the people living in the countries where U.S. wars have been fought since, and including, World War II, the so-called "battlefield" has quite clearly included and continues to include their hometowns and neighborhoods. In many cases, that is *all* the battlefield has consisted of. There hasn't been any other, non-residential area constituting part of the battlefield. While the battles of Bull Run or Manassas were fought in a field near Manassas, Virginia, the battles of Fallujah were fought in the city of Fallujah, Iraq. When Vietnam was a battlefield, all of it was a battlefield, or what the U.S. Army now calls "the battlespace." When U.S. drones shoot missiles into Pakistan, the suspected terror plotters the U.S. government is murdering are not positioned in a designated field; they're in houses, along with all of the other people the U.S. military "accidentally" kills as part of the bargain. (And at least some of those people's friends will indeed begin plotting terrorism, which is great news for the manufacturers of drones.)

It's Everywhere

At second glance, the battlefield or battlespace does include the United States. In fact, it includes your bedroom, your living room, your bathroom, and every other spot on the planet or off it, and possibly even the thoughts that are in your head. The notion of a battlefield has been expanded, to put it mildly. It now encompasses anywhere soldiers are when they're actively employed. Pilots speak of being on the battlefield when they have been great distances above anything resembling a field or even an apartment building. Sailors speak of being on the battlefield when they haven't set foot on dry land. But the new battlefield also encompasses anywhere U.S. forces might conceivably be employed, which is where your house comes in. If the president declares you an "enemy combatant," you will not only live on the battlefield—you will be the enemy, whether you want to be or not. Why should a desk with a joystick in Las Vegas count as a battlefield on which a troop is flying a drone, but your hotel room be off limits?

When U.S. forces kidnap people on the street in Milano or in an airport in New York and send them off to be tortured in secret prisons, or when the U.S. military pays a reward to someone in Afghanistan for handing over their rival and falsely accusing them of terrorism, and the United States ships the victims off to be imprisoned indefinitely in Guantanamo or right there in Bagram, all of those activities are said to take place on a battlefield. Anywhere someone might be accused of terrorism and kidnapped or murdered is the battlefield. No discussion of releasing innocent people from Guantanamo would be complete without expression of the fear that they might "return to the battlefield," meaning that they might engage in anti-U.S. violence, whether they had ever done so before or not, and *regardless of where they might do it.*

When an Italian court convicts CIA agents *in absentia* of kidnapping a man in Italy in order to torture him, the court is staking the claim that Italian streets are not located in a U.S. battlefield. When the United States fails to hand over the convicts, it is restoring the battlefield to where it now exists: in each and every corner of the galaxy. We will see in Chapter 12 that this conception of the battlefield raises legal questions. Traditionally, killing people has been deemed legal in war but illegal outside of it. Apart from the fact that wars are themselves illegal, should it be permissible to expand them to include an isolated assassination in Yemen? What about a massive bombing campaign with unmanned drones in Pakistan? Why should the smaller expansion of an isolated murder be less acceptable than the larger expansion that kills more people?

And if the battlefield is everywhere, it is in the United States as well. The Obama administration in 2010 announced its right to assassinate Americans, presuming to already possess by common understanding the right to assassinate non-Americans. But it claimed the power to kill Americans only outside the United States. Yet, active military troops are stationed within the United States and assigned to fight here if so ordered. The military is used to clean up, or at least guard, oil spills, to assist in domestic police operations, and to spy on U.S. residents. We live in the area of the globe policed by Northern Command. What's to stop a battlefield over yonder in Central Command from spreading to our towns?

In March 2010, John Yoo, one of the former lawyers in the Justice Department who had helped George W. Bush "legally" authorize aggressive war, torture, warrantless spying, and other crimes, spoke in my town. War criminals today usually go on book tours before the blood is dry, and sometimes they take questions from the audience. I asked Yoo if a president could shoot missiles into the United States. Or could a president drop nuclear bombs within the United States? Yoo refused to concede any limits to presidential power, except perhaps in time rather than place. A president could do anything he chose, even within the United States, as long as it was "wartime." Yet, if the "war on terrorism" makes it wartime, and if the "war on terrorism" lasts for generations, as some of its proponents desire, then there really are no limits.

On June 29, 2010, Senator Lindsey Graham (R-SC) questioned then solicitor general and successful Supreme Court nominee Elena Kagan. "The problem with this war," Graham said, "is that there will never be a definable end to hostilities, will there?" Kagan nodded and simply agreed: "That is exactly the problem, Senator." That takes care of the time constraints. What about place constraints? A bit later, Graham asked, "The battlefield, you told me during our previous discussions, that the battlefield in this war is the entire world. That is, if someone were caught in the Philippines, who was a financier of al Qaeda, and they were captured in the Philippines, they would be subject to enemy combatant determination. Um, because the whole world's the battlefield. Do you still agree with that?"[1] Kagan ducked and dodged, while Graham asked her this three times, before she made clear that, yes, she still agreed.

So a battlefield turns out to be more a state of mind than a physical location. If we are always in the battlefield, if marches for peace are in the battlefield too, then we had best be careful what we say. We wouldn't want to assist the enemy somehow, while living in the battlefield. Wars, even when the battlefield was not, like a god, present everywhere, have always had a tendency to eliminate hard-won rights. This tradition in the United States includes

President John Adams's Alien and Sedition Acts of 1798, Abraham Lincoln's suspensions of habeas corpus, Woodrow Wilson's Espionage Act and Sedition Act, Franklin Roosevelt's rounding up of Japanese Americans, the madness of McCarthyism, and the many developments of the Bush-Obama era that really took off with the first passage of the PATRIOT Act.

On July 25, 2008, the pressure for accountability for abuses of power had grown too great for silence to continue. The House Judiciary Committee finally agreed to hold a hearing on the impeachment of George W. Bush. Chairman John Conyers had held similar hearings in 2005 as the ranking minority member, advertising his aim to pursue accountability for the war on Iraq if he were ever given the power. He held that power from January 2007 forward, and in July 2008—having obtained the approval of Speaker Nancy Pelosi—he held this hearing. To make the similarity to the unofficial hearings he'd held three years earlier complete, Conyers announced before the hearing that, while the evidence would be heard, no impeachment proceedings would go forward. The hearing was just a stunt. But the testimony was deadly serious and included a statement from former Justice Department official Bruce Fein from which this is excerpted:

> After 9/11, the executive branch declared—with the endorsement or acquiescence of Congress and the American people—a state of permanent warfare with international terrorism, i.e., the war would not conclude until every actual or potential terrorist in the Milky Way were either killed or captured and the risk of an international terrorist incident had been reduced to zero. The executive branch further maintained without quarrel from Congress or the American people that since Osama bin Laden threatens to kill Americans at any time and in any location, the entire world, including all of the United States, is an active battlefield where military force and military law may be employed at the discretion of the executive branch.
>
> For instance, the executive branch claims authority to employ the military for aerial bombardment of cities in the United States if it believes that Al Qaeda sleeper cells are nesting there and are hidden among civilians with the same certitude that the executive branch knew Saddam Hussein possessed weapons of mass destruction....
>
> The executive branch has directed United States forces to kill or kidnap persons it suspects have allegiance to Al Qaeda in foreign lands, for instance Italy, Macedonia, or Yemen, but it has plucked only one United States resident, Ali Saleh Kahlah al-Marri, from his home for indefinite detention as a suspected enemy combatant. But if the executive branch's constitutional justification for its modest actions is not rebuked through impeachment or otherwise, a precedent of executive power will have been established that will lie around like a loaded weapon ready for use

by any incumbent who claims an urgent need. Moreover, the Founding Fathers understood that mere claims to unchecked power warranted stern responses.[2]

No stern responses were forthcoming, and President Obama maintained and expanded upon the powers established for presidents by George W. Bush.[3] War was now officially everywhere and eternal, thereby allowing presidents even greater powers, which they could use in the waging of even more wars, from which yet more powers could derive, and so forth to Armageddon, unless something breaks the cycle.

It's Nowhere

The battlefield may be all around us, but the wars are still concentrated in particular places. Even in those particular locations—such as Iraq and Afghanistan—the wars lack the two basic features of a traditional battlefield—the field itself and a recognizable enemy. In a foreign occupation, the enemy looks just like the supposed beneficiaries of the humanitarian war. The only people recognizable for who they are in the war are the foreign occupiers. The Soviet Union discovered this weakness of foreign occupations when it tried to occupy Afghanistan during the 1980s. Oleg Vasilevich Kustov, a veteran of 37 years of the Soviet and Russian military, described the situation for Soviet troops: "Even in the capital, Kabul...it was dangerous to go more than 200 or 300 meters from installations guarded by our troops or...the Afghan army...—to do so was to put one's life at risk. To be completely honest, we were waging war against a people."[4]

That sums it up perfectly. Wars are not waged against armies. Nor are they waged against demonized dictators. They are waged against peoples. Remember the U.S. soldier in Chapter 5 who shot a woman who had apparently been bringing a bag of food to the U.S. troops? She would have looked just the same if she had been bringing a bomb. How was the soldier supposed to tell the difference? What was he supposed to do?

The answer, of course, is that he was supposed to not be there. The occupation battlefield is full of enemies who look exactly like, but sometimes are not, women bringing groceries. It is a lie to call such a place a "battlefield."

One way to make this clear, and which often shocks people, is to note that a majority of those killed in wars are civilians. A better term is probably 'non-participants.' Some civilians participate in wars. And those who resist a foreign occupation violently are not necessarily military. Nor is there any clear moral or legal justification for killing those fighting a truly defensive war any more than there is for killing the non-participants.

Estimates of war deaths vary for any given war. No two wars are the same, and the numbers change if those who die later from injury or disease are included with those immediately killed. But by most estimates, even counting only those immediately killed, the vast majority of those killed in war in recent decades have been non-participants. And in wars involving the United States, the vast majority of those killed have been non-Americans. Both of these facts, and the numbers involved, will seem crazy to anyone getting their war news from American media outlets, which routinely report the "war dead" and list only Americans.

The "good war," World War II, is still the deadliest of all time, with military deaths estimated at 20 to 25 million (including 5 million deaths of prisoners in captivity), and civilian deaths estimated at 40 to 52 million (including 13 to 20 million from war-related disease and famine).[5] The United States suffered a relatively small portion of these deaths—an estimated 417,000 military and 1,700 civilian. That is a horrendous statistic, but it is small in relation to the suffering of some of the other countries.

The war on Korea saw the deaths of an estimated 500,000 North Korean troops; 400,000 Chinese troops; 245,000–415,000 South Korean troops; 37,000 U.S. troops; and an estimated 2 million Korean civilians.[6]

The war on Vietnam may have killed 4 million civilians or more, plus 1.1 million North Vietnamese troops, 40,000 South Vietnamese troops, and 58,000 U.S. forces.

In the decades following the destruction of Vietnam, the United States killed a lot of people in a lot of wars, but relatively few U.S. soldiers died. The Gulf War saw 382 U.S. deaths, the highest number of U.S. casualties between Vietnam and the "war on terrorism." The 1965–1966 invasion of the Dominican Republic didn't cost a single U.S. life. Grenada in 1983 cost 19. Panama in 1989 saw 40 Americans die. Bosnia-Herzegovina and Kosovo saw a total of 32 U.S. war deaths. Wars had become exercises that killed very few Americans in comparison to the large numbers of non-U.S. non-participants dying.

The wars on Iraq and Afghanistan similarly saw the other sides do almost all of the dying. The numbers were so high that even the proportionately tiny U.S. death counts climbed into the thousands. Americans hear through their media that over 4,000 U.S. soldiers have died in Iraq, but rarely do they encounter any report on the deaths of Iraqis. When news of Iraqi deaths is reported, the U.S. media usually cites totals collected from news reports by organizations that openly and prominently stress the likelihood that a large proportion of deaths are not reported. Fortunately, two serious studies have been done of Iraqi deaths caused by the invasion and occupation that began in March 2003. These studies measure the deaths that exceed the high death rate that existed under international sanctions before March 2003.

The *Lancet* published the results of household surveys of deaths through the end of June 2006. In 92 percent of households asked to produce a death certificate to verify a reported death, they did so. The study concluded that there had been 654,965 excess violent and nonviolent deaths. This included deaths resulting from increased lawlessness, degraded infrastructure, and poorer healthcare. Most of the deaths (601,027) were estimated to be due to violence. The causes of violent deaths were gunshot (56 percent), car bomb (13 percent), other explosion/ordnance (14 percent), air strike (13 percent), accident (2 percent), and unknown (2 percent).[7] Just Foreign Policy, a Washington-based organization, has calculated the estimated deaths through the time of this writing, extrapolated from the *Lancet* report based on the relative level of deaths reported in the media in the intervening years. The current estimate is 1,366,350.[8]

The second serious study of deaths caused by the war on Iraq was a poll of 2,000 Iraqi adults conducted by Opinion Research Business (ORB) in August 2007. ORB estimated 1,033,000 violent deaths due to the war on Iraq: "48 percent died from a gunshot wound, 20 percent from the impact of a car bomb, 9 percent from aerial bombardment, 6 percent as a result of an accident, and 6 percent from another blast/ordnance."[9]

Death estimates from the war on Afghanistan were much lower but rising swiftly at the time of this writing.

For all of these wars, one can add a much larger casualty figure for the wounded than those I've cited for the dead. It is also safe to assume in each case a much larger number for those traumatized, orphaned, made homeless, or exiled. The Iraqi refugee crisis involves millions. Beyond that, these statistics do not capture the degraded quality of life in war zones, the usual reduced life expectancy, the increased birth defects, the rapid spread of cancers, the horror of unexploded bombs left lying around, or even the U.S. soldiers poisoned and experimented upon and denied compensation.

Zeeshan-ul-hassan Usmani, an assistant professor at Ghulam Ishaq Khan Institute in Pakistan's North-West Frontier Province who recently completed five years as a Fulbright scholar in the U.S., reports that the ongoing and illegal U.S. drone strikes into Pakistan have killed 29 suspected terrorists, and 1,150 civilians, wounding 379 more.[10]

If the numbers above are correct, World War II killed 67 percent civilians, the war on Korea 61 percent civilians, the war on Vietnam 77 percent civilians, the war on Iraq 99.7 percent Iraqis (whether or not civilians), and the drone war on Pakistan 98 percent civilians.

On March 16, 2003, a young American woman named Rachel Corrie stood in front of a Palestinian home in the Gaza strip, hoping to protect it from demolition by the Israeli military which was seeking to expand Israeli settlements. She faced a Caterpillar D9-R bulldozer, and it crushed her to death. Defending against her family's civil suit in court in September 2010, an Israeli military training unit leader explained: "During war there are no civilians."

Women and Children First

One thing to remember about civilians is that they are not all military-age men. Some of them are senior citizens. In fact those in the weakest condition are most likely to be killed. Some are women. Some are children, infants, or pregnant women. Women and children combined probably make up a majority of war victims, even as we think of war as an activity primarily for men. If we thought of war as a means of killing large numbers of women and children and grandparents would we be less willing to allow it?

The primary thing war does to women is the very worst thing possible: it kills them. But there is something else war does to women that sells a lot more newspapers. So, sometimes we hear about it. War rapes women. Soldiers rape women in isolated, but usually numerous, incidents. And soldiers in some wars systematically rape all women as a form of planned terrorism.

"Hundreds, if not thousands, of women and girls have been and continue to be the victims of widespread and, at times, systematic rape and sexual assault committed by a range of fighting forces," said Véronique Aubert, deputy director of Amnesty International's Africa Program, in 2007, speaking about a war in Cote d'Ivoire.[11]

Taken by Force: Rape and American GIs in Europe during WWII by American sociologist Robert Lilly was finally published in 2007 in the United States. Back in 2001 Lilly's publisher had refused to publish the book because of the crimes of September 11, 2001. Richard Drayton summarized and commented on Lilly's findings in the *Guardian*: "Lilly suggests a minimum of 10,000 American rapes [in World War II]. Contemporaries described a much wider scale of unpunished sex crime. *Time Magazine* reported in September 1945: 'Our own army and the British army...have done their share of looting and raping...we too are considered an army of rapists.'"[12] In that war, as in many others, rape victims were not always provided assistance by their families, if their families were alive. They were often denied medical care, shunned, and even murdered.

Those who commit rape during war are often so confident of their immunity from the law (after all, they receive immunity and even praise for mass murder, so surely rape must be sanctioned too) that they brag about their crimes and, where possible, display photographs of them. In May 2009, we learned that photos of U.S. troops abusing prisoners in Iraq showed an American soldier apparently raping a female prisoner, a male translator raping a male prisoner, and sexual assaults on prisoners with objects including a truncheon, wire, and a phosphorescent tube.[13]

Numerous reports have surfaced of U.S. soldiers raping Iraqi women outside of prison as well. While not all accusations are true, such incidents are not always reported, and those reported to the military are not always made public or prosecuted. Crimes by U.S. mercenaries, including crimes against their own employees, have gone unpunished, since they have operated outside any rule of law. Sometimes we learn after-the-fact that the military has investigated rape allegations and dropped the case. In March 2005, the *Guardian* reported: "Soldiers from the 3rd Infantry Brigade...were under investigation last year for raping Iraqi women.... A U.S. Army investigator interviewed several soldiers from the military unit...but did not locate or interview the Iraqi women involved before shutting down the inquiry for lack of evidence."[14]

Then there was the gang rape participated in by Paul Cortez, mentioned in Chapter 5. The victim's name was Abeer Qassim Hamza al-Janabi, age 14. According to a sworn statement by one of the accused:

> The soldiers noticed her at a checkpoint. They stalked her after one or more of them expressed his intention to rape her. On March 12, after playing cards while slugging whisky mixed with a high-energy drink and practicing their golf swings, they changed into black civvies and burst into Abeer's home in Mahmoudiya, a town 50 miles south of Baghdad. They killed her mother Fikhriya, father Qassim, and five-year-old sister Hadeel with bullets to the forehead, and "took turns" raping Abeer. Finally, they murdered her, drenched the bodies with kerosene, and lit them on fire to destroy the evidence. Then the GIs grilled chicken wings.[15]

Female U.S. soldiers are even in serious danger of rape by their male comrades, and of retribution by their "superiors" if they report assaults.[16]

While rape is more common during a hot war, it's a regular occurrence during cold occupations as well. If the U.S. soldiers never leave Iraq, their rapes never will either. U.S. soldiers rape, on average, two Japanese women per month as part of their ongoing occupation of Japan, begun at the end of "the good war."[17]

Children make up a large percentage of the fatalities in war, possibly as many as half, thanks to their presence on the "battlefield." Children are also conscripted to fight in wars.[18] In such a situation, the child is legally a victim, although that doesn't stop the United States from throwing such children into prisons like Guantanamo without charge or trial. Primarily, however, children are non-participants killed by bullets and bombs, injured, orphaned, and traumatized. Children are also common victims of land mines, cluster bombs, and other explosives left behind after warfare.

During the 1990s, according to the United Nations Children's Fund, 2 million children died and over 6 million were permanently disabled or seriously injured in armed conflict, while wars uprooted over 20 million children from their homes.[19]

These aspects of war—the bulk, in fact, of what war is—make it sound rather less noble than an agreed upon duel between daring adversaries risking their lives in an effort to kill each other. Killing a brave adversary who is armed and attempting to kill you can absolve guilt in a sort of sportsmanship. A World War I British officer praised German machine gunners: "Topping fellows. Fight until they are killed. They gave us hell."[20] If their dying was noble then so was the killing of them.

This helpful mental trick is not so easily done when one is killing the enemy with long-range sniper fire or in ambushes or surprise attacks, actions that were once considered dishonorable. It's even harder to find nobility in killing people who very well may not be participating in your war at all, people who may be trying to bring you a bag of groceries. We still like to romanticize war, as discussed in Chapter 5, but the old ways of war are gone and were truly indecent while they lasted. The new ways involve very little jousting on horseback, even if groups of soldiers are still called "cavalries." There's also very little trench warfare. Instead, fighting on the ground includes street battles, house raids, and vehicle checkpoints, all in combination with the hurricane of death from above that we call aerial warfare.

Street Fights, Raids, and Checkpoints

In April 2010, a website called WikiLeaks posted online a video of an incident that had occurred in 2007 in Baghdad. U.S. helicopters are seen shooting a group of men on a street corner, killing civilians, including journalists, and wounding children. The voices of the U.S. troops in the helicopters are heard. They are not fighting on a battlefield but in a city in which both those trying to kill them and those they are supposedly defending are all around them, indistinguishable from each other. The soldiers clearly believe that if there's the slightest chance a group of men might be combatants, they should be killed. Upon discovering that they've hit children as well as adults, one U.S. troop comments, "Well it's their fault for bringing their kids into a battle."[21] Remember, this was an urban neighborhood. It's your fault for being on the battlefield, just as it's your fault Adam ate that forbidden apple: you're born at fault if you're born on this planet.

U.S. forces were also on the ground that day. Former army specialist Ethan McCord is seen in the video helping two wounded children after the attack. He talked in 2010 about what had happened. He said he was one of about six soldiers to first arrive at the scene:

It was pretty much absolute carnage. I had never seen anybody shot by a 30-millimeter round before, and frankly don't ever want to see that again. It almost seemed unreal, like something out of a bad B-horror movie. When these rounds hit you they kind of explode—people with their heads half-off, their insides hanging out of their bodies, limbs missing. I did see two RPGs on the scene as well as a few AK-47s.

But then I heard the cries of a child. They weren't necessarily cries of agony, but more like the cries of a small child who was scared out of her mind. So I ran up to the van where the cries were coming from. You can actually see in the scenes from the video where another soldier and I come up to the driver and the passenger sides of the van.

The soldier I was with, as soon as he saw the children, turned around, started vomiting and ran. He didn't want any part of that scene with the children anymore.

What I saw when I looked inside the van was a small girl, about three or four years old. She had a belly wound and glass in her hair and eyes. Next to her was a boy about seven or eight years old who had a wound to the right side of the head. He was laying half on the floorboard and half on the bench. I presumed he was dead; he wasn't moving.

Next to him was who I presumed was the father. He was hunched over sideways, almost in a protective way, trying to protect his children. And you could tell that he had taken a 30-millimeter round to the chest. I pretty much knew that he was deceased.

McCord grabbed the girl and found a medic, then went back to the van and noticed the boy moving. McCord carried him to the same vehicle to be evacuated as well. McCord went on to describe the rules he and his fellow troops were operating under in this urban war:

Our rules of engagement were changing on an almost daily basis. But we had a pretty gung-ho commander, who decided that because we were getting hit by IEDs [improvised explosive devices] a lot, there would be a new battalion SOP [standard operating procedure].

He goes, "If someone in your line gets hit with an IED, 360 rotational fire. You kill every motherfucker on the street." Myself and Josh [Stieber] and a lot of other soldiers were just sitting there looking at each other like, "Are you kidding me? You want us to kill women and children on the street?"

And you couldn't just disobey orders to shoot, because they could just make your life hell in Iraq. So like with myself, I would shoot up into the roof of a building instead of down on the ground toward civilians. But I've seen it many times, where people are just walking down the street and an IED goes off and the troops open fire and kill them.[22]

Former army specialist Josh Stieber, who was in the same unit with McCord, said that newly arrived soldiers in Baghdad were asked if they would fire back at an attacker if they knew unarmed civilians might get hurt in the process. Those who did not respond affirmatively, or who hesitated, were "knocked around" until they realized what was expected of them, added former army specialist Ray Corcoles, who deployed with McCord and Stieber.[23]

Although it is extremely difficult, when occupying a city, to distinguish violent resisters from civilians, the laws of war still distinguish between civilians and combatants. "What these soldiers are describing, tit-for-tat retaliation against civilians, is a clear war crime which has been successfully prosecuted after WWII in the case of German SS *Obersturmbannführer* Herbert Kappler," writes Ralph Lopez. "In 1944 Kappler ordered the mass execution of civilians in the ratio of 10 to 1 for every German soldier killed in a March 1944 hidden bomb attack by Italian partisans. The executions took place in the caves of Ardeatine in Italy. You may have seen a movie about it starring Richard Burton."[24]

One quick way to turn non-participants in a war into active combatants is to kick in their doors, smash their possessions, and insult and terrify their loved ones. Those who have resisted such frequent incidents in Iraq and Afghanistan have been shot or imprisoned—later, in many cases, to be released, often filled with a desire for vengeance against the occupiers. One such raid in Afghanistan is described by Zaitullah Ghiasi Wardak in Chapter 3. No accounts of any raids depict anything resembling a glorious battlefield.

In January 2010, the occupied government of Afghanistan and the United Nations both concluded that on December 26, 2009, in Kunar, U.S.-led troops had dragged eight sleeping children out of their beds, handcuffed some of them, and shot them all dead.[25] On February 24, 2010, the U.S. military admitted that the dead were innocent students, contradicting its initial lies about the incident. The killings led to student demonstrations across Afghanistan, a formal protest by the president of Afghanistan, and investigations by the Afghan government and the United Nations. The Afghan government called for the prosecution and execution of American soldiers who kill Afghan civilians. Dave Lindorff commented on March 3, 2010: "Under the Geneva Conventions, it is a war crime to execute a captive. Yet in Kunar on December 26, U.S.-led forces, or perhaps U.S. soldiers or contract mercenaries, cold-bloodedly executed eight hand-cuffed prisoners. It is a war crime to kill children under the age of 15, yet in this incident a boy of 11 and a boy of 12 were handcuffed as captured combatants and executed. Two others of the dead were 12 and a third was 15."[26] The Pentagon did not investigate, passing the buck to the U.S.-dominated NATO force in Afghanistan. Congress has no authority to compel testimony from NATO, as it does—at least in theory—with the Pentagon. When Lindorff contacted the House Armed Services Committee, the press officer was not familiar with the incident.

Another night raid, on February 12, 2010, targeted the home of a popular policeman, Commander Dawood, who was killed while standing in his doorway defending the innocence of his family. Also killed were his pregnant wife, another pregnant woman, and an 18-year-old girl. The United States and NATO claimed their soldiers had discovered the women tied up and already dead, and also claimed the soldiers had faced a firefight from several "insurgents."[27] In lying, sometimes less is more. Either lie would have worked, but both together smelled fishy. NATO later backed off the insurgents story and concisely stated the approach that the U.S. military takes to occupied nations, an approach that cannot possibly succeed: "If you have got an individual stepping out of a compound, and if your assault force is there, that is often the trigger to neutralise the individual. *You don't have to be fired upon to fire back* [italics added]."[28]

It took until April 2010 before NATO admitted to killing the women, revealing that U.S. special forces, in an attempt to cover up their crimes, had dug bullets out of the women's bodies with knives.[29]

In addition to raids, the new battlefield involves countless vehicle checkpoints. In 2007, the U.S. military admitted to having killed 429 civilians in a year at Iraqi checkpoints. In an occupied country, the occupier's vehicles must keep moving, or those inside might be killed. The vehicles belonging to the occupied, however, must stop to prevent their being killed. War on Iraq veteran Matt Howard remembers:

> An American life is always worth more than an Iraqi life. Right now, if you're in a convoy in Iraq, you do not stop that convoy. If a little kid runs in front of your truck, you are under orders to run him over instead of stopping your convoy. This is the policy that's set in how to deal with people in Iraq.
>
> I had this Marine friend who had set up a checkpoint. Car loaded with six people, family going on a picnic. It didn't stop immediately at the checkpoint. It was kind of coming to a rolling stop. And rules of engagement state, in a situation like that, you are required to fire on that vehicle. And they did. And they killed everyone in that car. And they proceeded to search the car, and just found basically a picnic basket. No weapons.
>
> And, yes, absolutely tragic, and his officer comes by and [my friend] is like, "You know, sir, we just killed a whole family of Iraqis for nothing." And all he said was, "If these hajis could just learn how to drive, this shit wouldn't happen."[30]

One frequent problem has been miscommunication. Soldiers were taught that a raised fist meant "stop," but nobody told the Iraqis, who had no idea and in some cases paid for that ignorance with their lives.

Checkpoints are also a frequent location for killing civilians in Afghanistan. Gen. Stanley McChrystal, then the senior American and NATO commander in Afghanistan, said in March 2010: "We have shot an amazing number of people, but to my knowledge, none has ever proven to be a threat."[31]

Bombs and Drones

One of the most significant legacies of World War II has been the bombing of civilians. This new approach to war brought the front lines much closer to home while allowing those doing the killing to be located too far away to see their victims. Two passages telling this story come from a collection of essays called *Bombing Civilians: A Twentieth Century History*, edited by Yuki Tanaka and Marilyn B. Young.[32]

> For the residents of German cities, survival "beneath the bombs" was a defining characteristic of the war. The war in the skies had erased the distinction between home and front, adding "air terror psychosis" and "bunker panic" to the German vocabulary. Urban dwellers could also claim "moments of a life at the front," in a war that had transformed Germany's cities into a "battlefield."

A U.S. pilot in the war on Korea had a different perspective:

> The first couple of times I went in on a napalm strike, I had kind of an empty feeling. I thought afterward, Well, maybe I shouldn't have done it. Maybe those people I set afire were innocent civilians. But you get conditioned, especially after you've hit what looks like a civilian and the A-frame on his back lights up like a Roman candle—a sure enough sign that he's been carrying ammunition. Normally speaking, I have no qualms about my job. Besides, we don't generally use napalm on people we can see. We use it on hill positions or buildings. And one thing about napalm is that when you've hit a village and have seen it go up in flames, you know that you've accomplished something. Nothing makes a pilot feel worse than to work over an area and not see that he's accomplished anything.

While the Germans had bombed Guernica, Spain, in 1937, the bombing of cities took on something closer to its current form and current motivation when the Japanese bombed Chongqing, China, from 1938 to 1941. This siege continued, with less intense bombing through 1943, and included the use of fragmentation and incendiary bombs, chemical weapons, and bombs with delayed fuses that caused long-term physical and psychological damage similar to the cluster bombs used 60 years later in Iraq. Just the first two days of this systematic bombing killed almost three times the number of people killed in Guernica. Unlike later bombing campaigns against Germany, England, and Japan, the bombing of China was a completely one-sided slaughter of people who had no real means to fight back, similar in this way to many later campaigns, including the bombing of Baghdad.

Proponents of aerial bombing have argued from the start that it could bring a faster peace, discourage a populace from continuing a war, or shock and awe them. This has always proved false, including in Germany, England, and Japan. The idea that the nuclear destruction of two Japanese cities would change the Japanese government's position was implausible from the start, given that the United States had already destroyed several dozen Japanese cities with firebombs and napalm. In March 1945, Tokyo consisted of "rivers of fire...flaming pieces of furniture exploding in the heat, while the people themselves blazed like 'matchsticks' as their wood and paper homes exploded in flames. Under the wind and the gigantic breath of the fire, immense incandescent vortices rose in a number of places, swirling, flattening, sucking whole blocks of houses into their maelstrom of fire."[33]

Mark Selden explains the importance of this horror to the decades of U.S. war making that would follow: "[E]very president from Roosevelt to George W. Bush has endorsed in practice an approach to warfare that targets entire populations for annihilation, one that eliminates all distinction between combatant and noncombatant with deadly consequences. The awesome power of the atomic bomb has obscured the fact that this strategy came of age in the firebombing of Tokyo and became the centerpiece of U.S. war making from that time forward."[34]

A spokesman for the Fifth Air Force put the U.S. military's view succinctly: "For us, there are no civilians in Japan."[35]

Unmanned drones are becoming the new centerpiece of war, distancing soldiers more than ever from those they kill, increasing the one-sidedness of casualties, and terrorizing everyone who must listen to the drones buzzing overhead as they threaten to explode one's house and end one's life at any moment. The drones are part of an array of deadly technologies imposed on the countries where the U.S. government takes its wars.

"My thoughts drift to the Emergency Surgical Center for Victims of War, in Kabul," Kathy Kelly wrote in September 2010.

> A little over two months ago, Josh [Brollier] and I met Nur Said, age 11, in the hospital's ward for young boys injured by various explosions. Most of the boys welcomed a diversion from the ward's tedium, and they were especially eager to sit outside, in the hospital garden, where they'd

form a circle and talk together for hours. Nur Said stayed indoors. Too miserable to talk, he'd merely nod at us, his hazel eyes welling up with tears. Weeks earlier, he had been part of a hardy band of youngsters that helped bolster their family incomes by searching for scrap metal and unearthing land mines on a mountainside in Afghanistan. Finding an unexploded land mine was a eureka for the children because, once opened, the valuable brass parts could be extracted and sold. Nur had a land mine in hand when it suddenly exploded, ripping four fingers off his right hand and blinding him in his left eye.

On a sad continuum of misfortune, Nur and his companions fared better than another group of youngsters scavenging for scrap metal in the Kunar Province on August 26th.

Following an alleged Taliban attack on a nearby police station, NATO forces flew overhead to "engage" the militants. If the engagement includes bombing the area under scrutiny, it would be more apt to say that NATO aimed to puree the militants. But in this case, the bombers mistook the children for militants and killed six of them, aged 6 to 12. Local police said there were no Taliban at the site during the attack, only children.

In Afghanistan, thirty high schools have shut down because the parents say that their children are distracted by the drones flying over-head and that it's unsafe for them to gather in the schools.[36]

The damage of our wars in the global battlefield outlasts the memories of elderly survivors. We leave landscapes pock-marked with bomb craters, oil fields ablaze, seas poisoned, ground water ruined. We leave behind, and in the bodies of our own veterans, Agent Orange, depleted uranium, and all the other substances designed to kill people quickly but carrying the side effect of killing people slowly. Since the United States' secret bombing of Laos that ended in 1975, some 20,000 people have been killed by unexploded ordnance.[37] Even the war on drugs begins to look like the war on terrorism when the spraying of fields renders regions of Colombia uninhabitable.

When will we ever learn? John Quigley visited Vietnam after the war and saw in downtown Hanoi, "a neighborhood we had bombed in December 1972, because President Nixon said that bombing would convince North Vietnam to negotiate. Here thousands had been killed in a short time.... An elderly man, a survivor of the bombing, was caretaker for the exhibit. As he showed it to me, I could see he was straining to avoid putting awkward questions to a guest whose country was responsible for the bombing. Finally, he asked me, as politely as he could, how America could do this to his neighborhood. I had no answer."[38]

WARS ARE NOT WON AND ARE NOT ENDED BY ENLARGING THEM

"I will not be the first president to lose a war," swore Lyndon Johnson.[1] Richard Nixon said, "I'll see that the United States does not lose. I'm putting it quite bluntly. I'll be quite precise. South Vietnam may lose. But the United States *cannot* lose. Which means, basically, I have made the decision. Whatever happens to South Vietnam, we are going to *cream* North Vietnam.... For once we've got to use the maximum power of this country...against this shit-ass little country: to win the war. We can't use the word 'win.' But others can."[2]

Of course, Johnson and Nixon "lost" that war, but they weren't the first presidents to lose wars. The war on Korea had not ended with a victory, just a truce. "Die for a tie," said the troops. The United States lost various wars with Native Americans and the War of 1812, and in the Vietnam era the United States proved repeatedly incapable of evicting Fidel Castro from Cuba. Not all wars are winnable, and the war on Vietnam may have had in common with the later wars on Afghanistan and Iraq a certain quality of unwinnability. The same quality might be detected in smaller failed missions like the hostage crisis in Iran in 1979, or in the efforts to prevent terrorist attacks on U.S. embassies and the United States prior to 2001, or the maintenance of bases in places that would not tolerate them, like the Philippines or Saudi Arabia.

I mean to indicate something more specific than simply that unwon wars were unwinnable. In many earlier wars, and perhaps through World War II and the war on Korea, the idea of winning consisted of defeating enemy forces on a battlefield and seizing their territory or dictating to them the terms of their future existence. In various older wars and most of the United States' more recent wars, wars fought thousands of miles from home against peoples rather than against armies, the concept of winning has been very hard to define. As the U.S. government finds itself occupying someone else's country, does that mean that it has already won, as Bush claimed about Iraq on May 1, 2003? Or can it still lose by withdrawing? Or does victory come when and if violent resistance is reduced to a particular level? Or does a stable government that obeys the wishes of Washington have to be established before there is victory?

That kind of victory, control over the government of another country with minimal violent resistance, is hard to come by. Wars of occupation or counter-insurgency are frequently discussed without mention of this central and seemingly crucial point: *they are usually lost.* William Polk made a study of insurgencies and guerrilla warfare in which he looked at the American Revolution, the Spanish resistance against the occupying French, the Philippine insurrection, the Irish struggle for independence, the Afghan resistance to the British and the Russians, and guerrilla fighting in Yugoslavia, Greece, Kenya, and Algeria, among others. Polk looked at what happens when we are the redcoats and the other people are the colonists. In 1963 he gave a presentation to the National War College that left the officers there furious. He told them that guerrilla warfare was composed of politics, administration, and combat:

> I told the audience that we had already lost the political issue—Ho Chi Minh had become the embodiment of Vietnamese nationalism. That, I suggested, was about 80 percent of the total struggle. Moreover, the Viet Minh or Viet Cong, as we had come to call them, had also so disrupted the administration of South Vietnam, killing large numbers of its officials, that it had ceased to be able to perform even basic functions. That, I guessed, amounted to an additional 15 percent of the struggle. So, with only 5 percent at stake, we were holding the short end of the lever. And because of the appalling corruption of South Vietnamese government, as I had a chance to observe firsthand, even that lever was in danger of breaking. I warned the officers that the war was already lost.[3]

In December 1963, President Johnson set up a working group called the Sullivan Task Force. Its findings differed from Polk's more in tone and intention than in substance. This task force viewed escalating the war with the "rolling thunder" bombing campaign in the North as "a commitment to go all the way." In fact, "the implicit judgment of the Sullivan Committee was that the bombing campaign would result in indefinite war, continuously escalating, with both sides embroiled in a perpetual stalemate."[4]

This should not have been news. The U.S. State Department had known the war on Vietnam could not be won *as early as 1946*, as Polk recounts:

> John Carter Vincent, whose career was subsequently ruined by hostile reaction to his insights on Vietnam and China, was then director of the Office of Far East Affairs in the State Department. On December 23,

1946, he presciently wrote the secretary of state that "with inadequate forces, with public opinion sharply at odds, with a government rendered largely ineffective through internal division, the French have tried to accomplish in Indochina what a strong and united Britain has found it unwise to attempt in Burma. Given the present elements in the situation, guerrilla warfare may continue indefinitely."[5]

Polk's research of guerrilla warfare around the world found that insurgencies against foreign occupations usually do not end until they succeed. This agrees with the findings of both the Carnegie Endowment for International Peace and the RAND Corporation, both cited in Chapter 3. Insurgencies arising within countries with weak governments are successful. Governments that take orders from a foreign imperial capital tend to be weak. The wars George W. Bush started in Afghanistan and Iraq are therefore almost certainly wars that will be lost. The main question is how long the U.S. military will spend doing it, and whether Afghanistan will continue to live up to its reputation as "the graveyard of empires."

One need not think about these wars solely in terms of winning or losing, however. If the United States was to elect officials and compel them to heed the public's wishes and retire from foreign military adventures, we would all be better off. Why in the world must that desired outcome be called "losing"? We saw in Chapter 2 that even the president's representative to Afghanistan can't explain what winning would look like. Is there, then, any sense in behaving as if "winning" is an option? If wars are going to cease to be the legitimate and glorious campaigns of heroic leaders and become what they are under the law, namely crimes, then a whole different vocabulary is needed. You cannot win or lose a crime; you can only continue or cease committing it.

More Shock Than Awe

The weakness of counter-insurgencies, or rather foreign occupations, is that they don't provide the people in occupied countries with anything they need or desire; on the contrary, they offend and injure people. That leaves a great opening for the forces of the insurgency, or rather the resistance, to win the people's support to their side. At the same time that the U.S. military makes feeble gestures in the general direction of comprehending this problem and mumbling some condescending crap about winning "hearts and minds," it invests enormous resources in an exactly contrary approach aimed not at winning people over, but at beating them down so hard that they lose all willingness to resist. This approach has a long and well-established history of failure and may be less a real motivation behind war plans than are such factors as economics and sadism. But it does lead to massive death and displacement, which can assist an occupation even if it produces enemies rather than friends.

The recent history of the myth of breaking the enemy's morale parallels the history of aerial bombing. Since before airplanes were invented and for as long as humanity has existed, people have believed, and they may continue to believe, that wars can be shortened by bombing populations from the air so brutally that they cry "uncle." (Yes, people theorized about aerial bombing campaigns long before the success of the Wright brothers in making an airplane fly.) That this doesn't work is no barrier to renaming and reinventing it as a strategy for each new war.

President Franklin Roosevelt told Secretary of the Treasury Henry Morgenthau in 1941: "The way to lick Hitler is the way I have been telling the English, but they won't listen to me." Roosevelt wanted to bomb small towns. "There must be some kind of factory in every town. That is the only way to break German morale."[6]

There were two key false assumptions in that view, and they have remained prominent in war planning ever since. (I do not mean the assumption that U.S. bombers could hit a factory; that they would miss was presumably Roosevelt's point.)

One key false assumption is that bombing people's homes has a psychological impact on them that is similar to that of a soldier's experience in war. Officials planning urban bombings in World War II expected herds of "gibbering lunatics" to wander out of the rubble. But civilians who survive bombings have not faced either the need to kill their fellow human beings, or the "wind of hate" discussed in Chapter 1—that intense horror of other human beings attempting to personally kill you. In fact, bombing cities doesn't traumatize everyone to the point of lunacy. Instead it tends to harden the hearts of those who survive and firm up their resolve to continue supporting the war.

Death squads on the ground *can* traumatize a population, but they involve a different level of risk and commitment than bombing does.

The second false assumption is that when people do turn against a war, their government is likely to give a damn. Governments lie their way into the wars in the first place, and unless the people threaten to remove them from power, they may very well choose to continue wars despite public opposition, something the United States itself has done in Korea, Vietnam, Iraq, and Afghanistan, among other wars. The War on Vietnam finally ended eight months after a president was forced out of office. Nor will most governments seek of their own accord to protect their own civilians, as the Americans expected the Japanese to do and the Germans expected the British to do. The United States bombed Koreans and Vietnamese even more intensely, and still they did not quit. Nobody was shocked and awed.

The warmonger theorists who coined the phrase "shock and awe" in 1996, Harlan Ullman and James P. Wade, believed that the same approach that had failed for decades would work, but that we might need *more of it*. The 2003 bombing of Baghdad fell short of what Ullman thought was needed to properly awe people. It's hard, however, to see where such theories draw the line between awing people as they have never been awed before, and *killing* most of the people, which has a similar result and has been done before.

The fact is that wars, once begun, are very difficult to control or predict, much less win. A handful of men with box cutters can take down your largest buildings, no matter how many nukes you have. And a small force of untrained rebels with homemade bombs detonated by disposable cell phones can defeat a trillion dollar military that has dared to set up shop in the wrong country. The key factor is where the passion lies in the people, and that grows ever harder to direct the more an occupying force tries to direct it.

Claim Victory While Fleeing

But there is no need to admit defeat. It's easy enough to claim to have wanted to leave all along, to escalate the war temporarily, and then to claim to be leaving because of the undefined "success" of the recent escalation. That story, elaborated to sound a little more complicated, can easily appear less like a defeat than does an escape by helicopter from the roof on an embassy.

Because past wars were winnable and losable, and because war propaganda is heavily invested in that theme, war planners think those are the only two choices. They obviously find one of those choices to be intolerable. They also believe that the world wars were won because of a surge of American forces into the fray. So, winning is necessary, possible, and can be achieved through a greater effort. That is the message to be put out, whether or not the facts cooperate, and anyone who says something different is hurting the war effort.

This thinking naturally leads to a great deal of pretense about winning, false claims that victory is just around the corner, redefinitions of victory as they are needed, and refusals to define victory so as to be able to claim it no matter what. Good war propaganda can make anything sound like progress toward victory while persuading the other side that they are headed for defeat. But with both sides constantly claiming progress, somebody has to be wrong, and the advantage in persuading people probably goes to the side that speaks their language.

Harold Lasswell explained the importance of victory propaganda in 1927: "The illusion of victory must be nourished because of the close connection between the strong and the good. Primitive habits of thought persist in modern life, and battles become a trial to ascertain the true and the good. If

we win, God is on our side. If we lose, God may have been on the other side....
[D]efeat wants a great deal of explaining, while victory speaks for itself."[7] So,
starting a war on the basis of absurd lies that won't be believed for a month
works, so long as within a month you can announce that you are "winning."

In addition to losing, something else that needs a great deal of explaining is endless stalemate. The United States' new wars go on longer than the
world wars did. The United States was in World War I for a year and a half,
in World War II for three and a half years, and in the war on Korea for three
years. Those were long and horrible wars. But the war on Vietnam took at
least eight and a half years—or much longer, depending on how you measure
it. The war on Afghanistan passed the 14 year mark in 2015, while U.S. war
on Iraq lessened between 2011 and 2014, but had been surging and lessening
for 25 years by 2015.

The war on Iraq was for a long time the larger and bloodier of the two
wars, and U.S. peace activists persistently demanded a withdrawal. Often we
were told by war proponents that the sheer logistics of bringing tens of thousands of troops out of Iraq, with their equipment, would require years. This
claim was proved false in 2010, when some 100,000 troops were rapidly withdrawn. Why couldn't that have been done years before? Why did the war have
to drag on and on and on, and escalate?

What will come of the two wars the United States is waging as I write
this (three if we count Pakistan), in terms of the agenda of the war makers,
remains to be seen. Those profiting from wars and "reconstruction" have been
profiting these several years. But will bases with large numbers of troops remain behind in Iraq and Afghanistan indefinitely? Or will some thousands
of mercenaries employed by the U.S. State Department to guard record-sized
embassies and consulates have to suffice? Will the United States exercise control over the governments or the nations' resources? Will the defeat be total
or partial? That remains to be determined, but what is certain is that the U.S.
history books will contain no descriptions of defeat. They will report that
these wars were successes. And every mention of success will include reference to something called "the surge."

Can You Feel the Surge?

We are winning in Iraq! —Senator John McCain (R-AZ)[8]

As a hopeless war drags on for year after year, with victory undefined and
unimaginable, there is always an answer to the lack of progress, and that answer is always "send more troops." When violence goes down, more troops
are needed to build on the success. When violence goes up, more troops are
needed to clamp down.

The constraint on the number of troops already sent has more to do with the military's lack of any more troops to abuse with second and third tours than with political opposition. But when a new approach, or at least the appearance of one, is needed, the Pentagon can find 30,000 extra troops to send, call it a "surge," and declare the war reborn as a completely different and nobler animal. The change in strategy suffices, in Washington, as an answer to demands for complete withdrawal: We can't leave now; we're trying something different! We're going to do slightly more of what we've been doing the past several years! And the result will be peace and democracy: we'll end the war by escalating it!

The idea was not completely new with Iraq. The saturation bombing of Hanoi and Haiphong mentioned in Chapter 6 is another example of ending a war with a pointless display of extra toughness. Just as the Vietnamese would have agreed to the same terms before the bombing that they agreed to afterward, the Iraqi government would have welcomed any treaty committing the United States to withdrawal years before the surge, just before it, or during it. When the Iraqi Parliament did consent to the so-called Status of Forces Agreement in 2008, it did so only on the condition that a public referendum be held on whether to reject the treaty and opt for immediate withdrawal instead of a three-year delay. That referendum was never held.

President Bush's agreement to leave Iraq—albeit with a three-year delay and uncertainty as to whether the United States would actually comply with the agreement—was not called a defeat purely because there had been a recent escalation that had been called a success. In 2007, the United States had sent an extra 30,000 troops into Iraq with tremendous fanfare and a new commander, General David Petraeus. So the escalation was real enough, but what about its supposed success?

The Congress and the president, the study groups and think tanks had all been setting "benchmarks" by which to measure success in Iraq since 2005. The president was expected by Congress to meet its benchmarks by January 2007. He did not meet them by that deadline, by the end of the "surge," or by the time he left office in January 2009. There was no oil law to benefit the big oil corporations, no de-Baathification law, no constitutional review, and no provincial elections. In fact, there was no improvement in electricity, water, or other basic measures of recovery in Iraq. The "surge" was to advance these "benchmarks" and to create the "space" to allow political reconciliation and stability. Whether or not that is understood as code for U.S. control of Iraqi governance, even cheerleaders for the surge admit it did not achieve any political progress.

The measure of success for the "surge" was quickly downsized to include only one thing: a reduction in violence. This was convenient, first because it erased from Americans' memories anything else the surge was supposed to have accomplished, and second because the surge had happily coincided with a longer-term downward trend in violence. The surge was extremely small, and its immediate impact may have actually been an *increase* in violence. Brian Katulis and Lawrence Korb point out that, "The 'surge' of U.S. troops to Iraq was only a modest increase of about 15 percent—and smaller if one takes into account the reduced number of other foreign troops, which fell from 15,000 in 2006 to 5,000 by 2008."[9] So, the surge added a net gain of 20,000 troops, not 30,000.

The extra troops were in Iraq by May 2007, and June and July were the most violent summer months of the entire war to that point. When the violence went down, there were reasons for the reduction that had nothing to do with the "surge." The decline was gradual, and the progress was relative to the horrendous levels of violence in early 2007. By the fall of 2007 in Baghdad there were 20 attacks per day and 600 civilians killed in political violence each month, not counting soldiers or police. Iraqis continued to believe the conflicts were mainly caused by the U.S. occupation, and they continued to want it to end quickly.[10]

Attacks on British troops in Basra dropped dramatically when the British stopped patrolling population centers and moved out to the airport. No surge was involved. On the contrary, because so much violence had in fact been driven by the occupation, scaling back the occupation predictably resulted in a reduction in violence.

Guerrilla attacks in al-Anbar province dropped from 400 per week in July 2006 to 100 per week in July 2007, but the "surge" in al-Anbar consisted of a mere 2,000 new troops. In fact, something else explains the drop in violence in al-Anbar. In January 2008, Michael Schwartz took it upon himself to debunk the myth that "the surge has led to the pacification of large parts of Anbar province and Baghdad." Here's what he wrote:

> Quiescence and pacification are simply not the same thing, and this is definitely a case of quiescence. In fact, the reduction in violence we are witnessing is really a result of the U.S. discontinuing its vicious raids into insurgent territory, which have been—from the beginning of the war—the largest source of violence and civilian casualties in Iraq. These raids, which consist of home invasions in search of suspected insurgents, trigger brutal arrests and assaults by American soldiers who are worried about resistance, gun fights when families resist the intrusions into their homes, and road side bombs set to deter and distract the invasions. Whenever Iraqis fight back against these raids, there is the risk of sustained gun battles that, in turn, produce U.S. artillery and air assaults that, in turn, annihilate buildings and even whole blocks.

The "surge" has reduced this violence, but not because the Iraqis have stopped resisting raids or supporting the insurgency. Violence has decreased in many Anbar towns and Baghdad neighborhoods because the U.S. has agreed to discontinue these raids; that is, the U.S. would no longer seek to capture or kill the Sunni insurgents they have been fighting for four years. In exchange the insurgents agree to police their own neighborhoods (which they had been doing all along, in defiance of the U.S.), and also suppress jihadist car bombs.

The result is that the U.S. troops now stay outside of previously insurgent communities, or march through without invading any houses or attacking any buildings.

So, ironically, this new success has not pacified these communities, but rather acknowledged the insurgents' sovereignty over the communities, and even provided them with pay and equipment to sustain and extend their control over the communities.[11]

The United States was finally doing more right than just reducing its raids on people's homes. It was communicating its intention to, sooner or later, get out of the country. The peace movement in the United States had built growing support in Congress for withdrawal between 2005 and 2008. The 2006 elections sent the clear message to Iraq that Americans wanted out. Iraqis may have listened more carefully to that message than did U.S. Congress members themselves. Even the pro-war Iraq Study Group in 2006 supported a phased withdrawal. Brian Katulis and Lawrence Korb argue that,"the message that America's [military] commitment to Iraq was not open-ended motivated forces such as the Sunni Awakenings in Anbar province to partner with the U.S. to combat Al Qaeda in 2006, a movement that began long before the 2007 surge of U.S. forces."[12]

As early as November 2005, leaders of the major Sunni armed groups had sought to negotiate peace with the United States, which wasn't interested.

The biggest drop in violence came with the late 2008 commitment by Bush to fully withdraw by the end of 2011, and violence fell further after the withdrawal of U.S. forces from cities in the summer of 2009. Nothing de-escalates a war like de-escalating a war. That this could be disguised as an escalation of the war says something about the United States' public communications system, to which we will turn in Chapter 10.

Another major cause of the reductions in violence, which had nothing to do with the "surge," was the decision by Moqtada al-Sadr, the leader of the largest resistance militia, to order a unilateral cease-fire. As Gareth Porter reported, "By late 2007, contrary to the official Iraq legend, the al-Maliki government and the Bush administration were...crediting Iran with pressuring Sadr to agree to the unilateral ceasefire—to the chagrin of Petraeus.... So it was Iran's restraint—not Petraeus's counterinsurgency strategy—that effectively ended the Shi'a insurgent threat."[13]

Another significant force limiting Iraqi violence was the provision of financial payments and weapons to the Sunni "Awakening Councils"—a temporary tactic of arming and bribing some 80,000 Sunnis, many of them the very same people who had recently been attacking U.S. troops. According to journalist Nir Rosen, a leader of one of the militias that were on the payroll of the United States "freely admit[ted] that some of his men belonged to Al Qaeda. They joined the American-sponsored militias, he sa[id], so they could have an identity card as protection should they get arrested."[14]

The United States was paying Sunnis to fight Shiite militias while allowing the Shiite-dominated national police to focus on Sunni areas. This divide-and-conquer strategy was not a reliable path to stability. And in 2010, at the time of this writing, stability was still elusive, a government had not been formed, the benchmarks had not been met and had largely been forgotten, security was horrible, and ethnic and anti-U.S. violence were still prevalent. Meanwhile water and electricity were lacking, and millions of refugees were unable to return to their homes.

During the "surge" in 2007, U.S. forces rounded up and imprisoned tens of thousands of military-age males. If you can't beat 'em, and you can't bribe 'em, you can put 'em behind bars. This almost certainly contributed to reducing violence.

But the biggest cause of reduced violence may be the ugliest and the least talked about. Between January 2007 and July 2007 the city of Baghdad changed from 65 percent Shiite to 75 percent Shiite. UN polling in 2007 of Iraqi refugees in Syria found that 78 percent were from Baghdad, and nearly a million refugees had relocated just to Syria from Iraq in 2007 alone. As Juan Cole wrote in December 2007, "this data suggests that over 700,000 residents of Baghdad have fled this city of 6 million during the U.S. 'surge,'.... Among the primary effects of the 'surge' has been to turn Baghdad into an overwhelmingly Shiite city and to displace hundreds of thousands of Iraqis."[15]

Cole's conclusion is supported by studies of light emissions from Baghdad neighborhoods. The Sunni areas darkened as their residents were killed or ejected, a process that peaked before the "surge" (December 2006–January 2007). By March 2007, "with much of the Sunni population left fleeing toward Anbar province, Syria, and Jordan, and the remainder holed up in the last Sunni stronghold neighborhoods in western Baghdad and parts of Adhamiyya in eastern Baghdad, the impetus for the bloodletting waned. The Shia had won...and the fight was over."[16]

Early in 2008, Nir Rosen wrote about conditions in Iraq at the end of 2007:

It's a cold, gray day in December, and I'm walking down Sixtieth Street in the Dora district of Baghdad, one of the most violent and fearsome of the city's no-go zones. Devastated by five years of clashes between American forces, Shiite militias, Sunni resistance groups and Al Qaeda, much of Dora is now a ghost town. This is what "victory" looks like in a once upscale neighborhood of Iraq: Lakes of mud and sewage fill the streets. Mountains of trash stagnate in the pungent liquid. Most of the windows in the sand-colored homes are broken, and the wind blows through them, whistling eerily.

House after house is deserted, bullet holes pockmarking their walls, their doors open and unguarded, many emptied of furniture. What few furnishings remain are covered by a thick layer of the fine dust that invades every space in Iraq. Looming over the homes are twelve-foot-high security walls built by the Americans to separate warring factions and confine people to their own neighborhood. Emptied and destroyed by civil war, walled off by President Bush's much-heralded "surge," Dora feels more like a desolate, post-apocalyptic maze of concrete tunnels than a living, inhabited neighborhood. Apart from our footsteps, there is complete silence.[17]

This does not describe a place where people were being peaceful. In this place people were dead or displaced. U.S. "surge" troops served to seal off newly segregated neighborhoods from each other. Sunni militias "awakened" and aligned with the occupiers, because the Shiites were close to completely destroying them.

By March 2009 Awakening fighters were back to fighting Americans, but by then the surge myth had been established. By then, Barack Obama was president, having claimed as a candidate that the surge had "succeeded beyond our wildest dreams."[18] The myth of the surge was immediately put to the use for which it had no doubt been designed—justifying the escalation of other wars. Having spun a defeat in Iraq as victory, it was time to transfer that propaganda coup to the war on Afghanistan. Obama put the surge hero, Petraeus, in charge in Afghanistan and gave him a surge of troops.

But none of the real causes of reduced violence in Iraq existed in Afghanistan, and an escalation by itself was likely to only make things worse. Certainly that was the experience following Obama's 2009 and 2010 escalations in Afghanistan. It's nice to imagine otherwise. It's pleasant to think that dedication and endurance will make a just cause succeed. But war is not a just cause, success in it should not be pursued even if plausibly obtainable, and in the kind of wars now waged the very concept of "success" makes no sense at all.

10

WAR NEWS DOES NOT COME FROM DISINTERESTED OBSERVERS

Virtually all of the war lies described in this book have been facilitated, if not created, by the news media. The CIA and other agencies have generated phony news.[1] The U.S. military has killed and imprisoned unfriendly reporters.[2] But for the most part government control of information is a much more subtle collaboration between propagandists and those who pass themselves off, even to themselves, as journalists.

War lies tend to be debunked much more quickly and thoroughly than most of us hear about (unless we frequent good blogs), because most of our news reaches us by way of a small number of corporations with interlocking boards. This cartel tends to prefer the war lies to the debunking. The pushing of war lies by major media outlets is not a new phenomenon, but the transmitters of the lies have grown more powerful in recent years. They monopolize the airwaves and print outlets, and they utilize the manipulative techniques of propaganda. Propaganda of the sort that appeared for World War I as it was needed, and then vanished when it wasn't, has now become a permanent fixture in the noise boxes in our living rooms. Interestingly, it was the propaganda and censorship during World War I that began the massive elimination of numerous small media outlets.[3]

The corporate bosses in the world of big media have financial interests that benefit from wars. These bosses seek to maintain access to those in power by not challenging lies, hope to please their advertisers, and prefer the higher viewership that comes with wars. But ordinary employees—I hesitate to use the term "journalists"—have an interest in war, too. They believe, or pretend to believe, that the pursuit of any given war is the most intelligent policy and that their professional standards require that they report what those in power say without disputing or even questioning it. In November 2004, *New York Times* reporter Elisabeth Bumiller spoke on a panel:

> **Bumiller:** That's why it's very hard to write those, because you can't say George Bush is wrong here. There's no way you can say that in the *New York Times*. So we contort ourselves up and say, "Actually"—I actually once wrote this sentence: "Mr. Bush's statement did not exactly..." It was some completely upside down statement that was basically saying he wasn't telling the truth. And I got an email from somebody saying, "What's wrong with you guys? Why can't you just say it plainly?" But there's just—
>
> **Lorean Ghiglione (Medill School of Journalism, moderator):** Why can't you say it plainly?
>
> **Bumiller:** You can't just say the president is lying. You don't just say that in the...you just say—
>
> **Ghiglione:** Well, why can't you?
>
> [laughter from the audience][4]

Bumiller spent some minutes trying to quiet the audience, to no avail. People thought a liar should be called a liar. They clearly imagined that journalism was different from stenography. You can get the president's statements off his website. Shouldn't a newspaper point out which parts are true and which are false? Bumiller ought to have explained that calling the president a liar would cost you your job at the *New York Times*.

Reporters who don't think wars are a good idea and don't show proper deference to the powerful don't get assignments or promotions or keep their jobs. A good example of this can be seen in MSNBC's cancellation of Jeff Cohen's debate segments in October 2002. MSNBC also canceled Phil Donahue's extremely popular program for being insufficiently pro-war, as was made clear in MSNBC executive memos.[5] The *New York Times* had no tolerance for reporter Chris Hedges when he dared to speak out against war in 2003.[6] Media workers who cheered for war, in contrast, kept their jobs or were even promoted.

Important and powerful guests are welcomed on talk shows and protected from any other guests who might challenge their propaganda. Norman Solomon's excellent book *War Made Easy: How Presidents and Pundits Keep Spinning Us to Death*, reviews studies done by FAIR (Fairness and Accuracy in Reporting) of the percentage of guests on television shows who have been supporters or opponents of wars. During the first two weeks of the Gulf War, 1.5 percent of sources were identified as American antiwar demonstrators. Eight years later, during the first two weeks of the 1999 bombing of Yugoslavia, 8 percent of the sources on ABC's *Nightline* and PBS's *News Hour*

With Jim Lehrer were critics of the bombing. During the first three weeks of the 2003 war on Iraq, 3 percent of U.S. sources were antiwar. In each case, however, a huge percentage of guests were current or former members of the U.S. military.[7]

The approach of the U.S. corporate media to war coverage is to feature lots of "experts" on war. By "experts" they clearly mean high-ranking military officials, current or retired. But if the question is whether or not to go to war, or whether or not to continue war, or whether or not to escalate war, then why aren't experts at peace making as relevant as experts at war making? In fact, why aren't they more relevant, given our supposed preference for peace, its legality, and the ongoing pretense of civilian control over our military? The military can offer expertise on *how* to start and fight a war, but should it be considered to have any authority on *whether* to start a war?

What about interviewing former members of the military who have turned against war, or historians who could give a broader view, or scientists who could assess the likely environmental and human damage? Why are there no economists to consider the question of what we'll pay for a war? Why are the only useful guests the people most interested in going to war? And then why must they be deferred to more as religious authorities than as apologists for controversial claims?

Cokie Roberts of ABC and NPR explained her approach to fact-checking:

> I am, I will confess to you, a total sucker for the guys who stand up with all the ribbons on and stuff, and they say it's true and I'm ready to believe it. We had General Shelton on the show the last day he was chairman of the Joint Chiefs of Staff and I couldn't lift that jacket with all the ribbons and medals. And so when they say stuff, I tend to believe it.[8]

With such criteria for determining truth, there would be no value in interviewing spokespersons for the antiwar position, even though a large percentage of Americans agree with them. It would be obvious that they were lying since our country offers no peace medals and ribbons with which to decorate them.

Cokie Roberts may have meant to say that medals made her want to support what a general said, whether or not it was true. War reporters for 150 years have more often seen their role as serving the military of their nations than as serving readers or viewers' need to know the facts. Sir Philip Gibbs, who reported on World War I for Britain's *Daily Telegraph*, recalled in 1923:

> We identified ourselves absolutely with the Armies in the field.... We wiped out of our minds all thought of personal scoops and all temptation to write one word which would make the task of officers and men more difficult or dangerous. There was no need of censorship of our despatches [*sic*]. We were our own censors.[9]

Two types of guests who are featured regularly on U.S. television are (1) current military officials, who can be expected to present the Pentagon's official position, and (2) former military officials, who will supposedly give their honest opinions, which will stand a very good chance of lining up nicely with the Pentagon's. In 2008, we learned that the distinction between these two major categories of guests was phony. The Pentagon had recruited 75 retired military officers and given them talking points, which they presented to the media as their own thoughts.[10] Unsurprisingly, the views of the retired generals were not dramatically different from the media norm and no one noticed that anything unusual was going on. The eventual revelation of what was going on went largely unnoticed as well, and few policies were reformed.

By the time of this writing, the Pentagon continued to spend over a half a billion dollars per year on propaganda, including the production of video and print "news" stories not labeled as having been produced by the military. There was no evidence of any significant shift in the types of guests permitted on the air, and some of the well-known liars about the grounds for launching the war on Iraq were now more than regular guests. They were actually employed by the media: Karl Rove at Fox News, the *Wall Street Journal,* and *Newsweek*; John Bolton at Fox News; John Yoo at the *Philadelphia Inquirer*; Newt Gingrich and Dick Morris at Fox News. The careers of those journalists who had pushed war lies in the media had not been harmed either. Charles Krauthammer was still at the *Washington Post* and Fox. Judith Miller was no longer at the *New York Times*, but was happily employed by Fox and a "think tank."

What did change is that active war commanders began to serve more as their own pundits, or what Tom Engelhardt called the wars' narrators. Stanley McChrystal and David Petraeus went on extended media tours, testifying unnecessarily before Congress, holding press conferences, and hitting all the talk show and interview venues, all while supposedly leading the troops in war. Making the "commanders on the ground" (to whom presidents routinely claimed to defer when making decisions) the media voices of war created a situation in which the commander-in-chief's subordinates could publicize their positions, thereby effectively giving the president orders rather than the other way around. In this way, the military compelled its commander to escalate the war on Afghanistan in 2010, and pressured him to delay or cancel planned withdrawals from Iraq and Afghanistan. Engelhardt noted that:

> [I]n late August [2010] commandant of the Marine Corps General James Conway, due to retire this fall, publicly attacked the president's "conditions-based" July 2011 drawdown date in Afghanistan, saying, "In some ways, we think right now it is probably giving our enemy sustenance."

Or consider that, while the Obama administration has moved fiercely against government and military leaking of every sort, when it came to the strategic leaking (assumedly by someone in, or close to, the military) of the "McChrystal plan" for Afghanistan in the fall of 2009, nothing at all happened even though the president was backed into a policy-making corner. And yet, as Andrew Bacevich pointed out, "The McChrystal leaker provid[ed] Osama bin Laden and the Taliban leadership a detailed blueprint of exactly how the United States and its allies were going to prosecute their war."[11]

Challenging a sainted active war commander is, of course, not just bad journalism but also a mortal sin of unpatriotism. You won't see it very often in the U.S. corporate media.

We Write What We're Told to Write, Sir

The U.S. corporate media (which, for you grammar mavens, I'll be glad to treat as plural when it gives me some reason to) certainly behaves as if it is in that deferential frame of mind, carrying its subservience so far as to readily obey the wishes of the Pentagon or the White House to no longer use words or phrases or concepts that it has used for decades. Prior to 2004, the *New York Times*, *Los Angeles Times*, *Wall Street Journal*, and *USA Today* almost always described waterboarding as torture. From that point forward they almost never did, and especially not when the waterboarding was done by the United States.[12] What had changed? Those in power in Washington had put out the propaganda that they did not torture but did waterboard, thereby making waterboarding no longer torture. The use of language in the media is determined by its use in the corridors of power. If a change in usage permits a gruesome crime to be committed with impunity, well that's just the price we have to pay for "objectivity."

Adding a phrase to the media's vocabulary is even easier than deleting one. During the five-and-a-half months leading up to the Gulf War in mid-January 1991, major U.S. media outlets printed and aired comparisons between Saddam Hussein and Adolf Hitler several times a day. Hussein had not become a worse dictator. Nothing new had been discovered about him or Hitler. The White House had simply ordered up a fresh supply of righteous and bloodthirsty indignation. And just three years after the *New Republic* had supported increased military "aid" to Saddam Hussein, the magazine obligingly altered a cover photo to make his mustache look more like Hitler's.[13]

Strict censorship is hardly necessary as a central tool of propaganda when the dominant media outlets are saturating the airwaves and newspapers with comparisons between your desired enemy and Adolf Hitler. As long as the war message is all over page one every day, inconvenient and contradictory facts can show up on page 18 once or twice without much harm being done, although the author of that back-page story will be unlikely to see his or her name on page one in the near future. An even stronger story can safely show up on the internet as long as most people don't hear about it. Censorship won't be required.

Of course, the war planners keep secrets. But the media outlets keep them as well, as part of the team. This wasn't always the case. When Daniel Ellsberg released secret records of the war on Vietnam, the *New York Times* published them because it feared the shame of someone's later finding out that it had not done so. By 2005, the media culture had changed—the *New York Times* was by then more fearful of the possible shame of having published a revelatory story. That year, the *Times* published a story on the government's illegal warrantless spying programs, explaining that it had sat on the story for a year out of fear that it might affect how people voted in elections. The *Times* eventually printed the story because one of its reporters was about to make it public in a book, a book that contained several other important revelations the *Times* never touched. When foreign newspapers or U.S. websites or international whistleblowers make secrets known, the U.S. corporate media tends to behave as if little or nothing has happened, except perhaps to report on efforts to prosecute whistleblowers.

Media outlets will suppress inconvenient news as long as possible. They're still suppressing the news that the attack on Pearl Harbor was expected and provoked. Nearly a dozen major print and television outlets suppressed the My Lai massacre in Vietnam for over a year until an independent news service forced the story out. The major media outlets similarly suppressed their knowledge that the Iraq War was based on lies, meanwhile promoting those lies and facilitating the war. When news that has been suppressed comes out years later, members of the media are not surprised by it and claim that it's boring, trivial, and old news, even though they've never published it. At the same time (forgetting that less can be more) they often claim that the information is false.

In May and June 2005, the most repeated excuse by U.S. media outlets, including the *Washington Post*, for not covering the Downing Street Minutes and related documents demonstrating the dishonesty of the planners of the war on Iraq, was that the documents told us nothing new, that they were old news. This conflicted, of course, with the second most common excuse, which was that they were false.

Those of us trumpeting the story as new and important scratched our heads. Of course we'd known the Bush-Cheney gang was lying, but did everyone know that? Had corporate media outlets reported it? Had they informed the public of confirmation of this fact in the form of memos from top government officials in the United Kingdom? And if so, when? When had this particular piece of news been *new* news?

At what point did it become stale and unnecessary to report that Bush had decided by the summer of 2002 to go to war and to use false justifications related to weapons of mass destruction and ties to terrorism? Judging by opinion polls in spring 2005, we hadn't reached that point yet. Much of the public still *believed* the lies.

If you went back, as I did, and reviewed all the issues of the *Washington Post* that had come out in June, July, and August 2002, you found that, while what was happening behind closed doors in Washington and London may have been known to the *Washington Post*, it certainly never informed its readers.[14] In fact, during that three month period, I found a flood of pro-war articles, editorials, and columns, many of them promoting the lies the debunking of which was supposedly old news.

On August 18, 2002, for example, the *Washington Post* ran an editorial, an ombudsman column, and three op-eds about a potential U.S. attack on Iraq, as well as three related "news" articles. One article, placed on the top of the front page, reported on a memo that Secretary of "Defense" Donald Rumsfeld had sent to the White House and the media. "Defense" officials were worried that countries such as Iraq or Iran could use cruise missile technology to attack "U.S. installations or the American homeland."

The article contained the admission that "no particular piece of new intelligence prompted the warning." What prompted the "reporting?"[15]

The second *Post* article—by Dana Milbank—urged Bush to hurry up and argue for an attack on Iraq before opponents of such an attack raised their voices too loudly. The headline was "White House Push for Iraqi Strike Is on Hold: Waiting to Make Case for Action Allows Invasion Opponents to Dominate Debate." While the article did touch on some of the opponents' arguments, it mainly focused on arguments about how best to persuade the American public and European politicians to support a war.

A third article—by Glenn Kessler—was called "Rice Details the Case for War With Iraq." It began:

> The United States and other nations have little choice but to seek the removal of Iraqi President Saddam Hussein from power, national security adviser Condoleezza Rice said.... "There is a very powerful moral case for regime change. We certainly do not have the luxury of doing nothing."[16]

The *Post*'s editorial on August 18 urged the White House to make its case for war, and advised it to do so on the grounds that Saddam Hussein had refused to get rid of weapons. Here's the last paragraph of the editorial:

A preemptive war carries another danger: that it will seem to legitimize aggression.... It has long seemed to us that targeting the weapons of Saddam Hussein carries a legitimacy that other such attacks would not...That is also a case that the administration must make more persuasively.[17]

The *Post*'s ombudsman column on the same day was titled "Covering the War Before it Starts," and lamented the *Post*'s biased coverage in favor of attacking Iraq. Unfortunately, this admirable observation was overshadowed by three much longer op-eds on the next page.

The best of them, David Broder's, questioned the accuracy of CIA information on Iraq, briefly mentioned a few concerns, and then joined the chorus urging Bush to make his case.

The worst of the op-eds—which was placed at the top and center of the page, illustrated by a clenched fist with an Uncle Sam sleeve pounding on a map of Iraq—was by former national security advisor Zbigniew Brzezinski. The title was "If We Must Fight...." It didn't call proponents of peace "assisters of terrorism," as a *Post* column had done some months earlier, but it did assume there was no reason to work for peace.

Brzezinski offered advice to the president in a list of five recommended steps to war: First, Brzezinski joined the chorus in suggesting that the president must articulate some sort of reason for attacking Iraq. Second, Brzezinski suggested that the reason the president articulates must be that Hussein is producing weapons in defiance of the Security Council. (Brzezinski was good enough to add that Hussein did not use chemical weapons in the last war and that some reason must be provided to believe he would use them in the future). Third, the United States must take the lead in a new proposal for weapons inspections. Europe would support this, and Hussein would not, giving the United States a good excuse to attack. (Here we have Brzezinski plotting publicly as Prime Minister Tony Blair was privately to "wrong-foot Saddam"—the phrase Britain's ambassador to the United States used privately in March 2002 to describe a process of manipulating Hussein into refusing inspections, thereby creating an excuse for war). Fourth, the United States must work for peace between Israel and Palestine, so that an attack on Iraq is not viewed together with the U.S.-backed Israeli assaults on Palestinians—a combination bound to anger quite a lot of people. And fifth, the United States should plan to occupy Iraq after demolishing it.

The *Post*'s final op-ed was by Charles "liberals are stupid" Krauthammer. He attacked the *New York Times* for its allegedly biased coverage against attacking Iraq. Krauthammer was upset that the *Times* had covered some of the stories that the *Post*'s ombudsman criticized the *Post* for not covering—including the expression of opposition to or concern about attacking Iraq on the part of various legislators and officials.

Remember this was the same "objective" media that had been so upset with President Clinton for missing a chance to launch a war on Iraq in 1998. This was the same media that didn't blink when Bush's Chief of Staff Andrew Card explained the delay until September 2002 of the most aggressive war propaganda by remarking, "You don't introduce new products in August."[18]

The war would be built on a planned marketing campaign, not resorted to as a last resort. This fact was not a scandal to be reported in the news or to legal authorities; this was what the *Washington Post* had repeatedly and publicly requested. The *Post* wanted war but wanted the President to sell the war well.

This was the same *Washington Post* that had written of the rising pro-war fever in the country in 1918: "In spite of excesses such as lynching [peace activists] it is a healthy and wholesome awakening."[19]

Ask the Wrong Questions, Find the Wrong Facts

Media outlets reveal their anti-democratic inclinations when they conduct polls, because the results of the polls have little or no influence on the reporting. If the majority of Americans oppose a war, the war is still described in the media as necessary and inevitable, exactly as it would be if everyone supported it, perhaps more so.

Often poll results are themselves misleadingly reported. In October 2006, *Newsweek* found that a majority of Americans wanted President Bush impeached. While other pollsters had found the same thing, this news had not made it into any headline, and it never would. *Newsweek* buried the finding in an article about other poll results and reported that compared to other demands, some things receive "less support, especially calls to impeach Bush: 47 percent of Democrats say that should be a 'top priority,' but only 28 percent of all Americans say it should be, 23 percent say it should be a lower priority and nearly half, 44 percent, say it should not be done."[20] Who could read that (and it continued with additional complicating statistics) and discover that a majority of Americans wanted Bush impeached? It says it, if you look closely enough, but you almost need a course in deciphering Newspeak.

Once in a while, a media outlet will actually claim to be checking the facts of a president's speech for accuracy. One problem with this is that assumptions that the president and the media share are not checked. The validity of the assumption that possession of weapons constitutes grounds for war, for example, is never checked in a review of whether or not there are any weapons. Another problem is that in a long speech important parts can be overlooked, even as less important parts are "fact checked." Nonetheless, it's interesting to fact-check the media's fact checkers.

After President Obama spoke from the Oval Office about the wars on Iraq and Afghanistan on August 31, 2010, Calvin Woodward and Robert Burns of the Associated Press published an article called "FACT CHECK: Is Iraq combat really over for US?" which included some facts of its own that were in dire need of checking. Woodward and Burns challenged the basic pretense that the "combat mission" was over, noting that "Peril remains for the tens of thousands of U.S. troops still in Iraq, who are likely if not certain to engage violent foes." But the authors failed to mention the mercenaries and contractors who were also in Iraq in large numbers. The authors maintained that Obama's claim to have met his responsibilities was debatable. They did not, however, consider the United States' legal or moral responsibilities to cease, desist, confess, and make reparations.

The reporters claimed that Iraq "is expected" to "need" the U.S. military for years. But the passive voice allowed them to avoid stating who was doing this expecting. In fact, the treaty that President Obama said he would comply with requires the removal of all U.S. forces by the end of 2011. There's a loophole for non-Department of "Defense" forces, such as those employed by the so-called State Department. There's no loophole for the military, no matter who expects one.

The AP fact checkers also claimed that Obama had opposed the war on Iraq from the start, failing to mention that he funded it repeatedly as a senator and insisted on continuing it as a president. Remarkably, in his speech, Obama mentioned the negative impact of the financial cost of wars, and the AP had this to say: "the costly Iraq and Afghanistan wars have contributed to the nation's budget deficit—but not by as much as Obama suggests. The current annual deficit is now an estimated $1.5 trillion. But as recently as 2007, the budget deficit was just $161.5 billion. And that was years after war expenses were in place for both the Afghanistan and Iraq conflicts. Most of the current deficit is due to the longest recession since the 1930s...."

War expenses "were in place?" Woodward and Burns mean to say that the wars were already draining hundreds of billions of dollars each year, but what a terrible way to say it! The fact that we've wasted such sums in one year in no way lessens the impact of doing so again in the next. And doing so is not "in place." It is a choice that must be made each time by Congress, even if Congress always makes the same choice.

Shifting the blame for budget deficits to the recession is also a bit slippery, since war and military spending, and their redirection of funds away from more useful areas, have no doubt contributed to causing the recession.

The AP noted that Obama had at one point promised to withdraw all troops in 2009 and had frequently promised to withdraw "combat troops" within 16 months—"a promise essentially kept." Actually, Obama's quick promise at rally after rally had been to make ending the war the first thing he did, and this speech (the one being fact-checked on August 31, 2010, by the Associated Press) came after 19 months, not 16, of Obama's presidency. Woodward and Burns also played along with the myth of the surge—on which see Chapter 9.

I don't mean to knock the novel idea of fact checking. The Associated Press should be applauded for trying at all. We just need someone to fact check the fact checkers.

Good Lies Never Die, They Just Fade Away

Congress members behave as if once a war begins, they must fund it forever. Similarly, many Americans behave as if once a war lie is given credence, it must be believed forever. Even once lies are thoroughly exposed as lies and a majority of Americans comes to believe a war was based on lies, as happened with Iraq, a significant minority goes right on believing the falsehoods. I know from personal experience, and imagine you do too, that presenting some people with facts has absolutely no impact. They simply dismiss the facts or explain them away, their goal clearly being to hang onto their beliefs, not to believe what's actually true.

Jacques Ellul may have figured this out by 1965, when he wrote: "He who acts in obedience to propaganda can never go back. He is now obliged to *believe* in that propaganda because of his past action."[21]

Some recent studies suggest that this is a widespread phenomenon. In March 2010, Brendan Nyhan and Jason Reifler reported on research they had done in 2005 and 2006.[22] They considered the fact that many Americans "failed to accept or did not find out that WMD were never found" in Iraq, and the possibility that "journalists failed to adequately fact-check Bush administration statements suggesting the U.S. had found WMD in Iraq." The researchers presented people with news articles correcting their misunderstanding. They found that among those who placed themselves to the right of center politically, exposure to the correction made them *more likely* to stick to their false belief.

In 2005, Nyhan and Reifler found this result among individuals on the right, but by 2006 it was only those who considered Iraq the most important issue facing the country who refused to have their erroneous beliefs corrected by the facts. The researchers hypothesize, reasonably enough, that the waning emphasis on Iraq WMDs in the media by 2006 and the Washington elite's shift to other justifications for the war may have caused some people to attach less importance to clinging to their erroneous beliefs, even though they would have insisted they were true a year earlier. These individuals had not necessarily dropped their belief that the war was a good thing, just their belief that the most prominent original justification for it was factual. Likewise, they had not necessarily begun to doubt the sincerity of those who had lied to them, just the accuracy of what had been claimed.

But how can we understand those who became *more* likely to believe a falsehood when their mistake was shown to them? Presumably they experience a combination of feeling threatened by the new information and distrusting the source of the written article containing the facts. Other studies have found that when an instructor orally, directly, and in an interactive manner confronts people with correct information they tend to accept it.

Studies have also found that individuals with higher levels of self-esteem are better able to accept information that contradicts what they had previously believed. This suggests, again, that people sometimes feel their reputation and image are threatened by the possibility that they might be wrong. This is a different sort of fear than a fear of communists, or of terrorists, or of the latest version of Adolf Hitler. It can perhaps be addressed more through early childhood education than through adult education.

Education of the adult population, however, is clearly the most important factor in shaping public opinion. If the war lies were not all over the media, people would not learn them in the first place. If the corrections were heard over and over again, they would get through. If our communications system allowed the presentation of a variety of voices and viewpoints and feared promoting falsehoods more than it feared being insufficiently militaristic, we wouldn't need to investigate the widespread phenomenon of engaged citizens certain of their beliefs but completely deluded.

Following World War II, the victors sought to prosecute Nazi propaganda as a war crime. The idea is not completely absurd. If freedom of speech does not permit you to shout "fire" in a crowded movie theater because somebody might get hurt, why should it permit you to shout things that will likely lead to much greater suffering? In fact, under Article VI of the U.S. Constitution, treaties to which our nation is party are the supreme law of the land, and since 1976 the United States has been party to the International Covenant on Civil and Political Rights, Article 20 of which states: "Any propaganda for war shall be prohibited by law."

Whether or not that prohibition is enforced and war lies are effectively banned from our media outlets, the lies can and must be banned from our minds. And those who seek to spread them must be shamed if not punished. We can counter the media's promotion of war lies by learning to spot them, rendering them ineffective from the start. That is the project to which this book is dedicated. The next chapter looks at what we will face if we do not take this step.

11

WAR DOES NOT BRING SECURITY
AND IS NOT SUSTAINABLE

Terrorist incidents have increased during and in response to the "war on terrorism." This shouldn't shock us. War has a history of provoking war, not peace. In our current society, war is now the norm, and eternal preparation for war is not viewed with the widespread horror it deserves.

When a public push begins to launch a new war, or when we discover that a war has quietly gotten underway without so much as a by-your-leave to the Constitution or we the people, that new condition of war does not stand out as significantly different from our normal existence. We don't have to raise an army from scratch. We have a standing army. In fact, we have an army standing in most corners of the globe, a fact that more likely than not explains the need for the new war. We don't have to raise the funds for a war. We (through our misrepresentatives) routinely dump over half of our discretionary public spending into the military, and any additional trillions will be found or borrowed—no questions asked.

We also have war on our minds. It's in our towns, in our entertainment, in our workplace, and all around us. There are bases everywhere, uniformed soldiers, Memorial Day events, Veterans Day events, Patriots Day events, discounts for soldiers, fund drives for soldiers, airport welcomings for soldiers, recruitment ads, recruitment offices, army-sponsored race cars, military band concerts. War is in our toys, our movies, our television shows. And it's a huge part of our economy and of our institutions of higher learning. I read a newspaper story about a family that moved from Virginia Beach because of the endless noise of military jets. They bought a farm in the countryside only to learn that the military would be opening a new airstrip right next door. If you really wanted to get away from the military in the United States, where would you go? Just try to get through a day without any contact with the military. It can't be done. And almost everything non-military that you might come into contact with is itself deeply involved in the military.

As Nick Turse has documented, unless you buy local and non-corporate, it is nearly impossible to purchase or use a product of any sort in the United States that is not produced by a Pentagon contractor. In fact, I am typing this on an Apple computer, and Apple is a major Pentagon contractor. But then, so is IBM. And so are most of the parent companies of most of the junk food and trinket stores and coffee stands I can see. Starbucks is a major military supplier, with a store even in Guantanamo. Starbucks defends its presence on Torture Island by claiming that to *not* be there would constitute taking a political position, whereas being there is simply standard American behavior. Indeed. Not only are traditional weapons manufacturers' offices now found alongside car dealers and burger joints in countless American suburban strip malls, but the car dealers and burger joints are owned by companies driven by Pentagon spending, just as are the media outlets that don't tell you about this.

The military funds and consults on Hollywood movies, sends souped-up Hummers with sexy models to trade fairs, dangles $150,000 signing bonuses around, and arranges (and pays) to be honored before and during major sporting events. Weapons companies, whose only possible customer in this country is a government that never listens to we the people, advertise as widely as beer or car insurance companies. Through this infiltration of every corner of our country, war is made to appear normal, sane, safe, and sustainable. We imagine that war protects us, that it can continue indefinitely without making the planet an inhospitable place to live, and that it is a generous provider of jobs and economic benefits. We suppose that war, and empire, are needed to preserve our extravagant lifestyle, or even our struggling lifestyle. That simply is not the case: war costs us in every way, and in return it provides nothing of benefit. It cannot go on forever without nuclear catastrophe, environmental collapse, or economic implosion.

Nuclear Catastrophe

Tad Daley argues in *Apocalypse Never: Forging the Path to a Nuclear Weapon-Free World* that we can choose to reduce and eliminate nuclear weapons or to annihilate all life on earth. There's not a third way. Here's why.

As long as nuclear weapons exist, they are likely to proliferate. And as long as they proliferate the rate of proliferation is likely to increase. This is because so long as some states have nuclear weapons, other states will want them. The number of nuclear states has jumped from six to nine since the end of the Cold War. That number is likely to go up, because there are now at least nine places a non-nuclear state can go for access to the technology and materials, and more states now have nuclear neighbors. Other states will choose to develop nuclear energy, despite its many drawbacks, because it will put them closer to developing nuclear weapons should they decide to do so.

As long as nuclear weapons exist, a nuclear catastrophe is likely to happen sooner or later, and the more the weapons have proliferated, the sooner catastrophe will come. There have been dozens if not hundreds of near misses, cases in which accident, confusion, misunderstanding, and/or irrational machismo have nearly destroyed the world.[1] In 1980, Zbigniew Brzezinski was on his way to wake up President Jimmy Carter to tell him the Soviet Union had launched 220 missiles when he learned that someone had put a war game into the computer system. In 1983 a Soviet lieutenant colonel watched his computer tell him the United States had launched missiles. He hesitated responding long enough to discover it was an error. In 1995, Russia's President Boris Yeltsin spent eight minutes convinced the United States had launched a nuclear attack. Three minutes before striking back and destroying the world, he learned the launch had been of a weather satellite. Accidents are always more likely than hostile actions. Fifty-six years before terrorists got around to crashing planes into the World Trade Center, the U.S. military accidentally flew its own plane into the Empire State Building. In 2007, six armed U.S. nuclear missiles were accidentally or intentionally declared missing, put on a plane in launch position, and flown across the country. The more near misses the world sees, the more likely we are to see the real launching of a nuclear weapon to which other nations will respond in kind. And all life on the planet will be gone.

This is not a case of "If guns were outlawed, only outlaws would have guns." The more nations that have nukes, and the more nukes they have, the more likely it is that a terrorist will find a supplier. The fact that nations possess nukes with which to retaliate is no deterrent whatsoever to terrorists who wish to acquire and use them. In fact, only someone willing to commit suicide and bring the rest of the world down at the same time can ever use nuclear weapons at all.

The U.S. policy of possible first-strike is a policy of suicide, a policy that encourages other nations to acquire nukes in defense; it is also a violation of the Nuclear Non-Proliferation Treaty, as is our failure to work for multilateral (not just bilateral) disarmament and elimination (not just reduction) of nuclear weapons.

There's no trade-off to be made in eliminating nuclear weapons, because they do not contribute to our safety. They do not deter terrorist attacks by non-state actors in any way. Nor do they add an iota to our military's ability to deter nations from attacking us, given the United States' ability to destroy anything anywhere at any time with non-nuclear weapons. Nukes also don't win wars, as can be seen from the fact that the United States, the Soviet Union, the United Kingdom, France, and China have all lost wars against non-nuclear powers while possessing nukes. Nor, in the event of global nuclear war, can any outrageous quantity of weaponry protect the United States in any way from apocalypse.

However, the calculation can look very different for smaller nations. North Korea has acquired nuclear weapons and has thereby greatly reduced bellicosity in its direction from the United States. Iran, on the other hand, has not acquired nukes, and is under steady threat. Nukes mean protection to a smaller nation. But the seemingly rational decision to become a nuclear state only increases the likelihood of a coup, or civil war, or war escalation, or mechanical error, or fit of rage somewhere in the world putting an end to us all.

Weapons inspections have been very successful, including in Iraq prior to the 2003 invasion. The problem, in that case, was that the inspections were ignored. Even with the CIA using the inspections as an opportunity to spy and to attempt to instigate a coup, and with the Iraqi government convinced that cooperation would gain it nothing against a nation determined to overthrow it, the inspections still worked. International inspections of all countries, including our own, could work as well. Of course, the United States is used to double standards. It's OK to check up on all the other countries, just not ours. But we're also used to living. Daley lays out the choice we have: "Yes, international inspections here would intrude upon our sovereignty. But detonations of atom bombs here would also intrude upon our sovereignty. The only question is, which of those two intrusions do we find less excruciating."[2]

The answer is not clear, but it should be.

If we want to be safe from nuclear explosions, we have to be rid of nuclear power plants as well as nuclear missiles and submarines. Ever since President Eisenhower talked about "atoms for peace" we've heard about the supposed advantages of nuclear radiation. None of them compete with the disadvantages. A nuclear power plant could very easily be detonated by a terrorist in an act that would make flying an airplane into a building seem almost trivial. Nuclear energy, unlike solar or wind or any other source, requires an evacuation plan, creates terrorist targets and toxic waste that lasts forever and ever, cannot find private insurance or private investors willing to take a risk on it, and must be subsidized by the public treasury. Iran, Israel, and the United States have all bombed nuclear facilities in Iraq. What sane policy would create facilities with so many other problems that are also bombing targets? We don't need nuclear power.

We may not be able to survive on a planet with nuclear power available anywhere on it. The problem with allowing nations to acquire nuclear power but not nuclear weapons is that the former puts a nation closer to the latter.

A nation that feels threatened may believe that nuclear weapons are its only protection, and it may acquire nuclear energy in order to be a step closer to the bomb. But the global bully will see the nuclear energy program as a danger, even if it is legal, and become all the more threatening. This is a cycle that facilitates nuclear proliferation. And we know where that leads.

A giant nuclear arsenal does not protect against terrorism, but a single suicidal killer with a nuclear bomb could begin Armageddon. In May 2010, a man tried to set off a bomb in Times Square, New York City. It was not a nuclear bomb, but it's conceivable that it could have been since the man's father had once been in charge of guarding nuclear weapons in Pakistan. In November 2001, Osama bin Laden said, "If the United States dares to attack us with nuclear or chemical weapons...we will retaliate by using the same kind of weapons. In Japan and other countries where the United States has killed hundreds of thousands of people, the U.S. does not regard their acts as a crime."[3]

If non-state groups begin to join the list of entities stockpiling nukes, even if everyone except the United States swears not to strike first, the possibility of an accident increases dramatically. And a strike or an accident could easily start an escalation. On October 17, 2007, after President Vladimir Putin of Russia rejected U.S. claims that Iran was developing nuclear weapons, President George W. Bush raised the prospect of "World War III."[4] Every time there's a hurricane or an oil spill, there are lots of I-told-you-sos. When there's a nuclear holocaust, there will be nobody left to say "I warned you," or to hear it.

Environmental Collapse

The environment as we know it will not survive nuclear war. It also may not survive "conventional" war, understood to mean the sorts of wars the U.S. government now wages. Intense damage has already been done by wars and by the research, testing, and production done in preparation for wars. At least since the Romans sowed salt on Carthaginian fields during the Third Punic War, wars have damaged the earth, both intentionally and—more often—as a reckless side-effect.

General Philip Sheridan, having destroyed farmland in Virginia during the Civil War, proceeded to destroy American bison herds as a means of restricting Native Americans to reservations. World War I saw European land destroyed with trenches and poison gas. During World War II, the Norwegians started landslides in their valleys, while the Dutch flooded a third of their farmland, the Germans destroyed Czech forests, and the British burned forests in Germany and France.

Wars in recent years have rendered large areas uninhabitable and generated tens of millions of refugees. War "rivals infectious disease as a global cause of morbidity and mortality," according to Jennifer Leaning of Harvard Medical School. Leaning divides war's environmental impact into four areas: "production and testing of nuclear weapons, aerial and naval bombardment of terrain, dispersal and persistence of land mines and buried ordnance, and use or storage of military despoliants, toxins, and waste."[5]

Nuclear weapons testing by the United States and the Soviet Union involved at least 423 atmospheric tests between 1945 and 1957 and 1,400 underground tests between 1957 and 1989. The damage from that radiation is still not fully known, but it is still spreading, as is our knowledge of the past. New research in 2009 suggested that Chinese nuclear tests between 1964 and 1996 killed more people directly than the nuclear testing of any other nation. Jun Takada, a Japanese physicist, calculated that up to 1.48 million people were exposed to fallout and 190,000 of them may have died from diseases linked to radiation from those Chinese tests.[6] In the United States, testing in the 1950s led to untold thousands of deaths from cancer in Nevada, Utah, and Arizona, the areas most downwind from the testing.

In 1955, movie star John Wayne, who avoided participating in World War II by opting instead to make movies glorifying war, decided that he had to play Genghis Khan. *The Conqueror* was filmed in Utah, and the conqueror was conquered. Of the 220 people who worked on the film, by the early 1980s 91 of them had contracted cancer and 46 had died of it, including John Wayne, Susan Hayward, Agnes Moorehead, and director Dick Powell. Statistics suggest that 30 of the 220 might ordinarily have gotten cancer, not 91. In 1953 the military had tested 11 atomic bombs nearby in Nevada, and by the 1980s half the residents of St. George, Utah, where the film was shot, had cancer.[7] You can run from war, but you can't hide.

The military knew its nuclear detonations would impact those downwind, and monitored the results, effectively engaging in human experimentation. In numerous other studies during and in the decades following World War II, in violation of the Nuremberg Code of 1947, the military and the CIA have subjected veterans, prisoners, the poor, the mentally disabled, and other populations to unwitting human experimentation for the purpose of testing nuclear, chemical, and biological weapons, as well as drugs like LSD, which the United States went so far as to put into the air and food of an entire French village in 1951, with horrific and deadly results.[8]

A report prepared in 1994 for the U.S. Senate Committee on Veterans Affairs begins:

> During the last 50 years, hundreds of thousands of military personnel have been involved in human experimentation and other intentional

exposures conducted by the Department of Defense (DOD), often without a servicemember's knowledge or consent. In some cases, soldiers who consented to serve as human subjects found themselves participating in experiments quite different from those described at the time they volunteered. For example, thousands of World War II veterans who originally volunteered to "test summer clothing" in exchange for extra leave time, found themselves in gas chambers testing the effects of mustard gas and lewisite. Additionally, soldiers were sometimes ordered by commanding officers to "volunteer" to participate in research or face dire consequences. For example, several Persian Gulf War veterans interviewed by Committee staff reported that they were ordered to take experimental vaccines during Operation Desert Shield or face prison.[9]

The full report contains numerous complaints about the secrecy of the military and suggests that its findings may be only scraping the surface of what has been hidden.

In 1993, the U.S. Secretary of Energy released records of U.S. testing of plutonium on unwitting U.S. victims immediately following World War II. *Newsweek* commented reassuringly, on December 27, 1993: "The scientists who had conducted those tests so long ago surely had rational reasons: the struggle with the Soviet Union, the fear of imminent nuclear war, the urgent need to unlock all the secrets of the atom, for purposes both military and medical."[10]

Oh, well that's all right then.

Nuclear weapons production sites in Washington, Tennessee, Colorado, Georgia, and elsewhere have poisoned the surrounding environment as well as their employees, over 3,000 of whom were awarded compensation in 2000. When my 2009–2010 book tour took me to more than 50 cities around the country, I was surprised that many of the peace groups in town after town were focused on stopping the damage that local weapons factories were doing to the environment and their workers with subsidies from local governments, even more than they were focused on stopping the wars in Iraq and Afghanistan.

In Kansas City, active citizens had recently delayed and were seeking to block the relocation and expansion of a major weapons factory. It seems that President Harry Truman, who had made his name by opposing waste on weaponry, planted a factory back home that polluted the land and water for over 60 years while manufacturing parts for instruments of death thus far used only by Truman. The private, but tax-break-subsidized factory will likely continue to produce, but on a larger scale, 85 percent of the components of nuclear weapons.

I joined several local activists in staging a protest outside the factory gates, similar to protests I've been part of at sites in Nebraska and Tennessee, and the support from people driving by was phenomenal: many more positive reactions than negative. One man who stopped his car at the light told us that his grandmother had died of cancer after making bombs there in the 1960s. Maurice Copeland, who was part of our protest, told me he'd worked at the plant for 32 years. When a car drove out of the gates containing a man and a smiling little girl, Copeland remarked that toxic substances were on the man's clothes and that he had probably hugged the little girl and possibly killed her. I can't verify what, if anything, was on the man's clothes, but Copeland claimed that such occurrences had been part of the Kansas City plant for decades, with neither the government, nor the private owner (Honeywell), nor the labor union (the International Association of Machinists) properly informing workers or the public.

With the replacement of President Bush with President Obama in 2009, opponents of the plant expansion deal hoped for change, but the Obama administration gave the project its full support. The city government promoted the effort as a source of jobs and tax revenue. As we'll see in the next section of this chapter, it was not.

Weapons production is the least of it. Non-nuclear bombs in World War II destroyed cities, farms, and irrigation systems, producing 50 million refugees and displaced people. The U.S. bombing of Vietnam, Laos, and Cambodia produced 17 million refugees, and as of the end of 2008 there were 13.5 million refugees and asylum seekers around the world.[11] A long civil war in Sudan led to a famine there in 1988. Rwanda's brutal civil war pushed people into areas inhabited by endangered species, including gorillas. The displacement of populations around the world to less habitable areas has damaged ecosystems severely.

Wars leave a lot behind. Between 1944 and 1970 the U.S. military dumped huge quantities of chemical weapons into the Atlantic and Pacific oceans. In 1943, German bombs had sunk a U.S. ship at Bari, Italy, that was secretly carrying a million pounds of mustard gas. Many of the U.S. sailors died from the poison, which the United States dishonestly claimed to have been using as a "deterrent," despite keeping it secret. The ship is expected to keep leaking the gas into the sea for centuries. Meanwhile the United States and Japan left over 1,000 ships on the floor of the Pacific, including fuel tankers. In 2001, one such ship, the USS Mississinewa was found to be leaking oil. In 2003 the military removed what oil it could from the wreck.

Perhaps the most deadly weapons left behind by wars are land mines and cluster bombs. Tens of millions of them are estimated to be lying around on the earth, oblivious to any announcements that peace has been declared. Most of their victims are civilians, a large percentage of them children. A 1993 U.S. State Department report called land mines "the most toxic and widespread pollution facing mankind." Land mines damage the environment in four ways, writes Jennifer Leaning: "fear of mines denies access to abundant natural resources and arable land; populations are forced to move preferentially into marginal and fragile environments in order to avoid minefields; this migration speeds depletion of biological diversity; and land-mine explosions disrupt essential soil and water processes."[12]

The amount of the earth's surface impacted is not minor. Millions of hectares in Europe, North Africa, and Asia are under interdiction. One-third of the land in Libya conceals land mines and unexploded World War II munitions. Many of the world's nations have agreed to ban land mines and cluster bombs. The United States has not.

From 1965 to 1971, the United States developed new ways of destroying plant and animal (including human) life; it sprayed 14 percent of South Vietnam's forests with herbicides, burned farmland, and shot livestock. One of the worst chemical herbicides, Agent Orange, still threatens the health of the Vietnamese and has caused some half-million birth defects. During the Gulf War, Iraq released 10 million gallons of oil into the Persian Gulf and set 732 oil wells on fire, causing extensive damage to wildlife and poisoning ground water with oil spills. In its wars in Yugoslavia and Iraq, the United States has left behind depleted uranium. A 1994 U.S. Department of Veterans Affairs survey of Gulf War veterans in Mississippi found 67 percent of their children conceived since the war had severe illnesses or birth defects.[13] Wars in Angola eliminated 90 percent of the wildlife between 1975 and 1991. A civil war in Sri Lanka felled five million trees.

The Soviet and U.S. occupations of Afghanistan have destroyed or damaged thousands of villages and sources of water. The Taliban has illegally traded timber to Pakistan, resulting in significant deforestation. U.S. bombs and refugees in need of firewood have added to the damage. Afghanistan's forests are almost gone. Most of the migratory birds that used to pass through Afghanistan no longer do so. Its air and water have been poisoned with explosives and rocket propellants.

To these examples of the types of environmental damage done by war must be added two key facts about how our wars are fought and why. As we saw in Chapter 6, wars are often fought for resources, especially oil. Oil can be leaked or burned off, as in the Gulf War, but primarily it is put to use polluting the earth's atmosphere, placing us all at risk. Oil and war lovers associate the consumption of oil with the glory and heroism of war, so that renewable energies that do not risk global catastrophe are viewed as cowardly and unpatriotic ways to fuel our machines.

The interplay of war with oil goes beyond that, however. The wars themselves, whether or not fought for oil, consume huge quantities of it. The world's top consumer of oil, in fact, is the U.S. military. Not only does the U.S. military fight wars in areas of the globe that happen to be rich in oil; it also burns more oil fighting those wars than we do in any other activity.

We pollute the air in the process of poisoning the earth with all variety of weaponry. The U.S. military burns through about 340,000 barrels of oil each day. If the Pentagon were a country, it would rank 38th in oil consumption.[14] If you removed the Pentagon from the total oil consumption by the United States, then the United States would still rank first with nobody else anywhere close. But you would have spared the atmosphere the burning of more oil than most countries consume, and would have spared the planet all the mischief the U.S. military manages to fuel with it.[15] No other institution in the United States consumes nearly as much oil as the military.

In October 2010, the Pentagon announced plans to try a small shift in the direction of renewable energy. The military's concern did not seem to be continued life on the planet or financial expense, but rather the fact that people kept blowing up its fuel tankers in Pakistan and Afghanistan before they could reach their destinations.[16]

How is it that environmentalists have not prioritized ending wars? Do they believe the war lies, or are they afraid to confront them? Each year, the U.S. Environmental Protection Agency spends $622 million trying to figure out how we can produce power without oil, while the military spends *hundreds of billions* burning oil in wars fought to control the oil supplies. The million dollars spent to keep each soldier in a foreign occupation for a year could create 20 green energy jobs at $50,000 each. Is this a difficult choice?

Economic Implosion

In the late 1980s, the Soviet Union discovered that it had destroyed its economy by spending too much money on the military. During a 1987 visit to the United States with President Mikhail Gorbachev, Valentin Falin, the head of Moscow's Novosti Press Agency, said something that revealed this economic crisis and presaged the post-9/11 era in which it would become obvious to all that inexpensive weaponry could penetrate to the heart of an empire militarized to the tune of a trillion dollars a year. He said:

> We won't copy [the United States] any more, making planes to catch up with your planes, missiles to catch up with your missiles. We'll take asymmetrical means with new scientific principles available to us. Genetic engineering could be a hypothetical example. Things can be done for which neither side could find defenses or counter-measures,

with very dangerous results. If you develop something in space, we could develop something on earth. These are not just words. I know what I am saying.[17]

And yet it was too late for the Soviet economy. And the strange thing is that everyone in Washington understands that and even exaggerates it, discounting any other factors in the demise of the Soviet Union. We forced them to build too many weapons, and that destroyed them. This is the common understanding in the very government that is now proceeding to build way too many weapons, while at the same time it brushes aside every sign of impending implosion.

War, and preparation for war, is our largest and most wasteful financial expense. It's eating our economy from the inside out. But as the non-military economy collapses, the remaining economy based around military jobs looms larger. We imagine that the military is the one bright spot and that we need to focus on fixing everything else.

"Military Towns Enjoy Big Booms," read a USA Today headline on August 17, 2010. "Pay and Benefits Drive Cities' Growth." While public spending on anything other than killing people would usually be vilified as socialism, in this case that description couldn't be applied because the spending was done by the military. So this seemed like a silver lining without any touch of gray:

> Rapidly rising pay and benefits in the armed forces have lifted many military towns into the ranks of the nation's most affluent communities, a USA TODAY analysis finds.
>
> The hometown of the Marines' Camp Lejeune—Jacksonville, N.C.—soared to the nation's 32nd-highest income per person in 2009 among the 366 U.S. metropolitan areas, according to Bureau of Economic Analysis (BEA) data. In 2000, it had ranked 287th.
>
> The Jacksonville metropolitan area, with a population of 173,064, had the top income per person of any North Carolina community in 2009. In 2000, it ranked 13th of 14 metro areas in the state.
>
> The USA TODAY analysis finds that 16 of the 20 metro areas rising the fastest in the per-capita income rankings since 2000 had military bases or one nearby....
>
> Pay and benefits in the military have grown faster than those in any other part of the economy. Soldiers, sailors and Marines received average compensation of $122,263 per person in 2009, up from $58,545 in 2000....
>
> After adjusting for inflation, military compensation rose 84 percent from 2000 through 2009. Compensation grew 37 percent for federal civilian workers and 9 percent for private-sector employees, the BEA reports....[18]

Okay, so some of us would prefer that the money for the good pay and benefits were going into productive, peaceful enterprises, but at least it's going *somewhere*, right? It's better than *nothing*, right?

Actually, it's worse than nothing. Failing to spend that money and instead cutting taxes would create more jobs than investing it in the military. Investing it in useful industries like mass transit or education would have a much stronger impact and create many more jobs. But even doing *nothing*, even cutting taxes, would be less harmful than military spending.

Yes, harm. Every military job, every weapons industry job, every war-reconstruction job, every mercenary or torture consultant job is as much a lie as any war. It appears to be a job, but it is not a job. It is the absence of more and better jobs. It is public money wasted on something worse for job creation than nothing at all and much worse than other available options.

Robert Pollin and Heidi Garrett-Peltier, of the Political Economy Research Institute, have collected the data. Each billion dollars of government spending invested in the military creates about 12,000 jobs. Investing it instead in tax cuts for personal consumption generates approximately 15,000 jobs. But putting it into healthcare gives us 18,000 jobs, in home weatherization and infrastructure also 18,000 jobs, in education 25,000 jobs, and in mass transit 27,700 jobs. In education the average wages and benefits of the 25,000 jobs created is significantly higher than that of the military's 12,000 jobs. In the other fields, the average wages and benefits created are lower than in the military (at least as long as only financial benefits are considered), but the net impact on the economy is greater due to the greater number of jobs. The option of cutting taxes does not have a larger net impact, but it does create 3,000 more jobs per billion dollars.[19]

There is a common belief that World War II spending ended the Great Depression. That seems very far from clear, and economists are not in agreement on it. What I think we can say with some confidence is, first, that the military spending of World War II at the very least did not prevent recovery from the Great Depression, and second, that similar levels of spending on other industries would very likely have improved that recovery.

We would have more jobs and they would pay more, and we would be more intelligent and peaceful if we invested in education rather than war. But does that prove that military spending is destroying our economy? Well, consider this lesson from post-war history. If you had that higher paying education job rather than the lower paying military job or no job at all, your kids could have the free quality education that your job and your colleagues' jobs provided. If we didn't dump over half of our discretionary government spending into war, we could have free quality education from preschool through college. We could have several life-changing amenities, including paid retirements, vacations, parental leave, healthcare, and transportation. We could have guaranteed employment. You'd be making more money, working fewer hours, with greatly reduced expenses. How can I be so sure this is possible? Because I know a secret that is often kept from us by American media: there are other nations on this planet.

Steven Hill's book *Europe's Promise: Why the European Way Is the Best Hope in an Insecure Age* has a message we should find very encouraging. The European Union (EU) is the world's largest and most competitive economy, and most of those living in it are wealthier, healthier, and happier than most Americans. Europeans work shorter hours, have a greater say in how their employers behave, receive lengthy paid vacations and paid parental leave, can rely on guaranteed paid pensions, have free or extremely inexpensive comprehensive and preventative healthcare, enjoy free or extremely inexpensive educations from preschool through college, impose only half the per-capita environmental damage of Americans, endure a fraction of the violence found in the United States, imprison a fraction of the prisoners locked up here, and benefit from democratic representation, engagement, and civil liberties unimagined in the land where we're teased that the world hates us for our rather mediocre "freedoms." Europe even offers a model foreign policy, bringing neighboring nations toward democracy by holding out the prospect of EU membership, while we drive other nations away from good governance at great expense of blood and treasure.

Of course, this *would* all be good news, if not for the extreme and horrible danger of higher taxes! Working less and living longer with less illness, a cleaner environment, a better education, more cultural enjoyments, paid vacations, and governments that respond better to the public—that all *sounds* nice, but the reality involves the ultimate evil of higher taxes! Or does it?

As Hill points out, Europeans do pay higher income taxes, but they generally pay lower state, local, property, and social security taxes. They also pay those higher income taxes out of a larger paycheck. And what Europeans keep in earned income they do not have to spend on healthcare or college or job training or numerous other expenses that are hardly optional but that we seem intent on celebrating our privilege to pay for individually.

If we pay roughly as much as Europeans in taxes, why do we additionally have to pay for everything we need on our own? Why don't our taxes pay for our needs? The primary reason is that so much of our tax money goes to wars and the military.

We also funnel it to the wealthiest among us through corporate tax breaks and bailouts. And our solutions to human needs like healthcare are incredibly inefficient. In a given year, our government gives roughly $300 billion in tax breaks to businesses for their employee health benefits. That's enough to actually pay for everyone in this country to have healthcare, but it's just a fraction of what we dump into the for-profit healthcare system that, as its name suggests, exists primarily to generate profits. Most of what we waste on this madness does not go through the government, a fact of which we are inordinately proud.

We are also proud, however, of shoveling huge piles of cash through the government and into the military-industrial complex. And that is the most glaring difference between us and Europe. But this reflects more of a difference between our governments than between our peoples. Americans, in polls and surveys, would prefer to move much of our money from the military to human needs. The problem is primarily that our views are not represented in our government, as this anecdote from *Europe's Promise* suggests:

> A few years ago, an American acquaintance of mine who lives in Sweden told me that he and his Swedish wife were in New York City and, quite by chance, ended up sharing a limousine to the theatre district with then-U.S. Senator John Breaux from Louisiana and his wife. Breaux, a conservative, anti-tax Democrat, asked my acquaintance about Sweden and swaggeringly commented about "all those taxes the Swedes pay," to which this American replied, "The problem with Americans and their taxes is that we get nothing for them." He then went on to tell Breaux about the comprehensive level of services and benefits that Swedes receive in return for their taxes. "If Americans knew what Swedes receive for their taxes, we would probably riot," he told the senator. The rest of the ride to the theater district was unsurprisingly quiet.[20]

Now, if you consider debt meaningless and are not troubled by borrowing trillions of dollars, then cutting the military and enlarging education and other useful programs are two separate topics. You could be persuaded on one but not the other. However, the argument used in Washington against greater spending on human needs usually focuses on the supposed lack of money and the need for a balanced budget. Given this political dynamic, whether or not you think a balanced budget is helpful in and of itself, wars and domestic issues are inseparable. The money is coming from the same pot, and we have to choose whether to spend it here or there.

In 2010, Rethink Afghanistan created a tool on Facebook that allowed you to spend, as you saw fit, the trillion dollars in tax money that had, by that point, been spent on the wars on Iraq and Afghanistan.[21] I clicked to add various items to my "shopping cart" and then checked to see what I'd acquired. I was able to hire every worker in Afghanistan for a year at $12 billion, build 3 million affordable housing units in the United States for $387 billion, and provide healthcare for a million average Americans for $3.4 billion and for a million children for $2.3 billion.

Still within the $1 trillion limit, I managed to also hire a million music/ arts teachers for a year for $58.5 billion, and a million elementary school teachers for a year for $61.1 billion. I also placed a million kids in Head Start for a year for $7.3 billion. Then I gave 10 million students a one-year university scholarship for $79 billion. Finally, I decided to provide 5 million residences with renewable energy for $4.8 billion. Convinced I'd exceed my spending limit, I proceeded to the shopping cart, only to be advised:

"You still have $384.5 billion to spare." Geez. What are we going to do with that?

A trillion dollars sure does go a long way when you don't have to kill anybody. And yet a trillion dollars was merely the direct cost of those two wars up to that point. On September 5, 2010, economists Joseph Stiglitz and Linda Bilmes published a column in the *Washington Post*, building on their earlier book of a similar title, "The True Cost of the Iraq War: $3 Trillion and Beyond." The authors argued that their estimate of $3 trillion for just the war on Iraq, first published in 2008, was probably low. Their calculation of the total cost of that war included the cost of diagnosing, treating, and compensating disabled veterans, which by 2010 was higher than they had expected. And that was the least of it:

> Two years on, it has become clear to us that our estimate did not capture what may have been the conflict's most sobering expenses: those in the category of "might have beens," or what economists call opportunity costs. For instance, many have wondered aloud whether, absent the Iraq invasion, we would still be stuck in Afghanistan. And this is not the only "what if" worth contemplating. We might also ask: If not for the war in Iraq, would oil prices have risen so rapidly? Would the federal debt be so high? Would the economic crisis have been so severe?
>
> The answer to all four of these questions is probably no. The central lesson of economics is that resources—including both money and attention—are scarce.[22]

That lesson has not penetrated Capitol Hill, where Congress repeatedly chooses to fund wars while pretending it has no choice.

On June 22, 2010, House Majority Leader Steny Hoyer spoke in a large private room at Union Station in Washington and took questions. He had no answers for the questions I put to him.

Hoyer's topic was fiscal responsibility, and he said that his proposals— which were all pure vagueness—would be appropriate to enact "as soon as the economy is fully recovered." I'm not sure when that was expected.

Hoyer, as is the custom, bragged about cutting and trying to cut particular weapons systems. So I asked him how he could have neglected to mention two closely related points. First, he and his colleagues had been increasing the overall military budget each year. Second, he was working to fund the escalation of the war in Afghanistan with a "supplemental" bill that kept the expenses off the books, outside the budget.

Hoyer replied that all such issues should be "on the table." But he did not explain his failure to put them there or suggest how he would act on them. None of the assembled Washington press *corpse* followed up.

Two other people asked good questions about why in the world Hoyer would want to go after Social Security or Medicare. One guy asked why we couldn't go after Wall Street instead. Hoyer mumbled about passing regulatory reform, and blamed Bush.

Hoyer repeatedly deferred to President Obama. In fact, he said that if the president's commission on the deficit (a commission apparently designed to propose cuts to Social Security, a commission commonly referred to as the "catfood commission" for what it may reduce our senior citizens to consuming for dinner) produced any recommendations, and if the Senate passed them, then he and House Speaker Nancy Pelosi would put them on the floor for a vote—no matter what they might be.

In fact, shortly after this event, the House passed a rule putting in place the requirement that it vote on any catfood commission measures passed by the Senate.

Later Hoyer informed us that only a president can stop spending. I spoke up and asked him "If you don't pass it, how does the President sign it?" The Majority Leader stared back at me like a deer in the headlights. He said nothing.

Another Way

The path of disarmament, clean energy, and investment in the peaceful economy is wide open before us. In the 1920s, Henry Ford and Thomas Edison proposed we create an economy based on carbohydrates rather than hydrocarbons. We have ignored that opportunity up to this point. In 1952, President Truman's Materials Policy Commission recommended a shift to solar power, predicting that three-quarters of homes would be solar powered by 1975. That opportunity has been sitting there waiting for us until now.

In 1963, Senator George McGovern (D-SD) introduced a bill, cosponsored by 31 senators, to establish a National Economic Conversion Commission, as did Congressmen F. Bradford Morse (R-MA) and William Fitts Ryan (D-NY) in the House. The bill, developed with Seymour Melman, the author of several books on conversion from a war economy to a peace economy, would have created a commission to begin that process. Unbeknownst to the country, our military at the time was conducting secret attacks and provocations against

North Vietnam, and strategizing on how to get Congress to pass a resolution that could be treated as authorization for war. A month later President Kennedy was dead. Hearings were held on the bill, but it was never passed. It lies there waiting for us to this day. Melman's books, too, are still widely available and highly recommended.

Benito Mussolini said, "Only war brings to the highest tension the energies of man and imprints the sign of nobility on those who have the virtue to confront it."[23] Then he wrecked his country and was murdered and hung upside down in the town square. As we saw in Chapter 5, war is not the only source of greatness or heroes. War has been made sacred, but need not be. Peace need not be boring. A sense of community can be created through projects other than mass murder.

William James in 1906 published *The Moral Equivalent of War*, proposing that we find the noble, courageous, and exciting aspects of war in something less destructive. No one alive, he wrote, would prefer that the U.S. Civil War had been resolved peacefully. That war had become sacred. And yet, no one would willingly start a new war either. We were of two minds, and only one of them deserved to be followed. "Modern war is so expensive that we feel trade to be a better avenue to plunder; but modern man inherits all the innate pugnacity and all the love of glory of his ancestors. Showing war's irrationality and horror is of no effect on him. The horrors make the fascination. War is the strong life; it is life in *extremis*; war taxes are the only ones men never hesitate to pay, as the budgets of all nations show us."[24]

James suggested that we needed the imagination and willingness "first, to envisage a future in which army-life, with its many elements of charm, shall be forever impossible, and in which the destinies of peoples shall nevermore be decided quickly, thrillingly, and tragically by force, but only gradually and insipidly by 'evolution,'" and in addition "to see the supreme theatre of human strenuousness closed, and the splendid military aptitudes of men doomed to keep always in a state of latency and never show themselves in action." We could not counter such desires, James counseled:

> by mere counter-insistency on war's expensiveness and horror. The horror makes the thrill; and when the question is of getting the extremest and supremest out of human nature, talk of expense sounds ignominious. The weakness of so much merely negative criticism is evident—pacifism makes no converts from the military party. The military party denies neither the bestiality nor the horror, nor the expense; it only says that these things tell but half the story. It only says that war is worth them; that, taking human nature as a whole, its wars are its best protection against its weaker and more cowardly self, and that mankind cannot afford to adopt a peace economy.[25]

James believed we could and should adopt a peace economy but would be unable to do so without preserving "some of the old elements of army-discipline." We could not build "a simple pleasure-economy." We would have to "make new energies and hardihoods continue the manliness to which the military mind so faithfully clings. Martial virtues must be the enduring cement; intrepidity, contempt of softness, surrender of private interest...."

James proposed universal conscription of young men—and today we would include young women—not for war, but for peaceful enterprise, for building a better world for the common good. James listed such projects as "coal and iron mines," "freight trains," "fishing fleets," "dishwashing, clotheswashing, and windowwashing," "road-building and tunnel-making," "foundries and stoke-holes," and "the frames of skyscrapers." He proposed a "warfare against nature."

Today we would propose the building of trains and windmills, solar arrays and projects to harness the energy of the tides and the earth's heat, the restoration of local agriculture and economies, a "war" if you insist against corporate greed and destruction, a humanitarian "war" if you like *on behalf of* nature.

James thought that young people returning from peaceful service would "tread the earth more proudly" and make better parents and teachers of the following generation.[26] I think so too.

12

WARS ARE NOT LEGAL

It's a simple point, but an important one, and one that gets overlooked. Whether or not you think a particular war is moral and good (and I would hope that you would never think that after reading the previous 11 chapters) the fact remains that war is illegal. Actual defense by a country when attacked is legal, but that only occurs once another country has actually attacked, and it must not be used as a loophole to excuse wider war that is not employed in actual defense.

Needless to say, a strong moral argument can be made for preferring the rule of law to the law of rulers. If those in power can do anything they like, most of us will not like what they do. Some laws are so unjust that when they are imposed on ordinary people, they should be violated. But allowing those in charge of a government to engage in massive violence and killing *in defiance of the law* is to sanction all lesser abuses as well, since no greater abuse is imaginable. It's understandable that proponents of war would rather ignore or "reinterpret" the law than properly change the law through the legislative process, but it is not morally defensible.

For much of U.S. history, it was reasonable for citizens to believe, and often they did believe, that the U.S. Constitution banned aggressive war. As we saw in Chapter 2, Congress declared the 1846–1848 war on Mexico to have been "unnecessarily and unconstitutionally begun by the president of the United States." Congress had issued a declaration of war, but later believed the president had lied to them. (President Woodrow Wilson would later send troops to war with Mexico *without* a declaration.) It does not seem to be the lying that Congress viewed as unconstitutional in the 1840s, but rather the launching of an *unnecessary* or aggressive war.

As attorney general Lord Peter Goldsmith warned British prime minister Tony Blair in March 2003, "Aggression is a crime under customary international law which automatically forms part of domestic law," and therefore, "international aggression is a crime recognized by the common law which can be prosecuted in the U.K. courts." U.S. law evolved from English common law, and the U.S. Supreme Court recognizes precedents and traditions based on it. U.S. law in the 1840s was closer to its roots in English common law than is U.S. law today, and statutory law was less developed in general, so it was natural for Congress to take the position that launching an unnecessary war was unconstitutional without needing to be more specific.

In fact, just prior to giving Congress the exclusive power to declare war, the Constitution gives Congress the power to "define and punish Piracies and Felonies committed on the high Seas, and Offenses against the Law of Nations." At least by implication, this would seem to suggest that the United States was itself expected to abide by the "Law of Nations." In the 1840s, no member of Congress would have dared to suggest that the United States was not itself bound by the "Law of Nations." At that point in history, this meant customary international law, under which the launching of an aggressive war had long been considered the most serious offense.

Fortunately, now that we have binding multilateral treaties that explicitly prohibit war, we no longer have to guess at what the U.S. Constitution says about war. Article VI of the Constitution explicitly says this: "This Constitution, and the Laws of the United States which shall be made in Pursuance thereof; *and all Treaties made, or which shall be made*, under the Authority of the United States, shall be the supreme Law of the Land; and the Judges in every State shall be bound thereby, any Thing in the Constitution or Laws of any State to the Contrary notwithstanding [italics added]."

So, if the United States were to make a treaty that banned war, war would be illegal under the supreme law of the land. The United States has in fact done this, at least twice, in treaties that remain today part of our highest law: the Kellogg-Briand Pact and the United Nations Charter.

We Banned All War in 1928

In 1928, the United States Senate, that same institution that on a good day can now get three percent of its members to vote against funding war escalations or continuations, voted 85 to 1 to bind the United States to a treaty by which it is still bound and in which all parties "condemn recourse to war for the solution of international controversies, and renounce it, as an instrument of national policy in [our] relations with" other nations. This is the Kellogg-Briand Pact. It condemns and renounces all war, and commits parties to the treaty to "agree that the settlement or solution of all disputes or conflicts of whatever nature or of whatever origin they may be, which may arise among them, shall never be sought except by pacific means." The U.S. secretary of state, Frank Kellogg, rejected a French proposal to limit the ban to wars of aggression. He wrote to the French ambassador that if the pact "were accompanied by definitions of the word 'aggressor' and by expressions and qualifications stipulating when nations would be justified in going to war, its effect would be very greatly weakened and its positive value as a guaranty of peace virtually destroyed."[1]

The treaty was signed with its ban on all war included, and was agreed to by dozens of nations. Kellogg was awarded the Nobel Peace Prize in 1929, an award already rendered questionable by its previous bestowal upon both Theodore Roosevelt and Woodrow Wilson.

When the U.S. Senate ratified the treaty it did not, contrary to common misunderstanding, add any modifications or reservations. It did, however, publish a report by the Foreign Relations Committee interpreting the treaty as allowing war for self-defense. The harm in placing that prerogative in law is, as Kellogg foresaw, a weakening of the idea that war is illegal. An argument could be made for U.S. participation in World War II under this reservation, for example, based on the Japanese attack on Pearl Harbor, no matter how provoked and desired that attack was. War with Germany could be justified by the Japanese attack as well, through predictable stretching of the loophole. Even so, wars of aggression—which is what we have seen in the preceding chapters most U.S. wars to be—have been illegal in the United States since 1929 when the treaty went into effect.

In 1945, the United States became a party to the United Nations Charter, which also remains in force today as part of the "supreme law of the land." The United States had been the driving force behind the UN Charter's creation. It includes these lines:

> All Members shall settle their international disputes by peaceful means in such a manner that international peace and security, and justice, are not endangered.

> All Members shall refrain in their international relations from the threat or use of force against the territorial integrity or political independence of any state, or in any other manner inconsistent with the Purposes of the United Nations.

This would appear to be a new Kellogg-Briand Pact with at least an initial attempt at the creation of an enforcement body. And so it is. But the UN Charter contains two exceptions to its ban on warfare. The first is self-defense. Here is part of Article 51: "Nothing in the present Charter shall impair the inherent right of individual or collective self-defence if an armed attack occurs against a Member of the United Nations, until the Security Council has taken measures necessary to maintain international peace and security."

So, the UN Charter contains the self-defense loophole. It also adds another. The Charter makes clear that the UN Security Council can choose to authorize the use of force. This further weakens the understanding that war is illegal, by making some wars legal. Other wars are then, predictably, justified by claims of legality. The architects of the 2001 and 2003 attacks on Afghanistan and Iraq claimed they were authorized by the United Nations, even though the United Nations disagreed.

The UN Security Council did authorize the War on Korea, but only because the U.S.S.R. was boycotting the Security Council at the time and China was still represented by the Kuomintang government in Taiwan. The Western powers were preventing the ambassador of the new revolutionary government of China from taking China's seat as a permanent member of the Security Council, and the Russians were boycotting the Council in protest. If the Soviet and Chinese delegates had been present, there is no way that the United Nations would have taken sides in the war that eventually destroyed most of Korea.

It seems reasonable to many, of course, to make exceptions for wars of self-defense. You can't tell people they're forbidden to fight back when attacked, even if nonviolent resistance has been proven more likely to succeed than violence. But what if they were attacked years or decades earlier and have been occupied by a foreign or colonial force against their will, albeit without recent violence? Many consider wars of national liberation to be a legal extension of the right to defense. The people of Iraq or Afghanistan don't lose their right to fight back when enough years go by, do they? But a nation at peace cannot legally dredge up centuries- or millennia-old ethnic grievances as grounds for war. The dozens of nations in which U.S. troops are now based cannot legally bomb Washington. Apartheid and Jim Crow were not grounds for war. Nonviolence is not just more effective in remedying many injustices; it is also the only legal choice. People cannot "defend" themselves with war any time they wish.

What people can do, under the UN Charter, if we ignore the Kellogg-Briand Pact, is fight back when attacked or occupied. Given that possibility, why wouldn't you also make an exception—as in the UN Charter—for the defense of other, smaller countries that are unable to defend themselves? After all, the United States liberated itself from England a long time ago, and the only way it can use this rationale as an excuse for war is if it "liberates" other countries by overthrowing their rulers and occupying them. The idea of defending others seems very sensible, but—exactly as Kellogg predicted—loopholes lead to confusion and confusion allows larger and larger exceptions to the rule until a point is reached at which the very idea that the rule exists at all seems ludicrous.

And yet it does exist. The rule is that war is a crime. There are two narrow exceptions in the UN Charter, and it is easy enough to show that any particular war does not meet either of the exceptions.

On August 31, 2010, when President Barack Obama was scheduled to give a speech about the war on Iraq, blogger Juan Cole composed a speech he thought the president might like to, but of course did not, give:

> Fellow Americans, and Iraqis...I have come here to apologize from the bottom of my heart for a series of illegal actions and grossly incompetent policies pursued by the government of the United States...in defiance of domestic US law, international treaty obligations, and...public opinion.[2]

Cole's imaginary Obama described the United Nations as an attempt to stop war, noting the two more often abused than used loopholes of "defense" or UN Security Council authorization. Cole credited former U.S. president Dwight Eisenhower with upholding the UN Charter by stopping France, Britain, and Israel from attacking Egypt in 1956–1957. This is from a speech by Eisenhower:

> If the United Nations once admits that international dispute can be settled by using force, then we will have destroyed the very foundation of the organization, and our best hope of establishing a real world order. That would be a disaster for us all.... If [the United Nations Security Council] does nothing, if it accepts the ignoring of its repeated resolutions calling for the withdrawal of the invading forces, then it will have admitted failure. That failure would be a blow to the authority and influence of the United Nations in the world and to the hopes which humanity has placed in the United Nations as the means of achieving peace with justice.[3]

Eisenhower was referring to an incident that began when Egypt nationalized the Suez Canal; Israel invaded Egypt in response. Britain and France pretended to step in as outside parties concerned that the Egyptian-Israeli dispute might jeopardize free passage through the canal. In reality, Israel, France, and Britain had planned the invasion of Egypt together, all agreeing that Israel would attack first, with the other two nations joining in later pretending they were trying to stop the fighting.[4] This illustrates the need for a truly impartial international body (something the United Nations has never become but someday could) and the need for a complete ban on war. In the Suez crisis, the rule of law was enforced because the biggest kid on the block was inclined to enforce it. When it came to overthrowing governments in Iran and Guatemala, shifting away from big wars to secret operations much as Obama would do, President Eisenhower held a different view of the value of law enforcement. When it came to the 2003 invasion of Iraq, Obama was not about to concede that the crime of aggression should be punished.

The National Security Strategy published by the White House in May 2010 declared:

> Military force, at times, may be necessary to defend our country and allies or to preserve broader peace and security, including by protecting civilians facing a grave humanitarian crisis.... The United States must reserve the right to act unilaterally if necessary to defend our nation and our interests, yet we will also seek to adhere to standards that govern the use of force.[5]

Try telling your local police that *you* may soon go on a violent crime spree, but that you will also seek to adhere to standards that govern the use of force.

We Tried War Criminals in 1945

Two other important documents, one from 1945 and the other from 1946, treated wars of aggression as crimes. The first was the Charter of the International Military Tribunal at Nuremberg, the institution that tried Nazi war leaders for their crimes. Among the crimes listed in the charter were "crimes against peace," "war crimes," and "crimes against humanity." Crimes "against peace" were defined as "planning, preparation, initiation or waging of a war of aggression, or a war in violation of international treaties, agreements or assurances, or participation in a common plan or conspiracy for the accomplishment of any of the foregoing."[6] The next year, the Charter of the International Military Tribunal for the Far East (the trial of Japanese war criminals) used the same definition. These two sets of trials deserve a great deal of criticism, but a great deal of praise as well.

On the one hand, they enforced victors' justice. They left out of the lists of prosecuted crimes certain crimes, such as the bombing of civilians, in which the allies had also engaged. And they failed to prosecute the allies for other crimes that the Germans and Japanese were prosecuted and hanged for. U.S. General Curtis LeMay, who commanded the firebombing of Tokyo, said, "I suppose if I had lost the war, I would have been tried as a war criminal. Fortunately, we were on the winning side."[7]

The tribunals claimed to start the prosecutions at the very top, but they gave the Emperor of Japan immunity. The United States gave immunity to over 1,000 Nazi scientists, including some who were guilty of the most horrendous crimes, and brought them to the United States to continue their research. General Douglas MacArthur gave Japanese microbiologist and lieutenant general Shiro Ishii and all the members of his bacteriological research units immunity in exchange for germ warfare data derived from human experimentation. The British learned from the German crimes they prosecuted how to later set up concentration camps in Kenya. The French recruited thousands of SS and other German troops into their Foreign Legion, so that about half of the legionnaires fighting France's brutal colonial war in Indochina were none other than the most hardened remnants of the German Army from World War II, and the torture techniques of the German Gestapo were widely used on French detainees in the Algerian War of Independence. The United States, also working with former Nazis, spread the same techniques throughout Latin America.[8] Having executed a Nazi for opening dikes to flood Dutch farmland, the United States proceeded to bomb dams in Korea and Vietnam for the same purpose.

War veteran and *Atlantic Monthly* correspondent Edgar L. Jones returned from World War II, and was shocked to discover that civilians back home thought highly of the war. "Cynical as most of us overseas were," Jones wrote, "I doubt if many of us seriously believed that people at home would start planning for the next war before we could get home and talk without censorship about this one." Jones objected to the sort of hypocrisy that drove the war crimes trials:

> Not every American soldier, or even one per cent of our troops, deliberately committed unwarranted atrocities, and the same might be said for the Germans and Japanese. The exigencies of war necessitated many so-called crimes, and the bulk of the rest could be blamed on the mental distortion which war produced. But we publicized every inhuman act of our opponents and censored any recognition of our own moral frailty in moments of desperation.
>
> I have asked fighting men, for instance, why they—or actually, why *we*—regulated flame-throwers in such a way that enemy soldiers were set afire, to die slowly and painfully, rather than killed outright with a full blast of burning oil. Was it because they hated the enemy so thoroughly? The answer was invariably, "No, we don't hate those poor bastards particularly; we just hate the whole goddam mess and have to take it out on somebody." Possibly for the same reason, we mutilated the bodies of enemy dead, cutting off their ears and kicking out their gold teeth for souvenirs, and buried them with their testicles in their mouths, but such flagrant violations of all moral codes reach into still-unexplored realms of battle psychology.[9]

On the other hand, there is a great deal to praise in the trials of the Nazi and Japanese war criminals. Hypocrisy not withstanding, surely it is preferable that some war crimes be punished than none. Many people intended that the trials establish a norm that would later be enforced equally for all crimes against the peace and crimes of war. The chief prosecutor at Nuremberg, U.S. Supreme Court Justice Robert H. Jackson, said in his opening statement:

> The common sense of mankind demands that law shall not stop with the punishment of petty crimes by little people. It must also reach men who possess themselves of great power and make deliberate and concerted use of it to set in motion evils which leave no home in the world untouched. The Charter of this Tribunal evidences a faith that the law is not only to govern the conduct of little men, but that even rulers are, as Lord Chief Justice Coke put it to King James, "under...the law." And let me make clear that while this law is first applied against German aggressors, the law includes, and if it is to serve a useful purpose it must condemn aggression by any other nations, including those which sit here now in judgment.[10]

The tribunal concluded that aggressive war was "not only an international crime; it is the supreme international crime, differing only from other war crimes in that it contains within itself the accumulated evil of the whole."[11] The tribunal prosecuted the supreme crime of aggression and many of the lesser crimes that followed from it.

The ideal of international justice for war crimes has not yet been achieved, of course. The U.S. House Judiciary Committee included a charge of aggression against President Richard Nixon for ordering the secret bombing and invasion of Cambodia in its draft articles of impeachment. Rather than including those charges in the final version, however, the Committee decided to focus more narrowly on Watergate, wire-tapping, and contempt of Congress.

In the 1980s Nicaragua appealed to the International Court of Justice (ICJ). That court ruled that the United States had organized the militant rebel group, the Contras, and mined Nicaragua's harbors. It found those actions to constitute international aggression. The United States blocked enforcement of the judgment by the United Nations and thereby prevented Nicaragua from obtaining any compensation. The United States then withdrew from the binding jurisdiction of the ICJ, hoping to ensure that never again would U.S. actions be subject to the adjudication of an impartial body that could objectively rule on their legality or criminality.

More recently, the United Nations set up tribunals for Yugoslavia and Rwanda, as well as special courts in Sierra Leone, Lebanon, Cambodia, and East Timor. Since 2002, the International Criminal Court (ICC) has prosecuted war crimes by the leaders of small countries. But the crime of aggression has loomed as the supreme offense for decades without being punished. When Iraq invaded Kuwait, the United States evicted Iraq and punished it severely, but when the United States invaded Iraq, there was no stronger force to step in and undo or punish the crime.

In 2010, despite U.S. opposition, the ICC established its possible, partial jurisdiction over future crimes of aggression. In what types of cases it will prosecute, and in particular whether it will ever go after powerful nations that have not joined the ICC, nations that hold veto power at the United Nations, remains to be seen. Numerous war crimes, apart from the overarching crime of aggression, have in recent years been committed by the United States in Iraq, Afghanistan, and elsewhere, but have not yet been prosecuted by the ICC.

In 2009, an Italian court convicted 23 Americans *in absentia*, most of them employees of the CIA, for their roles in kidnapping a man in Italy and shipping him to Egypt to be tortured. Under the principle of universal jurisdiction for the most terrible crimes, which is accepted in a growing number of countries around the world, a Spanish court indicted Chilean dictator Augusto Pinochet and 9/11 suspect Osama bin Laden. The same Spanish court then sought to prosecute members of the George W. Bush administration for war crimes, but Spain was successfully pressured by the Obama administration to drop the case. In 2010, the judge involved, Baltasar Garzón, was removed from his position for allegedly abusing his power by investigating the executions or disappearances of more than 100,000 civilians at the hands of supporters of Gen. Francisco Franco during the 1936–39 Spanish Civil War and the early years of the Franco dictatorship.

In 2003, a lawyer in Belgium filed a complaint against Gen. Tommy R. Franks, head of U.S. Central Command, alleging war crimes in Iraq. The United States quickly threatened to move NATO headquarters out of Belgium if that nation did not rescind its law permitting trials of foreign crimes. Charges filed against U.S. officials in other European nations have thus far failed to go to trial as well. Civil suits brought in the United States by victims of torture and other war crimes have run up against claims from the Justice Department (under the direction of Presidents Bush and Obama) that any such trials would constitute a threat to national security. In September 2010, the Ninth Circuit Court of Appeals, agreeing with that claim, threw out a case that had been brought against Jeppesen Dataplan Inc., a subsidiary of Boeing, for its role in "renditioning" prisoners to countries where they were tortured.

In 2005 and 2006 while Republicans held a majority in Congress, Democratic Congress members led by John Conyers (MI), Barbara Lee (CA), and Dennis Kucinich (OH) pushed hard for an investigation into the lies that had launched the aggression against Iraq. But from the time the Democrats took the majority in January 2007 up to the present moment, there has been no further mention of the matter, apart from a Senate committee's release of its long-delayed report.

In Britain, in contrast, there have been endless "inquiries" beginning the moment the "weapons of mass destruction" weren't found, continuing to the present, and likely extending into the foreseeable future. These investigations have been limited and in most cases can accurately be characterized as white-washes. They have not involved criminal prosecution. But at least they have actually taken place. And those who have spoken up a little have been lauded and encouraged to speak up a little more. This climate has produced tell-all books, a treasure trove of leaked and declassified documents, and incriminating oral testimony. It has also seen Britain pull its troops out of Iraq. In contrast, by 2010 in Washington, it was common for elected officials to praise the 2007 "surge" and swear they'd known Iraq would turn out to be a "good war" all along. Similarly, Britain and several other countries have been investigating their roles in U.S. kidnapping, imprisonment, and torture programs, but the United States has not—President Obama having publicly instructed the attorney general not to prosecute those most responsible, and Congress having performed an inspired imitation of a possum.

What if the Cops of the World Break the Law?

Political science professor Michael Haas published a book in 2009 the title of which reveals its contents: *George W. Bush, War Criminal? The Bush Administration's Liability for 269 War Crimes.* (A 2010 book by the same author includes Obama in his charges.) Number one on Haas's 2009 list is the crime of aggression against Afghanistan and Iraq. Haas includes five more crimes related to the illegality of war:

War Crime #2. Aiding Rebels in a Civil War. (Supporting the Northern Alliance in Afghanistan).

War Crime #3. Threatening Aggressive War.

War Crime #4. Planning and Preparing for a War of Aggression.

War Crime #5. Conspiracy to Wage War.

War Crime #6. Propaganda for War.[12]

The launching of a war can also involve numerous violations of domestic law. Many such crimes relating to Iraq are detailed in *The 35 Articles of Impeachment and the Case for Prosecuting George W. Bush*, which was published in 2008 and includes an introduction that I wrote and 35 articles of impeachment that Congressman Dennis Kucinich (D-OH) presented to Congress.[13] Bush and Congress did not comply with the War Powers Act, which requires a specific and timely authorization of war from Congress. Bush did not even comply with the terms of the vague authorization that

Congress did issue. Instead he submitted a report full of lies about weapons and ties to 9/11. Bush and his subordinates lied repeatedly to Congress, which is a felony under two different statutes. Thus, not only is war a crime, but war lies are a crime too.

I don't mean to pick on Bush. As Noam Chomsky remarked in about 1990, "If the Nuremberg laws were applied, then every post-war American president would have been hanged." Chomsky pointed out that General Tomoyuki Yamashita was hanged for having been the top commander of Japanese troops who committed atrocities in the Philippines late in the war when he had no contact with them. By that standard, Chomsky said, you'd have to hang every U.S. president.

But, Chomsky argued, you'd have to do the same even if the standards were lower. Truman dropped atomic bombs on civilians. Truman "proceeded to organize a major counter-insurgency campaign in Greece which killed off about one hundred and sixty thousand people, sixty thousand refugees, another sixty thousand or so people tortured, political system dismantled, right-wing regime. American corporations came in and took it over." Eisenhower overthrew the governments of Iran and Guatemala and invaded Lebanon. Kennedy invaded Cuba and Vietnam. Johnson slaughtered civilians in Indochina and invaded the Dominican Republic. Nixon invaded Cambodia and Laos. Ford and Carter supported the Indonesian invasion of East Timor. Reagan funded war crimes in Central America and supported the Israeli invasion of Lebanon. These were the examples Chomsky offered off the top of his head.[14] There are more, many of which have been mentioned in this book.

Presidents Don't Get to Declare War

Of course, Chomsky blames presidents for wars of aggression because they launched them. Constitutionally, however, the launching of a war is the responsibility of Congress. Applying the standard of Nuremberg, or of the Kellogg-Briand Pact—ratified overwhelmingly by the Senate—to Congress itself would require a lot more rope or, if we outgrow the death penalty, a lot of prison cells.

Until President William McKinley created the first presidential press secretary and courted the press, Congress looked like the center of power in Washington. In 1900 McKinley created something else: the power of presidents to send military forces to fight against foreign governments without congressional approval. McKinley sent 5,000 troops from the Philippines to China to fight against the Boxer Rebellion. And he got away with it, meaning that future presidents could probably do the same.

Since World War II, presidents have acquired tremendous powers to operate in secrecy and outside the oversight of Congress. Truman added to the presidential toolbox the CIA, the National Security Advisor, the Strategic Air Command, and the nuclear arsenal. Kennedy used new structures called the Special Group Counter-Insurgency, the 303 Committee, and the Country Team to consolidate power in the White House, and the Green Berets to allow the president to direct covert military operations. Presidents began asking Congress to declare a state of national emergency as an end run around the requirement of a declaration of war. President Clinton, as we saw in Chapter 2, used NATO as a vehicle for going to war despite congressional opposition.

The trend that moved war powers from Congress to the White House reached a new peak when President George W. Bush asked lawyers in his Justice Department to draft secret memos that would be treated as carrying the force of law, memos that interpreted actual laws to mean the opposite of what they had always been understood to say. On October 23, 2002, Assistant Attorney General Jay Bybee signed a 48-page memo to the president's counsel Alberto Gonzales titled *Authority of the President Under Domestic and International Law to Use Military Force Against Iraq*. This secret law (or call it what you will, a memo masquerading as a law) authorized any president to single-handedly commit what Nuremberg called "the supreme international crime."

Bybee's memo declares that a president has the power to launch wars. Period. Any "authorization to use force" passed by Congress is treated as redundant. According to Bybee's copy of the U.S. Constitution, Congress can "issue formal declarations of war." According to mine, Congress has the power "to declare war," as well as every related substantive power. In fact, there are no incidental formal powers anywhere in my copy of the Constitution.

Bybee dismisses the War Powers Act by citing Nixon's veto of it rather than addressing the law itself, which was passed over Nixon's veto. Bybee cites letters written by Bush. He even cites a Bush signing statement, a statement written to alter a new law. Bybee relies on previous memos produced by his office, the Office of Legal Counsel in the Department of Justice. And he leans most heavily on the argument that President Clinton had already done similar things. For good measure, he cites Truman, Kennedy, Reagan, and Bush Sr., plus an Israeli ambassador's opinion of a UN declaration condemning an aggressive attack by Israel. These are all interesting precedents, but they aren't *laws*.

Bybee claims that in an age of nuclear weapons "anticipatory self-defense" can justify launching a war against any nation that might conceivably acquire nukes, even if there is no reason to think that nation would use them to attack yours: "We observe, therefore, that even if the probability that Iraq itself would attack the United States with WMD, or would transfer such a weapon to terrorists for their use against the United States, were relatively low, the exceptionally high degree of harm that would result, combined with a limited window of opportunity and the likelihood that if we do not use force, the threat will increase, could lead the President to conclude that military action is necessary to defend the United States."[15]

Never mind the high degree of harm the "military action" produces, or its clear illegality. This memo justified a war of aggression and all the crimes and abuses of power abroad and at home that were justified by the war.

At the same time that presidents have assumed the power to brush aside the laws of warfare, they have publicly spoken of supporting them. Harold Lasswell pointed out in 1927 that a war could better be marketed to "liberal and middle-class people" if packaged as the vindication of international law. The British stopped arguing for World War I on the basis of national self-interest when they were able to argue against the German invasion of Belgium. The French quickly organized a Committee for the Defense of International Law.

> The Germans were staggered by this outburst of affection for international law in the world, but soon found it possible to file a brief for the defendant....The Germans...discovered that they were really fighting for the freedom of the seas and the rights of small nations to trade, as they saw fit, without being subject to the bullying tactics of the British fleet.[16]

The allies said they were fighting for the liberation of Belgium, Alsace, and Lorraine. The Germans countered that *they* were fighting for the liberation of Ireland, Egypt, and India.

Despite invading Iraq in the absence of UN authorization in 2003, Bush claimed to be invading in order to enforce a UN resolution. Despite fighting a war almost entirely with U.S. troops, Bush was careful to pretend to be working within a broad international coalition. That rulers are willing to promote the idea of international law while violating it, thereby risking endangering themselves, may suggest the importance they place on winning immediate popular approval for each new war, and their confidence that once a war has begun no one will go back to examine too closely how it happened.

The Accumulated Evil of the Whole

The Hague and Geneva Conventions and other international treaties to which the United States is a party ban the crimes that are always part of any war, regardless of the legality of the war as a whole. Many of these bans have been placed in the U.S. Code of Law, including the crimes found in the Geneva

Conventions, in the Convention Against Torture and Other Cruel, Inhuman or Degrading Treatment or Punishment, and in the conventions against both chemical and biological weapons. In fact, most of these treaties require signatory countries to pass domestic legislation to make the treaties' provisions part of each country's own legal system. It took until 1996 for the United States to pass the War Crimes Act to give the 1948 Geneva Conventions the force of U.S. federal law. But, even where the activities forbidden by treaties have not been made statutory crimes, the treaties themselves remain part of the "supreme law of the land" under the U.S. Constitution.

Michael Haas identifies and documents 263 war crimes in addition to aggression, that have occurred just in the current war on Iraq, and divides them into the categories of "conduct of the war," "treatment of prisoners," and "the conduct of the postwar occupation." A random sample of the crimes:

War Crime #7. Failure to Observe the Neutrality of a Hospital.

War Crime #12. Bombing of Neutral Countries.

War Crime #16. Indiscriminate Attacks Against Civilians.

War Crime #21. Use of Depleted Uranium Weapons.

War Crime #31. Extrajudicial Executions.

War Crime #55. Torture.

War Crime #120. Denial of Right to Counsel.

War Crime #183. Incarceration of Children in the Same Quarters as Adults.

War Crime #223. Failure to Protect Journalists.

War Crime #229. Collective Punishment.

War Crime #240. Confiscation of Private Property.[17]

The list of abuses that accompany wars is long, but it's hard to imagine wars without them. The United States seems to be moving in the direction of unmanned wars conducted by remote-controlled drones, and small-scale targeted assassinations conducted by special forces under the secret command of the president. Such wars may avoid a great many war crimes, but are themselves completely illegal. A United Nations report in June 2010 concluded that the U.S. drone attacks on Pakistan were illegal. The drone attacks continued.

A lawsuit filed in 2010 by the Center for Constitutional Rights (CCR) and the American Civil Liberties Union (ACLU) challenged the practice of targeted killings of Americans. The argument the plaintiffs made focused on the right to due process. The White House had claimed the right to kill Americans outside the United States, but it would of course be doing so without charging those Americans with any crimes, putting them on trial, or providing them with any opportunity to defend themselves against accusations. CCR and the ACLU were retained by Nasser al-Aulaqi to bring a lawsuit in connection with the government's decision to authorize the targeted killing of his son, U.S. citizen Anwar al-Aulaqi. But the secretary of the treasury declared Anwar al-Aulaqi a "specially designated global terrorist," which made it a crime for lawyers to provide representation for his benefit without first obtaining a special license, which the government at the time of this writing has not granted.

Also in 2010, Congressman Dennis Kucinich (D-OH) introduced a bill to prohibit the targeted killings of U.S. citizens. Since, to my knowledge, Congress had not up to that point passed a single bill not favored by President Obama since he entered the White House, it was unlikely that this one would break that streak. There was just not enough public pressure to force such changes.

One reason, I suspect, for the lack of pressure was a persistent belief in American exceptionalism. If the president does it, to quote Richard Nixon, "that means that it's not illegal." If our nation does it, it must be legal. Since the enemies in our wars are the bad guys, we must be upholding the law, or at least upholding ad hoc might-makes-right justice of some sort.

We can easily see the conundrum created if people on both sides of a war assume that their side can do no wrong. We would be better off recognizing that our nation, like other nations, can do things wrong, can in fact do things very, very wrong—even criminal. We would be better off organizing to compel Congress to cease funding wars. We would be better off deterring would-be war makers by holding past and current war makers accountable.

13

WARS CANNOT BE
BOTH PLANNED AND AVOIDED

A fundamental lie that keeps war going is the idea that we avoid war by preparing for it. "Speak softly and carry a big stick," said Theodore Roosevelt, who favored building a big military just in case, but of course not actually using it unless forced to.

This worked out excellently, with the few minor exceptions of Roosevelt's mobilization of forces to Panama in 1901, Colombia in 1902, Honduras in 1903, the Dominican Republic in 1903, Syria in 1903, Abyssinia in 1903, Panama in 1903, the Dominican Republic in 1904, Morocco in 1904, Panama in 1904, Korea in 1904, Cuba in 1906, Honduras in 1907, and the Philippines throughout Roosevelt's presidency.

The first people we know of who prepared for war—the Sumerian hero Gilgamesh and his companion Enkido, or the Greeks who fought at Troy— also prepared for the hunting of wild animals. Barbara Ehrenreich theorizes that:

> [W]ith the decline of wild predator and game populations, there would have been little to occupy the males who had specialized in hunting and anti-predator defense, and no well-trodden route to the status of "hero." What saved the hunter-defender male from obsolescence or a life of agricultural toil was the fact that he possessed weapons and the skills to use them. [Lewis] Mumford suggests that the hunter-defender preserved his status by turning to a kind of "protection racket": pay him (with food and social standing) or be subject to *his* predations.
>
> Eventually, the presence of underemployed hunter-defenders in other settlements guaranteed a new and "foreign" menace to defend against. The hunter-defenders of one band or settlement could justify their upkeep by pointing to the threat posed by their counterparts in

other groups, and the danger could always be made more vivid by staging a raid from time to time. As Gwynne Dyer observes in his survey of war, "pre-civilized warfare...was predominantly a rough male sport for underemployed hunters."[1]

In other words, war may have begun as a means of achieving heroism, just as it is continued based on the same mythology. It may have begun because people were armed and in need of enemies, since traditional enemies (lions, bears, wolves) were dying out. Which came first, the wars or the weapons? That riddle may actually have an answer. The answer appears to be the weapons. And those who do not learn from prehistory may be doomed to repeat it.

We like to believe in everyone's good intentions (despite the evidence "marshaled" in Chapter 6). "Be prepared" is the Boy Scouts' motto, after all. It's simply reasonable, responsible, and safe to be prepared. Not to be prepared would be reckless, right?

The problem with this argument is that it's not completely crazy. On a smaller scale it's not completely crazy for people to want guns in their homes to protect themselves from burglars. In that situation, there are other factors to consider, including the high rate of gun accidents, the use of guns in fits of rage, the ability of criminals to turn home owners' guns against them, the frequent theft of guns, the distraction the gun solution causes from efforts to reduce the causes of crime, etc.

On the larger scale of war and arming a nation for war, similar factors must be considered. Weapon-related accidents, malicious testing on human beings, theft, sales to allies who become enemies, and the distraction from efforts to reduce the causes of terrorism and war must all be taken into account. So, of course, must the tendency to use weapons once you have them. At times, more weapons can't be produced until the existing stock is depleted and new innovations are tested "on the battlefield."

But there are other factors to consider as well. A nation's stockpiling of weapons for war puts pressure on other nations to do the same. Even a nation that intends to fight only in defense, may understand "defense" to be the ability to retaliate against other nations. This makes it necessary to create the weaponry and strategies for aggressive war, and even "preemptive war," keeping the legal loopholes discussed in Chapter 12 open and enlarging them, and encouraging other nations to do the same. When you put a lot of people to work planning something, when that project is in fact your largest public investment and proudest cause, it can be difficult to keep those people from finding opportunities to execute their plans.

There Is No Way to Peace; Peace Is the Way

In the aftermath of World War I, a British military body called the Holland Committee reached this conclusion: "It is impossible to divorce the study of defence [sic] against gas from the study of the use of gas as an offensive weapon, as the efficiency of the defence depends entirely on an accurate knowledge as to what progress is being or is likely to be made in the offensive use of the weapon."[2] Even if military "defense" were not understood to include retaliation against a distant enemy, there is no way to develop defensive weapons without researching offensive weapons. In fact, there may be no way to develop defensive weapons at all. What weapon defends against box cutters on airplanes or a chemical weapon attack? In the 1930s, some argued that search lights, sound detectors, anti-aircraft guns, and wire nets to catch bombs, combined with gas masks and shelters could protect everyone from airplanes.[3] How'd that work out? Most war planners knew it was hopeless, and so backed a the-best-defense-is-to-go-on-offense-first approach.[4] War supporters still like to cite General George Patton as the source for "The best defense is a good offense," although I'm sure the idea predates him.[5] It turns out that researching weapons and potential weapons in the hopes that some technological, rather than diplomatic, means of defense will occur to you means, first and foremost, researching offensive weapons.

Attempting to deploy defensive weapons, such as a "missile defense" system creates other problems. That system has not been proven capable of defense, but it is clearly capable of offense. This leads to understandable skepticism about its true purpose. Deployment of the system's components in other countries creates targets for attack, serving the opposite purpose from defense. And the system, viewed with suspicion, is taken as a threat, thus antagonizing potential enemies in a way that something unequivocally defensive would not.

The way to peace turns out to lie not through war preparations, but through peace preparations. Preparing for war very often, though not always, leads to the launching of wars, wars that in many cases would probably not have happened without the preparations. Even the Project for the New American Century (the pro-war think tank discussed in Chapter 6) could not have advocated for the demonstration of the United States' military preeminence had the United States not built up a military dramatically larger than (though obviously not powerful enough to crush) anyone else's.

When Winston Churchill spoke in New York City on October 9, 1929, his $12,500 speaker's fee was paid by the chairman of African Explosives and deputy chairman of Imperial Chemical Industries, which manufactured bombs, ammunition, and poison gas. Imperial Chemical was a descendant of the company of Alfred Nobel (the arms manufacturer and creator of the eponymous "peace prize"), and it worked with DuPont in the United States and I.G. Farben in Germany, the latter being the supplier of gas for the Nazis' gas chambers. Churchill spoke in support of larger militaries.[6]

In President Franklin Roosevelt's office were an ashtray with a ship on it, a cigarette lighter in the shape of a ship's wheel, a barometer, a ship's clock, paintings of sea battles, and a model of a destroyer. Throughout the White House were ship models and paintings and lithographs of naval battles. A portrait of the president in the *New York Times Magazine* on April 3, 1938, carried the caption: "The sea and things of the sea, the navy and its ships and men and guns are probably the outstanding passions of the President's life."[7]

If instead of Churchill and Roosevelt, Britain and the United States had placed in power men or women who lacked affection for weapons and financial interests in weapons, would war have been as likely to occur and to take the form that it did?

And if war had to happen, would it have been as bloody had the United States and its future allies not armed the other side? In 1934, the French arms company Schneider sold 400 tanks to Hitler's Germany, and the British company Vickers sold Hitler 60 airplanes. Meanwhile, the U.S. company Boeing sold three two-engine airplanes to Germany. Pratt and Whitney sold BMW (Bavarian, not British, Motor Works) the rights to build one of its engines. The Sperry Corporation had a patent agreement with the German company Askania. Sperry made bombsights and gyroscopic stabilizers. American companies sold Germany crankshafts, cylinder heads, control systems for anti-aircraft guns, and enough components to produce a hundred planes a month. According to at least some monthly reports from the U.S. government during the 1930s, Germany was the third largest purchaser of U.S. weapons.

Beginning in 1938, Lockheed licensed the Tachikawa and Kawasaki companies in Japan to build 200 transport bombers.[8] Before the United States cut off oil to Japan, it had been—right up through 1940—shipping Japan tens of millions of dollars' worth of "aviation gas" each year, relabeling the substance "high-grade motor fuel" in order to avoid highlighting its purpose.[9]

Between June 1962 and January 1964 only 179 of approximately 7,500 weapons captured from the Vietcong had come from the Soviet bloc. The other 95 percent were U.S. weapons that had been provided to the South Vietnamese.[10]

So, perhaps stockpiling weapons can increase the likelihood of wars, and selling piles of weapons to the other side can make the wars bloodier, but didn't the accumulating mountain of weaponry during the Cold War lead to a bloodless victory?

No, it didn't. It led to endless and very bloody proxy wars fought with "conventional" weapons, not to mention the post–Cold War proliferation of nuclear weapons to additional nations—which can only look harmless up until the moment it eliminates all life on the planet.

The Cold War, just like the period that followed it, involved as much lying as any hot war. The way to build more weapons in an "arms race" is to pretend the other side is ahead of you. In May 1956, Curtis LeMay, head of Strategic Air Command, in testimony before a Senate subcommittee, claimed that Soviet aircraft production was outpacing that of the United States, creating a mad rush to "catch up." In fact, the exact opposite was true, and LeMay almost certainly knew it.[11] John Kennedy campaigned for president promoting a fictional "missile gap" with the Soviet Union, then boosted military spending by 15 percent in his first year. In reality, the United States had more missiles than the Soviet Union did, even before Kennedy doubled the production rate of land-based intercontinental ballistic missiles and increased the planned fleet of nuclear submarines.[12] This, of course, encouraged the Soviet Union to try to keep pace.

All of this is good news for weapons makers, but not for peace planners. Having built all kinds of weapons, people tend to start thinking about how they might use some of them. They focus their attention on war plans, war scenarios, and hypothetical war contingencies, but not on planning for peace. In 1936, an English subcommittee strategized an air war on Germany. They determined that bombing German cities would not cause Germany to surrender, but—importantly—in spite of that knowledge, they developed plans for bombing German cities. In contrast, in 1938, when Clarence Pickett, a leader of the American Friends Service Committee asked Roosevelt to talk directly with Hitler to try to avoid war, Roosevelt replied that he'd thought about that but was more concerned with building up a strong air force.[13] Planning for war was more important than working for peace. (More shocking to the contemporary eye, of course, is the phenomenon of a president communicating with a peace activist at all.)

In 2002, the British government produced a document known as the "Iraq Options Paper," which recommended the steps that would be necessary as a precursor to a military attack on Iraq. Britain and the United States would have to slowly build up pressure to frighten Saddam Hussein. A refusal to admit UN inspectors could serve as a justification, but intense diplomatic work would be needed first to win support from the UN Security Council and other nations. Re-energizing the peace process between Israel and Palestine could help sell the world on attacking Iraq. A major media campaign would be needed to prepare public opinion.[14] So much planning just to arrive at something the planners would claim was a last resort.

Of course, Iraq had no connection to al Qaeda, but the general and dangerously vague "war on terrorism" was driven by propaganda that substituted al Qaeda for the Cold War's Soviet Union, inflating reports of the al Qaeda threat and pursuing policies that actually helped to build al Qaeda. In September 2010, the London-based International Institute for Strategic Studies (IISS) produced a report overseen by a former deputy director of Britain's foreign intelligence agency, MI-6. The report found that the threat from al Qaeda and the Taliban had been "exaggerated" by the western powers. The occupation of Afghanistan had "ballooned" out of all proportion from its original aim of disrupting and defeating al-Qaeda and in fact constituted "a long-drawn-out disaster." The report admitted that the occupation was fuelling violence.[15]

Always innovating, the United States at about the same time found another way to fuel probable future violence. In the largest U.S. weapons sale ever, the Obama administration arranged to sell Saudi Arabia 60 billion dollars worth of aircraft. Apparently Saudi Arabia would need these to fend off the menace of Iran, which possessed a small air force consisting largely of old planes supplied by none other than—you guessed it—the United States.

Coming Soon to a Theater Near You

The most disturbing news about new weapons research and production usually comes from a terrific activist group called the Global Network Against Weapons and Nuclear Power in Space. At the time of this writing, these were their top concerns:

> The U.S. is encircling Russia and China with "missile defense" systems that are key elements in the Pentagon's "first strike" program. The U.S. is deploying Navy Aegis destroyers, with SM-3 interceptors on-board in Japan, South Korea, and Australia. Ground-based PAC-3 (Patriot) interceptors are being put in Japan, South Korea, and Taiwan.
>
> Obama is also deploying PAC-3 missiles in Poland, 35 miles from Russia's Kaliningrad border, and SM-3 missiles at a new U.S. base in Romania. Aegis destroyers will also be deployed in the Black Sea further surrounding Russia.
>
> All of these missile deployments will be directed by U.S. space technology from bases around the globe. U.S. "missile offense" makes it likely that a new arms race with Russia and China will move into space.[16]

How's *that* for bad news? I'll note also that in 2008, the United States shot down a Chinese spy satellite, justifying this successful test of new technology with a transparently false claim of concern over possible health risks. The claim was that if the satellite, which had gone off course, fell to earth its fuel tank could survive and present a toxic danger. The chances of a fuel tank surviving reentry were tiny, and someone would have had to breath its fumes at close range for some time to be affected. That seems a small risk for an institution that has no reservations about coating towns with white phosphorous, napalm, and depleted uranium to address with a $60 million missile.

On top of ending wars in Iraq and Afghanistan, advocates of peace now have to take on a global and galactic arms race. And that may all be the easy part. In addition, the United States appears to be developing and implementing a strategy of unmanned drone wars, secret wars fought by special forces, targeted assassinations and regime changes, and occupations enforced by an ever more privatized and mercenary army.

On June 4, 2010, the *Washington Post* reported that the Obama administration had "significantly expanded a largely secret U.S. war against al-Qaeda and other radical groups"[17] with so-called special operations in 75 countries, up from 60 in 2009. By 2015 Nick Turse was reporting this number as 135.[18] One of the nations where the *Post* reported on "special" operations in 2010 was Yemen, later cited as a success story by Obama, just before it collapsed into utter hell and became the target of intense bombing by Saudi Arabia using U.S. weapons.

"Plans exist," the *Post* reported, "for preemptive or retaliatory strikes in numerous places." The best part of this strategy, according to the *Post*, was that Obama could avoid criticism by not acknowledging what he was doing, even if it was reported in the media, which it likely would not be: "One advantage of using 'secret' forces for such missions is that they rarely discuss their operations in public."

The *Post* reported that Special Operations commanders had greater access to Obama than they'd had to Bush and were finding Obama willing to act more quickly and aggressively.[19] That, plus the increased size and budget, might satisfy some people. Not these guys. In 2010, Special Operations commanders were demanding that more of their operations be "outside war zones," meaning in nations other than Iraq and Afghanistan. By 2015, their wishes had been granted. Despite this information being publicly obtainable, it is little reported and little known. Yet the outlines of its existence, the fact that the president or the CIA can secretly kill, by drone missile or other means, may have by now contributed to the acceptance of presidential wars launched without Congress, including the 2011 war on Libya and the 2014 relaunched war on Iraq plus Syria.

Obama has claimed not to rely on Bush's belief in constitutionally inherent presidential war powers, preferring to claim that the 2001 authorization for the use of military force legalizes his wars, large and small, even though that authorization covered only those people responsible for 9/11 and everyone agrees that many current targets had nothing to do with 9/11.

How do people organize to put a stop to war making of this sort, war making often based on general lies about appropriate policy, but not based on any specific claims to justify each secret action?

Well, first of all, the massive and visible wars are not over yet. There are tens of thousands of troops, mercenaries, and contractors in Iraq and Afghanistan. Ending major hot wars and occupations would be a wonderful problem to have, but it is one we cannot count on having anytime soon. We'll have to keep working for it. Chances are that occupations will be reduced, but not ended. Failures to meet deadlines and comply with treaties will offer opportunities to mobilize antiwar activism or to attempt a spinal implant on Congress. We can use that energy to enlarge a movement aimed at shutting down all forms of warfare.

If we reach a point at which our wars are all small and secret, we may want to put some energy into exposing atrocities. Secret atrocities, when exposed, can make bigger scandals than public shock and awe-ings, especially if they are part of wars nobody even knew were happening. On September 8, 2010, *the Guardian* carried this headline: "US soldiers 'killed Afghan civilians for sport and collected fingers as trophies.'"[20] The theory behind the strategy of promoting awareness of such stories is not that the soldiers will be demonized and that hatred will drive activism. Rather, the hope is that people will be ashamed and horrified by such things being done in their names and with their funds, and will mobilize to put a stop to it. They'll put a stop to it by holding the top war planners accountable, and by defunding the military machine.

A campaign to defund the war machine can also be a campaign to fund jobs, schools, housing, transportation, green energy, and everything else that should be funded. Such a two-sided campaign can bring peace activists together with activists for domestic causes. When that happens in a big enough way, our culture will change, war lies will not seem credible, and war will be a thing of the past.

14

WAR IS OVER
IF YOU WANT IT

When President Barack Obama joined the ranks of Henry Kissinger and the other gentle souls who have received Nobel Peace Prizes, he did something that I don't think anyone else had previously done in a Peace Prize acceptance speech. He argued for war:

> There will be times when nations—acting individually or in concert—will find the use of force not only necessary but morally justified. I make this statement mindful of what Martin Luther King Jr. said in this same ceremony years ago: "Violence never brings permanent peace. It solves no social problem: it merely creates new and more complicated ones."... But as a head of state sworn to protect and defend my nation, I cannot be guided by [King's and Gandhi's] examples alone. I face the world as it is, and cannot stand idle in the face of threats to the American people. For make no mistake: Evil does exist in the world. A non-violent movement could not have halted Hitler's armies. Negotiations cannot convince al Qaeda's leaders to lay down their arms. To say that force may sometimes be necessary is not a call to cynicism—it is a recognition of history.... So yes, the instruments of war do have a role to play in preserving the peace.[1]

But, you know, I've never found any opponent of war who didn't believe there was evil in the world. After all, we oppose war because it is evil. Did Martin Luther King, Jr. stand idle in the face of threats? *Are you serious?* Did King oppose protecting and defending people? He worked for that very goal! Obama claims that his only choices are war or nothing. But the reason people know the names Gandhi (who was never given a Nobel Peace Prize) and King is that they suggested other options and proved that those other approaches could work. This fundamental disagreement cannot be smoothed over.

251

Either war is the only option or it is not—in which case we must consider the alternatives.

Couldn't we have halted Hitler's armies without a world war? To claim otherwise is ridiculous. We could have halted Hitler's armies by not concluding World War I with an effort seemingly aimed at breeding as much resentment as possible in Germany (punishing a whole people rather than individuals, requiring that Germany admit sole responsibility, taking away its territory, and demanding enormous reparations payments that it took Germany until 2010 to pay), or by putting our energies seriously into the League of Nations as opposed to the victor-justice of dividing the spoils, or by building good relations with Germany in the 1920s and 1930s, or by funding peace studies in Germany rather than eugenics, or by fearing militaristic governments more than leftist ones, or by *not* funding Hitler and his armies, or by helping the Jews escape, or by maintaining a ban on bombing civilians, or indeed by massive nonviolent resistance which requires greater courage and valor than we've ever seen in war.

We have seen such courage in the largely nonviolent eviction of the British rulers from India, in the nonviolent overthrow of the ruler of El Salvador in 1944, in the campaigns that ended Jim Crow in the United States and apartheid in South Africa. We've seen it in the popular removal of the ruler of the Philippines in 1986, in the largely nonviolent Iranian Revolution of 1979, in the dismantling of the Soviet Union in Poland, Lithuania, Latvia, Estonia, Czechoslovakia, and East Germany, and in dozens of other examples from all over the world. Why should Germany be the one place where a force more powerful than violence could not possibly have prevailed?[2] In fact, nonviolence has proven itself more likely to succeed and to achieve longer-lasting success.[3]

If you can't accept that World War II could have been avoided, there is still this crucial point to consider: Hitler's armies have been gone for the better part of a century but are still being used to justify the scourge of humanity that we outlawed in 1928: *WAR*. Most nations do not behave as Nazi Germany did, and one reason is that a lot of them have come to value and understand peace. Those that do make war still appeal to a horrible episode in world history that ended several decades ago to justify what they are doing—exactly as if nothing has changed, exactly as if King and Gandhi and billions of other people have not come and gone and contributed their bit to our knowledge of what can and should be done.

Negotiations cannot convince al Qaeda to lay down its arms? How would President Obama know that? The United States has never tried it. The solution cannot be to meet the demands of terrorists, thereby encouraging terrorism, but the grievances against the United States that attract people to anti-U.S.

terrorism seem extremely reasonable: *Get out of our country. Stop bombing us. Stop threatening us. Stop blockading us. Stop raiding our homes. Stop funding the theft of our lands.*

The United States ought to satisfy those demands even in the absence of negotiations with anyone. It ought to stop producing and selling most of the weapons we want other people to "lay down." And if it did so, you would see about as much anti-U.S. terrorism as the Norwegians giving out the prizes see anti-Norwegian terrorism. Norway has neither negotiated with al Qaeda nor murdered all of its members. Norway has just refrained (relatively, in fact less so than many countries) from doing what the U.S. military does.

Martin Luther King, Jr. and Barack Obama disagree, and only one of them can be right. I hope the arguments of this book have inclined you toward King's side of this disagreement. In his Nobel Peace Prize acceptance speech, King said:

> Civilization and violence are antithetical concepts. Negroes of the United States, following the people of India, have demonstrated that nonviolence is not sterile passivity ....[M]an must evolve for all human conflict a method which rejects revenge, aggression, and retaliation.[4]

King said the foundation for that method would be love. Love? I thought it was a big stick, a large Navy, a missile defense shield, and weapons in outerspace. King may in fact have been ahead of us. King's 1964 speech anticipated Obama's speech 45 years later, rejecting its arguments. I recommend reading King's whole speech. He explicitly rejects the "cynical" idea that war is sometimes necessary. What "self-centered men" have done with war, he says, "other-centered men" (and we might add women) can repair.[5]

Other-centered? How odd it sounds to imagine the United States and its people becoming other-centered. It sounds as outrageous as loving one's enemies. And yet there may just be something to it.

Don't Believe the Hype

There will be war lies as long as there is war. If the wars are launched without public process and debate or even public knowledge, we will have to force awareness and force debate. And when we do so, we will be confronting war lies. If we do not halt the war preparations in time, small wars will escalate, and we will be presented with a public argument for more war than ever before. I think we can be prepared to meet all war lies head-on and reject them. We can expect to encounter the same types of lies we've encountered in this book, always with slight variation.

We will be told how evil the opponent in our war is, and that our choices are war or acceptance of evil. We should be prepared to offer other courses of action and to expose the real motivations of the war makers. They will tell us they have no choice, that this war is defensive, that this war is an act of international humanitarianism, and that to question the launching of the war is to oppose the brave troops not yet sent off to kill and die. It will be yet another war for the sake of peace.

We must reject these lies, in detail, as soon as they appear. But we need not and must not wait for the war lies to come. The time to educate each other about the motives for war and the ways in which wars are dishonestly promoted is right now. We should educate people about the nature of war, so that the images that pop into our heads when we hear about war resemble the reality. We should increase awareness of the incredible dangers of escalating wars, of weapons production, of the environmental impact, of nuclear annihilation, and of economic collapse. We should make sure that everyone knows that war is illegal and that we all value the rule of law. We should create the educational and communications systems needed for all of this sharing of information. Some ideas on how to do those things can be found in my previous book *Daybreak*.

If we work to expose secret warfare and to oppose ongoing wars, while at the same time working to shrink the military machine and build peace and friendship, we could make war as shamefully backward an activity as slavery. But we will have to do more than educate. We cannot teach that wars are illegal without prosecuting the crimes. We cannot interest people in making the right decisions about wars unless we democratize war powers and allow people some influence on the decisions. We cannot expect elected officials in a system completely corrupted by money, the media, and political parties, to end war just because we want it ended and because we have made strong arguments. We will have to go beyond that to acquiring the power to compel our representatives to represent us. There are a lot of tools that may help in that project, but there are not any weapons.

What Do We Want? Accountability!
When Do We Want It? Now!

If our engagement is limited to opposing every proposed war and demanding that each current war end, we may prevent or shorten some wars, but more wars will be coming right behind. Crimes must be deterred, but war is currently rewarded.

Punishing war should not mean punishing an entire people, as was done to Germany after World War I and to Iraq after the Gulf War. Nor should we pick out a few low-ranking committers of colorful atrocities, label them "bad apples," and prosecute their crimes while pretending that the war itself was acceptable. Accountability must start at the top.

This means pressuring the first branch of our government to assert its existence. If you aren't sure what the first branch of our government is, get a copy of the U.S. Constitution and read what Article I is about. The whole Constitution fits on a single piece of paper, so this should not be a lengthy assignment.

This also means pursuing possible civil and criminal court actions at the local, state, federal, foreign, and international levels. It means sharing resources with our friends in other countries who are actively investigating their governments' complicity in our government's crimes or pursuing charges against our criminals under universal jurisdiction.

It means joining the International Criminal Court, making clear that U.S. officials are subject to its rulings, and supporting the prosecution of those for whom there is probable cause to believe they have committed war crimes.

There are those among us who invent and promote war lies, those who give deference to authority and believe whatever they are told to believe, those who are fooled, and those who go along because it's easier. There are government liars and volunteer liars helping out in the public relations industry or the news reportainment industry. And there are the great many of us who try our best to understand what is going on and to speak up when we need to.

We have to speak up a hell of a lot more, educate those who have been fooled, empower those who have kept quiet, and hold accountable those who create war lies.

Democratizing War Powers

The Ludlow Amendment was a proposed amendment to the U.S. Constitution requiring a vote by the American people before the United States could go to war. In 1938, this amendment appeared likely to pass in Congress. Then President Franklin Roosevelt sent a letter to the Speaker of the House claiming that a president would be unable to conduct an effective foreign policy if it passed, after which the amendment failed 209–188.

The Constitution from its inception and still today requires a vote in Congress before the United States can go to war. What Roosevelt was telling Congress was either that presidents needed to be free to violate the existing Constitution or that a public referendum might reject a war whereas Congress, in contrast, could be counted on to do as it was told. Of course, the public was indeed more likely to reject wars than Congress, and a public referendum could not have been held on a moment's notice. Congress declared war on Japan the first day after Pearl Harbor. The public would at least have been given a week to hold a referendum, during which time any sort of accurate knowledge might have been spread about by the sort of people White House press secretary Robert Gibbs in 2010 scornfully derided as "the professional left."

The public could conceivably vote for an illegal war, however. Then we would have a war approved by the true sovereigns of the nation, even though that war would have been banned by laws previously enacted through a process presumed to represent the public's wishes. But that wouldn't put us in any worse position than we are in now, with the people cut out of the loop and Congress members answering to their funders, their parties, and the corporate media. If we amended the Constitution, through Congress or through a convention called by the states, we could also take the money out of the electoral system and recover the possibility of being listened to in Washington.

If we were listened to in Washington, a lot of changes would be made. Having Congress listen to us wouldn't get us very far unless Congress took back some of the powers it has given to the White House over the centuries. We will need to abolish the CIA and all secret agencies and budgets for war, and to create real congressional oversight for the entire military. We will need to create in Congress the understanding that it can choose whether or not to fund wars, and that it must act in accordance with the public will.

It wouldn't hurt to strengthen the War Powers Act to eliminate exceptions and add time limits and penalties. It would also help to make aggressive war and war profiteering felonies in the U.S. Code, ban the use of mercenaries and private contractors in the military, get the recruiters out of schools, forbid involuntary extensions of military contracts, and various other reforms.

And then we'll need to move on to reforming, democratizing, and funding the United Nations, with which—by the way—most Americans ultimately agreed about Iraq. The United Nations was correct when it mattered; a lot of Americans came around to believing the war was a bad idea years later.

No Militarization Without Representation

Compelling governmental reforms requires a great deal of organizing and risk taking beyond education and persuasion. The peace movement can demand huge sacrifices. The experience of being a peace activist is a little bit like the thrill of going off to war, the main difference being that rich people don't support you.

The military reform that has been the most heavily funded campaign in recent years has been the effort to allow gay and lesbian Americans equal rights to participate in war crimes. Heterosexuals should be demanding equal rights to be excluded. The second biggest reform push at the moment is to allow immigrants to become citizens by joining the military, without offering them any non-violent alternative other than college, which most immigrants cannot afford. We should be ashamed.

We should be working, as many are, to build resistance within the military and to support those who refuse illegal orders. We should be strengthening our efforts to counter recruitment and assist young people in finding better career paths.

Can you set up a table outside a recruitment office, with copies of this book? Will you give one to your library? Your Congress member? Your local newspaper? Your brother-in-law with the "If you can read this, you're in range" bumper sticker? See http://warisalie.org.

We need people energized about working to dismantle the war economy and convert it to peace. This may not be as hard as it sounds when people find out that this is how we can create jobs and income. A broad coalition can and must be built to include those who want military funding reduced and war funding eliminated, together with those who want funding increased for jobs, schools, energy, infrastructure, transportation, parks, and housing. At the time of this writing, a coalition was beginning to come together that included on the one hand the peace movement (the people who knew where all the money was being misspent) and on the other hand labor and community and civil rights groups, housing advocates, and proponents of green energy (the people who knew where all the money was needed).

With Americans facing unemployment and foreclosure, their top priority is not ending wars. But a movement to move the money from the military to providing the human right to a home grabs everybody's attention. Bringing activists focused on international issues together with those working on the domestic side has the potential to combine major resources with radical and aggressive strategy—never an easy fit, but always a necessity.

If we build such a coalition, the peace movement will be able to add its strength in an organized way to struggles for domestic needs. Meanwhile, labor and community groups, and other activist coalitions could insist that they want only federal funding (for jobs, housing, energy, etc.) that is clean of war spending. This would avoid the situation we saw in 2010 when funding for teachers was included in a bill to fund an escalation of the war on Afghanistan. The teachers' unions apparently felt compelled to back any legislation that would keep their members employed for the time being, so they promoted the bill without mentioning that its biggest component was war funding, knowing full well that the war would keep eating away at our economy like a cancer while increasing the risks of terrorism.

How much larger, more passionate, principled, and energized would have been a unified front demanding money for schools instead of wars! How much larger would the available pot of money have appeared! A unified activist front would disarm the Congress. No longer could it push through war funding by tacking a little bit of disaster relief funding on top. Our collective voice would thunder through the Capitol Hill office buildings: *Use the money for the war to fund 10,000 times the proposed disaster relief, but do not fund the war!*

For this to happen, groups that have shied away from foreign policy would have to recognize that that's where all the money is going, that wars are driving politics away from domestic agitation for a better life, that wars are stripping away our civil liberties, and that wars endanger us all, whether we've been good little patriots and waved our war flags or not.

The peace movement would have to recognize that the money is where the action is. The wars have the money, and everybody else needs it. This would mean dropping the common focus on weak and arcane proposals for "benchmarks" or national intelligence estimates or unenforceable requests for unspecified "timetables" for withdrawal. It would mean focusing like a laser on the money.

To build such a coalition would require organizing outside the dominance of Washington's political parties. Most activist groups and labor unions are loyal to one of the two parties, both of which back policies the American people oppose, including war. The benchmark and timetable sort of rhetorical legislation originates in Congress, and then the peace movement promotes it. The demand to cut off the funding originates out among the people and must be imposed on Congress. That's a key distinction that should guide our organizing.

And the organizing should be doable. On October 2, 2010, a broad coalition held a rally at the Lincoln Memorial in Washington, D.C. The organizers sought to use the rally both to demand jobs, protect Social Security, and advance a hodgepodge of progressive ideas, and also to cheer for the Democratic Party, whose leadership was not on board with that program. An independent movement would back particular politicians, including Democrats, but they would have to earn it by supporting our positions.

The peace movement was included in the rally, if not given top billing, and many peace organizations took part. We found that, among all of those tens of thousands of union members and civil rights activists who showed up, virtually all of them were eager to carry anti-war posters and stickers. In fact the message "Money for Jobs, Not Wars," was immensely popular. If anyone at all disagreed, I haven't heard about it. The theme of the rally was "One Nation Working Together," a warm message but one so vague we didn't even offend anyone enough to produce a counter-rally. I suspect more people would have shown up and a stronger message would have been delivered had the headline been "Move War Dollars to Human Needs!"

One speech outshone all others that day. The speaker was 83-year-old singer and activist Harry Belafonte, his voice strained, scratchy, and gripping. These were some of his words:

> Martin Luther King, Jr., in his "I Have a Dream" speech 47 years ago, said that America would soon come to realize that the war that we were in at that time that this nation waged in Vietnam was not only unconscionable, but unwinnable. Fifty-eight thousand Americans died in that cruel adventure, and over two million Vietnamese and Cambodians perished. Now today, almost a half-a-century later, as we gather at this place where Dr. King prayed for the soul of this great nation, tens of thousands of citizens from all walks of life have come here today to rekindle his dream and once again hope that all America will soon come to the realization that the wars that we wage today in far away lands are immoral, unconscionable and unwinnable.
>
> The Central Intelligence Agency, in its official report, tells us that the enemy we pursue in Afghanistan and in Pakistan, the al-Qaeda, they number less than 50—I say 50—people. Do we really think that sending 100,000 young American men and women to kill innocent civilians, women, and children, and antagonizing the tens of millions of people in the whole region somehow makes us secure? Does this make any sense?
>
> The President's decision to escalate the war in that region alone costs the nation $33 billion. That sum of money could not only create 600,000 jobs here in America, but would even leave us a few billion to start rebuilding our schools, our roads, our hospitals and affordable housing. It could also help to rebuild the lives of the thousands of our returning wounded veterans.[6]

Making Lists

Shifting our spending priorities and getting clean votes in Congress on funding all the things we want also gets us straight, unencumbered (I can't say clean) votes on the war funding. And those votes provide us with two lists: the list of those who did what we told them and the list of those who did not. But these lists cannot remain, as they are today, lists of Congress members to thank and lists of Congress members to go meekly whining to. They have to become the lists of whom we are going to reelect and whom we are going to send packing. If you won't send a politician packing in a general election because of the party they belong to, then replace them in a primary. But send them packing we must, or they will never heed our demands, not even if we win over 100 percent of the country and reject every lie the day it's uttered.

Pressuring elected officials in between elections is going to be needed as well. Nonviolently shutting down the military-industrial-congressional complex can communicate our demands very strongly. But we can't sit in elected officials' offices demanding peace while promising to vote for them, no matter what they do—not if we expect to be heard.

If sitting in Congress members' offices and voting them out of office strikes you as exhibiting a naïve faith in the system, and if you want us to instead march in the street and appeal to the president, our views may not be as far apart as you imagine. We *do* need to march in the streets. We also need to create democratic media outlets and impact every segment of our culture and population. And we need to march in the suites, too, to disrupt what is happening and grab the attention of those responsible by letting them know that we can end their careers. If that's "working with the system" I certainly hope nobody tries working like that with me. We can neither ignore our government, nor obey it. We have to impose our will on it. That requires, in the absence of millions of dollars to "donate," millions of people dedicated to applying pressure. Those people need to know where to press. One important answer is on the public checkbook.

Appealing to presidents doesn't hurt. Really, that's just another way of saying that we need to reach everyone everywhere. And we do. But we have far less power over presidents than over members of the House of Representatives—and that's saying something! If we accept the idea that presidents, and only presidents, have the power to begin and end wars, we will guarantee ourselves a lot more wars from a lot more presidents, if the world survives that long.

The power of war must belong to us. If we can find a way to directly control presidents' war making, that will certainly work. If we can do so by controlling and re-empowering Congress, which seems at least slightly more likely, that will also work. As long as you're trying to influence someone away from war or toward peace, whether it's a Congress member, a president, a weapons maker, a soldier, a neighbor, or a child, you are doing work worthy of the highest honors on earth.

When the World Outlawed War

In 2011, the year after the publication of the first edition of *War Is a Lie,* I published a short book called *When the World Outlawed War.* It was the result of my reading materials from the peace movement of the 1920s that created the Kellogg-Briand Pact. The book became popular, at least among peace activists. Ralph Nader put it in one of his annual lists of the dozen or so books that everyone should read. In the book, I proposed marking August 27th as a peace holiday in remembrance of the signing of the Peace Pact in 1928, and groups and even city governments in some places have begun doing so.

The Kellogg-Briand Pact is a tool available to us. Getting the wealthy nations of the world on board a new treaty banning all war would be a steep climb indeed. How much easier to point out that they are on board already! The Pact is considered valid by the U.S. State Department's website, and by the Pentagon's 2015 Law of War Manual.[7] We can urge current parties to abide by the treaty and other nations to sign onto it.

But the real value of bringing back memory of the Kellogg-Briand Pact comes in bringing back understanding of how the people thought who created it—the vision of the world held by the Outlawry activists who imposed their will on Kellogg and Briand and the governments of the earth. These were people who looked at the banning of dueling and noted that defensive dueling had not been kept around. They looked at the ending (or major diminishment) of slavery, blood feuds, and other forms of barbarism, and proposed to add war to the list.

The very first time that the Kellogg-Briand Pact was used to prosecute the crime of war was, for whatever combination of reasons, the last time (thus far) that the wealthy nations of the world have gone to war directly with each other. If ineffectiveness were legal grounds for ignoring a law (and it isn't) that certainly wouldn't apply here.

But the wars on, through, and among poor countries roll on, and the world envisioned by the Outlawrists has yet to be made real—we still don't have the legal, economic, social, and cultural structures they thought would eliminate war from the world. And only to a limited extent do we have what they worked so hard to give us: the stigmatization of war as illicit, criminal, backward, and archaic.

World Beyond War

In 2013, I published a short book called *War No More: The Case for Abolition*. It argued that war can be ended, that war should be ended, that war is not going to end on its own, and that we have to end war. Part 3 (war is not going to end on its own) is a response to a phenomenon I call Pinkerism after one of its proponents, Steven Pinker.[8] The term is not ideal, because Pinker has written on many topics, on some of which I find his contributions quite valuable. Nonetheless, in this area, Pinkerists have created the widespread and false belief that war is going away on its own,[9] a belief that some of them, including Ian Morris,[10] combine with passionate support for war.

They manage this trick by treating U.S. and European wars as something other than wars, by miscounting casualties, by making misleading comparisons, by conflating war with other types of violence, and through various other sleights of hand. Their acknowledgment that war *could* go away is very helpful. Their false claim that it is going away is less than helpful. Their notion that war is going away thanks to Western warmaking is disastrous.

The publication of *War No More* led to the creation of a new organization called World Beyond War (http://worldbeyondwar.org) by some of us who believed the peace movement was missing something, that it was missing the forest of war abolition for the trees of particular wars or weapons. World Beyond War makes a case for dismantling the entire institution of war for a variety of reasons. As I wrote above in this book: "War would be the greatest evil on earth even if it cost no money, used up no resources, left no environmental damage, expanded rather than curtailed the rights of citizens back home, and even if it accomplished something worthwhile. Of course, none of these conditions is possible."

World Beyond War documents on its website that war kills more through how war funding is not spent than through how it is spent. A fraction of the money spent on war could alleviate massive suffering and death if spent instead on water, food, medicine, and environmental protection. Routine war preparations spending is the vast bulk of the spending, dwarfing the spending for any particular war or set of wars. Scaling back or eliminating military spending would make funding available for useful projects at home and abroad almost beyond comprehension. While we've been tricked into thinking that militarism is good economically, the opposite is true. It is hollowing out the U.S. economy.[11] As someone just posted to Twitter following news of some huge Pentagon purchase, "Our weapons now cost more than anything they're defending."[12] War is similarly catastrophic environmentally, in terms of civil liberties, and for the possibility of self-governance. Meanwhile it makes us less safe while killing large numbers of people.

At World Beyond War we've been detailing alternative means of avoiding and resolving conflict. We've created a whole calendar of peace holidays. We've developed a set of maps and an annual report laying out what militarism looks like around the globe. We've promoted the use of nonviolent action, which really is the answer to William James's question of how to replace war while keeping the positive bits, the camaraderie, the bravery, the heroism. And in the face of the general sentiment that you cannot change anyone's mind, we've been overwhelmed by the positive responses to surveys we pass around after speaking events, and by unsolicited comments from people whose minds have been changed about war.

Peace Is a Truth

In November 1943, six residents of Coventry, England, which had been bombed by Germany, wrote to the *New Statesman* to condemn the bombing of German cities, asserting that the "general feeling" in Coventry was the "desire that no other people shall suffer as they have done."

In 1997, on the 60th anniversary of the bombing of Guernica, the president of Germany wrote a letter to the Basque people apologizing for the Nazi-era bombing. The Mayor of Guernica wrote back and accepted the apology.

Murder Victims' Families for Human Rights is an international organization, based in the United States, of family members of victims of criminal murder, state execution, extra-judicial assassinations, and "disappearances," who oppose the death penalty in all cases.

Peaceful Tomorrows is an organization founded by family members of those killed on September 11, 2001, who say they have "united to turn our grief into action for peace. By developing and advocating nonviolent options and actions in the pursuit of justice, we hope to break the cycles of violence engendered by war and terrorism. Acknowledging our common experience with all people affected by violence throughout the world, we work to create a safer and more peaceful world for everyone."

So must we all.

Please get involved at http://warisalie.org

Epilogue:
War Lies 2010–2015

As of 2015 we have seen five more years of lying about war, interspersed with a few encouraging signs of the public recognizing and resisting lies about war. A 2013 effort to bomb Syria was stopped, at least temporarily, in large part by refusal to fall for the lies. The lies of generosity and noble motives (see Chapters 3 and 6) proved insufficient. The ongoing drawn-out effort to start a war on Iran continued to use lies of defense, unavoidability, and sustainability (Chapters 2, 4, and 11)—and to fail. But a 2014 renewal of U.S. war in Iraq, spilling over into Syria, found propaganda success using lies of evil, defense, unavoidability—and others, in particular the production of fear (Chapters 1, 2, and 4). And the lies (of legality, unbiased media, etc.) that prop up the routine militarism—which in turn generates the wars—still permeate our culture.

While some people are becoming more questioning of war and learning more about nonviolent alternatives, war is being made easier, less accountable, and less controllable, and the U.S. government is toying with the possibility of war with the nuclear nation of Russia, by antagonizing Russia and by telling lies about supposed evil Russian actions. China, too, is being once more built up as an enemy.

I have seen in the past five years that the lessons in this book can make a difference. People can learn to recognize war lies on sight. But a much greater number of people will need to do so during the coming years if it is to make the difference that's needed.

The most dangerous war lies are those that beautify a past war, because they make people trusting toward new wars. As we live through the centennial of World War I, the "war to end all wars," we witness governments like that in London going to great efforts to glorify a war heretofore almost universally recognized as pointless slaughter. Meanwhile, U.S. President Barack Obama has suddenly declared the Korean War a victory after so many decades of virtually everyone calling it a disastrous draw. And on May 25, 2012, Obama announced a 13-year, $65 million commemoration of the war on Vietnam:

> As we observe the 50th anniversary of the Vietnam War, we reflect with solemn reverence upon the valor of a generation that served with honor. We pay tribute to the more than 3 million servicemen and women who left their families to serve bravely, a world away.... They pushed through jungles and rice paddies, heat and monsoon, fighting heroically to protect the ideals we hold dear as Americans.[1]

Which ideals might those have been? Remember, this was the bad war in contrast to which World War II acquired the ridiculous label "good war." But the Pentagon is intent on undoing any accurate memory of Vietnam. Members of the wonderful organization, Veterans For Peace, meanwhile have launched their own educational campaign to counter the Pentagon's at VietnamFullDisclosure.org, and the Vietnam Peace Commemoration Committee has done the same at LessonsOfVietnam.com. Already, the Pentagon has been persuaded to correct some of its inaccurate statements. Evidence of the extent of the killing in Vietnam continues to emerge,[2] and it has suddenly become universally acceptable in academia and the corporate media to acknowledge that presidential candidate Richard M. Nixon secretly sabotaged peace talks in 1968 that appeared likely to end the war until he intervened. As a result, the war raged on and Nixon won election promising to end the war, which he didn't do.[3] There would seem to be at work here something like a 50-year limit on caring about treason or mass-murder; once 50 years have passed we can all admit that our elected officials have told the most awful lies to cover for the most murderous actions, but we aren't supposed to be bothered by it. Imagine what it might become acceptable to say about current wars 50 years hence!

The struggle to shape the memory of the U.S. war on Iraq and the overall "global war on terrorism" is already underway, even as the war on terrorism leads to an ongoing steady increase in terrorism.[4] President Obama has repeatedly praised the war on Iraq that he criticized as a candidate. Planners of the war on Iraq are claiming to have won it (what would losing it have looked like?!) and, in some cases, they are teaching courses about it, even as it continues in a different form.[5] They're also claiming that Obama created ISIS (also known as ISIL/Islamic State/Daesh), the new enemy, by recklessly withdrawing U.S. troops from Iraq, even though ISIS was created by the 2003 invasion and subsequent occupation,[6] and even though Obama broke his promise to withdraw rapidly, was compelled to withdraw by a treaty that former president Bush had signed and by Iraq's refusal to allow troops to remain with criminal immunity, and even though Obama left thousands of troops in place and quickly began sending more back in, which only strengthened ISIS.

U.S. State Department emails, published by WikiLeaks, show the U.S. government working with Sony Entertainment to create a caricatured image of the leader of North Korea in a film called *The Interview* and appealing to Sony for help with propaganda against ISIS. Leaked memos also show the CIA closely shaping another movie called *Zero Dark Thirty,* which falsely depicts torture as having been successful in obtaining information critical to locating and murdering Osama bin Laden. The killing of bin Laden itself was falsely depicted as a "capture or kill" operation by President Obama, whereas virtually every report makes clear that nothing but killing was ever considered, and bin Laden was murdered unarmed, not killed in a fight.

Meanwhile, pages of U.S. government reports covering Saudi Arabia's role in the crimes of September 11, 2001, remain secret, a serious and credible investigation of those crimes has never been done, and the announcement of bin Laden's death did nothing to end the ongoing wars that were begun with him as the supposed target, wars that have long since killed hundreds of times the people apparently killed by associates of bin Laden.

The Power of War Lie Preparedness

You'll recall from the lists mentioned in Chapter 6 that overthrow of the Syrian government had long been a U.S. government objective. U.S. State Department cables released by WikiLeaks trace U.S. efforts in Syria to undermine the government back to at least 2006. In 2013, the White House went public with plans to lob some unspecified number of missiles into Syria, which was in the midst of a horrible civil war already fueled in part by U.S. arms and training camps, as well as by wealthy U.S. allies in the region and fighters emerging from other U.S.-created disasters in the region. The excuse for the missiles was an alleged killing of civilians, including children, with chemical weapons—a crime that Obama claimed to have certain proof had been committed by the Syrian government. Watch the videos of the dead children, the President said, and support that horror or support my missile strikes. Those were the only choices, supposedly. It wasn't a soft sell, but it wasn't a powerful one either.

Secretary of State John Kerry made the ideal leading salesman for this war—that is to say, he was awful at it. The story never seemed to take hold with the U.S. public. No threat to the United States was seriously alleged. No imminent threat to anyone else was seriously alleged. Rather, because one side in a war that was constantly killing all kinds of people on both sides with all kinds of weapons, had used a particular type of weapon, the United

States was to kill a bunch more people with a different, more acceptable, type of weapon. In doing so, the United States would be jumping into a war on the same side as al Qaeda, the group that had been sold to the U.S. public as absolute evil for over a decade. And the missiles, according to Kerry but depending whom he was talking to, would have both a tiny and an enormous impact on the war. The whole thing made no sense, even to a country raised on war lies.

This new set of war lies failed to scare Americans or to properly demonize the president of Syria, although Kerry did call him the obligatory name ("Hitler"). The pretense of urgency was not well sold. The dead children were not coming back to life, after all, no matter who had killed them. And this war sales pitch came after over a decade of antiwar agitation around the war on Iraq. Congress members had seen supporters of that war go down in the 2006 Congressional elections and the 2008 Democratic presidential primaries. Congress members reportedly expressed concern in 2013 about going on record voting for "another Iraq." They'd also seen the disaster created by Obama's 2011 war on Libya, even if nobody talked about it very much.

Congress was right to worry, as Seymour Hersh would later reveal that the plan was for a massive bombing campaign.[7] And Robert Parry, among others, would report on the debunking of White House lies about the chemical weapons attack.[8] The White House never revealed its supposed evidence that proved the Syrian government guilty, and nobody else produced definitive evidence of that either. Various pieces of supposed evidence reported in the media were deeply flawed. So, while Syria might have been guilty, the White House almost certainly did not *know* that, and the U.S. public seemed to recognize that even such guilt would not justify entering the war.

The timing in 2013 was something of a perfect storm for stopping a war, with Congress members in their districts being confronted at town hall meetings. Britain and France were planned partners for the bombing, but the British public and the British Parliament decisively rejected the idea. Members of the U.S. military right up to the chairman of the Joint Chiefs of Staff were evidently opposed or reluctant. The U.S. "intelligence" services refused to back Obama's and Kerry's claims.

But Raytheon's stock was at a record high, the televisions and newspapers depicted the U.S. missile attack as imminent, the president insisted upon it, and the leaders of the two mega-political parties said they favored it. Then Congress members in both houses and parties started saying they'd never heard such a volume of voices and such a one-sided public position on any issue ever before. Congress made clear that it would vote no, and Obama made clear that he would allow Congress to vote. RootsAction.org, where I work, was part of a huge coalition that had flooded Congress with emails and phone calls.

A Russian proposal to eliminate Syria's chemical weapons had already been known to the White House and been rejected. When Kerry publicly suggested that Syria could avoid a war by handing over its chemical weapons, everyone knew he didn't mean it. In fact, when Russia called his bluff and Syria immediately agreed, Kerry's staff put out this statement: "Secretary Kerry was making a rhetorical argument about the impossibility and unlikelihood of [President Bashar al] Assad turning over chemical weapons he has denied he used. His point was that this brutal dictator with a history of playing fast and loose with the facts cannot be trusted to turn over chemical weapons, otherwise he would have done so long ago. That's why the world faces this moment."[9] In other words: stop getting in the way of our war!

By the next day, however, with Congress rejecting war, Kerry was claiming to have meant his remark quite seriously and to believe the process had a good chance of succeeding, as of course it did. Diplomatic alternatives are always available. What compelled Obama to accept diplomacy as the last resort was the public's and Congress's refusal to allow war, including the fact that the Iraq War had been made a badge of shame rather than honor.[10]

Once you allow that there is an option other than war, your effort to start a war is doomed, or at least must be delayed. Bush had said he would not attack Iraq if Iraq turned over its weapons. But he had quite possibly known that Iraq did not have the weapons and therefore would not be turning them over. Syria actually had the weapons that Kerry said it could turn over and avoid being bombed. Syria had proposed years earlier to turn over those weapons as part of establishing a WMD-free Middle-East, an initiative blocked by Israel.

In 2015, former Finnish president and Nobel Peace Prize laureate Martti Ahtisaari said that in 2012 Russia had proposed a process of peace settlement between the Syrian government and its opponents that would have included Assad stepping down. But, according to Ahtisaari, the United States was so confident that Assad would soon be violently overthrown that it rejected the proposal.[11] U.S. and European diplomats deny that this is what happened by claiming that the Russian diplomat making the proposal couldn't really speak for Moscow and shouldn't really have been taken seriously, but their denials make clear that they were not open to believing any possibility of peace was worth pursuing.[12] Incidents like this one—and the fact that Spain wanted the matter of the *Maine* to go to international arbitration, that Japan wanted peace before Hiroshima, that the Soviet Union proposed peace negotiations before the Korean War, and that the United States sabotaged peace proposals for Vietnam from the Vietnamese, the Soviets, and the French—wreak havoc with the public pretense that war is a "last resort." When a Spanish newspaper reported that Saddam Hussein had offered to leave Iraq before the 2003 invasion, U.S. media took little interest. When British media reported that the Taliban was willing to have Osama bin Laden put on trial before the 2001 invasion of Afghanistan, U.S. journalists yawned. Iran's 2003 offer to negotiate ending its nuclear energy program wasn't mentioned much during the 2015 debate over an agreement with Iran—which was itself nearly rejected as an impediment to war. The catastrophic Syrian civil war since 2012 has followed U.S. adherence to actual U.S. policy in which peaceful compromise is usually the last resort.

In January 2015, a scholarly study found that the U.S. public believes that whenever the U.S. government proposes a war, it has already exhausted all other possibilities. When a sample group was asked if they supported a particular war, and a second group was asked if they supported that particular war after being told that all alternatives were no good, and a third group was asked if they supported that war even though there were good alternatives, the first two groups registered the same level of support, while support for war dropped off significantly in the third group. This led the researchers to the conclusion that if alternatives are not mentioned, people don't assume they exist—rather, people assume they've already been tried.[13] So, if you mention that there is a serious alternative, the game is up. You'll have to get your war on later.

And that's exactly what the White House did in the case of Syria. It kept the arms and trainers flowing, even though in polls the U.S. public opposed sending arms and trainers even more strongly than it opposed the missiles, and even though a CIA report produced for President Obama found that arming and training rebels, in numerous cases in the past, had pretty much never worked, even on its own terms (an exception claimed as a success by the CIA was the arming of the Afghan rebels who later became al Qaeda; with that kind of success, who needs failure?).[14] The question of whether to send arms and trainers was never made into a public question in the media or Congress. The U.S. government refrained from any serious effort to resolve the crisis through disarmament, diplomacy, and aid. It bided its time, waiting for a better package of lies. The lies of generosity had not been enough. Something more was needed, even if it would require coming into the war in 2014 on the opposite side from that presented as a moral obligation in 2013.

But why were generosity and global policemanship not enough? Well, some people may be somewhat aware of numerous places where the U.S. government supports brutality rather than using it as an excuse for war: Saudi Arabia, Egypt, Bahrain, Yemen, Guantanamo, etc. During the Arab Spring of 2011 and after, the United States had done what it could to protect its loyal dictators while claiming to support democracy. So the pretense of generosity may not fool everyone. But polls also suggested that a large section of the U.S. public believed falsely that past wars, like that in Iraq, had benefitted the locals while harming Americans—and that the Iraqis were not even grateful. This delusion resulted in bizarre debates in 2013 between those opposing bombing because the Syrians would not even appreciate having their country bombed, and those favoring bombing because the Syrians are just as good as you and me.

While the lies aimed at justifying the bombing of Syria failed, and Syria has not yet—as of October 1, 2015—been bombed in the manner planned, another lie succeeded marvelously: the lie of powerlessness. Despite the obvious role that public pressure had played in blocking the war plans, and the willingness of peace groups to take credit (including in the film *We Are Many*), many activists ran from any notion that they might have been involved. If the all-powerful war machine didn't launch a war, they told each other, then it secretly never wanted to. With smug satisfaction, such activists then returned to antiwar activities that they clearly considered pointless gestures. It's important that we reject the lie of powerlessness. It is in fact common for activists to discover the extent of their impact many years after the fact.[15] And the full impact is never entirely measurable, but is usually much greater than imagined.

Another success in war lie preparedness is the holding off, thus far, of a U.S. war on Iran, including at a number of moments of crisis, including in 2007 and again with the negotiation of an agreement between Iran and Western nations in 2015. The longer this debate goes on, the more it should become clear that there is no urgent emergency that might help justify mass killing. But the longer it goes on, the more some people may accept the idea that whether or not to gratuitously bomb a foreign nation is a perfectly legitimate policy question. The *Washington Post* has already published an op-ed headlined "War With Iran Is Probably Our Best Option."[16] And the argument may also advance in the direction of favoring war for another reason: both sides of the debate promote most of the war lies. Yes, some peace groups are talking perfect sense on this issue as on most, but the debate between Democratic and Republican party leaderships is as follows—with many peace groups parroting the Democratic leadership. One side argues, quite illegally and barbarically, that because Iran is trying to build a nuclear weapon, Iran should be bombed. The other side argues, counterproductively if in a seemingly civilized manner, that because Iran is trying (or has tried and intends to try) to build a nuclear weapon, a diplomatic agreement should be reached to put a stop to it. The trouble with both arguments is that they reinforce the dubious idea that Iran is trying to build a nuclear weapon. As Gareth Porter makes clear in his book *Manufactured Crisis*,[17] there is no evidence for that.

U.S. "intelligence" agencies say Iran had no plans for a nuclear weapons program, even as both sides of the debate spoke as if such plans were established and menacing. Both arguments also reinforce the idea that there is something about Iranians that makes them unqualified to have the sort of weapon that it's alright to voluntarily spread to other nations. I don't actually think it's alright for anyone to have nuclear weapons or nuclear energy, but my point is the bias implicit in these arguments. It feeds the idea that Iranians are not civilized enough to speak with, even as one-half of the debate pushes for just that: speaking with the Iranians.

On the plus side, much of the push for a war on Iran was devoted for years to demonizing Iran's president until the Iranian people, for their own reasons, elected a different president, which threw a real monkey wrench into the gears of that old standby. Perhaps nations will learn the lesson that changing rulers can help fend off an attack as well as building weapons can. Also on the plus side, the ludicrous idea that Iran is a threat to the United States is very similar to the idea that Iraq was such a threat in 2002–2003. But on the negative side, memory of the Iraq war lies is already fading. Keeping past war lies well remembered can be our best protection against new wars. Also on the negative side, even if people oppose a war on Iran, several billionaire funders of election campaigns favor one.[18]

In the summer of 2015 as I was putting this epilogue together, the United States and other nations reached an agreement with Iran. U.S. activist efforts then focused on lobbying Congress not to kill the deal. A big coalition that I worked with put the focus on preventing a war. But many continued to hype the baseless claim that Iran was a threat to the United States and was pursuing a nuclear weapon. One organization filmed a bunch of celebrities for an online video urging support for the Iran deal after hyping the bogus Iranian nuclear threat, pretending that the United States gets "forced into" wars, making a bunch of sick jokes about how nuclear death can be better than other war deaths, suggesting that spies are cool, cursing, and mocking the very idea that war is a serious matter.[19] Another organization produced a video claiming that the deal would prevent the "Iranian regime" (never a government, always a regime) from "gaining a nuclear weapon."[20] When I questioned supporters of diplomacy and peace with Iran on why they focused their rhetoric on preventing Iran from getting nukes, even though at least some of them privately admitted that there was no evidence Iran was trying to, they didn't come out and say that they were cynically playing into popular beliefs, even false ones, because they have no choice. (A plausible argument along those lines might certainly have been attempted.) Rather, they told me that their language didn't actually state that Iran was trying to get nukes, only that if Iran ever did decide to try to get nukes, this deal would prevent it. That same position, I replied, could be maintained regarding the deal's effectiveness in preventing Iran from obtaining a ray gun that would strip you naked and convert you to Islam. In the long run, I maintained, we're going to more effectively prevent a war if we reject, rather than repeating, the pro-war propaganda.

Beyond that general problem, there were specific lies generated as this book was being prepared for publication. In August 2015, the Associated Press relied on a possibly forged document to claim falsely that under the nuclear agreement Iran would be doing its own inspections of a key nuclear facility. This was a huge story that fell apart in less than a day, providing great encouragement, I hope, to those who long to see war lies debunked swiftly and decisively. But how many people saw the original story and avoided seeing the debunking, I don't know.[21]

As this book neared publication, a sufficient number of U.S. senators publicly committed to the nuclear agreement to allow it to survive, at least for the moment. I drafted what I saw as the most important 10 lessons from this struggle:

1. There is never an urgent need for war. Wars are often begun with great urgency, not because there's no other option, but because delay might allow another option to emerge. The next time someone tells you a particular country must be attacked as a "last resort," politely ask the person to please explain why diplomacy was possible with Iran and not in this other case. If the U.S. government is held to that standard, war may quickly become a thing of the past.

2. A popular demand for peace over war can succeed, at least when those in power are divided. When much of one of the two big political parties takes the side of peace, the advocates of peace have a chance. And of course now we know which senators and Congress members will shift their positions with partisan winds. My Republican congressman opposed war on Syria in 2013 when President Obama supported it, but supported greater hostility toward Iran in 2015 when Obama opposed it. One of my two Democratic senators backed peace for a change, when Obama did. The other remained undecided, as if the choice were too complex.

3. The government of Israel can make a demand of the government of the United States and be told no. This is a remarkable breakthrough. None of the actual 50 states expects to always get its way in Washington, but Israel does—or did until now. This opens up the possibility of ceasing to give Israel billions

of dollars worth of free weapons one of these years, or even of ceasing to protect Israel from legal consequences for what it does with those weapons.

4. Money can make a demand of the U.S. government and be told no. Multibillionaires funded huge advertising campaigns and dangled major campaign "contributions." The big money was all on the side opposing the agreement, and yet the agreement prevailed—or at least now looks like it will. This doesn't prove we have a corruption-free government. But it does suggest that the corruption is not yet 100 percent.

5. Counterproductive tactics employed in this victorious antiwar effort may end up making this a Pyrrhic victory. Both sides in the debate over the agreement advanced baseless claims about Iranian aggression and Iranian attempts to create nuclear weapons. Both sides depicted Iranians as completely untrustworthy and menacing. If the agreement is undone or some other incident arises, the mental state of the U.S. public regarding Iran is in a worse position than it was before, as regards restraining the dogs of war.

6. The deal is a concrete step to be built on. It is a powerful argument for the use of diplomacy—perhaps even less hostile diplomacy—in other areas of the globe. It is also a verifiable refutation to future assertions of an Iranian nuclear threat. This means that U.S. weaponry stationed in Europe on the basis of that alleged threat can and must be withdrawn rather than remain as an open act of aggression toward Russia.

7. When given the choice, the nations of the world will leap at an opening for peace. And they will not easily be brought back again. U.S. allies are now opening embassies in Iran. If the United States backs away from Iran again, it will isolate itself. This lesson should be borne in mind when considering violent and non-violent options for other countries.

8. The longer a war with Iran is avoided, the stronger an argument we have for continuing to avoid it. When a U.S. push for war on Iran has been stopped before, including in 2007, this has not only put off a possible catastrophe; it has also made it more difficult to create. If a future U.S. government wants war with Iran, it will have to go up against public awareness that peace with Iran is possible.

9. The Nuclear Non-Proliferation Treaty (NPT) works. Inspections work. Just as inspections worked in Iraq, they work in Iran. Other

nations, such as Israel, North Korea, India, and Pakistan, should be encouraged to join the NPT. Proposals for a nuclear-free Middle East should be pursued.

10. The United States should itself cease violating the NPT and lead by example, ceasing to share nuclear weapons with other nations, ceasing to create new nuclear weapons, and working to disarm itself of an arsenal that serves no sane purpose but threatens apocalypse.

Preventing the bombing of Syria is still our best model going forward, even though everyone thinks it was a very temporary victory if they acknowledge the victory at all. I say this because in that instance we were up against both big political parties, and our opposition came from across the political spectrum—even to the point of including people who found each other's perspectives ridiculous. And while the Syrian crisis is ever worse and unpredictable, preventing that bombing prolonged many lives. Preventing a war on Iran is tremendous as well. Public pressure has even blocked a bill that would have committed the United States to join in any war between Israel and Iran. But this issue has been made partisan. President Obama and the Democrats, even while promoting the war lies, are on the antiwar side—hoping for Iranian help in a war in Iraq. Partisanship makes organizing and educating difficult in the extreme, and intentions hard to judge. Although presidential candidate Hillary Clinton has said she'd be willing to "totally obliterate" the people of Iran if Iran attacked Israel,[22] countless Democrats who support all kinds of wars argue that in the case of Iran a war should wait until diplomacy has had a chance. Well, why shouldn't every war wait for that?

On a side note, in 2015 the United States prosecuted and convicted a CIA whistleblower named Jeffrey Sterling who had gone to Congress, and allegedly to the media, with the fact that the CIA had in 2000 given Iran nuclear weapons plans, containing obvious flaws supposedly inserted to slow down Iran's nonexistent program. In the course of the trial, the CIA accidentally revealed that it had planned to similarly provide flawed nuclear blueprints and parts to Iraq, and for all we know it did so.[23] These were almost certainly efforts to plant incriminating evidence on targets of war.[24]

Getting What You Pay For

Preparing for war and expecting peace remains a national pastime in the United States. But the war funding creates wars, and if the public seems reticent, the wars are conducted without public or even congressional approval. Well into Barack Obama's presidency with its drone wars, proxy wars, coups, "special" forces active in 135 countries,[25] and the illegal war on Libya, George

W. Bush's willingness to bother lying about war to Congress and the public seemed downright respectful.

In 2001, U.S. military spending was $397 billion, from which it soared to a peak of $720 billion in 2010, and is now at $610 billion in 2015. These figures from the Stockholm International Peace Research Institute (in constant 2011 dollars) exclude debt payments, veterans costs, and civil defense, which raise the figure to over $1 trillion a year now, not counting state and local spending on the military.

Military spending is now 54 percent of U.S. federal discretionary spending according to the National Priorities Project. Everything else—and the entire debate in which liberals want more spending and conservatives want less!—is contained within the other 46 percent of the budget.

U.S. military spending, according to SIPRI, is 35 percent of the world total. U.S. and Europe together account for 56 percent of the world's spending. The U.S. and its allies around the globe (it has troops in 175 countries, and most countries are armed in great part by U.S. companies) make up the bulk of world spending.

Iran spends 0.65 percent of world military spending (as of 2012, the last year available). China's military spending has been rising for years and has soared since 2008 and the U.S. pivot to Asia, from $107 billion in 2008 to now $216 billion. But that's still just 12 percent of world spending.

Per capita the U.S. now spends $1,891 current U.S. dollars for each person in the United States per year, as compared with an average $242 per capita worldwide, or $165 per capita in the world excluding the United States, or $155 per capita in China.

The dramatically increased U.S. military spending has not made the United States or the world safer. Early on in the "war on terrorism" the U.S. government ceased reporting on terrorism, as it increased. The Global Terrorism Index records a steady increase in terrorist attacks from 2001 to the present.[26] A Gallup poll in 65 nations at the end of 2013 found the United States overwhelmingly viewed as the greatest threat to peace in the world. Iraq has been turned into hell, with Libya, Afghanistan, Yemen, Pakistan, and Somalia close behind. Newly embittered terrorist groups have arisen in direct response to U.S. terrorism and the devastation it's left behind. And arms races have been sparked that benefit only the arms dealers.

But the spending has had other consequences. The United States has risen into the top five nations in the world for disparity of wealth. The 10th wealthiest country on earth per capita doesn't look wealthy when you drive through many parts of it.[27] And you do have to drive, with 0 miles of high-speed rail built; but local U.S. police have weapons of war now. And you have to be careful when you drive. The American Society of Civil Engineers gives

U.S. infrastructure a D+. Areas of cities like Detroit have become wasteland. Residential areas lack water or are poisoned by environmental pollution— very often from military operations. The United States now ranks 35th in freedom to choose what to do with your life,[28] 36th in life expectancy,[29] 47th in preventing infant mortality,[30] 57th in employment,[31] and trails in education by various measures.[32, 33, 34] The percentage of Americans who think their country is the greatest one on earth has dropped to 28 percent.[35]

If U.S. military spending were merely returned to 2001 levels, which would still be much higher than any other country on earth, the savings of $213 billion per year could meet the following needs:

- End hunger and starvation worldwide—$30 billion per year.[36]
- Provide clean drinking water worldwide—$11 billion per year.[37]
- Provide free college in the United States—$70 billion per year (according to Senate legislation).[38]
- Double U.S. foreign aid—$23 billion per year.[39]
- Build and maintain a high-speed rail system in the United States—$30 billion per year.[40]
- Invest in solar and renewable energy as never before—$20 billion per year.
- Fund peace initiatives as never before—$10 billion per year.
- That would leave $19 billion left over per year with which to pay down debt.

The U.S. State Department cables published by WikiLeaks made clear how much of the State Department's time goes into persuading foreign governments to buy more U.S. weapons. Secretary of State Hillary Clinton, whose personal foundation has received huge "donations" from several major weapons makers, publicly accused governments of being soft on terrorism, and then oversaw the sales of more weaponry.[41] Nations banned from buying weapons because of their human rights abuses saw Clinton waive those restrictions after they "donated" to her foundation. These included: Algeria, Saudi Arabia, Kuwait, the United Arab Emirates, Oman, and Qatar.[42]

The U.S. military itself now has so much weaponry, including weaponry it doesn't even want that Congress funds anyway, that it sees advantages in giving it away to local police, and this is happening in combination with the U.S. and Israeli militaries training U.S. police to behave as if they are at war. U.S. police killings of unarmed African Americans made the news in 2014–2015. U.S. police kill more people than President Obama kills with drones, and a U.S. resident has a much greater chance of being killed by the police than by a foreign terrorist. Protests following a police killing in Ferguson, Missouri, led to the police creating a no-fly zone there, just as over a foreign nation.

This militarization of the police cannot be understood apart from racism, and it cannot be understood apart from these factors:

- A culture glorifying militarization and justifying it as global policing.
- A federal government that directs roughly $1 trillion every year into the U.S. military, depriving virtually everything else of needed resources.
- A federal government that still manages to find resources to offer free military weapons to local police in the U.S. and elsewhere.
- Weapons profiteers that eat up local subsidies as well as federal contracts while funding election campaigns, threatening the elimination of lots of jobs in congressional districts, and pushing for the unloading of weapons by the U.S. military on local police as one means of creating the demand for more.
- The use of permanent wartime fears to justify the removal of citizens' rights, gradually allowing local police to begin viewing the people they were supposed to protect as low-level threats, potential terrorists, and enemies of law and order—in particular when they exercise their former rights to speech and assembly. Notice that police "excesses," almost like war "excesses," are often not apologized for, as one does not apologize to an enemy.
- The further funding of abusive policing through asset forfeitures and SWAT raids.
- The further conflation of military and police through the militarization of borders, especially the Mexican border, the combined efforts of federal and local forces in fusion centers, the military's engagement in "exercises" in the United States, and the growth of the drone industry with the military, among others, flying drones in U.S. skies and piloting drones abroad from U.S. land.
- The growth of the profit-driven prison industry and mass incarceration, which dehumanize people just as boot camp and the nightly news do to war targets.
- Economically driven disproportionate participation in, and therefore identification with, the military by the very communities most suffering from its destruction of resources, rights, and lives.
- The attitude of war that comes with the war on crime, the war on drugs, etc., including the prioritization of protecting the police above all else, not protecting the enemy formerly known as the public.

The past five years have also seen an increase in government secrecy, surveillance, and retribution against whistleblowers. The justification for all of it is war and the idea of a war enemy. The actual motivations for much of it involve commercial espionage, imposing antidemocratic policies on the public, disrupting popular uprisings, etc. But without the idea of a war enemy, the excuse for secrecy and spying evaporates. And without the reality of militarism, its symptoms, its constituent "war crimes," largely vanish. Some day our human rights and civil liberties groups may recognize and act on that. U.S. hostility toward the world, including spying on foreign leaders, is isolating it as a rogue state. Reluctance of Americans to call their government out on its war-making is depriving every activist movement of huge opportunities. At the root of this madness is fear, as well as hate, greed, false pride, and blind loyalty.

This Is Your Brain on Fear

Why was the U.S. public willing to tolerate new U.S. war-making in Iraq and Syria in 2014–2015, after having opposed it in 2013? This time the advertised enemy was not the Syrian government, but terrorists scarier than al Qaeda, called ISIS. And ISIS was shown to be cutting the throats of Americans on videos. And something switched off in people's brains and they stopped thinking—with a few exceptions. A few journalists pointed out that the Iraqi government bombing Iraqi Sunnis was in fact driving the latter to support ISIS.[43] As if to hammer this point home, ISIS produced a 60-minute movie depicting itself as the leading enemy of the United States and virtually begging the United States to attack it. (When the United States did attack, recruitment soared, just as ISIS had expected.) Even *Newsweek* published a clear-eyed warning that ISIS would not last long unless the United States saved it by bombing it.[44] Matthew Hoh, whom we met in Chapter 3, warned that the beheadings were bait not to be taken.[45] And of course I shouted the warnings of this book everywhere I could. But the U.S. government and much of the public took the bait.

The fomenting of fear, and the characterization of ISIS as evil seem to have been key here in gaining the support of the American public to combat ISIS. Videos of beheadings were characterized as "barbaric" by the U.S. media, while killing done by the United States is considered necessary and often characterized as "surgical strikes" or "collateral damage." As if the U.S. government didn't kill people, as if the dictatorships it arms didn't kill people, as if ISIS had invented murder and something had to be done about it, even if that something was murder on a larger scale that would produce more murder by ISIS as well, people fell in line like obedient servants to their master, War.

And to make their war support more respectable, along came the supposed need to rescue civilians trapped on a mountaintop and awaiting death at the hands of ISIS. The story wasn't completely false, but its details were murky. Many of the people left the mountain or refused to leave the mountain where they preferred to stay, before a U.S. rescue mission could actually be created. And the U.S. seemed to drop bombs more with a goal of protecting oil than protecting people (four air strikes near the mountain, many more near oil-rich Erbil).[46] But, whether it helped those people or not, a U.S. war was created, and the war planners never looked back.

The world, as represented at the United Nations, didn't fall for it and didn't authorize this war or the proposed attack a year earlier, in large part because the UN had authorized a supposed humanitarian rescue in Libya in 2011 and seen that authorization predictably and swiftly misused to justify a wider war and the overthrow of a government.

In addition to the dubious claims about people needing to be rescued on a mountain, the United States also pulled out that old standby of saving U.S. lives, namely the lives of Americans in the oil-rush town of Erbil, all of whom could have been put onto a single airplane and flown out of there had there been a real need to rescue them.[47]

Completely false, on the other hand, was another story about evil. Just in case people were not sufficiently scared, the White House and Pentagon actually invented a non-existent terrorist organization, which they named the Khorasan Group, and which *CBS News* called "a more immediate threat to the U.S. Homeland." While ISIS was worse than al Qaeda and al Qaeda worse than the Taliban, this new monster was depicted as worse than ISIS *and* plotting the immediate blowing up of U.S. airplanes.[48] No evidence of this was offered, or apparently required by "journalists."

If you weren't frightened enough, and if you didn't care enough about people on a mountain to drop bombs on people in a valley, there was also your patriotic duty to overcome "intervention fatigue," of which U.S. ambassador to the United Nations Samantha Power began writing and speaking, actually warning that if we paid too much attention to what bombing places like Libya had done to them we'd fail in our obligation to support the bombing of new places like Syria.[49] Soon enough, the U.S. corporate media was hosting debates that ranged from advocacy for launching one type of war all the way to advocacy for launching a little bit different type of war.[50] A study by Fairness and Accuracy in Reporting found that inclusion of antiwar guests in the major U.S. media was even more lacking in the 2014 buildup to war than it had been in the 2003 run-up to the Iraq invasion.[51]

On September 23, 2014, I went on the Ed Schultz show on MSNBC, and this happened:

Ed Schultz: Has the President overstepped his Constitutional authority in your opinion?

David Swanson: Oh, there's no question. I agree with Congressman Garamendi and my own senator, Kaine. This is a blatant violation of Article I Section 8 of the Constitution. But even if Congress comes back and votes for it, it's a blatant violation of the UN Charter. This is illegal, to go into another country and bomb it. But more importantly it's counterproductive, it's almost knowingly counterproductive. There is no military solution, they keep saying that. And, by the way, candidate Barack Obama strongly agreed with everything I've just said; it's President Obama who's changed his mind. And we have to bring him back to that desire to end the mindset that gets us into war, because there are numerous useful nonmilitary actions here that don't involve doing what ISIS openly explicitly wants the U.S. military to do. And it's almost guaranteed to be counterproductive. Look at the disaster in Libya. Look at the past quarter-century and the past several years and the past six weeks in Iraq. It makes things worse to go in and bomb a bad situation.

Ed Shultz: What do you view the UN how the UN plays out here, I found it interesting that the UN informed the Syrian ambassador that these air strikes were taking place, and the UN has not formally said for this coalition to back off. What do you make of that?

David Swanson: I think the UN ought to, I think it is absolutely obliged to, but one of its permanent Security Council members with permanent veto status is involved in this. The UN needs to be reformed, it needs to be democratized, it needs to be strengthened, but the fact is that this is an operation going around the UN. And the fact that you can get five kings and dictators to say they're on your side shows that you have a great deal of influence over them. Why not get them on your side for an arms embargo? Seventy-nine percent of the weapons shipped into the Middle East, according to the United States Congress, are from the United States, not counting the U.S. military's weapons. An arms embargo would be three-quarters of the way, just with the United States initiating it. If it can get these Sunni governments to bomb Sunnis, it can get them to join an arms embargo, join discussions that include Iran and Russia and Syria and Iraq, which the U.S. government is willing to talk to about war but not about peace. And send in actual aid, a Marshall Plan scale of restitution to that region, which would be far cheaper than these $2 million missiles.

Ed Schultz: Dissenting voices, such as yourself, what are your expectations as all of this military action unfolds?

David Swanson: I think the public support for it is exaggerated and is likely to be short-lived. I think it's driven by irrational fear based on slick beheading videos and reports on beheading videos. I think people are going to realize that bombing the opposite side of the side they were told they had to bomb a year ago and arming the other side at the same time is madness, that this is benefitting ISIS, it's benefitting the weapons companies. It's not benefitting the people of Iraq or Syria or the world. And it's tearing down the rule of law, which we would like to uphold for this nation and every other nation going forward. And they are unwilling to say how many years and what cost in any measurement of the cost. People are not going to stand for this very long, and the Congress members have given themselves a little bit too lengthy of a vacation, I think. They're going to start hearing pressure from people who want this ended.

I have yet to be invited back on MSNBC.

Congress has begun hearing the opposition from people that I mentioned in that interview, and yet Congress has avoided ending or authorizing the war, allowing the president to go on waging it illegally. And the propaganda has never let up. Headlines about ISIS attacking within the United States have been relentless, despite such attacks not existing. The FBI has arrested some 50 people in locations all over the United States who communicated with FBI agents pretending to be ISIS and who in most cases were pushed into planning acts of terrorism by FBI plants—usually people hoping to see criminal charges dropped against themselves in exchange for setting up "ISIS terrorists." Meanwhile the FBI has publicly warned of imminent ISIS attacks some 40 times, and not once has any attack materialized.[52] On June 28, 2015, CNN reported that a black and white flag with odd symbols on it in a London gay pride parade was an ISIS flag indicating ISIS presence in London. Closer examination showed the flag to be one depicting a variety of sex toys.[53]

The U.S. "intelligence" agencies have always admitted that ISIS was no threat to the United States, but that fact hasn't seemed to matter. Reference to the fictional Khorasan Group, by the way, was abandoned as soon as the war started and has hardly been heard of since.

In June 2015, a white supremacist shot and killed nine people in a black church in Charleston, South Carolina. This was followed by a number of black churches being burned across the U.S. South. The media made no effort to create widespread panic. In truth, your chances of being shot or burned remained tiny compared to other dangers. But even more true, your chances of being killed by someone claiming allegiance to ISIS were also tiny, much less than dying of "a lightning strike on your birthday," as Stephen Kinzer put it, but panic was everywhere, at least to believe your television. Some people scared of ISIS are no doubt handling their fear right now by stuffing down food that contributes to heart disease and puffing on cigarettes that contribute to cancer. Diseases don't make good horror movies the way the wind of hate does (see Chapter 1), but they are what we should be most scared of. And of course the chance of being shot by an American imitating his federal government's manner of solving problems, while small, is far greater than that of being killed by a foreigner.

Being scared of foreign, dark-skinned, Arabic-speaking Muslims doesn't just come more readily than being scared of Americans, or of heart disease or Alzheimer's or nuclear war or climate change. It also allows the pretense that ISIS arose out of the irrational evil of *those people*. In fact, it arose out of the destruction, sectarian division, poverty, desperation, and an illegitimate government in Baghdad created by a U.S. war and the prior U.S. sanctions. It arose out of the disbanding of the Iraqi Army by Paul Bremmer. It arose out of the brutalization of its future leaders in U.S. prison camps. It arose out of the proliferation of U.S. weapons. It arose out of the arming and training of Syrian rebels by the United States in Turkey and Jordan. It arose out of the hell fire of the Hellfire missiles the United States kept giving the Iraqi government to use against its own people.

The creation of ISIS and its barbarous violence are directly related to the barbarous violence of others, including the Saudi government, the Iraqi government, and the U.S. government. When President Obama blew up a 16-year-old American boy whom nobody had ever accused of so much as jaywalking, and blew up six other kids who were too close to him at the time, we cannot imagine the boy's head remained on his body. And does it matter how a person is killed? Is murder by bomb more righteous than murder by a blade? The endless demand of "But what would you do about ISIS?" should be put into context, and then answered thus:

Disarm the region by ceasing to arm it and arranging an arms embargo with penalties for violators. Bring in aid on an unprecedented scale (which would be much cheaper than the war). Make one focus of that aid green energy. Empower people with agricultural assistance, education, cameras, and internet access. Apologize for past wrongs. Pull the U.S. military out of the region. Cease arming and propping up brutal governments, including Egypt and Israel. Open diplomatic negotiations on the topics of a WMD-free Middle East, peace in Syria, peace in Iraq, peace in Yemen, and equal rights for all in Israel/Palestine. End all economic sanctions. Send any willing and able doctors, nurses, journalists, aid workers, peace workers, human shields, and negotiators into crisis zones, understanding that this means risking lives, but fewer lives than further militarization risks. Launch a communications campaign in the United States to replace military recruitment campaigns, focused on building sympathy and desire to serve as critical aid workers, persuading doctors and engineers to volunteer their time to travel to and visit these areas of crisis. Sign the United States on to the International Criminal Court and voluntarily propose the prosecution of top U.S. officials of this and the preceding regimes for their crimes (and of course criminal officials of other nations as well, as the new leader of the Labour Party in the UK in 2015 correctly proposed prosecuting Tony Blair). Democratize the United Nations.

Those alternatives may be unappealing to some and extremely difficult to enact, but one can hardly argue that they don't exist at all, that the only options are dropping 500-pound bombs or doing nothing. In June 2015, on the same day that the U.S. House of Representatives voted not to end the war (see below), the chairman of the Joint Chiefs of Staff testified, along with the secretary of so-called defense, before a Congressional committee. He said there was "no military solution," and went on to explain that therefore they would be both using the U.S. military and training Iraqi soldiers. And how's that going, he was asked. It turned out they were having a very hard time finding Iraqis willing to be trained.

Meanwhile the CIA was spending some billion dollars a year training rebels for Syria and providing weaponry that not infrequently ended up in the hands of ISIS. Concerned that no actual plan existed for what in the world they were up to, and that the whole operation was likely counter-productive, some outraged Congress members proposed to cut the training operation's funding by 20 percent. The CIA argued that its trainees had captured a base, which would allow the United States or its proxies to stay in Syria once complete chaos had been established.[54] A couple of weeks after that exchange, the Secretary of so-called Defense Ash Carter admitted that only 60 rebels had been trained under the military's program (much smaller than the CIA's), bringing the price tag to $4 million per trainee.[55] In July 2015 came reports of these rebels all being captured.

Where's the Opposition?

There are many factors at work in creating the absence of a larger antiwar movement. The draft is gone. Taxes are no longer raised to pay for wars. U.S. casualties are minimized. Propaganda has become very skilled. People have been persuaded of their powerlessness. People are too busy working, too in debt to take risks, locked in cages or on probation, or drugged to cure rebelliousness. But one factor most explains the reversal from a growing movement in 2005 to a shrinking one in 2006.

A careful study makes clear that the U.S. peace movement grew in 2002–2003, during the long build-up to the invasion of Iraq, and virtually collapsed in 2007–2008, with attention diverted to a presidential election, largely because of the movement's association with the Democratic Party.[56]

Also gone AWOL is any serious and consistent opposition to war in Congress. On June 17, 2015, by a vote of 288–139, the U.S. House of Representatives voted down a resolution that would have required the President to withdraw all troops from Iraq and Syria.[57] A handful of members had forced a debate and vote, but the debate was dominated by those favoring war, with most of those favoring the resolution speaking only about the proper duties and procedures of the legislature. The only real exception was Congressman John Lewis of Georgia who said:

> For fourteen long years our nation has been at war. Our people are sick and tired of war. This resolution simply opens the door to bring American soldiers home.... The end of terrorism is not found through the barrel of a gun or more boots on the ground. More weapons cannot stamp out the root cause of terrorism, and more bombs cannot eradicate the seas of hate. Over and over again I have stood on this very floor and reminded my colleagues that the use of force cannot, must not be taken lightly.... Many years ago I shared my concern with you that young people in the Middle East would never forget the violence that they have experienced in their youth. I feared then and I said it then that they would grow up hating our children, our grandchildren, and generations yet unborn.... These young people must be our focus. We must lift them up and listen to regional voices for peace....[58]

There's a man in need of 217 colleagues and 51 senators.

But war opposition is missing from mainstream Democratic Party liberal politics, except in the case of Iran.[59] In part, perhaps, this is because of President Obama's broken promises on Iraq, and his kept promises on Afghanistan, a war he was widely given credit for "ending" even as he tripled the U.S. presence. The ongoing war on Afghanistan is more Obama's than Bush's in time spent, money spent, and people killed, and yet the admirable job of "ending" it (see Chapter 9) may be passed along to Obama's successor.

The Purloined Kill List

Like Edgar Allen Poe's purloined letter, hidden out in the open, Obama's kill list remains unknown. Perhaps if he'd been a Republican, or if the secret had been leaked, there would have been outrage, or at least awareness. But Obama, prior to his reelection in 2012, intentionally told the *New York Times,* which ran a front-page story on it, that on Tuesdays he goes through a list of men, women, and even children, and picks which ones to have murdered, using missiles from drones.[60]

The use of armed drones is an opportunity to expose the killing of war as murder, because drones bring it down to a scale people recognize as murder—if only they will look. The judicial death penalty is fading fast, but the extra-judicial death penalty has arisen without the level of resistance it clearly merits. There have been groups of dedicated peace activists slowly educating pockets of the United States in which drones are piloted. There have been activists, journalists, and artists in the nations under attack documenting the deaths, and in the United States and around the world noticeably moving public opinion in the right direction after years of dedicated effort. But still there is acceptance.

Apart from their use in other wars—like Afghanistan, Iraq, and Libya— drones have been used to create their own wars in places like Yemen and Pakistan. Some years ago, the common lie was that a drone war in Yemen was better than a ground war. My response was that, given time, it would create one, but it hadn't replaced one. The drone wars were new wars. "But what would you do instead?" was the insistent question. Considering that drone killings have proven themselves to actually be counter-productive, creating many more enemies than those killed, I certainly wouldn't continue them. Nor would I replace them with something else similar. As some of us warned, the drone war on Yemen helped to create a ground and air war, with Saudi Arabia heavily bombing its neighbor with U.S. weapons including cluster bombs, about a year after Obama had claimed Yemen as a model for war success. Also providing cover for the Saudi war on Yemen were lies about Iranian involvement in the war there.[61]

You would never know it from the reporting in the *New York Times,* but a May 13, 2015, editorial in that paper blurted out the obvious: "Of course, we already know that torture and drone strikes pose a profound threat to America's national security and the safety of its citizens abroad. After all, the murderers of the Islamic State did not dress their victims in orange jumpsuits for no reason; they did it to evoke the horrors of the Guantánamo prison camp."[62] An internal CIA document, leaked in December 2014, made clear that the CIA understood its own drone-murder program to be counterproductive.[63] In fact, this is a common admission regarding U.S. wars in general, and drone wars in particular, especially by recently retired U.S. officials.[64]

Acceptance of murder-by-president has been created in part by totally avoiding the subject, and in part by creating a debate narrowly targeted to the question of legality. Never mind morality or even military strategy, focus on the legal question, we're told. Of course, the government blatantly lies about particular drone murders, sometime unable to even get its own story straight.[65] It claims it had to kill people who clearly could have been arrested. And when it provides legalistic excuses, it defines "imminent" to mean eventually theoretically conceivable, and "combatant" to mean military-aged male.

But the root of the problem is the idea that a president should have the power to create his own rules for legal murder sprees and to claim to secretly be abiding by his rules. Never mind what the rules are or whether he's abiding by them![66] The spectacle of law professors telling Congress that a drone murder is murder if it's not part of a war, but fine if it's part of a war, and that the question of its war status is unknowable because contained in a secret memo written by the president responsible for the drone murder—that ought to make us all ashamed, and willing to at long last ban state murder, a.k.a. war.[67]

Or, if you're willing to allow murder, what do you say to those who want to know why torture, or any other crime, isn't acceptable as well?

Where Israel Leads

In 2014, as in 2012 and 2008, Israel again attacked the people of Gaza, using weapons provided for free by the U.S. government, which can be counted on to defend Israel's crimes at the United Nations. Practicing what's been called the Dahiya Doctrine (disproportionate force, destruction of civilian infrastructure), Israel's policy is one of collective punishment. After all, Israel is not trying to take anything from the Gazans who are already defeated and trapped, and installing democracy is the opposite of what Israel aims for.[68]

The whole thing was kicked off when Prime Minister Benjamin Netanyahu lied that three murder victims might be still alive (when he knew they weren't), blamed their kidnapping on Hamas, and began raiding West Bank houses and rounding up Palestinians.[69] Once Israel and the United States had rejected out-of-hand quite reasonable ceasefire demands from Hamas, the war was on for 51 days—with great popular support in Israel. Some 2,200 Gazan people were killed, over 10,000 injured, and 100,000 made homeless by a very one-sided war.[70] There were 66 Israeli soldiers and 6 Israeli civilians reported killed.

The stories in the U.S. media were completely one-sided and focused on Israelis' fears. The deaths of Gazans were explained as intentional sacrifices by a people with a "culture of martyrdom" who sometimes choose to die because it makes good video footage. After all, Israel was phoning people's houses and giving them five-minute warnings before blowing them up. The fact that it was also blowing up shelters and hospitals they might flee to was glossed over or explained as somehow involving military targets.

But the Israeli media and internet were full of open advocacy by top Israeli officials of genocide. On August 1, 2014, the deputy speaker of Israel's Parliament posted on his Facebook page a plan for the complete elimination of the Gazan people using concentration camps, to take one of many examples.[71]

Is this where the United States is headed culturally and with its own wars? One reason to hope not is that opposing Israel's wars is one of the few places where U.S. youth are engaged in antiwar activism.[72]

Non-Hostile Bombs

White House lawyer Harold Koh told Congress that an aerial attack on Libya would not be a real war or even "hostilities" because U.S. troops would not be on the ground, even though he'd just invented that definition of wars and hostilities, and even though U.S. troops were already on the ground stirring up trouble. Ed Schultz demanded war against the evil of formerly U.S.-backed dictator turned too independent Muammar Ghadafi (which is why I brought up Libya when I was on his show). Juan Cole and Chris Hedges favored the same war for humanitarian reasons (though Hedges turned around and opposed it later, writing an excellent article against it six months in).[73]

The White House claimed that Ghadafi had threatened to massacre the people of Benghazi with "no mercy," but the *New York Times* reported that Ghadafi's threat was directed at rebel fighters, not civilians, and that Ghadafi promised amnesty for those "who throw their weapons away." Ghadafi also offered to allow rebel fighters to escape to Egypt if they preferred not to fight to the death. Yet President Obama warned of imminent genocide.

In March 2011, the African Union had a plan for peace in Libya but was prevented by NATO, through the creation of a "no fly zone" and the initiation of bombing, to travel to Libya to discuss it. In April, the African Union was able to discuss its plan with Ghadafi, and he expressed his agreement. NATO, which had obtained UN authorization to protect Libyans alleged to be in danger but no authorization to continue bombing the country or to overthrow the government, continued bombing the country and overthrowing the government. "We came. We saw. He died!" laughed a triumphant Hillary Clinton,[74] whose emails, later released, showed her concern in Libya to be more about oil than human rights.[75]

The U.S. public opposed the war (in polls), as did Congress, as did the United Nations. But nobody stopped it, and Libya was reduced to violence, chaos, and refugee crises.[76]

Outsourced Imperialism

The leaders of the 2009 coup that overthrew President Manuel Zelaya of Honduras had all trained at the School of the Americas in the United States (which has changed its name to Western Hemisphere Institute for Security Cooperation). The United States assisted in the coup and in recognition of the coup government. Hillary Clinton and Barack Obama were part of and are part of this ongoing crime, and U.S. military supply shipments to Honduras are at record levels now as the military has merged with the police and turned its weaponry against the people.[77]

When the people of Egypt rose up in the Arab Spring, leaders of the Egyptian military were attending a meeting at the Pentagon. When the Egyptian military carried out a brutal coup in 2012, the U.S. military maintained its relationship as if nothing had happened. The United States is arming the Egyptian coup government for free, out of the goodness of its heart.

Obama has overseen a major build-up of troops around and hostility toward China. More quietly, and on a smaller scale, he's been militarizing Africa as well. Five to eight thousand U.S. troops plus mercenaries are training, arming, and fighting alongside and against African militaries and rebel groups in nearly every nation in Africa. Major land and water routes to bring in the U.S. armaments, and all the accoutrements of bases housing U.S. troops, have been established, as well as local agreements to make use of 29 international airports.[78]

The U.S. militarization of Africa includes airstrikes and commando raids in Libya; "black ops" missions and drone murders in Somalia; a proxy war in Mali; secretive actions in Chad; anti-piracy operations that result in increased piracy in the Gulf of Guinea; wide-ranging drone operations out of bases in Djibouti, Ethiopia, Niger, and the Seychelles; "special" operations out of bases in the Central African Republic, South Sudan, and the Democratic Republic of Congo; CIA bungling in Somalia; over a dozen joint training exercises a year; arming and training of soldiers in places like Uganda, Burundi, and Kenya; a "joint special operations" operation in Burkina Faso; base construction aimed at accommodating future "surges" of troops; legions of mercenary spies; the expansion of a former French foreign legion base in Djibouti and joint warmaking with France in Mali.[79]

The spreading of the U.S. empire through militarism is justified, when it's noticed at all, by the example of Rwanda as a place where the opportunity for a humanitarian war, to prevent the Rwanda Genocide, was supposedly missed. But the United States backed an invasion of Rwanda in 1990 by a Ugandan army led by U.S.-trained killers, and supported their attacks for three-and-a-half years, applying more pressure through the World Bank, International

Monetary Fund (IMF), and USAID. U.S.-backed and U.S.-trained warmak-
er Paul Kagame—now president of Rwanda—is the leading suspect behind
the shooting down of a plane carrying the then-presidents of Rwanda and
Burundi on April 6, 1994. As chaos followed, the United Nations might have
sent in peacekeepers (not the same thing, be it noted, as dropping bombs) but
Washington was opposed. President Bill Clinton wanted Kagame in power,
and Kagame has now taken the war into the Democratic Republic of Congo,
with U.S. aid and weapons, where 6 million have been killed. And yet nobody
ever says "We must prevent another Congo."[80]

I'm Not Saying We Wouldn't Get Our Hair Mussed

> Mr. President, I'm not saying we wouldn't get our hair mussed. But I do
> say no more than ten to twenty million killed, tops. Uh, depending on
> the breaks.
>
> —General "Buck" Turgidson in *Dr. Strangelove*

Many members of the public didn't see the first two world wars coming, because they didn't look into the matter.[81] The danger of a third is apparent,
as those were, to anyone who really chooses to look. With some 17,000 nuclear bombs in the world, the United States and Russia have about 16,000 of
them. Breaking its promise to Russia, the United States has expanded NATO
to Russia's borders, as well as having pulled out of the Anti-Ballistic Missile
treaty.

Western leaders met repeatedly in 2012 and 2013 to plot the fate of
Ukraine. Neo-Nazis and other nationalists from Ukraine were sent to Poland
to train for a coup. NGOs operating out of the U.S. embassy in Kiev organized trainings for coup participants. On November 24, 2013, three days
after Ukraine refused an IMF deal, including refusing to sever ties to Russia,
protesters in Kiev began to clash with police. The protesters used violence,
destroying buildings and monuments, and tossing Molotov cocktails, but
President Obama warned the Ukrainian government not to respond with
force.[82]

U.S.-funded groups organized a Ukrainian opposition, funded a new
TV channel, and promoted regime change. The U.S. State Department spent
some $5 billion. The U.S. assistant secretary of state who handpicked the new
leaders, openly brought cookies to protesters. When those protesters violently
overthrew the government in February 2014, the United States immediately declared the coup government legitimate. That new government banned
major political parties, and attacked, tortured, and murdered their members.
The new government included neo-Nazis and would soon include officials

imported from the United States. The new government repealed a law allowing the use of the Russian language—the first language of many Ukrainian citizens (although the president didn't sign the repeal). Russian war memorials were destroyed. Russian-speaking populations were attacked.

Crimea, an autonomous region of Ukraine, had its own parliament, had been part of Russia from 1783 until 1954, had publicly voted for close ties to Russia in 1991, 1994, and 2008, and its parliament had voted to rejoin Russia in 2008. On March 16, 2014, 82 percent of Crimeans took part in a referendum, and 96 percent of them voted to rejoin Russia. This nonviolent, bloodless, democratic, and legal action, in no violation of a Ukrainian constitution that had been shredded by a violent coup, was immediately denounced in the West as a Russian "invasion" of Crimea. Reports allege improper influence by Crimean or Russian troops. An easy way to put doubts about the referendum to rest would be to hold a new one; the result seems unlikely to change.

Novorossiyans, too, sought independence and were attacked by the new Ukrainian military the day after CIA Director John Brennan visited Kiev and, according to deposed president Viktor Yanukovich, sanctioned that crime.[83] Civilians were attacked by jets and helicopters for months in possibly the worst killing in Europe since World War II. Russian president Vladimir Putin, whom Hillary Clinton has labeled "Hitler," repeatedly pressed for a ceasefire and negotiations. A ceasefire finally came on September 5, 2014.

Remarkably, contrary to what we've all been told, Russia didn't invade Ukraine any of the numerous times we were told that it had just done so. It always had a military base in Crimea, and it introduced more troops to Crimea, while reportedly supplying weaponry to east-Ukrainian rebels (while the United States supplied weaponry to the now-western-focused Ukrainian government). But a serious invasion of the Russian military into Ukraine has been repeatedly announced without ever being documented. We've graduated from mythical weapons of mass destruction, through wildly exaggerated threats to Libyan civilians, and unsupported accusations of chemical weapons use in Syria, to false accusations of launching invasions that were never launched. The "evidence" of the invasion(s) was usually, if not always, left devoid of location or any verifiable detail.

The downing of the MH17 airplane in Ukraine on July 17, 2014, was blamed on Russia with no evidence to uphold that claim made public,[84] and even a year later still no evidence has been made public.[85]

None of this should suggest holding either Russia or Ukrainian rebels blameless. Not just Hillary Clinton, but even U.S. peace activists whom I respect, compare Putin to Hitler after analyzing his domestic agenda and consolidation of power.[86] And some who recognize Putin's behavior as a response to U.S. aggression nonetheless fault him for his own imperial dreams.[87] No party resorting to violence or the threat of violence is blameless from a perspective that views war as counterproductive in addition to being immoral. Yet, I sense in these critiques of Putin and Russia both the idea that domestic evil augurs international threat, which is not necessarily the case—and an acceptance of NATO's existence and expansion as neutral facts, morally indifferent, unworthy of radical critique as aggressive, destructive, and indefensible.

In July 2015, the Joint Chiefs of Staff published "The National Military Strategy of the United States of America—2015."[88] It gave as its justification for militarism lies about four countries, beginning with Russia, which it accused of "using force to achieve its goals," something the Pentagon would never do! Next it lied that Iran was "pursuing" nukes. Next it claimed that North Korea's nukes would someday "threaten the U.S. homeland." Finally, it asserted that China was "adding tension to the Asia-Pacific region." This "strategy" admitted that none of the four nations wanted war with the United States. "Nonetheless, they each pose serious security concerns," it said.[89]

What Is It Good For?

I have not sought to include mention of every recent war here. All wars are not equal in terms of their propaganda value for producing more wars. In fact, all wars combined are but a drop in the sea of propaganda compared to the one war that still dominates U.S. thinking and entertainment: World War II—about which I have a few closing words (see also Chapter 4 in particular, as well as Chapters 1, 2, 6, 10, and 11).

The danger of World War II was warned of immediately upon the creation of the Treaty of Versailles that ended World War I by brutally punishing all Germans. From there decades of what wise observers saw as policies that risked war were pursued until war arose. The crisis ought to have been avoided, and today we know a lot more about avoiding such crises. But even in the midst of it, alternative approaches were available.

The idea that the Nazis, as insanely dedicated militarists, never responded to nonviolent public pressure is easily disproved. When Hitler first asphyxiated mentally ill Germans, a few prominent voices raised in opposition led to the cancellation of that program, known as T4. When many in the German population and abroad were displeased by the Crystal Night attacks on Jews, those tactics were abandoned, and Hitler released a handful of Jews from concentration camps.[90] When non-Jewish wives of Jewish men began demonstrating in Berlin to demand their release, and others joined in the demonstrations, those men and their children were released. What might a far larger, better-planned nonviolent resistance campaign have accomplished?

It was never attempted, but it is not hard to imagine. A general strike had reversed a rightwing coup in Germany in 1920. German nonviolence had ended a French occupation in the Ruhr region in the 1920s, and nonviolence would later remove a ruthless dictator from power in East Germany in 1989. In addition, nonviolence proved moderately successful against the Nazis in Denmark with little planning, coordination, strategy, or discipline. In Finland, Denmark, Italy, and especially Bulgaria, and to a lesser extent elsewhere, non-Jews successfully resisted German orders to kill Jews. And what if the Jews in Germany had understood the dangers earlier and nonviolently resisted, managing somehow to use techniques developed and understood in the decades that followed, and the Nazis had begun to slaughter them in the public streets rather than in distant camps? Would millions have been saved by the reaction of the German and world public, or would most of the public have looked away? We cannot know because it wasn't tried.[91]

We can try nonviolent alternatives today. A terrific organization called Nonviolent Peaceforce is currently training 2,000 people in Syria in preventing violence for a cost of $2 million, which can be compared to the U.S. military's $4 million to train each violent "rebel"—with each such rebel standing a 99 percent chance of deserting and a 100 percent chance of making matters worse if he doesn't.

Six months after Pearl Harbor, in the auditorium of the Union Methodist Church in Manhattan, the executive secretary of the War Resisters League Abraham Kaufman argued that the United States needed to negotiate with Hitler. To those who argued that you couldn't negotiate with Hitler, he explained that the Allies were already negotiating with Hitler over prisoners of war and the sending of food to Greece.[92] For years to come, peace activists would argue that negotiating a peace without loss or victory would still save the Jews and save the world from the wars that would follow the current one. Their proposal was not tried, millions died in the Nazis' camps, and the wars that followed that one have not ended.

But belief in the inevitability of war can end. One can easily understand how wiser behavior in the 1920s and 1930s would have avoided World War II. The current crisis in Syria and Iraq could be resolved with great difficulty but far more successfully by talking than by supplying even more weaponry.

Most nations are much closer, in fact *all* other nations are closer, to Costa Rica's $0 investment in war than they are to the United States' $1 trillion annually. To hit the world's average national spending on militarism, the United States would need to slash its spending by 99 percent. The mad pursuit of war after war after war is only "human nature" if we avoid looking at the 96 percent of humanity outside the United States. Let's try looking at all of humanity. Let's try thinking of ourselves as humans rather than citizens of a national government. We may find far more cause for pride and satisfaction.

I'm working on abolishing war at WorldBeyondWar.org and hope you'll join me there.

Notes

Chapter 1

1. Dave Grossman, *On Killing: The Psychological Cost of Learning to Kill in War and Society* (New York: Back Bay Books, 1995).
2. Harold Lasswell, *Propaganda Technique in World War I* (Cambridge, MA: The M.I.T. Press, 1971).
3. George Orwell, *Essays* (London: Penguin Books, 2000).
4. Howard Zinn, *A People's History of the United States* (New York: Harper Perennial, 1995).
5. Phillip Knightley, *The First Casualty: The War Correspondent as Hero and Myth-Maker from the Crimea to Iraq* (Baltimore, MD: Johns Hopkins University Press, 2004), 88.
6. Alan Axelrod, *Selling the Great War: The Making of American Propaganda* (New York: Palgrave MacMillan, 2009).
7. Knightley, *The First Casualty*, 88.
8. Barak Kushner, *The Thought War: Japanese Imperial Propaganda* (Honolulu: University of Hawaii Press, 2006), 100.
9. Grossman, *On Killing*, 217.
10. Kushner, *The Thought War*, 149.
11. Mickey Z., *There Is No Good War: The Myths of World War II* (Brooklyn, NY: Vox Pop, Inc., 2005).
12. Ibid.
13. Cynthia Wachtell, *War No More: The Antiwar Impulse in American Literature 1861–1914* (Baton Rouge: Louisiana State University Press, 2010), 50.
14. Susan Brewer, *Why America Fights: Patriotism and War Propaganda from the Philippines to Iraq* (New York: Oxford University Press, 2009).
15. Garth S. Jowett and Victoria O'Donnell, *Propaganda and Persuasion*, 3rd ed. (Thousand Oaks, CA: Sage Publications, 1999), 328.

16. Barbara Ehrenreich, *Blood Rites: Origins and History of the Passions of War* (London: Virago Press, 1998).

17. Wachtell, *War No More.*

18. Ibid.

19. William McKinley, "William McKinley's Imperial Gospel," in *Major Problems in American Foreign Relations,* ed. Thomas G. Paterson and Dennis Merrill (Lexington, MA: D.C. Heath, 1995), 424.

20. Lasswell, *Propaganda Technique.*

21. Karim H. Karim, "War, Propaganda, and Islam in Muslim and Western Sources," in *War, Media, and Propaganda: A Global Perspective,* ed. Yahya R. Kamalipour and Nancy Snow (Lanham, MD: Rowman & Littlefield, 2004), 112.

22. Paul Sullivan and Mikey Weinstein, "Vets for Common Sense and Religious Freedom Org Slam Christian Proselytizing in U.S. Military, Going to God Won't Make it for PTSD Victims," *Veterans Today,* accessed December 6, 2015, http://bit.ly/1OBmE84.

23. Albert J. Beveridge, "Albert J. Beveridge's Salute to Imperialism," in *Major Problems in American Foreign Relations,* vol. I, ed. Thomas G. Paterson and Dennis Merrill (Lexington, MA: D.C. Heath, 1995).

24. Lasswell, *Propaganda Technique,* 69.

25. "President Signs Declaration of War," *New York Times,* December 8, 1917.

26. Grossman, *On Killing,* 161.

27. Ehrenreich, *Blood Rites,* 207.

28. Ibid., 220.

29. Brewer, *Why America Fights,* 191.

30. Elisabeth Bumiller, "Records Show Doubts on '64 Vietnam Crisis," *New York Times,* July 14, 2010.

31. Ehrenreich, *Blood Rites,* 13.

32. Norman Solomon, *War Made Easy: How Presidents and Pundits Keep Spinning Us to Death* (Hoboken, NJ: John Wiley & Sons, 2005), 12.

33. Ibid., 70.

34. Stefan Zweig, *The World of Yesterday* (Lincoln: University of Nebraska Press, 1964), 210–11.

35. Jowett and O'Donnell, *Propaganda and Persuasion.*

36. Howard Zinn, *A People's History of the United States* (New York: Harper Perennial, 1995), 59.

37. Robert Fantina, *Desertion and the American Soldier: 1776–2006* (New York: Algora Publishing, 2006).

38. James Carroll, "Remembering the Heroes, Victims," *Boston Globe,* May 31, 2010.

39. Murray Polner and Thomas Woods, Jr., "The Civil War," in *We Who Dared to Say No to War: American Antiwar Writing from 1812 to Now,* eds. Murray Polner and Thomas Woods, Jr. (New York: Basic Books, 2008), 56–8.

40. Douglas Blackmon, *Slavery by Another Name* (New York: Anchor Books, 2009).

41. Ibid., 45.

42. Zinn, *A People's History,* 400.

43. Nicholson Baker, *Human Smoke: The Beginnings of World War II, the End of Civilization* (New York: Simon & Schuster, 2008).

44. Ralph Stavins, Richard J. Barnet, and Marcus G. Raskin, *Washington Plans an Aggressive War: A Documented Account of the United States' Adventure in Indochina* (New York: Random House, 1971), 44.

45. Jeremy R. Hammond, "Newly Discovered Documents Shed More Light on Early Taliban Offers, Pakistan Role," *Foreign Policy Journal*, September 20, 2010.

46. Ibid.

47. William Goodell, "This Is a War for Slavery," in *We Who Dared to Say No to War: American Antiwar Writing from 1812 to Now*, ed. Murray Polner and Thomas Woods Jr. (New York: Basic Books, 2008), 43.

48. J. William Fullbright, *The Arrogance of Power* (New York: Random House, 1966).

49. Walter Isaacson, "Madeleine's War," *Time Magazine*, May 9, 1999.

50. Andrew Bacevich, *Washington Rules: America's Path to Permanent War* (New York: Metropolitan Books, 2010), 205.

51. Harry S. Truman, "Statement by the President Announcing the Use of the A-Bomb at Hiroshima," August 6, 1945, Public Papers of the President Harry S. Truman, 1945–1953.

52. United States Strategic Bombing Survey Summary Report (Pacific War) (Washington, DC, July 1946), http://bit.ly/1OBqE8G.

53. Howard Zinn, *The Bomb* (San Francisco, CA: City Light Books, 2010).

54. Harry S. Truman, "Radio Report to the American People on the Potsdam Conference," August 9, 1945, Public Papers of the President Harry S. Truman, 1945–1953.

55. Daniel Ellsberg, *Secrets: A Memoir of Vietnam and the Pentagon Papers* (New York: Penguin, 2002).

Chapter 2

1. "Text: President Bush Addresses the Nation," http://wapo.st/My0Lh0.

2. Paul Chappell, *The End of War: How Waging Peace Can Save Humanity, Our Planet, and Our Future* (Westport, CT: Easton Studio Press, 2010).

3. Harold Lasswell, *Propaganda Technique in World War I* (Cambridge, MA: The M.I.T. Press, 1971), 57.

4. "Security Spending Primer: Getting Smart About the Pentagon Budget," National Priorities Project, 2009, accessed October 7, 2010, http://bit.ly/1VVYaeH.

5. "Where Your Income Tax Money Really Goes," War Resisters League, accessed October 7, 2010, http://bit.ly/1QvIZtY.

6. Jacqueline Cabasso, "StratCom in Context: The Hidden Architecture of U.S. Militarism," accessed October 7, 2010, http://bit.ly/1nMIiQr.

7. John Quigley, *The Ruses for War: American Interventionism Since World War II* (Amherst, NY: Prometheus Books, 1992).

8. Samuel Taggart, "With Good Advice Make War," in *We Who Dared to Say No to War: American Antiwar Writing from 1812 to Now*, eds. Murray Polner and Thomas Woods Jr. (New York: Basic Books, 2008), 15.

9. *Meet the Press*, March 16, 2003.

10. Oleg Vasilevich Kustov, "We Were Waging War Against a People," in *The Case for Withdrawal from Afghanistan*, ed. Nick Turse (Brooklyn, NY: Verso, 2010), 25.

11. Norman Thomas, *War: No Glory, No Profit, No Need* (New York: Frederick A. Stokes Company, 1935), 88.

12. James W. Douglass, *JFK and the Unspeakable: Why He Died and Why it Matters* (Maryknoll, NY: Orbis Books, 2008).

13. "Put the White House Memo into the Media," accessed October 7, 2010, http://bit.ly/1OBqNsJ.

14. Norman Solomon, *War Made Easy: How Presidents and Pundits Keep Spinning Us to Death* (Hoboken: John Wiley & Sons, 2005), 22–24.

15. Quigley, *Ruses for War*, 17.

16. David Wildman and Phyllis Bennis, *Ending the US War in Afghanistan: A Primer* (New York: Olive Branch Press, 2010).

17. Peter Bergen and Paul Cruickshank, "The Iraq Effect: War Has Increased Terrorism Sevenfold Worldwide," *Mother Jones*, March 1, 2007.

18. Paul Richter, "Obama Losing Support in War Effort; The Lack of Progress in Afghanistan Weighs on Lawmakers as They Consider a Bill for Emergency Funding," *Los Angeles Times*, July 21, 2010.

19. Ibid.

20. News Transcript: DOD News Briefing with Gen. McChrystal from the Pentagon, May 13, 2010," accessed October 7, 2010, *http://1.usa.gov/1Zgw1RX*.

21. Martin Gilbert, *The Churchill War Papers*, vol. 3 (London: Heinemann, 1993–2000), 556.

22. Robert Menzies, *Dark and Hurrying Days: Menzies' 1941 Diary* (National Library of Australia, 1993), 126–29.

23. "Japanese General Finds Us 'Insolent,'" *New York Times*, August 5, 1934.

24. *Harper's Magazine*, October 1934.

25. Smedley Butler, *War Is a Racket* (Port Townsend, WA: Feral House, 2003), 41.

26. Thomas, *War: No Glory*, 84.

27. Nicholson Baker, *Human Smoke: The Beginnings of World War II, the End of Civilization* (New York: Simon & Schuster, 2008). Most of the details in this account of U.S. actions toward Japan come from this source.

28. Ibid.

29. General Claire Lee Chennault, "The Flying Tigers: American Volunteer Group, Chinese Airforce, A Brief History With Recollections and Comments by General Claire Lee Chennault," accessed October 7, 2010, http://bit.ly/1Yr1ezM.

30. Baker, *Human Smoke*.

31. Ibid. Most of the details in this account of U.S. actions toward Japan come from this source.

32. Jeanette Rankin, "Two Votes Against War: 1917 and 1941," in *We Who Dared to Say No to War: American Antiwar Writing from 1812 to Now*, eds. Murray Polner and Thomas Woods Jr. (New York: Basic Books, 2008), 168–169.

33. Ibid.

34. John Nichols, *The Genius of Impeachment: The Founders' Cure for Royalism* (New York: The New Press, 2006).

35. Bruce Fein, *American Empire: Before the Fall, Campaign for Liberty* (CreateSpace, 2010), 84.

36. Abraham Lincoln, "The Half-Insane Mumbling of a Fever Dream," in *We Who Dared to Say No to War: American Antiwar Writing from 1812 to Now*, eds. Murray Polner and Thomas Woods Jr. (New York: Basic Books, 2008), 30.

37. Howard Zinn and Anthony Arnove, *Voices of a People's History of the United States* (New York: Seven Stories Press, 2004), 154.

38. Ibid.

39. Robert Fantina, *Desertion and the American Soldier: 1776–2006* (New York: Algora Publishing, 2006).

40. Howard Zinn, *A People's History of the United States* (New York: Harper Perennial, 1995).

41. Songwriter David Rovics website, www.davidrovics.com.

42. Phillip Knightley, *The First Casualty: The War Correspondent as Hero and Myth-Maker from the Crimea to Iraq* (Baltimore, MD: Johns Hopkins University Press, 2004), 58.

43. Butler, *War Is a Racket*, 41.

44. Baker, *Human Smoke*.

45. Faiz Shakir, "To Provoke War, Cheney Considered Proposal to Dress Up Navy Seals As Iranians and Shoot at Them," *Think Progress*, July 31, 2008, accessed October 7, 2010, http://bit.ly/1Nu9YSD.

46. Solomon, *War Made Easy*, p. 135.

47. Alan Axelrod, *Selling the Great War: The Making of American Propaganda* (New York: Palgrave MacMillan, 2009), 57.

48. Anne Goodwin Sides, "New Clues in Lusitania's Sinking," *National Public Radio*, November 22, 2008, accessed October 7, 2010, http://n.pr/1BsVTkR.

49. "Conspiracy or Foul-Up?" The Lusitania Resource, http://bit.ly/1IZqQ4V.

50. Knightley, *The First Casualty*, 117.

51. Chris Hedges, *The Death of the Liberal Class* (New York: The Nation Books, 2010), 65.

52. This is a very famous quote appearing in many sources, among them http://bit.ly/1lXNQY3.

53. Thomas, *War: No Glory*, 169.

54. Quigley, *The Ruses for War*, 36.

55. Bruce Cumings, *The Korean War: A History* (Random House, 2010).

56. Ibid., 56.

57. Ibid., 64.

58. Dave Chaddock, *This Must Be the Place: How the U.S. Waged Germ Warfare in the Korean War and Denied it Ever Since* (Bennett and Hastings, 2013).

59. Michael Christopher Carroll, *Lab 257: The Disturbing Story of the Government's Secret Germ Laboratory*.

60. H.P. Albarelli, Jr., *A Terrible Mistake: The Murder of Frank Olson and the CIA's Secret Cold War Experiments*.

61. Susan Brewer, *Why America Fights: Patriotism and War Propaganda from the Philippines to Iraq* (New York: Oxford University Press, 2009).

62. Juan Cole, "Obama's Domino Theory," *Slate*, March 30, 2009, accessed October 10, 2010, http://bit.ly/1msoIsk.

63. Jeff Cohen and Norman Solomon, "30-Year Anniversary: Tonkin Gulf Lie Launched Vietnam War," Fairness and Accuracy in Reporting (FAIR), July 27, 1994,
http://bit.ly/1d6nDBJ.

64. Solomon, *War Made Easy*, 5.

65. Mickey Z., *There Is No Good War: The Myths of World War II* (Brooklyn, NY: Vox Pop, Inc., 2005), 110.

66. "Wolfowitz Comments Revive Doubts over Iraq's WMD," last updated June 1, 2003, http://usat.ly/1Nua8ta.

67. Ralph Stavins, Richard J. Barnet, and Marcus G. Raskin, *Washington Plans an Aggressive War: A Documented Account of the United States' Adventure in Indochina* (New York: Random House, 1971), 99.

68. *Newsweek,* March 8, 1999.

69. Seth Ackerman, "Media Advisory: What Reporters Knew About Kosovo Talks—But Didn't Tell: Was Rambouillet Another Tonkin Gulf?", Fairness and Accuracy in Reporting (FAIR), June 2, 1999, accessed October 7, 2010, http://bit.ly/1RujKIn.

70. Ibid.

71. Solomon, *War Made Easy*, 42.

72. Max Arax, "Suddenly, the Israel Lobby Discovers a Genocide," *Salon*, June 16, 2010, accessed October 7, 2010, http://bit.ly/1NuaY9n.

Chapter 3

1. "War in the Gulf: The President; Transcription of the Comments by Bush on the Air Strikes Against the Iraquis," January 17, 1991, http://nyti.ms/1Od8ppB.

2. "Clinton: 'We Did the Right Thing,'" Federal Document Clearing House, June 11, 1999, page A31, http://wapo.st/1Vh5TDJ.

3. Woodward, Bob, Plan of Attack *(2004),* 150.

4. *60 Minutes,* May 12, 1996.

5. "Poll of Iraqis: Public Wants Timetable for US Withdrawal, but Thinks US Plans Permanent Bases in Iraq, World Public Opinion," January 31, 2006, http://bit.ly/1ULflQ4.

6. Harold Lasswell, Propaganda Technique in World War I (Cambridge, MA: The M.I.T. Press, 1971), 191.

7. *George W. Bush, Book 1: January 1 to June 30, 2005* (Government Printing Office), http://bit.ly/1OBoXbd.

8. Minxin Pei and Sara Kasper, "Lessons from the Past: The American Record on Nation Building," Carnegie Endowment for International Peace, 2003.

9. Ben Connable and Martin C. Libicki, "How Insurgencies End," RAND National Defense Research Institute, 2010, accessed October 7, 2010, http://bit.ly/1QRnt14.

10. Sanjeev Miglani, "Kandahar Trusts Taliban More than Govt—US Army Poll," April 22, 2010, http://reut.rs/1IZrTls.

11. George McGovern and William R. Polk, *Out of Iraq* (New York: Simon & Schuster, 2006), 29.

12. Susan Brewer, *Why America Fights: Patriotism and War Propaganda from the Philippines to Iraq* (New York: Oxford University Press, 2009), 26.

13. McGovern and Polk, *Out of Iraq*, 99–100.

14. Ralph Stavins, Richard J. Barnet, and Marcus G. Raskin, *Washington Plans an Aggressive War: A Documented Account of the United States' Adventure in Indochina* (New York: Random House, 1971), 41.

15. "Transcript of President Clinton's Speech on Bosnia," CNN, November 27, 1995, http://cnn.it/1ULfEdz.

16. "Emancipation of Afghan Women Not Attainable as Long as the Occupation, Taliban and "National Front" Criminals Are Not Sacked!" Statement of the Revolutionary Association of the Women of Afghanistan (RAWA) on the International Women's Day, March 8, 2010, accessed October 7, 2010, http://bit.ly/1OdMlRG.

17. "Guantanamo at Home: Muslim American Syed Fahad Hashmi Held in 23-Hour Solitary Pretrial Confinement for over Two Years in Case Resting on Plea-Bargaining Government Informant," *Democracy Now!*, June 5, 2009, accessed October 7, 2010, http://bit.ly/1PeDEpb.

18. Ann Jones, "Meet the Afghan Army: Is it a Figment of Washington's Imagination?" in *The Case for Withdrawal from Afghanistan*, ed. Nick Turse (Verso, 2010), 79.

19. One of many possible sources is Michael Powell, "Obama Addresses Critics on 'Centrist' Moves," *New York Times The Caucus* (blog), July 8, 2008, http://nyti.ms/1PbR9V0.

20. Howard Zinn and Anthony Arnove, *Voices of a People's History of the United States* (New York: Seven Stories Press, 2004), 145.

21. Source is a video made by Rethink Afghanistan.

22. Ambrose Bierce, *The Devil's Dictionary*.

Chapter 4

1. Douglas P. Fry, *Beyond War: The Human Potential for Peace* (New York: Oxford University Press, 2007), 66.

2. Ibid.

3. Barbara Ehrenreich, *Blood Rites: Origins and History of the Passions of War* (London: Virago Press, 1998).

4. Fry, *Beyond War*.

5. Ibid., 18.

6. Institute for Economics and Peace, "Global Peace Index 2010 Methodology, Results, and Findings," accessed October 7, 2010,http://bit.ly/1msnf5u.

7. Norman Solomon, *War Made Easy: How Presidents and Pundits Keep Spinning Us to Death* (Hoboken: John Wiley & Sons, 2005).

8. Nicholson Baker, *Human Smoke: The Beginnings of World War II, the End of Civilization* (New York: Simon & Schuster, 2008), 144.

9. Ibid., 7.

10. Ibid., 420–21.

11. "President Franklin Delano Roosevelt Address over the Radio on Navy Day Concerning the Attack upon the Destroyer U.S.S. Kearny, October 27, 1941," American Merchant Marine at War, http://bit.ly/1OdPW2o.

12. Robert Fantina, *Desertion and the American Soldier: 1776–2006* (New York: Algora Publishing, 2006).

13. Ralph Lopez, "WikiLeaks Soldier Who Found Rocket Launcher at Scene Says No Attack Was Imminent," WarIsACrime.org, August 13, 2010, accessed October 7, 2010, http://bit.ly/1mspWnF.

14. These and other first-person accounts can be found in Studs Terkel, *My American Century* (New York: New Press, 1997).

15. Ibid.

16. Edwin Black, "The Horrifying American Roots of Nazi Eugenics," originally published in the San Francisco Chronicle, History News Network, November 24, 2003, accessed October 7, 2010, http://bit.ly/1Yr3aIk.

17. Here's one place to read the ruling in Buck v. Bell: http://bit.ly/1MmaZbA.

18. Mickey Z., *There Is No Good War: The Myths of World War II* (Brooklyn, NY: VoxPopNet, 2005), 62.

19. Ibid., 12.

20. Mickey Z., "June 6 Is D(isinformation) Day: The 'Good War' Lie," June 3, 2013, Countercurrents.org, http://bit.ly/1T74NJZ

21. Mickey Z., *There Is No Good War.*

22. Peter Ackerman and Jack Duvall, *A Force More Powerful: A Century of Nonviolent Conflict* (New York: Palgrave Macmillan, 2001).

23. Michael Walzer, "What a Little War in Iraq Could Do," *The New York Times*, March 7, 2003, http://nyti.ms/1Yn5ple.

Chapter 5

1. "Thucydides, Pericles' Funeral Oration,"University of Minnesota Human Rights Library, http://bit.ly/1RXSMrL.

2. "The Gettysburg Address," Abraham Lincoln Online, http://bit.ly/1bFJewr.

3. "John F. Kennedy Presidential Library & Museum, Historical Resources, Archives, Reference Desk, Quotations of John F. Kennedy," John F. Kennedy Presidential Library & Museum, retrieved November 21, 2008. http://bit.ly/1rtk2U3

4. Safire, William, "ON LANGUAGE; Warrior," *The New York Times*, August 27, 2007.

5. Ambrose Bierce, *The Devil's Dictionary.*

6. Joshua Kors, "Disposable Soldiers," *The Nation*, April 8, 2010, accessed October 7, 2010, http://bit.ly/1Mmbhz8.

7. Katie Drummond, "Looting, Cannibalism and Death Blows: The 'Shock and Awe' of Ant Warfare," *Wired*, August 3, 2010, accessed October 7, 2010, http://bit.ly/1TV0yBg.

8. Steve Connor, "Scientists Abuzz at Wasp's Anti-Ant Warfare," *The Independent*, June 4, 2002, accessed October 7, 2010, http://ind.pn/1mdmVad.

9. Peter Phillips and Andrew Roth, eds., "Censored 2009: The Top 25 Censored Stories of 2007–08," http://bit.ly/1OdNcSx.

10. Norman Thomas, *War: No Glory, No Profit, No Need* (New York: Frederick A. Stokes Company, 1935), 106.

11. Hearings: Developments in Afghanistan, Rayburn-2118, United States House of Representatives House Armed Services Committee Democrats website, http://1.usa.gov/23kXQLW.

12. History News Network Staff, "Have Presidents in the Past Attended the Funerals of Dead Soldiers?" History News Network, accessed October 7, 2010, http://bit.ly/1Yr3xmk.

13. This was on July 15, 1815, to the captain of HMS Bellerophon, according to "Napoleon Quotes—Napoleon Bonaparte," Military Quotes, http://bit.ly/1lXQNrL.

14. Cynthia Wachtell, *War No More: The Antiwar Impulse in American Literature 1861–1914* (Baton Rouge: Louisiana State University Press, 2010).

15. Phillip Knightley, *The First Casualty: The War Correspondent as Hero and Myth-Maker from the Crimea to Iraq* (Baltimore, MD: Johns Hopkins University Press, 2004) 66.

16. Susan Brewer, *Why America Fights: Patriotism and War Propaganda from the Philippines to Iraq* (New York: Oxford University Press, 2009) 49.

17. Knightley, *The First Casualty*, 116.

18. Jorge Mariscal, "The Poverty Draft: Do Military Recruiters Disproportionately Target Communities of Color and the Poor?" *Sojourners*, June 2007, accessed October 7, 2010, http://bit.ly/1T75cfj.

19. Ibid.

20. Andrew Bacevich, "Unequal Sacrifice," *The Nation*, September 1, 2010, accessed October 7, 2010, http://bit.ly/1IegSwk.

21. This is quoted in a great many books and articles, such as Mark Smith, *Treblinka Survivor: The Life and Death of Hershl Sperling*, http://bit.ly/1RuhgtD.

22. Barbara Ehrenreich, *Blood Rites: Origins and History of the Passions of War* (London: Virago Press, 1998).

23. Ibid.

24. James Gilligan, *Violence: Reflections on a National Epidemic* (Vintage, 1997).

25. Ibid.

26. Dave Grossman, *On Killing: The Psychological Cost of Learning to Kill in War and Society* (New York: Back Bay Books, 1995), xxii.

27. Ibid.

28. Associated Press, "Alabama Judge Sentences Man to Join Military," August 27, 2010, accessed October 7, 2010, http://bit.ly/1IZt6Jv.

29. Margaret E. Noonan and Christopher J. Mumola, "Bureau of Justice Statistics Special Report: Veterans in State and Federal Prison, 2004," Bureau of Justice Statistics, May 2007, accessed October 7, 2010, http://1.usa.gov/1Ied5zm.

30. R. Jeffrey Smith, "Crime Rate of Veterans in Colo. Unit Cited: Soldiers Tell Newspaper of Sharp Rise in Violent Incidents After Iraq Deployments," *Washington Post*, July 28, 2009.

31. Mark Thompson, "Is the U.S. Army Losing Its War on Suicide?" *Time*, April 13, 2010.

32. Brewer, *Why America Fights*, 67.

33. Dennis Kucinich, *The 35 Articles of Impeachment and the Case for Prosecuting George W. Bush* (Port Townsend, WA: Feral House, 2008), http://bit.ly/1OdNysr.

34. "2004: Highlights and Lowlifes," Ann Coulter website, December 29, 2014, http://http://bit.ly/1QvMpNf.

35. "Iraq Veterans Against the War," in *Winter Soldier: Iraq and Afghanistan: Eyewitness Accounts of the Occupations*, ed. Aaron Glantz (Chicago, IL: Haymarket, 2008).

36. "Press Release: U.S. Troops in Iraq: 72 percent Say End War in 2006," Zogby International, February 28, 2006, accessed October 7, 2010, http://bit.ly/1NucjNw.

37. Michael Prysner, "Fort Hood Soldiers Protest Repeated Deployments," MichaelMoore.com, August 7, 2010, accessed October 7, 2010, http://bit.ly/1ULb2nU.

Chapter 6

1. Letter to President Clinton, January 26, 1998, Project for the New American Century, http://bit.ly/1QyKtDk.

2. "Rebuilding America's Defenses—PNAC," a report of the Project for the New American Century, September 2000, http://bit.ly/1QRnamY.

3. Robert Parry, "Blair Reveals Cheney's War Agenda," *Consortium News*, September 6, 2010, accessed October 7, 2010, http://bit.ly/1NYfLBu.

4. Ralph Stavins, Richard J. Barnet, and Marcus G. Raskin, *Washington Plans an Aggressive War: A Documented Account of the United States' Adventure in Indochina* (New York: Random House, 1971), 214.

5. John Quigley, *The Ruses for War: American Interventionism Since World War II* (Amherst, NY: Prometheus Books, 1992), 284.

6. "Smedley Butler," Wikipedia, http://bit.ly/1QLdBbl.

7. Harold Lasswell, *Propaganda Technique in World War I* (Cambridge, MA: The M.I.T. Press, 1971).

8. Carl von Clausewitz, *On War, Indexed Edition*, reprint ed. (NJ: Princeton University Press, 1989).

9. Quigley, *The Ruses for War*, 109.

10. Ibid.

11. Ibid.

12. Ibid.

13. Norman Thomas, *War: No Glory, No Profit, No Need* (New York: Frederick A. Stokes Company, 1935), 78.

14. Howard Zinn, *A People's History of the United States* (New York: Harper Perennial, 1995), 32.
15. Susan Brewer, *Why America Fights: Patriotism and War Propaganda from the Philippines to Iraq* (New York: Oxford University Press, 2009).
16. Quigley, *The Ruses for War*, 273.
17. George McGovern and William R. Polk, *Out of Iraq* (New York: Simon & Schuster, 2006), 34.
18. Robin Beste, "All Neptune's Oceans Could Not Wash the Blood from Blair's Hands," Stop the War Coalition, August 16, 2010, accessed October 7, 2010.
19. Zinn, *A People's History*, 350.
20. Barbara Ehrenreich, *Blood Rites: Origins and History of the Passions of War* (London: Virago Press, 1998), 30.
21. Daniel Yergin, *The Prize: The Epic Quest for Oil, Money and Power* (New York: Touchstone, 1992), 395.
22. Jimmy Carter, "The State of the Union Address Delivered Before a Joint Session of the Congress," January 23, 1980, http://bit.ly/1om5yys.
23. Mickey Z., *There Is No Good War: The Myths of World War II* (Brooklyn, NY: Vox Pop, Inc., Drench Kiss Media Corp., 2005), xii.
24. Antonia Juhasz, "AFRI(OIL)COM—Will the Next War for Oil be in Africa?" *Foreign Policy in Focus*, June 17, 2008, accessed October 8, 2010, http://bit.ly/1QRoRRm.
25. Howie Hawkins, "Bombing Yugoslavia: A 'Humanitarian War' for an Imperialist Peace," *Synthesis/Regeneration* 20, Fall 1999, accessed October 7, 2010, http://bit.ly/1OBxv1N.
26. Robert Scheer, *The Great American Stickup* (New York: Nation Books, 2010), 120.
27. Nicolas J.S. Davies, *Blood on Our Hands: The American Invasion and Destruction of Iraq* (Nimble Books, 2010).
28. Hawkins, "Bombing Yugoslavia."
29. Quigley, *The Ruses for War*, 22.
30. "Afghanistan and Iraq: Must They Be Wars Without End?" *The Economist*, December 13, 2007, http://econ.st/1k7re5G.
31. Tariq Ali, "Afghanistan: Mirage of the Good War," *New Left Review* 50, March–April 2008, 20.
32. Zinn, *The Bomb* (City Lights Books, 2013).
33. Stavins, Barnet, and Raskin, *Washington Plans an Aggressive War*, 224.
34. Source is the Pentagon Papers http://1.usa.gov/1migZWG.
35. Stavins, Barnet, and Raskin, *Washington Plans an Aggressive War*, 142.
36. Quigley, *The Ruses for War*, 154.
37. Zinn, *A People's History*, 290.
38. Russ Baker, "Bush Wanted to Invade Iraq If Elected in 2000," Guerrilla News Network, October 27, 2004, accessed October 7, 2010, http://bit.ly/1IZCH2Y.
39. Stavins, Barnet, and Raskin, *Washington Plans an Aggressive War*.
40. Jim Lobe, "So, Did Saddam Hussein Try to Kill Bush's Dad?" Inter Press Service, October 19, 2004, accessed October 7, 2010, http://bit.ly/1IZCH2Y.

41. Ewen MacAskill, "George Bush: 'God told me to end the tyranny in Iraq,'" *Guardian*, October 7, 2005, accessed October 7, 2010, http://bit.ly/1ZgGQUd.

42. Dennis Perrin, *Savage Mules: The Democrats and Endless War* (Brooklyn, NY: Verso, 2008).

43. Marilyn B. Young, "Bombing Civilians from the Twentieth to the Twenty-First Centuries," in *Bombing Civilians: A Twentieth Century History*, eds. Yuki Tanaka and Marilyn B. Young (The New Press, 2009), 165.

44. Ehrenreich, *Blood Rites*, 76.

45. One of many possible sources is David McCullough, *Truman*, reprint ed. (New York: Simon & Schuster, 1993).

46. Stavins, Barnet, and Raskin, *Washington Plans an Aggressive War*, 111.

47. Mark Selden, "A Forgotten Holocaust: U.S. Bombing Strategy, the Destruction of Japanese Cities, and the American Way of War from the Pacific War to Iraq," in *Bombing Civilians: A Twentieth Century History*, eds. Yuki Tanaka and Marilyn B. Young (The New Press, 2009), 95.

48. Stavins, Barnet, and Raskin, *Washington Plans an Aggressive War*, 206.

49. Ibid., 240.

50. Propaganda, http://bit.ly/1PuMP0q.

51. Chris Hedges, *The Death of the Liberal Class*, (New York: The Nation Books, 2010), 68.

52. Final Report: Foreign and Military Intelligence, U.S. Senate, Select Committee to Study Governmental Operations with Respect to Intelligence Activities, Book I, 94th Congress, Second session, April 26, 1976, 9.

Chapter 7

1. Norman Solomon, *War Made Easy: How Presidents and Pundits Keep Spinning Us to Death* (Hoboken: John Wiley & Sons, 2005) 155.

2. Fairness and Accuracy in Reporting, "Using 'Pro-Troops' to Mean 'Pro-War' Is Anti-Journalistic," by Fairness and Accuracy in Reporting (FAIR), March 26, 2003, accessed October 7, 2010, http://bit.ly/1RY7gIb.

3. "Press Release: U.S. Troops in Iraq: 72 percent Say End War in 2006," Zogby International, February 28, 2006. Accessed October 7, 2010, http://bit.ly/1NucjNw.

4. Ralph Stavins, Richard J. Barnet, and Marcus G. Raskin, *Washington Plans an Aggressive War: A Documented Account of the United States' Adventure in Indochina*, (New York: Random House, 1971), 273.

5. David Swanson, *Daybreak: Undoing the Imperial Presidency and Forming a More Perfect Union* (New York: Seven Stories Press, 2009), 158.

6. Susan Brewer, *Why America Fights: Patriotism and War Propaganda from the Philippines to Iraq* (New York: Oxford University Press, 2009).

7. Stavins, Barnet, and Raskin, *Washington Plans an Aggressive War*, 42.

8. Ted Rall, "Don't Support Our Troops: Win or Lose, War on Iraq Is Wrong," Common Dreams, March 13, 2003, accessed October 7, 2010, http://bit.ly/1k7sl6q.

9. Solomon, *War Made Easy*, 157.

10. Ibid., 160.

11. Colby Hall, "Bill Maher: We Love the Troops the Way Michael Vick Loves Dogs," Mediaite, February 13, 2010, http://bit.ly/1VhbfPr.

12. John Caruso, "Support the Troops?" A Tiny Revolution, http://bit.ly/1k7s16q.

Chapter 8

1. Emptywheel, "Elena Kagan and Lindsey Graham on the Global Battlefield, the Sequel," Fire Dog Lake, June 29, 2010, accessed October 7, 2010, http://bit.ly/1QyUl05.

2. Bruce Fein, "Statement of Bruce Fein before the House Judiciary Committee Re: Impeachment," July 25, 2008, accessed October 7, 2010, http://1.usa.gov/1NYmpHY.

3. David Swanson, "Bush's Third Term?" TomDispatch, September 1, 2009, accessed October 7, 2010, http://bit.ly/1NYmoUo.

4. Oleg Vasilevich Kustov, "We Were Waging War Against a People," in *The Case for Withdrawal from Afghanistan*, ed. Nick Turse (Verso, 2010), 25.

5. "World War II casualties," Wikipedia, accessed October 7, 2010, http://bit.ly/1d08eLy.

6. "Korean War," Wikipedia, accessed October 7, 2010, http://bit.ly/1IepGma.

7. "Casualties of the Iraq War," Wikipedia, accessed October 7, 2010, http://bit.ly/RdNsoF.

8. "Iraq Deaths," Just Foreign Policy, accessed October 7, 2010, http://bit.ly/1MmjXp0.

9. "Casualties of the Iraq War," Wikipedia.

10. "Pakistan Body Count," accessed October 7, 2010, http://bit.ly/1mdwDcy.

11. "Women Are the Forgotten Victims of War," *Infosud Human Rights Tribune*, March 16, 2007, accessed October 7, 2010, http://bit.ly/1T7d00E.

12. Richard Drayton, "An Ethical Blank Cheque," *Guardian*, May 10, 2005, accessed October 7, 2010, http://bit.ly/1T7d00E.

13. Duncan Gardham, "Abu Ghraib Abuse Photos 'Show Rape'," *Telegraph*, May 27, 2009, accessed October 7, 2010, http://bit.ly/1oaz5NG.

14. "U.S. Soldiers Accused of Raping Iraqi Women Escape Prosecution," *Democracy Now!*, March 29, 2005, accessed October 7, 2010, http://bit.ly/1IZDzo6.

15. Excerpted with the author's permission from Robin Morgan, "Manhood and Moral Waivers," The Women's Media Center, August 8, 2006, http://bit.ly/1T-V9AhF. Copyright 2006 by Robin Morgan.

16. Anne Gearen, "Military Rape Reports Rise, Prosecution Still Low," *Huffington Post*, March 17, 2009, accessed October 7, 2010, http://huff.to/1RY8gfs.

17. Chalmers Johnson, "How to Deal with America's Empire of Bases," *TomDispatch*, July 2, 2009, accessed October 7, 2010, http://bit.ly/1Yray6x.

18. "Children and Armed Conflict, Report of the Secretary-General, United Nations," April 13, 2010, accessed October 7, 2010, http://bit.ly/1Yraynd.

19. "Children as War Victims," *Frontline* volume 19, issue 06 (March 16–29, 2002.

20. Dave Grossman, *On Killing: The Psychological Cost of Learning to Kill in War and Society* (New York: Back Bay Books, 1995), 197.

21. "Collateral Murder," WikiLeaks, April 5, 2010, http://bit.ly/1yvPUdW.

22. Bill Van Auken, "U.S. Soldier in WikiLeaks Massacre Video: 'I Relive This Every Day,'" World Socialist Web Site, April 28, 2010, accessed October 7, 2010, http://bit.ly/1mdx2M8.

23. Sherwood Ross, "Army Ordered Massive Return Fire When Civilians Present," OpEdNews, August 13, 2010, accessed October 7, 2010, http://bit.ly/1QvXnT4.

24. Ralph Lopez, "U.S. Soldiers Ordered to Kill Iraq Civilians," WarIsACrime.org, August 13, 2010, accessed October 7, 2010, http://bit.ly/1ULz16m.

25. David Swanson, "Shooting Handcuffed Children," WarIsACrime.org, January 2, 2010, accessed October 7, 2010, http://bit.ly/1QyVo02.

26. Dave Lindorff, "Where Are This War's Heroes, Military and Journalistic?" WarIsACrime.org, March 3, 2010, accessed October 7, 2010, http://bit.ly/1Nuj3Lc.

27. Dave Lindorff, "This Time it's Pregnant Women: Another US Atrocity in the Bush/Cheney War in Afghanistan," WarIsACrime.org, March 14, 2010, accessed October 7, 2010, http://bit.ly/1OdYMNp.

28. Jerome Starkey, "US Special Forces 'Tried to Cover-Up' Botched Khataba Raid in Afghanistan," *The Sunday Times*, April 5, 2010, accessed October 7, 2010, http://thetim.es/1Pc2MLw.

29. Ibid.

30. Cathy Resmer, "Peace Talks: Three Vermont Veterans Share Their (Anti) War Stories," Seven Days: Vermont's Independent Voice, April 24, 2007, accessed October 7, 2010, http://bit.ly/1NYnmjA.

31. Richard Oppel, Jr., "Tighter Rules Fail to Stem Deaths of Innocent Afghans at Checkpoints," *New York Times*, March 26, 2010.

32. *Bombing Civilians: A Twentieth Century History*, eds. Yuki Tanaka and Marilyn B. Young (The New Press, 2010).

33. Mark Selden, "A Forgotten Holocaust: U.S. Bombing Strategy, the Destruction of Japanese Cities, and the American Way of War from the Pacific War to Iraq," in *Bombing Civilians: A Twentieth Century History*, eds. Yuki Tanaka and Marilyn B. Young (The New Press, 2009), 83.

34. Ibid., 92.

35. Mickey Z., *There Is No Good War: The Myths of World War II* (Brooklyn, NY: Vox Pop, Inc., Drench Kiss Media Corp., 2005), 67.

36. Kathy Kelly, "The Indefensible Drones: A Ground Zero Reflection," WarIsACrime.org, September 8, 2010, accessed October 7, 2010, http://bit.ly/1IeqGGE.

37. Melody Kemp, "New Case for US Reparations in Laos," *Asia Times*, September 4, 2010.

38. John Quigley, *The Ruses for War: American Interventionism Since World War II* (Amherst, NY: Prometheus Books, 1992), 116.

Chapter 9

1. James Reston, "Private Behavior, Public Responsibility," *New York Times*, December 25, 1987, http://nyti.ms/1Nujg15.
2. Nixon's oval office tapes, May 4, 1972.
3. William R. Polk, *Violent Politics: A History of Insurgency, Terrorism & Guerrilla War, From the American Revolution to Iraq* (New York: HarperCollins, 2007), xvi.
4. Ralph Stavins, Richard J. Barnet, and Marcus G. Raskin, *Washington Plans an Aggressive War: A Documented Account of the United States' Adventure in Indochina* (New York: Random House, 1971), 110.
5. Polk, *Violent Politics*, 165.
6. Nicholson Baker, *Human Smoke: The Beginnings of World War II, the End of Civilization* (New York: Simon & Schuster, 2008), 374.
7. Harold Lasswell, *Propaganda Technique in World War I* (Cambridge, MA: The M.I.T. Press, 1971), 102.
8. Associated Press video, http://bit.ly/1RY9ojd.
9. Brian Katulis and Lawrence Korb, "Today's Iraq Redeployment Made Possible by Our Deadline," AmericanProgress.org, August 31, 2010, accessed October 7, 2010, http://ampr.gs/1lY2nTF.
10. Juan Cole, "Top Ten Myths about Iraq 2007," *Informed Comment*, December 26, 2007, accessed October 7, 2010, http://ampr.gs/1lY2nTF.
11. Michael Schwartz, "The Top Eleven Myths about Iraq, 2007," *Huffington Post*, January 4, 2008, accessed October 7, 2010, http://huff.to/1k7ttWp.
12. Katulis and Korb, "Today's Iraq Redeployment."
13. Gareth Porter, "Biden Embraces Myth that Surge Turned Iraq into Good War," *Foreign Policy in Focus*, September 7, 2010, accessed October 7, 2010, http://bit.ly/22f0TEZ.
14. Nir Rosen, "The Myth of the Surge," *Rolling Stone*, March 6, 2008.
15. Cole, "Top Ten Myths."
16. John Agnew and Claudio Guler, "False Advertising about the Iraq Surge," *Truthout*, June 13, 2010, accessed October 7, 2010, http://bit.ly/1k7tycH.
17. Rosen, "Myth of the Surge."
18. The O'Reilly Factor, FOX News, September 3, 2008.

Chapter 10

1. John Quigley, *The Ruses for War: American Interventionism Since World War II* (Amherst, NY: Prometheus Books, 1992), 275.
2. Robert Fisk, "Does The U.S. Military Want to Kill Journalists," Znet: The Spirit of Resistance Lives, April 9, 2003, accessed October 7, 2010, http://bit.ly/1Ynbqyu.
3. Chris Hedges, *The Death of the Liberal Class* (New York: The Nation Books, 2010), 70.
4. "You Can't Just Say the President Is Lying: The Limits of Honesty in the Mainstream Press," From a panel discussion in Washington, D.C. sponsored

by Northwestern's Medill School of Journalism, November 4, 2004, accessed October 7, 2010, http://bit.ly/1OdZA53.

5. Jeff Cohen, *Cable News Confidential: My Misadventures in Corporate Media* (San Francisco, CA: Polipoint, 2006).

6. Hedges, *Death of the Liberal Class*, 130.

7. Norman Solomon, *War Made Easy: How Presidents and Pundits Keep Spinning Us to Death* (Hoboken, NJ: John Wiley & Sons, 2005), 124.

8. Ibid., 170.

9. Philip Knightley, *The First Casualty: The War Correspondent as Hero and Myth-Maker from the Crimea to Iraq,* (Baltimore: John Hopkins Paperback, 2004).

10. "Investigating the Pentagon's Pundits," *Source Watch*, accessed October 7, 2010, http://bit.ly/1IerxY6.

11. Tom Engelhardt, "The Pentagon Triumphant on the Media Battlefield," *TomDispatch*, September 7, 2010, accessed October 7, 2010, http://bit.ly/1nMIiQr.

12. Harvard Students, "Torture at Times: Waterboarding in the Media," Joan Shorenstein Center on the Press, Politics, and Public Policy, April 2010, accessed October 7, 2010, http://bit.ly/1RYa7AS.

13. Solomon, *War Made Easy*, 65.

14. David Swanson, "Remember When Bush's Lies Weren't 'Old News?'" June 20, 2005, accessed October 9, 2010, http://bit.ly/1NCsRRj.

15. Bradley Graham, "Cruise Missile Threat Grows, Rumsfeld Says; Bush Urged to Boost Defense Against Low-Flying Weapon," *Washington Post*, August 18, 2002, A1, http://bit.ly/1RuvSci.

16. Glenn Kessler, "Rice Details the Case for War with Iraq," *Washington Post*, August 18, 2002.

17. "The Iraq Debate Continues," *Washington Post* Editorial, August 18, 2002.

18. *New York Times* quotation of the day, September 7, 2002, http://nyti.ms/1QyWNUi.

19. Hedges, *Death of the Liberal Class*, 80.

20. Marcus Mabry, "Are the Faithful Losing Faith?" *Newsweek*, October 21, 2006.

21. Jacques Ellul, *Propaganda: The Formation of Men's Attitudes* (New York: Vintage Books, 1969), 29.

22. Brendan Nyhan and Jason Reifler, "When Corrections Fail: The Persistence of Political Misperceptions," published online, March 30, 2010, accessed October 7, 2010, http://bit.ly/1IerSdi.

Chapter 11

1. Tad Daley, *Apocalypse Never: Forging the Path to a Nuclear Weapon-Free World* (Piscataway, NJ: Rutgers University Press, 2010).

2. Ibid.

3. Tetsuo Maeda, "Strategic Bombing of Chongoing by Imperial Japanese Army and Naval Forces," in *Bombing Civilians: A Twentieth Century History*, eds. Yuki Tanaka and Marilyn B. Young (The New Press, 2009), 152.

4. Brian Knowlton, "Nuclear-Armed Iran Risks 'World War III,' Bush Says," *New York Times*, October 17, 2007.

5. Jennifer Leaning, "Environment and Health: 5. Impact of War," *Canadian Medical Association Journal* 163(9):1157–61 (2000), accessed October 8, 2010, http://bit.ly/1k7ucH7.

6. Michael Sheridan, "Revolt Stirs among China's Nuclear Ghosts," *Sunday Times*, April 19, 2009.

7. Cecil Adams, "Did John Wayne Die of Cancer Caused by a Radioactive Movie Set?" *The Straight Dope*, October 26, 1984, accessed October 8, 2010, http://bit.ly/1MmlT0Y.

8. H.P. Albarelli, Jr., *A Terrible Mistake: The Murder of Frank Olson and the CIA's Secret Cold War Experiments* (Walterville, OR: Trine Day, 2009).

9. Military Human Experimentation, Congressional Committee Report 103-97, 103d Congress, 2d Session—Committee Print—S. Prt. 103-97, "Is Military Research Hazardous to Veterans' Health? Lessons Spanning Half a Century, a Staff Report Prepared for the Committee on Veterans' Affairs," United States Senate, December 8, 1994.

10. "America's Nuclear Secrets," *Newsweek*, December 27, 1993, http://bit.ly/1QyXmxd.

11. World Refugee Survey 2009, by the U.S. Committee for Refugees and Immigrants, accessed October 8, 2010, http://bit.ly/1TVb1g5.

12. Leaning, "Environment and Health."

13. Mickey Z., *There Is No Good War: The Myths of World War II* (Brooklyn, NY: Vox Pop, Inc., Drench Kiss Media Corp., 2005), 87.

14. Naomi Klein, "Fight Climate Change, Not Wars," December 10, 2009, accessed June 29, 2015, http://bit.ly/1Mmm8ZZ.

15. Michael Klare, "The Pentagon v. Peak Oil: How the Wars of the Future May Be Fought Just to Run the Machines that Fight Them," *TomDispatch*, June 14, 2007, accessed October 8, 2010, http://bit.ly/1MmmcJ2.

16. Elisabeth Rosenthal, "U.S. Military Orders Less Dependence on Fossil Fuels," *New York Times*, October 4, 2010.

17. Brian Jones, *Failing Intelligence: The True Story of How We Were Fooled into Going to War in Iraq* (London: Biteback Publishing Ltd., 2010).

18. "Military Towns Enjoy Big Booms," *USA Today*, August 17, 2010.

19. "Security Spending Primer: Getting Smart about the Pentagon Budget," National Priorities Project, 2009, accessed October 8, 2010, http://bit.ly/1NYp8Bf.

20. Steven Hill, *Europe's Promise: Why the European Way Is the Best Hope in an Insecure Age* (University of California Press, 2010).

21. "What's Your Trillion Dollar Plan?" Facebook, accessed October 8, 2010, http://bit.ly/1OBAFTh.

22. Joseph Stiglitz and Linda Bilmes, "The True Cost of the Iraq War: $3 Trillion and Beyond," *Washington Post*, September 5, 2010.

23. Benito Mussolini, "The Doctrine of Fascism," from *Encyclopedia Italiana* volume XIV.

24. William James, "The Moral Equivalent of War," Constitution Society, 1906, accessed October 7, 2010, *http://www.constitution.org/wj/meow.htm*.

25. Ibid.

26. Ibid.

Chapter 12

1. Ralph Stavins, Richard J. Barnet, and Marcus G. Raskin, *Washington Plans an Aggressive War: A Documented Account of the United States' Adventure in Indochina* (New York: Random House, 1971), 295.
2. Juan Cole, "The Speech President Obama Should Give about the Iraq War (But Won't)," *Informed Consent*, August 31, 2010, accessed October 8, 2010, http://bit.ly/1msxUwX.
3. Televised speech by President Dwight Eisenhower, February 21, 1957.
4. John Quigley, *The Ruses for War: American Interventionism Since World War II* (Amherst, NY: Prometheus Books, 1992), 262.
5. National Security Strategy, May 2010, http://1.usa.gov/1K7rnRU.
6. "Charter of the International Military Tribunal at Nuremberg," http://bit.ly/1TVbEGv.
7. "Curtis LeMay," World War II Database, http://bit.ly/1YrcKLu.
8. Richard Drayton, "An Ethical Blank Cheque," *Guardian*, May 10, 2005.
9. Edgar L. Jones, "One War Is Enough," *Atlantic Monthly*, February 1946.
10. Robert Jackson, opening statement before the International Military Tribunal, The Robert H. Jackson Center, http://bit.ly/1QRpFFG.
11. "Judgment of the International Military Tribunal at Nuremberg," http://bit.ly/1lY5qeo.
12. Michael Haas, *George W. Bush, War Criminal? The Bush Administration's Liability for 269 War Crimes* (Praeger, 2009).
13. Dennis Kucinich, *The 35 Articles of Impeachment and the Case for Prosecuting George W. Bush* (Port Townsend, WA: Feral House, 2008).
14. "Noam Chomsky: The Crimes of U.S. Presidents," YouTube video, posted by Resident Dissident, January 2, 2015, http://bit.ly/1wSGVwn.
15. Assistant Attorney General Jay Bybee, "Authority of the President Under Domestic and International Law to Use Military Force Against Iraq," memo to President's Counsel Alberto Gonzales, October 23, 2002.
16. Harold Lasswell, *Propaganda Technique in World War I* (Cambridge, MA: The M.I.T. Press, 1971), 66.
17. Haas, *George W. Bush, War Criminal?*

Chapter 13

1. Barbara Ehrenreich, *Blood Rites: Origins and History of the Passions of War* (London: Virago Press, 1998), 123.
2. Brian Jones, *Failing Intelligence: The True Story of How We Were Fooled into Going to War in Iraq* (Biteback Publishing, 2011), 14.
3. Norman Thomas, *War: No Glory, No Profit, No Need*, (New York: Frederick A. Stokes Company, 1935), 66.
4. Ibid., 68.
5. Lt. Col. Anthony Shaffer, *Operation Dark Heart* (New York: St. Martin's Press, 2010), 45.

6. Nicholson Baker, *Human Smoke: The Beginnings of World War II, the End of Civilization* (New York: Simon & Schuster, 2008), 18.
7. Ibid., 83.
8. Ibid.
9. Mickey Z., *There Is No Good War: The Myths of World War II*, (Brooklyn, NY: VoxPopNet, 2005), 17.
10. Chris Hedges, *The Death of the Liberal Class*, (New York: The Nation Books, 2010), 166.
11. Andrew Bacevich, *Washington Rules: America's Path to Permanent War* (New York: Metropolitan Books, 2010), 51.
12. Ibid., 63.
13. Baker, *Human Smoke*, 98.
14. Jones, *Failing Intelligence.*
15. Eric S. Margolis, "Bombshell from London," *Toronto Sun*, September 18, 2010.
16. Newsletter of the Global Network Against Weapons and Nuclear Power in Space, 2010, http://space4peace.org.
17. Karen DeYoung and Greg Jaffe, "U.S. 'Secret War' Expands Globally as Special Operations Forces Take Larger Role," *Washington Post*, June 4, 2010.
18. Nick Turse, "U.S. Special Ops Forces Deployed in 135 Nations: 2015 Proves to Be Record-Breaking Year for the Military's Secret Military," *TomDispatch*, September 24, 2015, http://bit.ly/1Ruy7MH.
19. DeYoung and Jaffe, "U.S. 'Secret War' Expands Globally."
20. Chris McGreal, "US Soldiers 'Killed Afghan Civilians for Sport and Collected Fingers as Trophies'," *Guardian*, September 8, 2010, http://bit.ly/1NCuVZv.

Chapter 14

1. Barack Obama, "Remarks by the President at the Acceptance of the Nobel Peace Prize," December 10, 2009, http://1.usa.gov/1KRp85w.
2. Peter Ackerman and Jack Duvall, *A Force More Powerful* (St. Martin's Griffin, 2000).
3. Erica Chenoweth and Maria J. Stephan, *Why Civil Resistance Works: The Strategic Logic of Nonviolent Conflict* (New York: Columbia University Press, 2011).
4. "Martin Luther King Jr.—Acceptance Speech," Nobelprize.org, Nobel Media AB 2014, Website November 21,2015, http://bit.ly/1dnnBQn.
5. Ibid.
6. One source would be the C-Span video of the One Nation Rally, October 2, 2010, http://cs.pn/1T7h1Ch.
7. David Swanson, "Pentagon Admits that War Is Illegal," http://bit.ly/1QyZODS.
8. David Swanson, "War Is Not Going to End on its Own," http://bit.ly/1ULGBhv.
9. Edward S. Herman and David Peterson, "Steven Pinker's Apologetics for Western-Imperial Violence," WarIsACrime.org, http://bit.ly/1NCvfHz.
10. David Swanson, "War Is Good for Us, Dumb New Book Claims," http://bit.ly/1QyZRQj.

11. Robert Pollin and Heidi Garrett-Peltier, "The U.S. Employment Effects of Military and Domestic Spending Priorities: 2011 Update," http://bit.ly/1ZgKcqn.
12. U.S. Dept. of Fear, Twitter, June 29, 2015, http://bit.ly/1msyNWo.

Epilogue

1. Barack Obama, "Presidential Proclamation—Commemoration of the 50th Anniversary of the Vietnam War," May 25, 2012, http://1.usa.gov/1TVcKC0.
2. Nick Turse, *Kill Anything that Moves: The Real American War in Vietnam* (Picador, 2013).
3. David Swanson, "Nixon's Treason Now Acknowledged," http://bit.ly/1RuyOWj.
4. Ewen MacAskill, "Five-Fold Increase in Terrorism Fatalities Since 911, Says Report," *Guardian*, http://bit.ly/1AaUU7C.
5. "Former Bush Officials Teaching Course on Iraq War 'Decision Making'," *The Hill*, http://bit.ly/1SY6fyM.
6. Phyllis Bennis, *Understanding ISIS and the New Global War on Terror, A Primer* (Chicago, IL: Olive Branch Press, 2015).
7. Seymour M. Hersh, "The Red Line and the Rat Line," *London Review of Books*, January 25, 2001, http://bit.ly/1lO8WVV.
8. Robert Parry, "The Collapsing Syria-Sarin Case," *Consortium News*, April 7, 2014, http://bit.ly/1ULHmqM.
9. One possible source of many is "Kerry Speaking Rhetorically over Syria Turning in Weapons: State Department," Reuters, September 9, 2013, http://reut.rs/1T7hLau.
10. David Swanson, "They Never Announce When You Prevent a War," http://bit.ly/1NCvH8I.
11. Julian Borger and Bastien Inzaurralde, "West 'Ignored Russian Offer in 2012 to Have Syria's Assad Step Aside'," *Guardian*, September 15, 2015, http://bit.ly/1iLsRWu.
12. Colum Lynch and Dan de Luce, "Did the West Really Miss a Chance to End the Syrian War?" *Foreign Policy*, September 15, 2015, http://atfp.co/1IevtYP.
13. David Swanson, "Study Finds People Assume War Is Only Last Resort," http://bit.ly/1NumqSw.
14. Mark Mazzetti, "C.I.A. Study of Covert Aid Fueled Skepticism About Helping Syrian Rebels," *New York Times*, October 14, 2014, http://nyti.ms/1z93zrD.
15. David Swanson, "Why Even Failed Activism Succeeds," http://nyti.ms/1z93zrD.
16. David Swanson, "The Washington Post Will Kill Us All," http://bit.ly/1IZI1Dy.
17. Gareth Porter, *Manufactured Crisis: The Untold Story of the Iran Nuclear Scare* (Charlottesville, VA: Just World Books, 2014).
18. Medea Benjamin, "US Lobby Groups Try to Squash Iran Deal Despite Public Support," Telesur, July 6, 2015, http://bit.ly/1gnnjQM.
19. "Jack Black and Morgan Freeman Drop the Mic on the #IranDeal," YouTube video, posted by globalzerochannel, July 28, 2015, http://bit.ly/1JLbPhg.
20. "Reza Aslan Wants You to Take Action for Peace - NIAC Action," YouTube video, posted by NIAC, July 20, 2015, http://bit.ly/1Pc67u1.

21. "AP's Supposed Iran Deal Leak Full of Holes," Atomic Reporters, August 21, 2015, http://bit.ly/1Mmp2Oe.
22. "Hillary Clinton Cannot Be Less(er) Evil than Anyone," video posted by David Swanson, May 16, 2013, http://bit.ly/22f52Ja.
23. David Swanson, "In Convicting Jeff Sterling, CIA Revealed More than it Accused Him of Revealing," http://bit.ly/1IZI9CN.
24. Marcy Wheeler, "The Sterling Trial: Merlin Meets Curveball," ExposeFacts.org, January 15, 2015, http://bit.ly/1KNtlF7.
25. Nick Turse, "Tomgram: Nick Turse, A Secret War in 135 Countries," *TomDispatch*, September 24, 2015, http://bit.ly/1Ruy7MH.
26. Ewen MacAskill, "Fivefold Increase in Terrorism Fatalities Since 911, Says Report," *Guardian*, November 17, 2014, http://bit.ly/1AaUU7C.
27. "List of Countries by GDP (PPP) per Capita," Wikipedia, http://bit.ly/1odJPK8
28. Jon Walker, "America Ranks 36th in Feeling Free to Choose What to Do With Your Life," Shadowproof.com, July 1, 2014, http://bit.ly/1ULIDhw.
29. "List of Countries by Life Expectancy," Wikipedia, http://bit.ly/1LjieDy; "List of countries by infant mortality rate," Wikipedia, http://bit.ly/1JfLj5i.; "List of Countries by Unemployment Rate," Wikipedia, http://bit.ly/1Pc6moQ.
30. Joe Weisenthal, "Here's the New Ranking of Top Countries in Reading, Science, and Math," *Business Insider*, December 23, 2013, http://bit.ly/1mdBvly.
31. "Best Education in the World: Finland, South Korea Top Country Rankings, U.S. Rated Average," *Huffington Post*, updated January 27, 2013, http://huff.to/1dTZZWD.
32. Jessica Shepherd, "World Education Rankings: Which Country Does Best at Reading, Maths and Science?" *Guardian*, December 7, 2010, http://bit.ly/1eVyURu.
33. "Best Education in the World: Finland, South Korea Top Country Rankings, U.S. Rated Average," Huffington Post, updated January 27, 2013, http://huff.to/1dTZZWD.
34. Jessica Shepherd, "World Education Rankings: Which Country Does Best at Reading, Maths and Science?" *The Guardian*, December 7, 2010, http://bit.ly/1eVyURu.
35. Alec Tyson, "Most Americans Think the U.S. Is Great, but Fewer Say it's the Greatest," Pew Research Center, July 2, 2014, http://pewrsr.ch/1TVdCGQ.
36. "The World Only Needs 30 billion Dollars a Year to Eradicate the Scourge of Hunger," FAONewsroom, http://bit.ly/TbavBV.
37. "Costs and Benefits of Water and Sanitation Improvements at the Global Level (Evaluation of the)," World Health Organization, http://bit.ly/15P2ZTd
38. Michael Schramm, "Bernie Sanders Issues Bill to Make 4-year Colleges Tuition-Free," *USA Today*, May 19, 2015, http://usat.ly/1di7jOK
39. Mattea Kramer, "How Much Foreign Aid Does the U.S. Give Away?," National Priorities Project, May 6, 2013, http://bit.ly/23l065R.
40. U.S. High Speed Rail Association, http://bit.ly/1S2htVJ.
41. David Sirota and Andrew Perez, "Clinton Foundation Donors Got Weapons Deals From Hillary Clinton's State Department," *International Business Times*, May 26, 2016, http://bit.ly/1LCV5uT.

42. Ibid.

43. "Journalist: Indiscriminate Bombing of Civilians by Iraqi Gov't Has Helped ISIS Recruit Supporters," *Democracy Now!*, September 3, 2014, http://bit.ly/1lY8KGx.

44. Kurt Eichenwald, "ISIS's Enemy List: 10 Reasons the Islamic State Is Doomed," *Newsweek*, September 8, 2014, http://bit.ly/1s0sXNa.

45. Matthew Hoh, "The Beheadings Are Bait," *Huffington Post*, September 4, 2014, http://huff.to/1lD3SEY.

46. Bennis, *Understanding ISIS*.

47. Ibid.

48. Glenn Greenwald and Murtaza Hussain, "The Fake Terror Threat Used to Justify Bombing Syria," *The Intercept*, September 28, 2014, http://bit.ly/1Br9ggo.

49. Molly O'Toole, "UN Ambassador Warns Against Intervention Fatigue," *Defense One*, November 19, 2014, http://bit.ly/11xHOSV.

50. David Swanson, "ISIS Derangement Syndrome," http://bit.ly/1QRq5vV.

51. "No Debate and the New War: Study Finds Little Opposition to US Attacks on Iraq, Syria," Fairness & Accuracy in Reporting, November 14, 2014, http://bit.ly/1xzAJwT.

52. Adam Johnson, "Zero for 40 at Predicting Attacks: Why Do Media Still Take FBI Terror Warnings Seriously?" Fairness & Accuracy in Reporting, July 1, 2015, http://bit.ly/1HId3Pp.

53. Andres Jauregui"CNN Mistakes Sex Toy Flag For ISIS Flag At London Gay Pride," *Huffington Post*, June 27, 2015, http://huff.to/1LvhwEP.

54. Greg Miller and Karen DeYoung, "Secret CIA Effort in Syria Faces Large Funding Cut," *The Washington Post*, June 12, 2015, http://wapo.st/1RYfu30.

55. Austin Wright, "Price Tag for Syrian Rebels: $4 Million Each," *Politico*, July 8, 2015, http://politi.co/1JWumK1.

56. Michael T. Heaney and Fabio Rojas, *Party in the Street: The Antiwar Movement and the Democratic Party after 9/11* (MA: Cambridge University Press, 2015).

57. David Swanson, "U.S. House Debates and Votes Down Withdrawal from Iraq/Syria," http://bit.ly/1QRq8b8.

58. Proceedings of the U.S. House of Representatives, June 17, 2015.

59. David Swanson, "The 16 Core Progressive Policies, Really?" http://bit.ly/1Pc6ZPc.

60. Jo Becker and Scott Shane, "Secret 'Kill List' Proves a Test of Obama's Principles and Will," *New York Times*, May 29, 2012, http://nyti.ms/1Gh7LGF.

61. Gareth Porter, "How False Stories of Iran Arming the Houthis Were Used to Justify War in Yemen," Truthout, http://bit.ly/1YRkQCA.

62. New York Times Editorial Board, "Overkill on a C.I.A. Leak Case," *New York Times*, May 13, 2015, http://nyti.ms/1msA7s8.

63. Jon Queally, "Leaked Internal CIA Document Admits US Drone Program 'Counterproductive'," *Common Dreams*, December 18, 2014, http://bit.ly/1uZLqEH.

64. "Even the Warriors Say the Wars Make Us Less Safe," WarIsACrime.org, http://bit.ly/1RuAKOz.

65. Jameel Jaffer, "The CIA Can't Keep its Drone Propaganda Straight," Just Security, June 20, 2015, http://bit.ly/1TIUVYH.

66. David Swanson, "Why I Don't Want to See the Drone Memo," http://bit.ly/1Qw5eQr.
67. David Swanson, "A Liberal Lawyer Gives Up on Preventing Murder," http://bit.ly/1Pc7hWq.
68. Max Blumenthal, *The 51 Day War* (Nation Books, 2015), 47.
69. Ibid.
70. David Swanson, "The 51 Day Genocide," http://bit.ly/22f6Kdm.
71. David Swanson, "If a Genocide Falls in the Forest," WarIsACrime.org, August 5, 2014, http://bit.ly/1Pc7lFL.
72. David Swanson, "Students Save Palestine," http://bit.ly/1T7jYCO.
73. Chris Hedges, "Libya: Here We Go Again," *TruthDig*, September 5, 2011, http://bit.ly/1RYgnsv.
74. "Hillary Clinton Cannot Be."
75. Sarah Westwood, "Six Things We Learned from the Blumenthal Emails," *Washington Examiner*, June 24, 2015, http://washex.am/1NCxz1l.
76. Robert Parry, "Hillary Clinton's Failed Libya 'Doctrine'," *Consortium News*, July 1, 2015, http://bit.ly/1Iey19o.
77. David Swanson, "Resistance in Honduras Alive and Jumping," http://bit.ly/1Qw5z5O.
78. David Swanson, "A Preview of Coming Wars: Do Black Lives Matter in Africa?" http://bit.ly/1RuBbIN.
79. Ibid.
80. David Swanson, "Lies about Rwanda Mean More Wars if Not Corrected," http://bit.ly/1OdoHyL.
81. David Swanson, "Public Didn't See Last Two World Wars Coming Either," http://bit.ly/1k7z0fL.
82. David Swanson, "Ukraine and the Apocalyptic Risk of Propagandized Ignorance," http://bit.ly/1RuBgMu.
83. "Ukraine on Brink of Civil War After Blood Was Spilt in East—Yanukovich," Russia TV, http://bit.ly/1TVeRWH.
84. Swanson, "Ukraine and the Apocalyptic Risk."
85. "Obama Should Release MH-17 Intel," *Consortium News*, July 22, 2015, http://bit.ly/1Ji9GKz.
86. John Feffer, "Brown Is the New Black in Russia," *Huffington Post*, May 27, 2014, http://huff.to/1QRreUb.
87. John Feffer, "Can Ukraine Gnaw its Way Out of Trouble?" *Huffington Post*, April 21, 2015, http://huff.to/1Ji9I5l.
88. Joint Chiefs of Staff, The National Military Strategy of the United States of America 2015, http://1.usa.gov/1Itrd5v.
89. Ibid.
90. Eve Spangler, *Understanding Israel/Palestine: Race, Nation, and Human Rights in the Conflict* (Sense Publishers, 2015).
91. Timothy Bratz, *Peace Lessons* (The Disproportionate Press, 2015).
92. Nicholson Baker, "Why I'm a Pacifist," *Harper's Magazine*, May 2011.

INDEX

ACKNOWLEDGMENTS

I remain grateful to everyone who helped with the first edition of this book. I also need to acknowledge that my thinking has advanced over the past five years thanks to countless people I've worked with, as I hope is reflected in the epilogue and in the new additions to Chapter 14.

Thank you to Helena Cobban, Diana Ghazzawi, and Kimberly MacVaugh of Just World Books for putting this second edition together and, I hope, getting it to a whole new readership.

Thank you to Patrick Hiller, Nicolas Davies, Medea Benjamin, Leah Bolger, Jeff Cohen, Coleen Rowley, John Feffer, Jean Bricmont, Lawrence Wittner, and Norman Solomon for their helpful comments on the epilogue. Thank you also to John Horgan, Emanuel Yi Pastreich, Linda Swanson, Dahr Jamail, Cindy Sheehan, and Daniel Ellsberg for reading over the epilogue for me.

All shortcomings are my own, and quite likely several people pointed them out but I ignored the warnings.

Thank you, above all, to Anna, Wesley, and Oliver.

ABOUT THE AUTHOR

David Swanson is an author, activist, journalist, and radio host. His books include *When the World Outlawed War* and *War No More: The Case for Abolition*. Swanson serves as director of World Beyond War and host of Talk Nation Radio. He blogs at DavidSwanson.org and WarIsACrime.org. He was a 2015 Nobel Peace Prize nominee. Swanson was instrumental in exposing the Downing Street Minutes and other evidence of Iraq war lies.